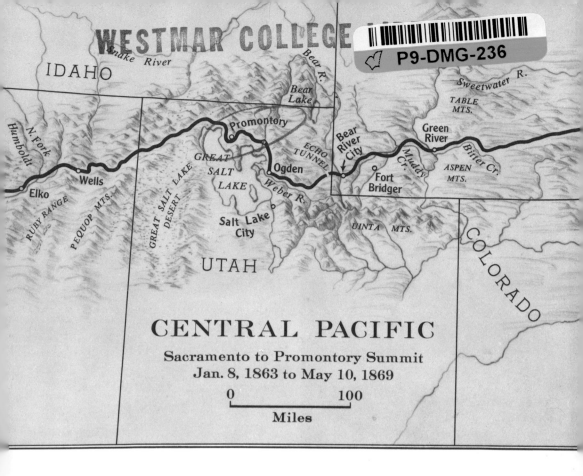

IDAHO

Snake River

Bear R.

Humboldt

N. Fork

Elko

Wells

RUBY RANGE

PEQUOP MTS.

GREAT SALT LAKE DESERT

GREAT
SALT
LAKE

Bear
Lake

Promontory

*ECHO
TUNNEL*

Ogden

Weber R.

Salt Lake
City

UTAH

Sweetwater R.

TABLE
MTS.

Bear
River
City

Green
River

Muddy Cr.

Bitter Cr.

ASPEN
MTS.

Fort
Bridger

UINTA MTS.

COLORADO

CENTRAL PACIFIC

Sacramento to Promontory Summit
Jan. 8, 1863 to May 10, 1869

0   100

Miles

A WORK OF GIANTS

By Wesley S. Griswold

This profusely illustrated and richly detailed story of the first American transcontinental railroad tells the great saga of the Union Pacific Railroad and the rival Central Pacific Railroad as they bridged two-thirds of North America.

Both companies shared the responsibility for the cross-country line—the Union Pacific pushing westward from Omaha, and the Central Pacific starting from Sacramento toward the unknown point where they would meet. The tremendous task of spanning the vast lands, of financing and equipping so immense and unprecedented a venture, and the harsh demands made on everyone concerned are described by Wesley Griswold in this vivid, dramatic account.

From the start, both railroads were beset by financial problems, which were further complicated by personal conflicts and political difficulties. On the Central Pacific side, none of the chief officers had any knowledge of railroad building. After ground-breaking, the Union Pacific was stalled for two and a half years before it was able to acquire General Dodge, war hero and top-notch engineer, who drove it full steam ahead. General William Tecumseh Sherman, one of the nation's most ardent enthusiasts for the huge railroad project—and the man who first described the undertaking as a "work of giants,"— stated that even he did not expect to see it completed in his lifetime.

Overcoming the enormous financial and material obstacles imposed by Civil War shortages and the months-long delivery route around South America, the Central Pacific began work early in January, 1863. Step by step, the author follows the great bands of workers as they start out, illustrating his dramatic story with rare photographs that have been treasured for a century and carefully selected for *A Work of Giants*.

The Union Pacific was more fortunate, both in terms of terrain and in financial support, which resulted from government interest. However, political turmoil and intrigues plagued the company, and the notorious Credit Mobilier scandal, involving the principals of the Union Pacific, ruined the careers of several key participants.

Despite political chicanery and wartime obstacles, work went ahead. At one time the Central Pacific employed 12,000 men (10,000 were Chinese, imported for the task), working in fierce summer heat and through record winter blizzards as they struggled with snow plows, built trestles, and blasted their way through mountains. The Union Pacific's army of workers lived in portable towns, each known as "hell on wheels," which were moved as the track advanced. As graphic as the pictures that fill the pages are Mr. Griswold's descriptions of the lawlessness that characterized these wild, transient communities.

It was finally in May of 1869, with hundreds of workers dead, and millions of dollars spent or wasted, that the magnificent dream of spanning the continent by rail was realized. *A Work of Giants* tells one of the most stirring chapters in the nation's history, and with the rich anecdotes and legends that enliven his fine account, Mr. Griswold offers an unusually colorful excursion into a high order of Americana.

The Central Pacific's first locomotive, the Governor Stanford, being tested after assembly in November, 1863, before it had even acquired a headlight.

A WORK OF GIANTS

The Union Pacific's first locomotive, Major-General Sherman, was brought to Omaha on a Missouri River steamboat in June, 1865.

(Above, top) *William Henry Jackson took this photograph of the Union Pacific's shops and water-pumping windmill at North Platte, Nebraska, in 1869.*

(Above) *Freight train on reinforced Devil's Gate bridge in summer of 1869. Jackson photo.*

(Top right) *U.P. engineering survey party in Wasatch Mountains, 1866.*

(Right) *Dale Creek Bridge, Wyoming, soon after completion, with guy ropes still steadying it against frequent gales. This was the U.P.'s biggest trestle.*

U.P.

U.P.

(Top) *Looking from the interior toward the west entrance of C.P. Tunnel No. 10, just east of the summit of the Sierra Nevada. This was excavated entirely by black powder, as were all C.P. tunnels except the long one at the summit.*

(Middle) *Framework of one of the C.P. snowsheds in the process of construction. Tree trunks are its main supports, sawed timbers its roof beams.*

(Below) *Only photo in existence of the entire Stanford special train en route to Promontory Summit for driving of last spike in May, 1869.*

(Right) *A Shoshone Indian gazes down upon the C.P. track in the dramatic Palisades section of the Humboldt River, 435 miles east of Sacramento.*

With the tracks joined, Chief Engineers Montague (left) and Dodge shook hands, C.P.'s Jupiter (left) and U.P.'s No. 119 touched pilots, and champagne was broken out.

A
WORK
OF
GIANTS

Building the First
Transcontinental Railroad

By
Wesley S.
Griswold

McGraw-Hill Book Company, Inc.

New York   Toronto   London

U.P.

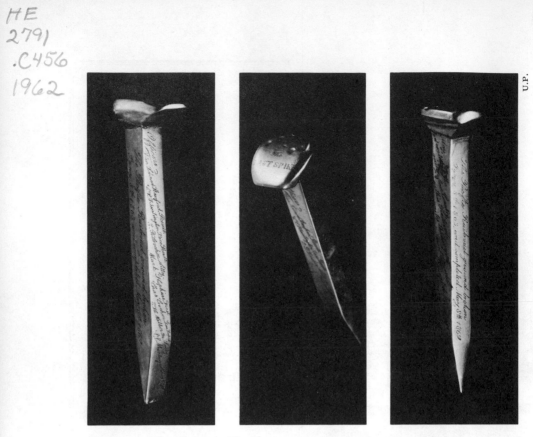

Closeups of the Hewes gold spike presented to the Central Pacific for ceremonial use at Promontory Summit, May 10, 1869. It is now at Stanford University.

A WORK OF GIANTS

To the bright memory of

STEWART JOHNSON

PREFACE

The building of the first "transcontinental" railroad—an amalgam of the 690-mile Central Pacific, cornerstone of the vast future Southern Pacific Co., and the first, 1,086-mile segment of the eventual great Union Pacific system—was truly "a work of giants," just as Gen. William Tecumseh Sherman predicted it would be. The General didn't specify the sort of giant he had in mind. It must have impressed him particularly that they turned out to be rather small in stature, on the whole: Chinese lads from the moist fields around Canton, Irish boys not long removed from the worn-out farms of their deceptively green island, and the occasionally martyred engineers who laid out a path for them to follow.

In telling their story, I have not allowed my awareness that today's Southern Pacific and Union Pacific are two of this nation's most respected, prosperous, and efficient railroads, with their original debts to the United States Government long since repaid, to obscure the fact that their ancestors often represented the antithesis of those qualities.

W.S.G.

ACKNOWLEDGMENTS

I am grateful, first, to unknown persons long dead who were incapable of throwing away diverting tangibles of their times, the fateful 1860s. The fact that they could not bring themselves to discard a vast and often curious potpourri of things printed and unprinted, the latter ranging from the Central Pacific's first locomotive to the scalp lock of Bill Thompson, Union Pacific telegraph repairman, has made easier and livelier my retelling of an important chapter in the story of America's past.

Fortunately, instead of being hoarded in barns and attics, the diversified acquisitions of those ghostly collectors have found their way into the solicitous care of libraries and museums. It is to these latter-day custodians of the evidence that I am presently indebted.

Foremost among them is the Department of Special Collections, University of California, Los Angeles, and its unflaggingly helpful staff. I also wish to acknowledge in particular the generous assistance of the staffs of the Bancroft Library, University of California, Berkeley; California Division, California State Library; Department of Special Collections and the Stanford Collection, Stanford University Libraries; Union Pacific Historical Museum; and Free Public Library, Council Bluffs, Iowa. Others to whom I owe appreciative thanks are the Departments of Public Relations of the Union Pacific Railroad and the Southern Pacific Company; Henry E. Huntington Library; Stanford University Museum; Wyoming State Archives and Historical Department; University of Wyoming Library; California Historical Society; Nevada Historical Society; Transportation Library, University of Michigan; Society of California Pioneers; Manuscript Division, N. Y. Public Library; Manuscript Division, Library of Congress; The National Archives; and the reference librarians of the Los Angeles and Santa Monica Public Libraries.

For distinguished professional advice and encouragement, I am deeply thankful to Mrs. Catherine Drinker Bowen, Dr. Allan Nevins, Frank Rowsome, Jr., and Edward Kuhn, Jr., and, for deft editing, to Robert Mabry. Other individuals to whom I owe a debt of gratitude for a wide variety of special deeds of helpfulness in the preparation of this book include Howard Allaway, James V. Mink, F. Brooke Whiting II, Allan R. Ottley, Miss Margaret Dennison, Mrs. Irene Authier Keeffe, Dr. V. R. Easterling, Prof. James C. Carey, John Barr Tompkins, Miss Ruth Scibird, Terry Bender, Julius P. Barclay, Richard D. Tincher, Miss Mildred K. Smock, Mrs. John S. Ames, Ian M. Ferguson, Hon. Ezra Taft Benson, William W. Whitney, Gilbert H. Kneiss, Mrs. Thomas B. Russell, Frank N. Winton, Robert Hancocks, Edward K. Strobridge, Jr., Mrs. Marion Welliver, Paul A. Bissell, H. P. O'Leary, Corrine and Derek Povah, and Marjorie and Arthur Griswold.

For the initial challenge that set me at this long task, for stern intellectual prods when my courage faltered, and for wise counsel, I am forever indebted to a fine writer and irreplaceable comrade, the late Stewart Johnson.

To Prof. James D. Hart, Acting Director, Bancroft Library, University of California, I wish to express my gratitude for his permission to quote from the library's manuscripts of Collis P. Huntington, Charles Crocker, and Mrs. Theodore D. Judah.

To the Stanford University Libraries, I am grateful for having been allowed to quote from the Huntington-Hopkins correspondence in their possession.

Cordial thanks are due, finally, to John S. Casement, of Padroni, Colorado, for allowing me to quote from the few surviving personal letters of his grandfather, Gen. John S. Casement.

CONTENTS

Maps showing routes of Central Pacific and Union Pacific appear on front and rear endpapers.

Photographs appear on front-matter pages i-viii and following pages 86, 134, 198, 246, 278, and 326.

A WORK OF GIANTS

CHAPTER ONE

A BEGINNING
IN THE WEST

It was a few minutes past noon on a balmy, sunlit Thursday, the eighth day of January, 1863. Sacramento, the young capital of California, was expectant and excited. Along muddy Front Street, within a few yards of the flooded Sacramento River, most of the inhabitants of the town had gathered to watch a ceremony whose promise stirred the whole West.

After a generation of dreaming, a dozen years of widespread editorial prodding, and many fruitless debates in state and territorial legislatures and in Congress, work on the yearned-for Pacific Railroad was about to begin. The hope for this seemingly legendary track—that would someday link the West Coast with the dishearteningly remote East—had long helped to sustain homesick Western settlers. Now their daydream was going to materialize. At last they could look forward to a way to revisit homes that had seemed as far off as the other side of the world. Families that had thought themselves separated forever could look forward to reunion.

In a simmer of anticipation, the women of Sacramento crowded the second-floor balconies of Front Street's low brick and wooden business buildings, or sat in a half-circle of carriages whose wheels were partly lost in muck. The men clustered in the potholed street, trampling soggy bales of hay that had been scattered about a rough, flag-adorned platform of new boards near the river bank. It was messy and uncomfortable there. But as the local correspondent for the San Francisco *Bulletin* wrote, "If a man is going to be frightened by a little mud, he'd better go under a glass case at once and be set on a parlor table."

A ten-piece band that the Sacramento *Union* sponsored was puffing through a program of patriotic songs and marches on the porch of the American Exchange Hotel. It kept repeating a short, lively popular tune called "Wait for the Wagon." This was a musical joke, and the capering listeners enjoyed it. Everybody was aware that at the northern fringe of the crowd, two horse-drawn carts, loaded with dirt and draped with bunting, stood in line, as if about to move onto a stage. On the audience's side of the first cart hung a banner that displayed huge hands clasped across the American continent, and above them the slogan "May the Bond Be Eternal."

The chill, tainted scent of freshet was in the air drifting in from the drowned meadows to the west. It made many people remember uneasily the fearful flood that had come upon them a year before. At that time, the little town where the American and Sacramento Rivers meet had been nearly submerged in a vast lake of melted snow from the peaks of the Sierra Nevada, which stood palely along the eastern horizon, 90 miles away and more. They recalled that young Governor Leland Stanford, who was to be the chief speaker today, had had to ride to his inaugural in a rowboat. When the Stanfords had returned home, they had found their brand-new square piano soaking in the parlor among the floating, plush-covered chairs. Since then, Sacramento's levees had been strengthened and raised.

The impatient throng jostled and chattered. There was some anxious talk about the ominous recent Indian raids on forest settlements in northwest California. Casual references were made to the latest news from the comfortably distant battlefronts of the Civil War. An old man reminded those around him that this day already had a certain significance, for fifty years ago Andy Jackson had whipped the British at New Orleans. A few listeners nodded respectfully, but no one had much thought for the heroic past. The ceremony they were waiting for was the matter of overriding interest, an event of intense personal importance. None but the children present had been born in California. Nearly every adult had made his way there by a perilous, months-long journey by land or sea, a journey that seemed impossible to repeat. All had left behind them tearful relatives or mourning friends whom they had only the thinnest hope of ever seeing again.

Stanford himself had first brought his wife to the West only a little more than seven years before. Preferring to risk storms at sea rather than submit to the dangers and delays of the overland stage route, they had traveled by a relay of steamers, crossing Central America in Nicaragua instead of Panama. Both oceans had been rough, and Mrs. Stanford was frequently seasick. "Never mind," her husband had said as he tried to comfort her. "I will build a railroad one of these days for you to go back on." [1]

Now, as the assembled Sacramentans looked toward the bareheaded men in dirty boots who were mounting the steps of the speakers' stand, they felt a lift of affection for them that was as cheering and comforting as the day's sunlight, which followed a spell of cold rain. For in that knot of men at the platform stood four fellow-citizens—Stanford, the grocer who had become their governor; Charles Crocker, a drygoods merchant; Mark Hopkins, a hardware dealer; and Theodore D. Judah, an engineer with a consuming vision—who were really going to build a railroad that everyone could "go back on" if he chose. At least they were going to construct the western end of it—a track of indeterminate length on which future cars of their newly formed Central Pacific Railroad Co. would run. A fifth Sacramentan in the enterprise, Collis P. Huntington, who was Hopkins' partner in the hardware business, was already in faraway New York, grimly trying to raise money and buy equipment for the job. Only one member of the group knew anything whatever about building a railroad. The funds in prospect were far from bountiful. The self-confidence of the collaborators, nonetheless, was unlimited.

"We all said to each other that if anyone could do it, we could," Crocker had declared.[2] In just such a mood, he had contracted to build the first 18 miles of the Central Pacific himself. When someone jeeringly asked him what experience he, a dealer in yard goods, had had to justify the undertaking, he had answered, "All the experience necessary: I know how to manage men." [3]

Crocker now moved to the front railing of the platform. He was popular with the ladies for his friendliness at the counter and his dependable memory for names and family particulars. Men liked his breezy good humor and rather envied him his cockiness. A fairly tall, bulging forty-year-old with chin whiskers, Crocker stood for a moment grinning and waving as the crowd roared its welcome. A few individuals standing below him shouted, "Hurray for Charlie!" Then he gestured for silence, and in his loud, folksy way proceeded to introduce the Governor, who was also president of the Central Pacific.

Stanford, only thirty-eight, but looking older because he was thickset and bearded, stepped forward. His swarthy skin and shaggy, dark hair gave him a somewhat sinister aspect. Nonetheless, his 6-foot, straight-backed figure, massive head, high forehead, firm jaw, and tight mouth commanded a wide measure of respect. The façade was impressive; what lay behind it was less so. Stanford's friend and successor as Governor, Frederick F. Low, always thought him very mediocre, but said he had at least unusual tenacity of purpose and stout faith in his enterprise. Stanford was a rather plodding speaker. Despite that, most people seemed to like to hear him talk. His voice had a pleasant sound, and he used all the rotund phrases that they thought a public man should employ.

Fellow citizens [he now began], I congratulate you upon the commencement of the great work which, in its results to the State of California and the Pacific Coast, and to the nation itself, is to be what the Erie Canal was to New York and the Western States [he was referring to the present Midwest]. The work will go on, from this side, to completion—as rapidly as possible. There will be no delay, no halting, no uncertainty in its continued progress. . . .[4]

When he had finished, a local minister prayed at some length. Then the first of the two waiting carts was ordered forward and the ornamented horses plodded clumsily to a position close to the platform.

Stanford reached for the handle of a shovel that protruded from the cart and began tossing heaps of dirt, the beginning of a railroad embankment, into the puddles below.

There were some cynics who snickered as the cascading earth splashed and sank. ("Underlying all the enthusiasm, there was . . . a fear that it was a farce and not a fact which was being inaugurated,"[5] the *Union* recalled.) Most of the crowd responded with happy vigor, however, when Crocker, with typical boisterousness, called for nine cheers in place of the usual three.

Various state senators and assemblymen then made short speeches, giving the enterprise a reassuring legislative benediction. And Charlie

Crocker once more bustled to the fore, this time to bring the ceremony to a close.

"Now, then," he said briskly, "the talk is through and the labor commences." [6] In fact, he pointed out, it had already begun. Even while he was talking, he said, a pile driver was at work out in the American River, preparing the foundation of a railroad bridge.

The air quivered with cheers.

Tomorrow, Crocker continued, the teams they saw in front of the platform would be busy at grading, across the river.

"It is going right on, gentlemen, I assure you!" he concluded. "All that I have—all of my own strength, intellect, and energy—is devoted to the building of this section which I have undertaken." [7]

There was a final, prolonged din of applause, and the crowd began to scatter. The principals—all but two—headed for the little offices of the Central Pacific nearby to open some bottles of champagne and drink toasts to the railroad.

One of the abstainers was Mark Hopkins, a thin, sad-faced, bearded man of forty-nine. Hopkins was the oldest and most conservative of these neophyte railroad builders. He loved horses, dogs, and bookkeeping, but he was ill-at-ease with people, especially when they were holding a celebration. There was always the likelihood that, widely respected as he was for his uncommonly shrewd judgment, he might be called upon to make a speech. "Uncle Mark has a long head," [8] friends often said, and they liked to hear what was in it. Hopkins, however, hated being made conspicuous, and dodged all occasions when it might happen. So did his absent partner, Collis Huntington. At forty-one, Huntington was a bold, spare, towering individual of rare strength and intelligence. He had a passion for going his own way and explaining it to no one.

The other abstainer from the champagne party was Theodore Judah, without whom there would have been no cause for celebrating this day. Judah was a mannerly but restless young man, short and solid, with dark, curly hair and a well-trimmed Vandyke. He was a proud and sensitive man who played the organ as a hobby. For years he had been obsessed by a conviction that a railroad linking the East and West could, and must, be built right away. "Neighbors laughed at him," wrote Horace Greeley's best reporter, Albert D. Richardson, "but earnestness is always contagious." [9] Many people half-jokingly said he was crazy, but they had listened to him. Judah resented the party today as a waste of time that had far better been used to push the railroad forward. He was also fast coming to resent his chief associates as well.

This handsome, idealistic son of an Episcopal clergyman was at thirty-six already distinguished. He had engineered the spectacular Niagara Gorge Railroad, in New York State, and the 22-mile Sacramento Valley Railroad, California's first. He was the youngest founder of the Central Pacific. Indeed, he thought of it, with a great deal of justification, as *his* railroad. He had made all the surveys for it. When he could get no financial backing elsewhere, he had talked Stanford, Huntington, Hopkins, Crocker, and a few other gentlemen, more pliable but less well-heeled, into forming a company with him to build it. Now, though, his principal partners seemed to him irritating encumbrances. They had money, and through their connections could doubtless gather more, but they were, he felt, unimaginative men. Already they had made it quite clear that their caution and preoccupation with profit were likely to impede the progress and curb the scope of his grandiose scheme. They were interested primarily in luring the rich freight traffic between the Sacramento River and Nevada's Comstock Lode away from a swarm of teamsters. Judah was impatient with these short-range notions when there was more than half a continent to be spanned and glory to be won.

His impatience was excusable. Theodore Judah had been to a very large extent personally responsible for the fact that, seven months before, in the early summer of 1862, Congress had at last passed a law to create a railroad that would reach from the Missouri River to the Sacramento. The railroad would cross nearly 1,800 miles of plain, desert, and mountain, and connect the isolated West with the outreaching rail lines of the rapidly growing East. It would span two-thirds of the nation—the territories of Nebraska, Wyoming, Utah, and Nevada, and the state of California. Once it had been joined to Eastern tracks, it would enable travelers for the first time to ride all the way from the Atlantic to the Pacific by train.

Imaginative men had begun proposing to build a railroad from the Eastern communities of the United States to the Pacific Coast in 1830, soon after the first American locomotive made its appearance. But no one backed such a scheme with enough fervor and funds, however, until Asa Whitney came along. Whitney was a wealthy New York merchant who had traveled in the Far East, and saw a Pacific Railroad as a means of developing trade with Asia. He set out alone in 1845 to convince state legislatures and Congress that he should be permitted to build it himself. "You will see that it will change the whole world," [10] he assured them.

It was Whitney's loosely conceived idea that the railroad should start at some point between Lake Michigan and the Arkansas Valley, and find its way through a more or less central pass in the Rockies. Beyond the mountains, it was to sprout branches that would reach to Oregon and to Mexico. The main line would head for San Francisco or Monterey, California.

Whitney said that if the government itself were to build this railroad, it would cost the taxpayers $200 million. Instead of seeking Federal funds, he asked Congress to let him buy a strip of public land 60 miles wide, reaching from Lake Michigan to the Pacific, at the rate of 10 cents an acre. He estimated that this purchase would cost him $8 million. But as he sold the land, he thought, he could make enough profit to pay for constructing a railroad across it. The settlers on the land would create business for the line as it inched its way westward. By the time the railroad was finished, it would be all paid for and operating successfully. Whitney then anticipated giving it to the nation.

"I shall have got my profit, the Union will have the line, and the people who use it must keep it in repair," he concluded. "That is my notion, and the thing is plain." [11]

Though chortling critics figured that it would take several hundred years for Whitney's plan to work, his "notion" won official endorsement from sixteen state legislatures in the course of ten years. In various versions, it was even introduced several times in Congress.

But the powerful forces of sectionalism that eventually precipitated the Civil War were already beginning to tear Congress apart. Stubborn arguments between senators and representatives from the South and the North as to where a transcontinental railroad line should run accomplished nothing but the wrecking of bill after bill that might have got the railroad started.

Asa Whitney wound up, broke and forgotten, on a milk route in Washington, D.C.

But contention between slavery and anti-slavery advocates in the Senate and House of Representatives could not drown out repeated demands for a Pacific Railroad. After the Gold Rush had transplanted scores of thousands of Easterners to the Far West, and California had become a state, the demands grew more insistent.

Finally, in 1853, Congress voted to investigate all the principal routes that had been suggested for the railroad by Northerners and Southerners alike. Jefferson Davis, then Secretary of War, dispatched five exploring parties. They were led by officers of the Corps of Engineers, including Capt. George B. McClellan and Lieut. John Pope, future commanders of the Army of the Potomac. Along with surveyors, cartographers, and engineers went geologists, naturalists, and botanists. Their reports contained, in addition to a vast amount of fascinating information that has nothing to do with railroads, five possible routes.

The first was the Northern Trail, 1,854 miles long, from St. Paul to Vancouver, by way of the upper Missouri River. Its cost was estimated at $117,121,000. Next came the Mormon Trail, 2,032 miles long, from Council Bluffs to San Francisco. This crossed the Rockies through South Pass and touched Salt Lake City. It would cost $116,095,000 to build a railroad along this route, the explorers estimated. Considerably farther south lay the Buffalo Trail, which started at Kansas City, and stretched 2,080 miles to San Francisco by way of Cochetopa Pass, in the Rockies of southern Colorado. This route was dismissed as wholly impracticable. It would cost altogether too much to put a railroad there.

Next to be considered was the Thirty-fifth Parallel Trail. It led from Fort Smith, Arkansas, through the northern parts of Texas, New Mexico, and Arizona, to Los Angeles, then known as San Pedro. This route was 1,892 miles long, but it would involve very heavy construction work. The cost of building the railroad there was set at $169,210,222.

The shortest and least expensive route of the five was the Southern Trail, from Fulton, Arkansas, through central Texas and southern New Mexico and Arizona, to San Diego. Length: 1,618 miles. Cost: $68,970,000.

Secretary Davis and other Southern leaders promptly espoused the Southern Trail. The exploring parties had pointed out that heavy snows might make the Northern and Mormon Trails unfeasible. There was no snow to worry about along the Southern Trail. Moreover, argued its advocates, the construction cost would be much less on this route.

In Congress, however, the issue was caught in the great debate over slavery. Southerners feared that the selection of a central or northern route for the railroad would guarantee the development of additional free states. Northerners were equally convinced that the choice of a southern route would place California and perhaps the entire West in the proslavery camp.

It was even suggested in later years that Davis already had at this time a plan for forming a separate republic in the South, and had in mind how he might secure future military support for it from England. Those who believed this of Davis declared that his idea had been to enlist British capital to construct the Pacific Railroad along the Southern Trail. Then, in the event of war between the North and South, the British government would feel obliged to intervene to protect the rights of its citizens who were investors in the railroad.

Senator Thomas Hart Benton, the massive, pugnacious Missourian who was the leading spokesman in Congress for the ideas and aims of the frontier settlers, strongly favored a central route. A powerful advocate of the Pacific Railroad, he proved himself to be amazingly prescient about how long it would take to build it if the job were tackled with sufficient will and strength.

In a public letter to the people of Missouri, printed in March, 1853, at his own expense, he had written, "I should be in favor of seeing an army of laborers employed upon it at once, and the work done in seven years, instead of piddling at it for a lifetime. And why not? We can have the money and the men, and . . . there would be room for 50,000 men to work without elbowing each other." [12]

But the Pacific Railroad was stalled until the coming of the Civil War eliminated all Southern members from Congress. Then the question of routes narrowed to a choice between the Mormon Trail and the Northern Trail. The former won out and became, in a considerably shortened version, the route of the first transcontinental railroad. (It is interesting to note, however, that eventually the Northern Pacific and Great Northern Railroads took the general direction of the Northern Trail. The Santa Fe followed the Thirty-fifth Parallel Trail rather closely. The Southern Pacific laid its track along large sections of the Southern Trail.)

It was the Mormon Trail that Theodore Judah had favored for the Pacific Railroad since the mid-1850's, when he was not yet thirty years old. It had been almost entirely a one-man campaign, paid for out of his own scanty funds. Judah launched it nationally in 1857, with a pamphlet he had written called A Practical Plan for Building the Pacific Railroad. He sent copies of his Practical Plan to all members of Congress.

Early in January, 1860, Judah arrived in Washington from California to try personal persuasion. But his eloquence was lost in a roar of secession talk. He dejectedly sailed for home, but he was back in Washington by late fall of 1861. This time, his position was remarkably strengthened. He had an exciting new route to talk about, proving that the mountain wall along the eastern border of California would not be an impassable barrier for locomotives. In addition, he was now chief engineer and accredited agent of the Central Pacific Railroad.

Judah was present for the turbulent special session of the Thirty-seventh Congress. He remained for the far more fruitful sessions of the following winter and spring. Meanwhile, he enjoyed more enviable prerogatives than perhaps any other lobbyist has ever had. He was made secretary of the Select Committees for the Pacific Railroad in both House and Senate, helping to draft the legislation in which he was so deeply interested and being given floor privileges in both chambers. Furthermore, the old Vice-President's Room in the Capitol was turned over to him. He used it as an office and as a kind of outsize sample case of maps, profiles, and pencil sketches, all pertinent to his well-reinforced argument that it would be entirely feasible for trains to climb over the abrupt, lofty Sierra Nevada.

Judah's proof rested upon repeated surveys that he had begun making in the spring of 1860. At that time, when he had just returned to Sacramento from his futile winter trip to Washington, he had received a compelling letter. It came from a druggist and impromptu doctor named Daniel W. Strong, who lived in Dutch Flat, a thriving mining community in steeply hilly country about 65 miles to the east. "Doc" Strong, as everybody in town called him, said he could show Judah a likely place for a railroad to cross the Sierra. Strong was a surveyor as well as a druggist, so his views seemed worth investigating.

The engineer took the next stagecoach to Dutch Flat. When he arrived, the driver introduced him to Strong. Soon afterward, Strong led Judah out on horseback to look over his discovery. It was a long, continuous, gradually inclined ridge between deep river valleys, that appeared to lead, like an elevated path, most of the way from the Sacramento plain to Donner Summit, more than 7,000 feet above sea level. This westward-flung arm of the Sierra lay between the north fork of the American River and the south forks of the Yuba and Bear Rivers—all three of them tumbling streams that had worn deep gorges in the mountain slopes.

Judah's interest and enthusiasm grew as the two men moved up the ridge over a rough trail first marked by the survivors of the ill-fated Donner Party thirteen years earlier. From the summit, overshadowed by Crested Peak, which towered 2,000 feet above them to the south, the pair gazed down upon Donner Lake, cupped in a broad, forested basin 1,200 feet below their feet. Eastward from the lake, a valley tilted downward through a jumble of mountains toward Nevada Territory. Strong had only casually investigated the country beyond. But he answered Judah's eager questions as well as he could.

Judah knew that the Sierra Nevada range, for much of its 430-mile length, has two rows of summits, separated by a trough sometimes 35 miles across. He had not previously found a pass that did not involve a crossing of both summits. What about this one?

Strong replied that the Truckee River, flowing north out of Lake Tahoe, turned east not far beyond Donner Lake and cut a gate right through the second summit of the Sierra. From there its descent to the Truckee Meadows in Nevada was certainly not steep. Strong surmised that its valley would be suitable for a railroad track to follow. Judah was convinced that it would be, and he urged Strong back to Dutch Flat as fast as they could travel. They rode through a spring snowstorm that turned to soaking rain as they headed down the west flank of the mountains.

As soon as they were back in "Doc" Strong's drugstore, Judah asked for a pencil and paper. He began drawing up "articles of association" for organizing a railroad to cross the Sierra by the Dutch Flat and Donner Lake route.

This was the simple beginning of the Central Pacific. But before anything more substantial could be accomplished, Judah knew that he must confirm his hasty observations of the route with at least a few basic instrument readings. This would require an outlay of around $500. Judah didn't have the money to spare. Neither did Strong. So they set out to raise it by public subscription.

Together, the engineer and the druggist canvassed Dutch Flat and the considerably larger community of Auburn. By the end of June, only forty-seven people had contributed to the project. One was a woman, who gave $2.50. The other contributions ranged from $1 to $15. Their total fell considerably short of the needed $500.

Judah and Strong moved on to Sacramento and began trying to find men who would subscribe for stock in their proposed railroad. State law demanded that before any railroad company could be organized, subscriptions equal to $1,000 a mile for the anticipated length of the line must be signed for and 10 per cent of that sum paid in.

"Merchants, saloon men, draymen . . . everybody, in fact, took an interest in the matter," [13] recalled Strong much later. They also took a few shares, but far too few.

The earnest canvassers then tackled San Francisco. It proved to be hopeless. "The people there laughed at the idea," Strong said. Only two men in the city subscribed for stock—25 shares apiece—"and they were men belonging in the mountains anyway." [14]

Greatly discouraged, Judah and Strong returned to Sacramento for a final attempt to launch the railroad. Judah arranged to hold a public meeting at the St. George Hotel.

Collis Huntington was among those who attended. "Some subscribed a barrel of flour, others a sack of potatoes or some kind of stores, and some, money," he related. "I gave nothing, and when the meeting was about to break up, someone said to me, 'Huntington, you are the man to give to this enterprise.'" But Huntington did no more than express interest. As he was leaving, he said to Judah, "If you want to come to my office some evening, I will talk with you about the railroad." [15]

Judah responded eagerly, of course. The next night, they met in the rooms above the Huntington & Hopkins hardware store, at 54 K Street. In the course of answering Huntington's searching questions about the project, Judah had said it would cost $35,000 to make a thorough instrumental survey of the prospective route, all the way from downtown Sacramento to the Nevada border. At the end of the discussion, Huntington said he would find the money for it. "But I said that although I would carry the survey through," he declared later, "I would not agree to do anything further than that." [16]

Huntington rounded up several other local men who agreed to put as much money into the survey as he did. Stanford was first. Then came James Bailey, a jeweler, who was a friend of Judah's; Lewis A. Booth, a grocer; and Charles Marsh, a mine owner from little Nevada City, California. Judah was accepted as an equal contributor with the others, his professional services to count as a fair substitute for cash. Hopkins proved hardest to persuade. "He thought it a great mountain and that it offered a vast amount of hard work," [17] Huntington explained. But Hopkins finally gave in. Crocker then agreed to join the group, saying to Huntington, "I think that anything that you and Uncle Mark undertake is worthy of some attention." [18]

Judah jubilantly began the survey a few days later, starting on Front Street, in view of the hotel room where he and his wife were temporarily residing.

"If you want to see the first work done on the Pacific Railroad, look out of your bedroom window," he said to Mrs. Judah that day. "I am going to work there this morning, and I am going to have these men pay for it."

"I'm glad," she replied. "It's about time somebody else helped." [19]

The engineer could not move on into the mountains until the following spring. When he did, he took his wife along. She made pencil sketches while he and his assistants proceeded with their surveying and the driving of stakes at 100-foot intervals.

By the late spring of 1861, Judah was able to demonstrate, with a fat accumulation of maps, profiles, and statistics, that the route he had looked over with "Doc" Strong a year before was indeed practicable for a railroad to follow. It led up the long granite spur at a steady diagonal whose grade never exceeded 105 feet to the mile, and was usually less than that. Stakes marked out a so-called "side hill" line, which kept close to the tops of the successive humps in the ridge but largely clung to their north slopes. Judah proposed to cross the gaps between humps with trestles. There was no deep canyon in the way.

Along the approach to the summit, and in crossing it, Judah estimated that eighteen tunnels would have to be cut, most of them over 1,000 feet long. He decided that the best way to descend from the summit to the valley floor east of Donner Lake was to slant down along the steep northerly slopes of the mountains that formed the south rim of the lake basin. To his great delight, he found that once this line had met the Truckee River, the stream itself angled toward Nevada at an easy pitch. A track could comfortably follow it. The distance from Sacramento to the Truckee by the staked-out route was 123 miles; to the Nevada line, 145 miles. Beyond lay the Truckee Meadows, the Nevada desert, and nothing formidable for railroad builders to encounter until they reached the Wasatch Mountains, in eastern Utah.

There was the troublesome question of snowfall, however. Every Californian knew that tremendous blizzards occasionally buried the summits of the Sierra. But from studying the bark on the north sides of trees and by questioning the few mountain dwellers whom they met, Judah and his men estimated that the greatest depth of level snow to be anticipated near Donner Summit would be around 13 feet. That, of course, was much more than any other railroad in the United States had ever had to contend with. Still, since the Central Pacific's track would largely lie along a shelf notched in a steep slope, the engineer felt that snows would slide off it, or at least be readily disposed of by plows—a woeful underestimation, as the future would show.

The Central Pacific Railroad Co. was formally organized at Sacramento on June 28, 1861. The railroad's directors, in addition to Stanford, Huntington, Hopkins, and Crocker, included Booth, Judah, "Doc" Strong, Marsh, and Bailey. The directors chose Stanford to be the railroad's president. Huntington was made vice-president. At the same time, he conveyed to at least two men present the impression that he felt he should have headed the enterprise. He had a nagging feeling that Stanford was not quite the man for the job. Hopkins was elected secretary-treasurer. Judah, naturally, was named chief engineer.

It was a measure of the ambition of these men—or at least of Judah—that they almost immediately asked Nevada for the right to extend their non-existent track across that territory. They asked as the incorporators of a paper organization called the Nevada Rail Road Co. The first Territorial Legislature, eager for a rail link to the Pacific, promptly granted their request, giving the Nevada Rail Road a charter to build from the western boundary of the territory to its eastern border.

Judah had estimated that it would cost about $12,500,000, or a little more than $88,500 a mile, to extend the Central Pacific as far as the California-Nevada line. The organizers of the railroad, though most of them were successful businessmen, could not contemplate raising more than a small portion of that sum from their own resources. They spent a good deal of time during the summer of 1861 considering how they might obtain the rest of the money they would need. They agreed to seek most of it from the United States government. They even drafted proposals for Congress to consider. Finally, on October 9, the directors voted to send Judah to Washington, by a steamer leaving two days later. He went "as the accredited agent of the Central Pacific Railroad Company of California, for the purpose of procuring appropriations of land and U.S. Bonds from Government, to aid in the construction of this Road."

It was a month in which the pace of the nation's scientific and industrial progress seemed suddenly very swift and certain. Before Judah's ship reached Panama, the first transcontinental telegraph line was opened. By the time he had docked in New York, the romantic Pony Express was officially dead. Its glamorous life of only a year and a half had already been ended by the new, instantaneous means of sending messages from coast to coast.

After Judah arrived in Washington, he became secretary of the special Pacific Railroad committees of the Senate and House. Moreover, he buttonholed every congressman who would stand still.

"His knowledge of his subject was so thorough, his manners so gentle and insinuating, his conversation on the subject so entertaining, that few resisted his appeals," [20] wrote Representative John C. Burch of California, who was one of the first lawmakers to fall under Judah's spell. And the persuasive young engineer helped powerfully to convince Congress that the railroad, which would be many times longer and more difficult to construct than any other in the world at that time, could be built.

It would, however, be "a work of giants," as William Tecumseh Sherman had declared in 1857 to his brother John, a congressman from Ohio. "And Uncle Sam is the only giant I know who can grapple the subject," [21] the future Civil War general had added. Many congressmen felt, as W. T. Sherman did, that private enterprise would be unequal to the task, even if it could be entrusted with it.

In the winter and spring of 1862, there were heavier pressures on Congress than Theodore Judah's to do something right away about the Pacific Railroad. Several members were afraid that if California were not soon given firm proof that an end to its isolation was in sight, the large Southern element there would seize the state for the Confederacy. It was also rumored that if war should break out between the North and England, as then seemed possible, the British fleet in the Pacific would attack San Francisco. Without a railroad on which to rush troops and munitions to the defense of California, Oregon, and Washington Territory, the entire West Coast would surely be forced to surrender to the invaders.

Representative Aaron A. Sargent of California, a former small-town editor and attorney, even raised the spectre of his state's eventual secession, if it were left isolated. Sargent, a Republican, was a friend and political crony of the Central Pacific's officials. A fast and able talker, he was the most persistent advocate of the Pacific Railroad in the House. He was also a new member of the committee then hammering out a bill to aid its construction. In time, he was rewarded by having a Central Pacific locomotive named for him.

The Pacific Railroad bill, Sargent now told the House, ought to be passed at once. If it were delayed until the Civil War was paid for, as some suggested, it might not be built for thirty or forty years. Meanwhile, a whole new generation would have grown up in a California that was still segregated from the rest of the Union. Without the loyalties and family ties of his own generation, these future citizens of the West might decide to form a separate republic. "You must break down this barrier and assimilate the different portions of the country," [22] Sargent declared.

Querulous old Thaddeus Stevens of Pennsylvania, ever mindful of his ironmaking constituents and of his own thriving little foundry at Chambersburg, then rose to bring the debate around to a matter of more immediate concern. The railroad, he said, would be a whale of a good thing for the iron industry. Then, unwilling to be thought preoccupied with the pocketbooks of Pennsylvanians alone, he hastened to expand his picture of the railroad's potentialities.

"The Western soil is but a platform on which to lay the rails to transport the wealth of the furthest Indies to Philadelphia, Boston, and Portland," he said, "scattering its benefits on its way to St. Louis, Chicago, Cincinnati, Buffalo, and Albany. Then our Atlantic seaports will be but a resting place between China, Japan, and Europe." [23]

The House of Representatives passed the enabling act, 79 to 49, on May 8, 1862. The Senate, where there were fewer skeptics, approved a nearly identical version of the bill, 35 to 5, on June 20th.

Congress had decreed that the railroad should be built from both ends. The Central Pacific Railroad Co. was to run a track eastward from Sacramento as far as it could go. Another company, to be called the Union Pacific Railroad and Telegraph Co., was to be organized to thrust a track westward to meet it. But not from the Missouri River. Oddly, the law stated that the Union Pacific's main line was to begin at a point on the 100th Meridian of West Longitude in south-central Nebraska. Today that point is close to the little town of Cozad. Then it was just an arbitrary dot on a blank map, 247 miles west of Omaha. It was approximately in the middle of nowhere.

This strange decision was made in an effort to quiet a wrangle among half a dozen Missouri River towns for the prize of becoming the eastern terminus of the U.P.'s main line. Sioux City, Omaha, Council Bluffs, St. Joseph, Atchison, Leavenworth, and Kansas City were in the bitter fight, which had resounded clamorously in Congress. In framing the Pacific Railroad Act of 1862, congressmen had tried to please them all. The law stipulated that branch lines were to be built from Sioux City and Kansas City to converge on the main line at the 100th Meridian. Short spurs from St. Joseph and Leavenworth were to connect with the Kansas City branch.

There was to be a central branch, beginning somewhere on the western boundary of Iowa, at a place to be chosen by the President of the United States. Finally, out in California, a track was to be built to link Sacramento with San Francisco.

Instead of creating general satisfaction, the provisions for branch lines at the eastern end of the road merely stirred up more trouble. It was clear to almost everyone that the central branch was likely to have the shortest, most direct route to the starting point of the Union Pacific's main line. Therefore, it would stand the best chance of becoming the vital link between the main line and the Missouri River, and inherit the bulk of the East-West traffic. This would be especially true if the President were to name Omaha or Council Bluffs as the initial point. And rumors were lively that he would do just that.

To make matters worse, while various railroad companies were authorized to build the other branches, the law stated that the Union Pacific Co. itself was to construct the central branch as well as the main line. Out along the Missouri, this looked like blatant favoritism, except to the people of Omaha and Council Bluffs. And even they couldn't be sure of triumph. So until Lincoln decided where the central branch was to start, each town likely to be affected by his choice would strive mightily to win his favor for itself.

Having created this prickly problem for the President, the Pacific Railroad Act went on to specify the extent of financial help that the railroad builders might expect from the government. Most lawmakers considered it generous.

Each company was granted a 400-foot right-of-way along "the most direct, central, and practicable route" that could be determined. It could help itself to earth, stone, timber, and other construction materials that lay at hand. It was denied access to mineral lands, but if trees grew there, they could be cut if needed. For each mile of track completed, the company would receive 6,400 acres of public land within 20 miles of the line, and a thirty-year loan in government bonds, with interest at 6 per cent to be paid by the U.S. Treasury until the bonds matured. At the end of thirty years, principal and accumulated interest were to be repaid. The financial subsidy would amount to $16,000 a mile where the going was easy—west of the Sierra Nevada and east of the Rockies. It would be raised to $48,000 a mile for the mountain crossings, estimated to encompass 150 miles of the heaviest kind of work over each of those mighty ranges. It was set at $32,000 a mile for the high, barren land that lay between the mountain barriers.

In return for this support from the U.S. Treasury, expected to amount to about $50 million in bonds and 20 million acres of land for the main line, the government would hold a first mortgage on the completed railroad and all its appurtenances.

To make certain that the nation would be getting what it expected for its money, bonds and lands would be doled out in strict accord with the progress of the railroad builders. Trios of government inspectors, men of integrity and engineering background who would know a good railroad when they saw one, were to ride over specific sections of track as they were completed. Their approval of the work would be required before the public bounty could be tapped. In territory where the subsidy was $16,000 a mile, these official inspections would be made every 40 miles; elsewhere, at 20-mile intervals.

Congressmen concluded that the Central Pacific, faced at the start with the soaring rise of the Sierra Nevada, a granite wave that swelled from nearly sea level to more than 7,000 feet in altitude within 100 miles, would be lucky to reach the eastern border of California before it encountered the rails of the Union Pacific. With this in mind, they provided that if the Union Pacific got there first, it could, with California's consent, push on until it connected with the Central Pacific. However, with scrupulous regard for the off chance, they also inserted in the law permission for the Central Pacific, in case it should accomplish a miracle of construction, to build eastward indefinitely if it hadn't met the Union Pacific at the western edge of Nevada Territory.

The Central Pacific was required to complete 50 miles of its road within the next two years, and build at least 50 additional miles a year thereafter. The Union Pacific must do twice as well as that. The penalty for lagging: confiscation of the dawdling railroad. No matter where the completed tracks might meet, they must form "a connected, continuous line of railroad" and be ready for use at the end of fourteen years, by July 1, 1876.

Despite the heights that had to be climbed, grades should nowhere be allowed to exceed the steepest (116 feet to the mile) on the Baltimore & Ohio, the oldest U.S. railroad of importance, nor should curves anywhere be sharper than the B.&O.'s maximum of 10 degrees. The gauge of the track, certain to be a matter of stubborn contention if debated in Congress, since existing railroads in the nation varied in width from 4 feet, 8½ inches, to 7 feet, was left for President Lincoln to decide.

Having described the financial assistance that the United States would provide for the building of a railroad to the Pacific Coast, congressmen proceeded to shrink their bounty with restrictive phrases. When the government was able to transport troops, supplies, and mails on the railroad, the charges for these services would not be paid in cash but applied on the road's indebtedness. Furthermore, at least 5 per cent of net earnings must be applied each year to reducing the debt.

This was only the beginning. One-quarter of all bonds issued on the initial, easy miles of track, and 15 per cent of those to be loaned on the vast sections in between, were to be withheld until the railroad was completed to the government's satisfaction.

Thaddeus Stevens had insisted on inserting a requirement that all rails and other ironwork be of American origin. This clause raised the future cost of construction enormously.

Finally, the national legislators chilled the interest of most potential investors by placing an implied ceiling on earnings. They stipulated that whenever net earnings of a participating railroad company exceeded 10 per cent of the cost of building its portion of the line, exclusive of the 5 per cent already earmarked for trimming debt, "Congress may reduce the rates of fare thereon, if unreasonable in amount, and may fix and establish the same by law."

Having thus laid in the path of the railroad-builders impediments that would have to be removed by an amended law before the project could take on more than feeble life, the members of both Houses sent the Railroad Act of 1862 to President Lincoln, who signed it on July 1st.

Later that month, in a gesture without precedent, forty-four representatives, seventeen senators, and the Secretary of the Senate sent a heartwarming testimonial to Theodore Judah:

We cannot let this opportunity pass without tendering to you our warmest thanks for your valuable assistance in aiding the passage of the Pacific Railroad bill through Congress.

Your explorations and surveys in the Sierra Nevada Mountains have settled the question of practicability of the line, and enabled many members to vote confidently on the great measure, while your indefatigable exertions and intelligent explanations of the practical features of the enterprise have gone very far to aid in its inauguration.[24]

CHAPTER TWO

1863

OFF TO A
LONG CLIMB

After the Central Pacific's lighthearted ground-breaking ceremonies on January 8, 1863, when champagne kept an afternoon party bubbling for hours, unexpected troubles sprouted and flourished. Obtaining money was, of course, a basic problem. Finding laborers, however, was a more pressing concern at the moment. Newspaper advertisements and hand-bills produced only a trickle of reluctant applicants, but even at that, rounding them up was easier than keeping them on the job.

"Most of the men working on the road were merely working for a stake," Stanford recalled. "When they got that, they would go off to the mines, and we could not hold them, except in rare instances, more than a very little while." [1]

Charles Crocker, in a move to dodge possible legal backfire later, had resigned from the railroad's board of directors late in December, 1862, in order to sign a $400,000 contract to build the first 18 miles of track. He was to be paid $250,000 in cash, $100,000 in Central Pacific bonds, and $50,000 in the company's stock, then representing little but hope. Along with the contract, he was given the title of General Superintendent of the railroad.

His oldest brother, Edward B. Crocker, trained both as an engineer and as a lawyer, took Charles' place on the Central Pacific board. Here was a smart move. E. B. Crocker, a fat, graying, moon-faced man, with chin whiskers that looked like a small, limp whiskbroom, was liberally endowed with brains and cunning. He was regarded as much more able than Charles, and took hold of any undertaking with a determined grasp. He was already handling the Central Pacific's legal affairs. He continued to do so even after Governor Stanford, sometimes hazy about ethics, appointed him in May, 1863, to fill out a short, unexpired term on the State Supreme Court. After this temporary elevation, E. B. Crocker was always called "Judge" by his associates.

Upon becoming superintendent, Crocker at once sublet the construction work to three local firms with the required experience—something he altogether lacked. They in turn parcelled out segments of their labor to four lesser contractors. This set off brisk competitive bidding for men and one-horse dump carts, which casually migrated wherever the working conditions seemed most inviting. The average pay for a man with a team was $4 a day at first. Before the summer was over, many of the workers struck for $1 a day more, and got it.

Though the Sacramento *Union* announced with zest at the end of February, 1863, that there were 200 men at work on the grading, in five places between the American River and the foothills, the results were disheartening to the Central Pacific's officials.

Widely separated mounds of fresh earth, some of them 12 feet high, lay dribbled across the valley floor. There was little indication that they would ever be united to support a railroad track.

Most of the subcontractors had discovered that the easily moved topsoil was only a foot or two deep. Beneath it lay a crust of sand, pebbles, and rocks, called "concrete," which was nearly as unyielding as pavement. The graders had to scrape much wider areas than anticipated, and the cost shot up to more than double their estimates. Some of the smaller firms engaged began to protest that they could not afford to go on with the work.

The movement of migrating laborers showed a pronounced drift toward the mines. As a result, the grading and culverts farthest from the river front at Sacramento, and thus nearest the gold and silver diggings, were being completed first.

This situation was worrisome indeed. It was essential to the success of

the enterprise that the Central Pacific should become an operating railroad as soon as possible. Unless the track could be laid consecutively from
Sacramento eastward, it could not carry income-producing trains of passengers and freight, to say nothing of supply trains moving to the
construction front.

Charles Crocker, whom Stanford called "a man of a great deal of energy
and force of character," [2] decided very soon to take command of the disorderly operation and learn railroad construction by doing it. As he told
his son, Charles, many years later, "If it becomes necessary to jump off
the dock in the service of the company, instead of saying, 'Go, boys!,'
you must pull off your coat and say, 'Come, boys!,' and let them follow." [3]

He shed his drygoods business. Selling part of the inventory to former
competitors, he let his clerks purchase the rest, at low cost and with plenty
of time to pay for it. Then off he went, surprisingly agile for a man who
weighed 244 pounds, to bring efficiency and dynamism to a wholly unfamiliar undertaking. As it turned out, he had an extraordinary aptitude
for the job. He even gained weight under the stress of it.

The people of Sacramento were soon encouraged by what they could
see of the results of Crocker's energy and drive. Redwood pilings up to
30 feet long, to support the future railroad bridge across the American
River, had begun to arrive at the Front Street dock. Schooners brought
them from coastal groves near Santa Cruz, California. Timbers for trestles
came by ship from the vast forests encircling Puget Sound, in Washington
Territory. Ties were being imported, too, to push the track toward the
mountains. By midyear there would be an immense pile of them on Front
Street, increasing at the rate of a schooner load a day.

The *Union* pointed to the noisy accomplishments of the little 10-horse-
power pile driver out in the American River. At work on the foundations
of the bridge, the huffing machine was lifting a 1,900-pound hammer
three times a minute and pounding 30-foot pilings into the river bed at
the rate of seven a day. The *Union's* editor, Lauren Upson, had long been
a crony of Theodore Judah, the Central Pacific's chief engineer. He lost
no opportunity to print a friendly paragraph about the railroad.

Rolling stock for the Central Pacific was being built in the East. Six
locomotives, a practical assortment of forty-two freight cars, six first-class
coaches, and enough frogs, switches, turntables and other track equipment for the first 50 miles had been ordered from firms in New Jersey,
Pennsylvania, and Massachusetts more than six months earlier. Judah had

done the shopping. Collis Huntington, who had joined the engineer in Washington early in 1862, sent him on to New York to place the orders as soon as the Pacific Railroad Act had got through both House and Senate. Huntington announced the outcome of the voting to his distant colleagues in a characteristically sardonic telegram: "We have drawn the elephant. Now let us see if we can harness him." [4]

Steel rails were not yet known in the United States, except as rare and very costly imports from England, where they had originated in 1855. Huntington, acting on Judah's advice after the latter had returned to California, bought the heaviest wrought-iron rails available. They weighed 60 pounds per yard. On March 30, 1863, he telegraphed Stanford the encouraging news that he had obtained commitments for 5,000 tons of them. They would be delivered at the rate of 500 tons a month. No mill owner could say exactly when the first cargo would arrive at Sacramento, though. The Federal armies and rapidly expanding navy were demanding iron in staggering quantities. Their requirements, naturally, must be satisfied ahead of all others.

In addition, the success of raids by Confederate privateers was boosting the cost of insurance. All too often, these swift harriers slipped through the Federal blockade of Southern ports and intercepted cargoes bound to or from the West Coast. The threat of loss by this means primarily shadowed shipping lanes along the Eastern seaboard.

Sacramento newspaper readers were reminded of this threat in July, 1863. "The Pacific Railroad has large shipments of iron afloat," the *Union* announced. It added cautiously that the iron could be expected to arrive at a convenient time "if it does not fall into the hands of the pirates [of?] Alabama or Florida." [5]

No cargo destined for the Central Pacific was ever lost to the Southern "pirates," though at one time during the Civil War there were thirty ships at sea carrying materials consigned to the railroad. But the United States government once confiscated two C.P. locomotives from a vessel bound for Sacramento, feeling that its own desperate need of the moment was greater than the railroad's.

The pinch of rising insurance and freight costs was hurtful enough to the men who were trying to build the Central Pacific, but it was responsible for only part of their financial distress.

Their fundamental problem, a fearful one, was where to raise $3,-221,496. That was what the first 50 miles of the railroad would cost to build, according to Judah's careful estimates. Those 50 miles must be completed within two years, according to the Pacific Railroad Act, and 40 of them must be ready for use before the builders would get a cent from the government for having built them. There were the Central Pacific's own bonds, of course. But the bonds, despite Huntington's bold, airy salesmanship, were regarded by Eastern financiers as almost too speculative to be tempting. They were, after all, second-mortgage bonds. The government itself was to hold a first mortgage on the railroad in return for its financial aid to the builders.

Central Pacific bonds could not be sold at all except at prices well below their par value of $1,000. Moreover, the buyers paid for their bonds in the new U.S. Treasury banknotes, which, because of their unaccustomed color, were earning the nickname "greenbacks." This paper currency was not depreciated seriously in the markets where Huntington was paying for rolling stock and equipment for the Central Pacific and chartering vessels to deliver it. But no one on the West Coast would touch the stuff. In the isolated part of the nation where gold and silver were mined, those precious metals were the medium of exchange. Laborers insisted on being paid in gold, and so did all merchants. The loss incurred in exchanging greenbacks for gold in New York and Boston, where Huntington conducted his vital end of the railroad's business, ranged from regrettable to appalling. The value of gold fluctuated crazily with the wobbly tone of news from the battlefronts. During the first year that the Central Pacific was under construction, $100 in greenbacks never bought more than $81.88 in gold. At one particularly gloomy point, it purchased only $57.97 worth.

This situation put an excruciating squeeze on the slim resources of the Central Pacific. It was a source of delight, though, to many California merchants and traders. They made huge profits by buying goods with greenbacks in the East and selling them for gold on the West Coast.

It was most fortunate for the Central Pacific at this austere and anxious time in its young life that Collis Huntington was negotiating its securities and making its major purchases. He had been a daring and successful trader since he was a boy. He had a sharp eye for opportunity, and always moved confidently to take advantage of it when it appeared.

Arriving in New York by steamer early in 1863, as vice-president and financial agent of the Central Pacific Railroad, Huntington set up shop at 54 William Street. From there, he wrote scrawling, barely legible letters to "Friend Stanford," "Friend Crocker," and "Mr. Hopkins; Dear Sir" on ruled white letterheads only slightly larger than the pages of a pocket notebook.[6] In the upper left-hand corner was a diminutive block of lettering that contained the name of the railroad, the address of its New York office, and a tiny line that read "C.P. Huntington, V.P."

It is curious that Huntington's letters to Hopkins, which form the bulk of his correspondence that has been preserved, often began with a formal salutation. Presumably this was a reflection of his respect for the older man, who had been his esteemed partner since 1854, and of the restraining influence of Hopkins' distant manner. There was certainly no lack of warmth in Huntington's feelings for his closest associate. "Mark Hopkins was one of the truest and best men that ever lived," [7] he said of him in later years.

Collis Huntington was thoroughly at home in New York City. He knew it well from the days before he went West. Then he used to come down from his general store in upstate Oneonta to walk the streets tirelessly peddling butter and other country commodities. Though twenty years older now than he was when he first made his rounds in lower Manhattan seeking customers, Huntington was still in remarkably youthful physical condition and as erect as a Sierra pine. Six feet, two inches tall, his body almost as lean and muscular as it had been when he used to saw and pile firewood before breakfast each day to keep in trim, he was a most impressive figure. Now that he was a leading California businessman, half-owner of the West's biggest hardware firm as well as an official of a fledgling railroad, his connections were no longer with clerks but with the city's leading merchants and bankers. But he was still peddling. Central Pacific bonds were firmer than his old wares, but their value showed a distressing tendency to melt under the hard scrutiny of potential buyers.

In a situation like this, a diffident salesman would have been lost. Huntington, as was natural for him, took the opposite approach. When he strode into a prospect's office with his quick, light step, shook hands firmly, and stated his case in a brisk manner, while his keen blue-gray eyes looked confidently into those of the man he was addressing, he conveyed an impression of strength, dependability, and purposefulness that was disarming.

That untypically chatty banker, Henry Clews, who wrote his reminiscences of the financial life of New York during this period, paid a wondering tribute to Huntington's sales technique:

Many, at such a time, would have gone to speculators, begging for aid and pledging his bonds for railroad material with which to commence the great line. He did nothing of the kind. He was always bold. He coolly announced that he would not dispose of his bonds except for cash, and, strange as it may have seemed, he capped the climax by refusing to sell any at all unless $1,500,000 worth were taken. He was again successful, but the purchasers required more security. Thereupon, Mr. Huntington made himself and his [hardware] firm responsible for the whole amount.[8]

Huntington had come prepared for this situation. He had brought with him powers of attorney to pledge the personal credit of each of his associates along with his own, if that became necessary. Huntington, Hopkins, Stanford, and Crocker had all been for several years large purchasers of goods in Eastern markets, for their respective businesses. They had promptly paid their bills and repaid their loans. They had no debts. Their credit ratings were uniformly reassuring. As an added inducement to Easterners to buy Central Pacific bonds, Huntington had brought with him a letter of recommendation from Darius Ogden Mills, the West's chief banker. (Mills had declined to invest in the railroad himself, but he gladly testified to the responsibility and honor of the men who were going to try to build it!) But the cautious buyers still demanded further, and more tangible, assurance. As a result, Huntington and his chief associates pledged that they would personally guarantee the payment of interest on the Central Pacific bonds for a period of ten years.

With these various desperate measures of reinforcement, Huntington managed to sell enough of the bonds in the first six months of 1863 to pay for a goodly assortment of rolling stock and sufficient rails to lay 70 miles of track.

Meanwhile he was making his debut as the railroad's lobbyist in Washington as well as its financial and purchasing agent in New York and Boston. Traveling repeatedly from one of those cities to another in his urgent hunt for money and political support, he rode certain Eastern trains almost as often as their crews did.

What the Central Pacific wanted of the government at this juncture was a ruling that the first transcontinental railroad should have a 5-foot gauge. That was already the width of California tracks. It had been legally established when the brief Sacramento Valley Railroad and the equally short California Central were built. It would be a serious financial handicap to the Central Pacific if a national edict should force it to be narrower than those two little local railroads. Its officers hoped to utilize them as feeders, and as soon as possible.

All the lines in the South had a 5-foot gauge. This uniformity was proving of great value to the Confederates in concentrating soldiers and supplies. Northern railroads, on the other hand, varied disconcertingly in width. Some, especially in the Midwest, were narrower, some considerably wider, than 5 feet. All New England tracks and those of the New York Central, Pennsylvania Railroad, and Baltimore & Ohio were 4 feet, 8½ inches wide.

The framers of the Pacific Railroad Act had left the decision about gauge up to President Lincoln. Huntington later claimed that he had influenced them to do so during the debates in the spring of 1862. If this was true, Judah had undoubtedly done his persuading for him. What Huntington had had in mind was that if the issue were permitted to be settled in Congress, pressure by legislators from the populous regions served by the principal Eastern railroads might well overwhelm the proponents of other gauges. He thought that it would be easier to persuade Lincoln to see the matter his way than to win over a majority of congressmen. To see if he could turn the trick, Huntington had headed for Washington very shortly after debarking from the steamer that brought him to New York from California in January, 1863.

His maneuvers were wily. Knowing that the member of the Administration who was in closest touch with all matters pertaining to the Pacific Railroad was John P. Usher, Secretary of the Interior, he first found out where Usher boarded. Then he arranged not only to take his meals at the same place but at the same table with the Secretary. In casual conversation over their food, Huntington encouraged Usher to talk at length about the transcontinental railroad. Without disclosing his own anxious desire for a 5-foot gauge, the Central Pacific official led Usher to reveal that he was going to recommend to the President a gauge of 4 feet, 8½ inches. Usher said that he had letters from the heads of several leading Eastern railroads in support of this choice.

Spurred by the adverse news, Huntington quickly organized an opposing campaign. By telegraph, he enlisted the services of a prominent engineer of the Hudson River Railroad in New York. The engineer was to arm himself with all possible data in behalf of a 5-foot gauge and come to Washington at once. When he had arrived and had his documentation ready, Huntington and California's then senior senator, Milton S. Latham, whose term ended shortly afterward, called on Lincoln. They asked that he let the Central Pacific present its case for a 5-foot gauge after Secretary Usher had made his report. Lincoln told Huntington to drop in at the White House the following Tuesday morning at eleven o'clock.

Huntington then went to Col. George T. M. Davis, the railroad-equipment dealer. Davis, he knew, was an old friend of Lincoln's. He was also an obvious authority on railroad gauges, since they were basic to his work. Huntington asked Davis to accompany him to the interview with the President. He also asked him to be his spokesman and present the statistics that the New York engineer had assembled. Davis, understandably reluctant to oppose the wishes of a prospective large buyer of railroad equipment, agreed to do so.

On Tuesday, January 20, when Huntington arrived at the White House, he found Davis already in Lincoln's office, delivering his speech. Huntington interrupted to explain to the President why he had asked Davis to present the case for a 5-foot gauge. "I had not considered my own knowledge sufficient," he told Lincoln. Davis was then allowed to resume.

By now, however, it was apparent that Lincoln had deliberately chosen the hour of a Cabinet meeting for this interview. Cabinet members began dropping in, one by one, and quietly took their seats while Davis was talking. Finally, Secretary Usher spoke up. "Mr. President, what kind of a meeting have we here today?" he asked, with obvious irritation.

"Mr. Usher, this is a meeting of the Cabinet and their friends. Go on, Mr. Davis," Lincoln blandly replied, according to Huntington's later recollection. And Huntington added, "This incident endeared the President to me more than anything else that happened during the interview."

Huntington, whose remarkably good memory was the envy and wonder of his friends and associates, recalled the President's remarks in full detail twenty-five years later:

Colonel Davis, I have known you a long time, and I believe you are a friend of mine. But there are other men I have believed in who have come to me and talked to me as earnestly and seemingly as honestly as you are doing. They have called upon me to advise me—men that I thought as highly of as I do of you— and they have advised me on matters that they well knew that I knew I was unfamiliar with. And I have decided according to what I supposed to be their honest judgment. Subsequently, I have learned that they counselled me to do what was for their own personal interest, without any regard to the interests of their country.[9]

Secretary of the Navy Gideon B. Welles jotted in his diary afterward that when the "California committee," as he called it, had left, the President had asked for a secret vote of the Cabinet. Without further discussion, they were to write on slips of paper whether or not they thought the gauge of the transcontinental railroad should be 5 feet. Welles reported that he had voted against it and in favor of 4 feet, 8½ inches. He said he thought that a majority of the Cabinet had done the same. Lincoln did not announce the result of the balloting, but on the following day he signed an order decreeing that the gauge should be 5 feet.

Huntington must have preened himself on an easy victory, but his triumph was brief. Within a few days, in defiance of the President, bills were introduced in the House and Senate to establish a gauge of 4 feet, 8½ inches for the Pacific Railroad and its branches. The Senate, despite opposition loyally led by California's two senators, voted 26 to 9 to overrule the President. The House concurred without debate. President Lincoln, accepting the rebuff of Congress without protest, signed the measure on March 3, 1863. The gauge thus established not only fixed the width of the first transcontinental railroad but determined the standard for every other major railroad in the United States. Eventually all their tracks, North and South, were made to match.

The contrary action of Congress cost the Central Pacific many thousands of dollars that were desperately painful to lose. Huntington at once had to request readjustments in the rolling stock and equipment that had been confidently ordered to fit a 5-foot track. The alterations also delayed delivery of the goods.

While Huntington was trying his bold but inexperienced hand at influencing legislators in Washington, Stanford was having considerably greater success, as was due his position and experience, in Sacramento. His effort to obtain favors from the State Assembly and Senate stemmed from the Central Pacific's aching need for money.

Attempts to obtain funds from private sources had already been abandoned as hopeless. The standard adverse reaction of local financiers was once described by Alfred A. Cohen, later the Central Pacific's chief attorney, in these words: "I have sat here in bank parlors in San Francisco and heard bankers say, 'Don't you have anything to do with those men, Stanford, Hopkins, and Huntington. Don't you put any money into their schemes. They are bound to come to grief. Nobody in the world could get that road through.' " [10]

In addition, there was a universal awareness among the West Coast's principal businessmen that the advent of a transcontinental railroad would raise hob with a whole array of monopolies on which they had fattened for years. These men obstructed its progress by every means short of armed intervention. One of the Central Pacific's bitterest and busiest enemies from the first was the Sacramento Valley Railroad, whose principal backers did not hesitate to circulate scandalous lies about their impending competitor.

Beaten in the effort to win financial backing from any individuals but themselves, the railroad's directors had fallen back upon a scheme of Stanford's. As a successful politician, the Governor had decided that their best chance lay in taking their case to the people. He well knew that the average citizen of California had an almost obsessive desire for a railroad to the East. If Californians weren't willing to invest their own money in it, they might favor putting county funds into the enterprise.

The obvious counties to be asked to invest in the Central Pacific were those it would pass through, serve, and benefit. They were San Francisco, Sacramento, and Placer. But before the voters there could be asked to express themselves on the question at the polls, the State Legislature must first grant the counties permission to exchange their bonds for railroad stock.

In the early winter of 1863, Stanford had gone to work to rally support for the idea among his fellow-Republicans and friends in the Assembly and Senate. There was little tendency to question the ethics of this move, for it was generally felt that whatever was good for the railroad was good for California.

Meanwhile, casting about worriedly for any feasible source of extra money, Stanford remembered a crucial fact. The government had assured the Central Pacific of a loan of $48,000 a mile for the most difficult and mountainous 150 miles of construction east of the western base of the Sierra Nevada. This was three times as much as it would receive for the flat miles along the approach to the mountains. The sum seemed especially mouth-watering right now, even though it couldn't be collected until 40 miles of the railroad had been built.

Where *was* that western base? To the eye of the traveler, there was no apparent rise in the ground east of Sacramento until one had gone 20 miles or more. But Stanford recalled that the celebrated Professor James Dwight Dana, in his *Manual of Geology*, had pointed out that the base of the Rocky Mountains began at the Mississippi River. Anyone who had ever crossed that mid-continent region knew that the steady upward tilt of the land was imperceptible, except to measuring instruments, for 600 miles west of the Mississippi. Perhaps, thought Stanford, the plain east of Sacramento might be found to have similarly hidden assets.

According to the Pacific Railroad Act, Lincoln was to declare officially where the east base of the Rockies and the west base of the Sierra Nevada began. But he would obviously rely on professional advice. Stanford sought out Professor Josiah W. Whitney, California's first State Geologist and the man for whom the state's highest peak was soon to be named. He also went to E. F. Beale, U.S. Surveyor-General for California, and J. F. Houghton, the state's Surveyor-General. All three men were asked to give their official, written opinions of where the west slope of the Sierra began its rise.

Whitney's decision arrived first, on March 23, 1863, and it was stimulating. He had chosen the point where the line of the railroad crossed Arcade Creek, only 7 miles east of Sacramento. "From there commences a regular and continuous ascent," [11] he wrote, though he admitted that it wasn't noticeable. The other experts independently concurred.

Stanford, elated, sent the opinions to the Secretary of the Interior for delivery to the President. He also impatiently spurred Representative Aaron Sargent to bring the matter to Lincoln's attention himself. Sargent finally succeeded. Lincoln obligingly named Arcade Creek as the western base of the mountains.

This was a joke to the home folks, who regarded the Central Pacific's owners as sly dogs for having won this debatable point. It was a joke, too, to Noah Brooks, the Sacramento *Union's* Washington correspondent, who gleefully reported what Aaron Sargent had said when he heard the news. "Here, you see," Sargent had remarked, with a chuckle, "my pertinacity and Abraham's faith moved mountains." [12]

Still, the geologists' decision was legitimate, and the Central Pacific was within its legal rights in asking for—and receiving—the highest amount of government aid for each mile of its route that lay within the area now officially declared to be part of the Sierra Nevada, whether it looked mountainous or not.

In the course of three jubilant weeks in April, 1863, Stanford's campaign to win legislative help also succeeded to a gratifying degree. The Legislature voted by wide majorities to authorize various county purchases of Central Pacific stock. Placer County was permitted to buy $250,000 worth; the city and county of Sacramento, $300,000; and the city and county of San Francisco, $600,000. As a topping for their largesse, the legislators added a gift of $500,000 from the state. It was to be given in installments: $200,000 apiece for the first two 20-mile sections of track completed, and $100,000 when 50 miles of the railroad were ready for use.

Dates only a few weeks ahead were promptly set for the referendums in Placer, Sacramento, and San Francisco Counties. Just as promptly, the commercial interests that dreaded the construction of the Central Pacific began a sharp battle to defeat the railroad's hopes. Vicious circulars appeared in the little mountain settlements of Placer County. A typical one contained this paragraph:

The whole matter resolves itself simply into this: Leland Stanford & Co. have, by log-rolling and political juggling, bamboozled the Government and the people out of a stupendously magnificent franchise, worth hundreds of millions of dollars if they can but build the road. It is to them, and to them alone, that all the benefits, all the profits inure.[13]

Quoting this canard, the editor of the Sacramento *Union* sensibly retorted, "If it is worth so many millions, why should not the county of Placer become a subscriber, and thus obtain an interest in those millions?" [14] He surmised that the envious owners of the Sacramento Valley Railroad had inspired the circular.

The voters of Placer and Sacramento Counties were unruffled by scurrilous pamphlets. They firmly demonstrated at the polls in May that they agreed with the editor of the *Union*. At the same time, the citizens of Sacramento gave the Central Pacific 30 acres of city land for its use, including 1,300 feet of waterfront. The Legislature had previously granted the railroad right-of-way through certain streets in the capital, along its levee, and across public lands outside.

Even in San Francisco, headquarters of the enemy, the vote in May was 2 to 1 in favor of investing city funds in the railroad. Here, though, where most of the newspapers had already been mobilized against the Central Pacific, the issue was not so easily settled. The aroused opposition resorted to the courts, and kept the matter in dispute for nearly two years.

In June, Collis Huntington sailed home from New York, having for a time accomplished all that he was capable of doing in the East. His arrival brought about a swift deterioration in the relationship between Chief Engineer Judah and the other principals on the railroad's board of directors. There were several sources of friction. The chief one was the fundamental clash of ideas between Judah and Huntington, the dominant personality among the Central Pacific's officers. "I never build castles in the air," [15] Huntington once declared. Judah had been erecting them for years, though in no way damaging his high reputation as an engineer.

Huntington had made no attempt to hide his wholly pragmatic attitude toward the railroad. In fact, he had persistently tried to instill it in his associates. "Now, don't let's talk about a *Pacific* road," he used to say. "Don't spread yourselves. Let's go slow and steady and own what we build." [16]

This must have produced anguish in the mind of Judah, who never for an instant allowed himself to forget the greater goal, the creation of a transcontinental railroad.

He was nettled, too, by the way in which the various subcontractors were messing about with the grading. He was skeptical of Crocker's ability to improve the situation, and suspected that he would sacrifice quality in his urge to get the foundation for the ties and rails ready in a rush.

What annoyed and alarmed Judah most, though, was the preoccupation of his associates with a toll road that they were planning to build in the mountains, along part of the route that the railroad would eventually take. This wagon road would connect Dutch Flat, 65 miles east of Sacramento, with Nevada's Carson Valley, near Virginia City. A lengthy eastern section of the toll road had already been constructed and was in heavy use. It carried a burgeoning two-way traffic of teams. Over it, supplies and fancy goods moved eastward to the free-spending miners of Virginia City; ponderous loads of gold and silver bars creaked westward to San Francisco. At the present time, the only course open to this traffic was a rambling one 25 miles south of the Central Pacific's chosen route. It was a road that led through Placerville and Shingle Springs. At the latter settlement, it met the track of the Sacramento Valley Railroad.

With a greedy eye on this lucrative trade, the chief backers of the Central Pacific had devised a shrewd scheme to capture it. They reasoned that if they were to build a highway from Dutch Flat, a future station on their railroad, to meet the main road as it emerged from the Carson Valley, and were to buy that eastern stem, they could provide and control a more direct route across the Sierra Nevada than the one then in use. Thus they would certainly divert some of the freight that the Sacramento Valley Railroad now carried. In due time, when the Central Pacific track reached Dutch Flat, they could expect to capture it all.

This plan was a legitimate piece of business strategy. Judah chose to regard it as a serious threat to the progress of the Central Pacific. He even suspected the planners of intending to content themselves with building the railroad only as far as Dutch Flat.

The young engineer, a proud, forceful man, was understandably jealous of his Eastern renown as the man most responsible for making a transcontinental railroad possible. Now he was bitterly conscious that his creation, the Central Pacific, was being pried out of his hands.

"I cannot make these men—some of them—appreciate the 'elephant' they have on their shoulders," he told his wife after one of the directors' meetings in the spring of 1863. "They won't do what I want and must do. We shall just as sure have trouble in Congress as the sun rises in the East if they go on in this way. They will not see it as it is. Something must be done. I will not be satisfied before Congress and the world!" [17]

In May he had complained in a letter to his good friend "Doc" Strong, the druggist at Dutch Flat, that he had "a pretty hard row to hoe" . . .

I had a blow-out about two weeks ago and freed my mind, so much so that I looked for instant decapitation [he wrote]. I called things by their right name and invited war, but counsels of peace prevailed and my head is still on. My hands are tied, however. We have no meetings of the board nowadays, except the regular monthly meeting, which, however, was not had this month, but there have been any quantity of private conferences to which I have not been invited.[18]

Rather pathetically he added, "I try to think it is all for the best, and devote myself with additional energy to my legitimate portion of the enterprise." A good deal of this additional energy was being expended in night work. He and his youthful assistant, Lewis M. Clement, a future chief engineer of the Central Pacific, were at the railroad offices regularly until midnight and after. They were making estimates of the costs of eventual repair shops and other essential buildings.

By July, Judah was discouraged enough to consider quitting. At any rate, he must have demanded a suitable financial settlement for his great contribution to the Central Pacific up to that time. For on July 1, 1863, the directors voted to pay him $25,000 worth of capital stock "for his services as agent in the Atlantic States, and prior to the organization of the company." [19] Then, three days later, they issued an additional $66,000 worth of C.P. stock to him.

On July 10th he again shared his troubles with Strong.

Huntington has returned, and seems to possess more than usual influence. . . . Stanford, who I told you was all right, is as much under their influence [that of the Huntington-dominated group] as ever. . . . The wagon road seems to be a tie which unites them, and its influence seems to be paramount to everything else. . . . They have been consulting and looking over the way every day, and do not hesitate to talk boldly, openly before me, but not to me, about it. They talk as though there was nobody in the world but themselves who could build a wagon road. . . .[20]

Far more exasperating to Judah, however, was the way in which Huntington at once began to meddle with the railroad construction. On an inspection walk to the north edge of town, Huntington had discovered a hundred teams at work preparing grade for the track along a section of levee that had to be protected against flood by expensive rip-rap. He ordered them to stop at once. Judah happened along a few minutes later. He angrily protested that the board of directors had ordered the work done there. Huntington brusquely replied, "It will cost $200,000 at least to put the road here. It must go up I Street." [21] And he told the contractor to shift his force.

A short time later, Huntington precipitated a complete stoppage of all grading. The crisis arose from a dispute he had with James Bailey, who had become secretary of the Central Pacific in the summer of 1863 and was one of its seven directors. It had been agreed that all members of the board would share equally in footing expenses that could not be met from other sources. Bailey refused to pay up, probably out of loyalty to Judah, whose views he supported. Huntington offered to take over his interest in the railroad, or let Bailey buy him out. Bailey rejected both suggestions. "Then there's only one alternative," said Huntington coldly.

"The work must stop at once." [22] Off he rode to the contractors' outfits strung across the valley. By nine o'clock that night he had halted all grading and was back in Sacramento. Bailey, with Judah's help, then tried to find the means to buy Huntington out, while Sacramento buzzed with gossip. Huntington granted them two weeks in which to make the purchase. Meanwhile, not a shovel was lifted to advance the Central Pacific.

Within two or three days, Bailey wired from San Francisco that he had a customer for Huntington's stock: Charles McLaughlin, a wealthy man from Boston. This was an overly hasty conclusion. McLaughlin at first had not known who was offering to sell. When he found out, he said, "If Old Huntington is going to sell out, I am not going in. Just what sends him out will keep me out." [23]

With their scheme collapsed, the dissenters returned to Sacramento. Judah made the best of his discomfiting position for a couple of months longer. Bailey resigned as secretary and director at once, and sold his stock. In October, E. H. Miller, Jr., who had migrated to California on the same vessel with Hopkins in 1849 and had been a business partner of his before Hopkins teamed up with Huntington, succeeded Bailey in both official positions with the railroad. Before long, Miller, who kept an account book in which the tiniest item of office expense was faithfully entered, was carefully noting that the Central Pacific had spent 25 cents for glue, 37 cents for "carrying wood," 50 cents for a desk eraser, and, curiously, 25 cents for "camphor for blankets." [24]

In mid-August, Huntington, Stanford, Hopkins, and Charles Crocker organized the Dutch Flat and Donner Lake Wagon Road Co. Its announced purpose was

constructing, completing and maintaining a wagon road and collecting compensation for the use thereof, over the Sierra Nevada Mountains from Dutch Flat . . . to Washoe Valley . . . with such extensions and branches as the said Company shall determine. . . .[25]

Judah was now fully convinced that the fate of the transcontinental railroad was at stake. In acute frustration at these various maneuvers, he had begun a campaign to take the Central Pacific away from the men who then controlled it. He wrote letters to various Eastern financiers whom he knew, seeking to enlist their help in buying out the little band of Sacramento merchants. The Easterners to whom Judah appealed have never been identified. Only fragmentary glimpses of his activities during the late summer and early fall of 1863 are obtainable.

The final dissolution of his financial interests in the Central Pacific came on September 28th. On that day, for the sum of $10,000, evidently in cash, Judah conveyed to Charles Crocker all his rights in the Nevada Rail Road Company.[26] That was the company chartered by the Territorial Legislature of Nevada on November 25, 1861, "to construct a rail road from the Western to the eastern boundary of the territory of Nevada." Judah, Stanford, Huntington, Hopkins, Crocker, and Bailey had all been equal incorporators. Bailey sold his rights in the Nevada Rail Road to Crocker on the same day that Judah did, and for the same amount.

Judah and his wife sailed for New York in October, 1863. Crossing Panama, en route, he caught yellow fever.

It rained, [wrote his widow] and he got wet in helping the women and children board the steamer from the cars and hotels. His last purchase was a big umbrella with which to shield them. He could not see them exposed to the rain and not try to do his part, and more, for women and children who had no one to help them. I feared for him, and remonstrated, for I knew he was doing too much, but he replied, "Why, I must, even as I would have someone do for you—it's only humanity!" That night, he had a terrible headache, and from that time grew worse and worse. All those eight days to New York, I stood by his berth night and day, as it were, to care for him—but it was terrible; there is no use in my writing of it. He lived just one week after we arrived in New York, at the Metropolitan Hotel. . . . We buried him in the quiet country cemetery outside Greenfield, Mass., only a stone's throw from the old home and where I have always lived.[27]

Judah died, in a delirium, on November 2, 1863, four months before his thirty-eighth birthday. The first rail of the Central Pacific had been laid only seven days before, and the organizers of the Union Pacific had not yet done much but argue.)

In a memorial tribute to Judah fourteen years later, his old friend former Congressman John C. Burch stated that the engineer had intended to combine his capital with a great deal more, which he had already lined up. The plans, wrote Burch, were "fully matured, his coadjutors selected and meetings arranged." [28] Judah's scheme, he continued, was to buy the Central Pacific and place its management in the hands of "a new set of men of known public spirit, who would, without other designs to hinder or obstruct them, prosecute diligently the main work of completing the railway from ocean to ocean."

Mrs. Judah, wistfully recalling in 1889 the last days of her husband's life, wrote:

He had secured the right and had the power to buy out the men opposed to him and the true interests of the Pacific railroad at that time. Everything was arranged for a meeting in New York City on his arrival—gentlemen from New York and Boston who were ready to take their places.[29]

The only direct, contemporary evidence of Judah's intentions is contained in a letter that he wrote to "Doc" Strong from the steamer *St. Louis* at San Francisco on Oct. 9, 1863:

I have a feeling of relief in being away from the scenes of contention and strife which it has been my lot to experience for the past year, and to know that the responsibilities of events, as far as regards Pacific Railroad, do not rest on my shoulders. If the parties who now manage hold to the same opinion three months hence that they do now, there will be a radical change in the management of the Pacific Railroad, and it will pass into the hands of men of experience and capital. If they do not, they may hold the reins for awhile, but they will rue the day they ever embarked in the Pacific Railroad.[30]

Judah was exuberantly confident of the success of his plans. One day, en route to Panama, he had roused himself suddenly from his berth and exclaimed to his wife, "Anna, what can I not do in New York now! I have always had to set my brains and will too much against other men's money. Now, with money—equal—what can I not do!"[31]

His break with Huntington and his other former associates had not been complete, however. He remained on the Central Pacific payroll as chief engineer, at $10,000 a year, until the day he died.

Ten days before the Judahs had steamed away from San Francisco, a fast clipper with a lovely and prophetic name, *Herald of the Morning*, had dropped anchor in that harbor. Aboard it were 100 tons of iron rails for the Central Pacific, the first consignment to arrive. A couple of days later, the rails were being unloaded at Sacramento.

Three thousand tons were on the way, the *Union* proudly announced. Its story added that grading for the first 18 miles of the railroad was nearly finished. The wood-and-iron bridge across the American River, just outside of town, would be ready in time for the rails. This was an impressive structure. Its two main spans were each 192 feet long, and 6 feet above the highest water level ever recorded. They were nearly dwarfed, however, by the great stretches of trestle that led to them across the swamps on both sides of the stream. The timbered approach from the city was 2,200 feet long; the northern approach, 615 feet long.

On October 5th the schooner *Artful Dodger* slid up to the levee at Sacramento. On board was the Central Pacific's first locomotive, the Governor Stanford, soon to be a vehicle of gleaming brass and blazing beauty but now only a scattering of parts. An inclined track to the dock's edge made it easier to unload them.

By the morning of October 26th Charlie Crocker was ready to spike the first rails to their ties.

"Nothing looks to the public as much like making a railroad as the work of laying down the iron on the road bed," the *Union's* editor commented. He was obviously puzzled, though, that while a few people had gathered to watch, "those engaged in the enterprise did not choose to have any ceremony over the affair." [32]

Some of the Central Pacific officials had suggested a suitable celebration. Huntington chilled their eagerness:

Now, if you want to jubilate over driving the first spike here, go ahead and do it. I don't. Those mountains over there look too ugly, and I see too much work ahead of us. We may fail, and if we do, I want to have as few people know it as we can. And if we get up a jubilation, everybody will remember it. Anybody can drive the first spike, but there are many months of labor and unrest between the first and last spike.[33]

His subdued associates abandoned their plan for a ceremony.

A few days afterward, W. S. Siddons, who ran the Occidental Saloon, came home from a shopping trip in San Francisco with a new French cannon, a 12-pounder. He christened it Union Boy, and said he intended to use it to celebrate good news from the battlefronts.

Union Boy rattled the town's windows a morning or two later, but not for a Federal victory. On November 9th the cannon saluted the Governor Stanford in a heart-stirring suit of paint, as it chuffed along the track for the first time. The wood-burning locomotive, about twice the height of a tall man and 50 feet long, including its maroon tender, was a splendid sight. Its four driving wheels, 4½ feet in diameter, were bright red, with a gold star painted on each hub. The driving rods and pistons were of brass, butter-colored and glowing in the sunlight. So were the bell, with its orange clapper, and the bands that girdled the gray-blue boiler. The locomotive's cab was maroon outside and apple green inside. Its name was painted in gold letters beneath the windows, whose frames were the color of ripe lemons. Vivid green fenders hooded the driving wheels, and above them on each side of the cab was an orange step for the crew to use for climbing aboard. The smokestack and wooden slats of the cowcatcher were as red as the driving wheels. The headlight was maroon, with a fat kerosene lamp sitting inside in front of a glistening reflector. Huge gold initials, "C.P.R.R.," decorated the tender's dark-red sides, which bore a chirpy stripe of orange along their base. Locomotive and tender, when carrying a full load of water and wood, weighed 46 tons.

This resplendent vehicle delighted its beholders. Its debut was, however, a flop. A small group of leading citizens—state officers, bankers, merchants, editors, a general, and a popular priest, Father Gallagher—had received invitations from Central Pacific officials to take the first ride on the railroad, now 2 miles long. They waited eagerly beside the track, with two baskets of champagne at their feet. But before the locomotive could reach them, its tender was crowded to capacity. Excited boys and young men, who had been hanging about daily while the engine was being assembled, in the open beside a machine shop and foundry on I Street, scrambled aboard as soon as the Governor Stanford began to move. When the locomotive wheezed alongside the invited guests, there was no room for them. More disappointing than that, though, was the discovery that there was something wrong with the engine's valves.

The inaugural trip had to be postponed for a day, while the engineer and helpers went to work on the faulty machinery. By eight-thirty that night the trouble had been found and corrected. The Governor Stanford then made several short trial runs, loaded with hangers-on, who cheered themselves out of voices as they rode through the shadowy town.

On the following afternoon, the distinguished guests of the previous day reassembled with the champagne baskets. This time the locomotive, trimmed with flags and with its shrieking whistle offending every dog in the city, carried them smoothly to Twenty-first Street. That was as far as the rails went. There the passengers broke out the bottles. They drank a score of toasts. Glasses were lifted to Stanford, Crocker, Huntington, and "the memory of T. D. Judah, late Engineer of the Pacific Railroad." His death had been front-page news in Sacramento three days after it occurred. Finally, the day's fun ended with a toast "To the Governor Stanford: May her boiler never, like the glass of Father Gallagher at present, become empty!" [34]

After Judah's death, his thirty-three-year-old assistant Samuel S. Montague, a rangy, slim, black-bearded New Hampshireman with fine eyes and a wide brow, became acting chief engineer of the Central Pacific. The "acting" remained in his title until March, 1868. When he succeeded Judah as Chief Engineer of that railroad, his first job was to continue surveying the future route as far as the Big Bend of the Truckee River, in Nevada Territory, more than 40 miles east of the California border. Montague and a small crew of surveyors completed this assignment in December, 1863. Though little was made of it publicly at the time, it was ample evidence that there was no foundation whatever in the stories, later spread by the Central Pacific's detractors, that the railroad was going to end at Dutch Flat, 65 miles from Sacramento.

On December 4th the *Union* duly noted that the Union Pacific had held ground-breaking ceremonies at Omaha two days earlier. It reminded its readers, so that they might not be led later to make unfair comparisons, that "the labor of building a railroad up the valley of the Platte is very light when compared with that required to construct one over the Sierra Nevada Mountains." It quoted an authority who had said that "for five hundred miles up the Platte the ties and rails could be laid on the natural surface of the ground."

If the builders of the Central Pacific were downhearted because of the discouragements and delays encountered in the first year of construction, and the grave uncertainties ahead, they hid their feelings well. Stanford's annual report to the Secretary of the Interior for 1863 sounded jaunty. It made the most of the little that had been accomplished.

In turn, Secretary Usher wrote a sunny report to the House of Representatives at the close of 1863.

The California branch of the Pacific Railroad is being constructed with all practicable dispatch, and there is every reason to believe that the work will not be permitted to languish, but that, at an earlier day than would have been reasonably anticipated, the entire line will be completed.[35]

CHAPTER THREE

1863

THE UNION PACIFIC
TAKES FORM

The Union Pacific had a clumsy birth and showed every evidence of being sickly. By the Railroad Act of 1862, Congress had arranged a ponderous delivery for it. It involved 158 commissioners from twenty-five states and territories, and five more, to be chosen by the Secretary of the Interior, to represent the government's interests. They—or, at least, a quorum of twenty-five—were to meet at Chicago within three months of the passage of the Railroad Act. There they were to elect officers and open subscription books for the company's stock in all the leading cities of the North and West.

The Union Pacific was to be permitted $100 million of capital stock. The stock was to cost $1,000 a share, and no subscriber would be allowed to own more than 200 shares. When 2,000 shares had been signed for, and a down payment of $100 per share securely tucked away in the company's treasury, the commissioners were to elect thirteen directors from among their number. President Lincoln would then nominate two government directors to join the others on the board. The directors were to elect a president, vice-president, secretary, and treasurer. Then the Board of

Commissioners could turn the Union Pacific Railroad Co. over to these officers and consider its midwifely chores done.

A skeptical group of commissioners, politicians, and railroad contractors gathered at Chicago on September 2, 1862. They picked over the clauses of the Pacific Railroad Act with as little enthusiasm as buyers of second-hand goods. The gist of their talks was that the Union Pacific, important as it might be to the nation, would never be built unless Congress could be induced to offer more liberal support. Right now, however, the commissioners must make the best of what they considered to be a very bad bargain and invite the public to take shares in the Union Pacific. This they did.

An active participant in the gloomy discussions at Chicago was Senator James A. McDougall, of California, Democratic chairman of the Senate's Select Committee on the Pacific Railroad. An old friend of Lincoln's in Illinois, where he had been the state's attorney general before moving to the West, McDougall was one of the best orators in Congress. He was also one of its heaviest drinkers. But in lucid moments he was an effective mouthpiece for his Republican friends of the Central Pacific management.

When the Chicago meeting was over, many of its delegates entrained for New York. There they continued their discussions, with McDougall again on hand. Afterward, the Senator returned to Washington and immediately began drafting legislation to provide the railroad-builders with more lucrative encouragement.

Two days before Christmas, he proposed to the Senate that the Pacific Railroad Act of 1862 be amended. He gave his fellow senators no clues as to what he had in mind, merely stating that amendments were essential if the road were to be constructed. He asked that the Select Committee on the Pacific Railroad be given the task of framing the amending legislation. There were a few grumbles, but the Senate granted McDougall's request with scarcely a pause in its consideration of ominous matters pertaining to the war.

In this same month of December, 1862, Union Pacific stock had been on sale for more than ninety days. Yet hardly anyone in the United States seemed interested in buying it. Too many financiers knew that even in flat Illinois and Iowa, railroads were costing twice as much per mile to build as the Act of 1862 would provide in loans for track on similar terrain. Judah's Sacramento Valley Railroad, on floor-like land, had cost $51,707 a mile. And that was five years before the Civil War had exploded the cost of everything.

The prospect for builders of a railroad across the Western plains and mountains was most discouraging, and the Central Pacific faced the greater share of difficulties. But problems of the same sort harassed the Union Pacific as well, though they varied somewhat in detail. The need for replenishing and equipping the Northern armies, rather than the lure of fortunes in mining, drained the labor markets of the East and Midwest. Construction materials destined for the Union Pacific could travel routes far shorter than those bound for the Central Pacific, but the paths were as frustrating. There were three railroad lines reaching across Iowa toward Council Bluffs, on the Missouri River opposite Omaha, but they were making little progress. The longest of them, the Chicago & North Western, was still more than 150 miles short of its goal. Supplies taking this road would have to be transferred to wagons for a slow journey of several days across open prairie, a course marked by mires and broken axles. An alternative route was largely by water down the Ohio to the Mississippi, up the Mississippi to the Missouri, a few miles north of St. Louis, and then on up the Missouri to wherever Mr. Lincoln might decide that the railroad should commence, probably Omaha. A third possibility, and the best of a poor lot, was that of utilizing the Hannibal & St. Joseph Railroad, a carrier so rickety that it had been nicknamed the Horrible St. Joe. Bad as it was, it did cross the narrowest part of Missouri. At St. Joseph cargoes bound for the Union Pacific could be shifted to river boats for a relatively short haul. There was still the Missouri itself to contend with—too thick to swim in and not quite thick enough to walk on, Senator Benton had called it. This stream was studded with submerged trees and wrecks. It thrashed about so in its valley that its channel was a continuing mystery.

A final complication for both the Central Pacific and the Union Pacific was the fact that nearly every pound of material required to build them, and all the food and a good deal of the water needed to sustain the thousands of men and animals that would do the job, must be carried to the moving point of construction over their own single tracks as they grew.

If one's enthusiasm for buying shares in the Union Pacific were exuberant enough to survive a close study of such drastic handicaps as these, it tended to shrivel when one considered the country that the railroad was to cross. The precise route was still to be surveyed when the Board of Commissioners met at Chicago in the fall of 1862, but everyone knew that for the most part it would roughly follow the 41st parallel of latitude. That lay through land that was empty, except for nomadic Indian tribes and enormous, drifting herds of wild animals. "Ruinous space—a dead void," [1] the editor of a Boston newspaper had called it.

For 500 miles west of Omaha, there was gently rising grassland, creased by infrequent streams. The only trees to be found there were low cottonwoods, which grew along the streams. They were too soft to make durable railroad ties. Beyond the plains stood the main range of the Rockies, continent-deep. If engineers could find a practical pass through this mountain wall, they would merely emerge upon a sterile plateau that stretched for several hundred miles beyond. Along the western edge of this plateau lay the heavily wooded Wasatch Mountains, and, at the foot of their far side, Salt Lake City. That was the only settlement of any consequence between Omaha and Sacramento. West of the irrigated lands of the Salt Lake Valley, no more than an oasis, there were hundreds of miles of bleak and bitter desert to cross before the Sierra Nevada could be reached.

It was hardly surprising, then, that when the entire nation was invited to sign up for stock in the Union Pacific, just seven subscribers stepped forward. Altogether, they ordered 31 shares, out of the 2,000 required to organize the company. Only two of the purchasers were commissioners. They were William M. McPherson, a lawyer and railroad builder of sorts from St. Louis, and Augustus Kountze, an eager young banker from Omaha. The one buyer of note was Brigham Young, the Mormon Moses, head of the Church of Jesus Christ of Latter-Day Saints. Young, who had the look of a small-town banker and was as shrewd as any, subscribed for only five shares of U.P. stock, but he was the first to pay in full for his purchase. At that time, he confidently expected that the railroad would eventually run through Salt Lake City, capital of his secluded empire.

As the Union Pacific's stock-subscription books lay open, and largely blank, in thirty-five cities of the land, one man began a frenetic campaign to mobilize enough subscribers to take the company out of the hands of its 163 commissioners and place it largely in his own. He was Thomas C. Durant of New York City, a former doctor of medicine who had long ago discovered that he had a greater flair for speculating than for healing. Now the only trace of his Aesculapian past that lingered was the tendency of a few close associates to call him "the doctor." Durant, forty-two, a lean, immensely energetic 6-footer with a marked stoop, large, intense eyes, thin brown hair, straggly mustache and goatee, and a jutting jaw that warned of his stubborn, rather testy nature, was convinced that the Union Pacific was worth a gamble. He had already had a bold but bungling hand in the promotion and partial construction of three railroads: the Michigan Southern, Chicago & Rock Island, and Mississippi & Missouri. Now, almost alone, and by mortgaging nearly everything he owned, he launched the Union Pacific. Durant knew it wouldn't do, however, to let a suspicious Congress get the notion that a railroad so national in character was in danger of becoming one man's property. He must round up other sponsors, men whose names were more distinguished than his own, men who would succumb to the patriotic plea that the charter for the first railroad to the Pacific must not be allowed to lapse because of the disinterest of public-spirited individuals. If he could not persuade enough of these to comply with the terms of the Railroad Act, then he would corral friends and associates who would be willing to subscribe for stock if he paid the first installment for them. They couldn't lose by this arrangement, he argued. Congress would almost certainly increase the subsidies rather than let the Union Pacific die in its infancy. If the friends he staked weren't encouraged by subsequent developments to repay him eventually for their stock, they could simply turn it over to him. He'd run the risk that the 200-share limit on individual ownership would be eliminated in time.

While Durant was rounding up co-sponsors for the Union Pacific, the U.S. Senate's Select Committee for the Pacific Railroad reported back Senator McDougall's bill to amend the Railroad Act of 1862. On February 23, 1863, it was read to the assembled Senate. It contained nothing to get excited about. The railroad interests evidently had not yet generated sufficient legislative pressure to suit their desires, or else they lacked boldness.

There was a proposal in the bill to increase the number of shares in the Union Pacific from 100,000 to 1,000,000 and reduce their cost from $1,000 to $100 per share. This left the capitalization unchanged but greatly broadened the field of potential investors.

Another important clause was one that would let the railroad builders get all the government bonds that were coming to them at the end of every 100 miles of continuous track. The original bill had required a frustratingly large percentage of aid bonds to be withheld until the entire transcontinental line was finished and had satisfied the government's inspectors.

Some anti-railroad sentiment had apparently been aired in committee sessions, for the width of the right-of-way had been trimmed from 400 feet to 200. The cut was not as severe as it sounded. The new bill provided for additional land to be granted where it was needed for stations, sidings, or other functional uses.

The debate that followed did not stir up objections to what had been read. Rather, it dealt almost entirely with matters that were not in the bill. Take the labor problem, for instance, said Senator S. C. Pomeroy of Kansas, always attentive to the needs of the Leavenworth, Pawnee & Western Railroad Co., which was to build the southernmost branch of the transcontinental. Why not enlist workers on a military basis, he asked, with stern penalties for failing to show up on the job and even stiffer ones for desertion?

This extraordinary proposal stimulated more laughter than censure. Senator Morton Wilkinson of Minnesota drew the merriest response when he asked Pomeroy if the Fugitive Slave Law would apply to any railroad laborers that ran away. After a gust of guffaws, the Senate smacked down the proposed amendment.

Pomeroy had a far better idea. Let's allow the railroad companies to buy iron abroad when the price goes above $60 a ton in the local market, he suggested. Indeed not, retorted Pennsylvania's senators and their fellow-protectionists. Let the railroad people pay the going price for American iron, wherever it climbed. If they needed more money to foot the cost, the government could lend it to them.

With this hint that greater financial aid might be had if the pleas were shrill enough, the debate ended. The Senate passed the bill on February 25, 1863, and sent it along to the House, which hadn't bothered to prepare one of its own.

But the last session of the Thirty-seventh Congress was in its final hours. Nearly every representative had a favorite bill he was trying to push through before adjournment. The proposed amendment to the Railroad Act of 1862 was buffeted by a storm of parliamentary objections, with apparently no one steering it, and became a derelict. The House never voted on it. Congress adjourned on March 4th. The railroad promoters would have to start all over again, nine months later.

Collis Huntington, who had been a one-man lobby for the Central Pacific during the congressional discussions, went back to New York and the discouraging task of trying to market his railroad's bonds. Thomas Durant continued his equally depressing effort to persuade men of ample means and reputation to buy shares in the Union Pacific. He also attempted once more to induce young Brig. Gen. Grenville M. Dodge, of Council Bluffs, Iowa, to give up fighting for his country and return to his profession of railroad engineering.

Durant had been trying repeatedly to lure Dodge into the formative Union Pacific organization for more than a year. The time had seemed particularly ripe in March, 1862, just after the crucial battle of Pea Ridge, in Arkansas. In that battle, Dodge had had three horses killed under him, the knuckles of one hand dislocated by a flying fragment of grapeshot, and his clothes ripped by half a dozen bullets. Even after that sobering taste of warfare, Dodge had turned Durant down.

Now thirty-two years old, the short, spare, tough-fibred engineer was at present in Mississippi. There he was greatly impressing Generals Grant and Sherman by the energy, skill, and speed with which he was putting together railroads for them that the Confederates had done their best to take apart.

Durant had regarded Dodge with increasing favor over a period of ten years. They had first met in 1853. Durant, already a successful speculator in grains and other commodities, was then beginning to dabble in railroads. He had come out to the Midwest from New York to join Henry Farnam, builder of the Chicago & Rock Island Railroad, in promoting a logical westward extension of that line. The extension, called the Mississippi & Missouri Railroad, was to cross Iowa from Davenport, opposite Rock Island, Illinois, to Council Bluffs. This was a distance of about 280 miles. At the time, it was a five-day journey by stagecoach.

This enterprise brought together several men who were to figure importantly in the building of the Union Pacific. Farnam's key employees on the M.&M. were Peter A. Dey, chief engineer, and Samuel B. Reed, construction boss. They later held those respective positions on the U.P., Dey for a year only, Reed for most of the construction period. At the time Durant became Farnam's partner, Dey had just hired Grenville Dodge, fresh out of Norwich University, to be his own assistant.

In the spring of 1853, the principal task before Dey and Dodge was that of surveying a route for the Mississippi & Missouri to take across Iowa. Dey delegated most of the field work to his eager assistant, who seemed to relish both the responsibility and the adventure of it. By the time Dodge's survey had reached Council Bluffs, Durant, forever dazzling himself with a bigger scheme than the one immediately at hand, had persuaded Farnam to let him keep going. Durant was already dreaming of the possibility of the M.&M.'s becoming a link in the Pacific Railroad, which had been talked about so long. Why not let Dodge explore the country west of the Missouri and find out what the prospects were for extending the route he was working on?

Dodge, in the fall of that year, took his small surveying crew across the Missouri in a flatboat, led them up past the few sod-roofed cabins that comprised Omaha, and headed out upon the vast prairie beyond.

This initial reconnaissance was necessarily brief, for the bitter winter of the plains was warning of its approach. It was of lasting significance in Dodge's life, however. It convinced him that he had found, in the grand Platte Valley of Nebraska, a superlatively fine route for a railroad to the West. Moreover, he fell in love with the countryside, and especially with Council Bluffs, where he determined to live.

"We are on the way to the Pacific, and we intend to go there," [2] John A. Dix, then president of the Mississippi & Missouri, had bravely assured a crowd in Davenport in June, 1854. But the railroad's progress had been feeble and spasmodic. After only 120 miles, its track had come to a full stop at Grinnell, 160 miles east of Council Bluffs.

Durant's chronic urge to take speculative plunges had been over-stimulated by the prospect of the M.&M. The results were disastrous. He nearly ruined himself, and Farnam as well.

Meanwhile, Dodge had to turn to other means of earning a living. In the customary way of businessmen in a frontier settlement, he tried his hand at a variety of enterprises. At one time or another, he was active in freighting, banking, real estate, milling, merchandising, and contracting.

Twice again, though, Farnam and Durant sent him out on additional explorations of the Platte Valley and of the country as far west as the Rockies. The surveys were made on widely separate occasions when reviving strength in the national economy led the promoters of the M.&M. to try to resuscitate the railroad. With each survey, Dodge's conviction grew that here was the place where the Pacific Railroad must go. "The Lord had so constructed the country that any engineer who failed to take advantage of the great open road . . . would not have been fit to belong to the profession," [3] he once wrote.

The buffalo had first trampled open the way, instinctively following the path of least resistance. Indians had followed them. The harassed Mormons, intent on putting as many miles as possible between themselves and persecuting Gentiles, had wisely taken the same westward course. Pioneers bound for California and Oregon had trailed after the Mormons, desirous only of pushing far beyond them. All had indeed found the Platte Valley "the great open road" that Dodge called it.

Dodge made his third investigation of this territory for Farnam and Durant in the spring and summer of 1859. He got back to Council Bluffs in mid-August. The next day, Abraham Lincoln arrived in town on a river boat from Kansas, where he had been making speeches. On his way back to Illinois, he decided to take a look at some lots on the flood plain of the Missouri at Council Bluffs. His friend Norman B. Judd wanted to borrow $3,000 from him, and was offering the lots as security for the loan. Lincoln had been an attorney for the Mississippi & Missouri on a few occasions and knew that the railroad was headed for this point. Its precise location might have a vital bearing on the value of those lots of Judd's—which, incidentally, Dodge had sold to him. Lincoln wanted all the information he could get on the matter.

He was persuaded to talk informally to the citizens of the town on political matters that night. On the following afternoon, a sweltering one, Lincoln sat for a while on a shady bench on the uneven porch of the Pacific House and chatted with a wilted group that gathered around him. He mentioned his special interest in railroad prospects. Someone spotted young Dodge on the fringe of the crowd, and told Lincoln that there was the man who could tell him everything he wanted to know about railroad plans. Dodge was introduced to Lincoln, and for two hours the future President casually but persistently questioned him. "He shelled my woods completely," Dodge recalled afterward, "and got all the information I'd collected for Henry Farnam, my employer." [4]

They first discussed the various routes explored during the War Department surveys of 1853. Then Dodge told Lincoln all about the special merits of the Platte Valley, and why Council Bluffs, in his opinion, should become the actual starting point for the Pacific Railroad. The engineer pointed out that the town had a special strategic advantage quite apart from its geography. Three railroads were reaching toward it from the East. When comfortably crammed with facts, Lincoln rose and thanked his informant, who had made a deep impression by the thoroughness of his knowledge. The meeting was "a milestone in my life," Dodge said in later years, "and Mr. Lincoln never forgot it." [5]

President Lincoln had a particular reason for remembering Dodge in the spring of 1863. He was then being beset by delegations from all the Missouri River towns that wanted to be designated as the eastern terminus of the Union Pacific.

The feud for this prize involved a great deal more than mere local rivalry. The powerful financial and political influence of Chicago, already a key railroad center, was being exerted vigorously in favor of Omaha–Council Bluffs. That of St. Louis, which was nearly as weighty, was working stubbornly for Kansas City. A third storm center of widening propaganda and intrigue was Leavenworth.

All that the law required of Lincoln was that he decide where the central branch of the Union Pacific was to start. The rivals of Omaha and Council Bluffs all seemed to feel that no matter what Lincoln's choice, he could somehow be persuaded to notify the nation that the main line would actually begin in one of their communities. So, intent upon convincing him, "they came flocking from all quarters," [6] reported Secretary Usher, who had to listen to his share of their arguments in Washington.

Harassed and confused by the uproar, Lincoln thought of Dodge, and sent for him. The summons came to Dodge, at his headquarters in Corinth, Mississippi, in late April, 1863, only a couple of months before Vicksburg fell. It arrived in the form of a telegram from General Grant, ordering him to report to the Adjutant General in Washington at once, but not explaining why. When he reached the capital, the Adjutant General told him it was Lincoln who wanted to see him.

At the White House, the President greeted Dodge with great cordiality and came straight to his point. He wanted Dodge's advice, he said, on the matter of naming "an initial point for the Union Pacific." [7] (Lincoln, at least, was convinced that the starting place of the central branch would become that of the main line.) He explained that Peter Dey had already been to see him on behalf of the company, and had recommended Council Bluffs. Dodge promptly endorsed that suggestion. Then he and Lincoln went over the pertinent maps together. Dodge was impressed to find that the President knew all about the rival claims. But Lincoln revealed something further that encouraged and delighted the engineer. That was that none of the contending groups had explored west of the Missouri. All of them lacked reliable information to bolster their pretensions.

Then the talk with Lincoln took an even more significant turn. The question of the Union Pacific's apparently fruitless effort to get private financial backing came up. Dodge told the President that he thought the government itself should build the railroad. He said it was just too big a job for private enterprise. Lincoln shook his head. The government couldn't take on any more burdens than it already had, he said. But he'd do anything he could to make the project more enticing to private capital.

Dodge then passed along a bold idea that Durant had originally proposed in a letter to him. He suggested that the government relinquish its law-given prior claim to the future Union Pacific system as security for its subsidy bonds. Once the U.P. was organized, why not let the railroad's own bonds constitute a first mortgage on the property? Otherwise, the company's bonds would surely be a drug on the market. Lincoln's response to this suggestion was a dramatic surprise. He said that reversing the liens would be all right with him.[8]

Dodge took the next train for New York. There he brought the stimulating news to his old friends of the Mississippi & Missouri, three of whom —Dix, Durant, and Farnam—were now busy trying to free the Union Pacific from the control of the commissioners and set it on its own corporate feet. This trio saw in the railroad that Congress had chartered in 1862 the brightest hope of restoring their moribund M.&M. to life. The latter could become one of the most important links between the Union Pacific and Eastern railroads. But it was only for the sake of the M.&M. that Farnam had permitted himself to be teamed once more, even loosely, with Durant, who had so nearly bankrupted him only seven years earlier. Farnam had discovered that Durant lacked a "high sense of honor, sound judgment, and financial skill." [9]

It was a chilling experience for Henry Farnam to watch Durant, in the late summer of 1863, begin to gather control of the Union Pacific organization. As soon as the new railroad was incorporated, at the end of October, Farnam withdrew from it and from Durant.

At the time of Dodge's excited arrival from his interview with Lincoln, however, the old M.&M. triumvirate was still holding together. Dodge's news left them vastly encouraged. They decided to petition the new Congress to improve the status and the investment appeal of Union Pacific bonds.

When Dodge was about to leave them, Durant took him aside and renewed his persuasive argument that the general had done enough for his country on the battlefield; now let him aid it by building a railroad to California. But Dodge said he must get back to his duty, and headed for Mississippi.

Once there, he was stricken with malaria. In deep exhaustion from the stern demands of his military railroad-building, he seemed unable to regain strength and conquer the fever. Finally, in August, it became necessary to send him home to Council Bluffs to recuperate.

Dodge had no sooner arrived in Iowa than a letter brought fresh evidence that Durant hadn't given up hope of getting him out of uniform. This time, the approach was indirect. The letter came from Peter Reed, an Illinois politician and old friend of Dodge.

Writing from New York on August 20, 1863, Reed said he had just seen Durant. "He asked me this afternoon if you could be induced to leave the army and take hold of the Union Pacific Railroad," Reed reported. Exerting a bit of pressure himself, he continued, "I told him you could." Then, referring to the squabble over the starting point of the central branch, Reed added, "There's got to be hard work done to guard against the efforts north and south of us. Durant wants you to write him your opinion of the Platte Valley as a place to build the road, so he can show your letter to conflicting interests here in New York. You know the St. Louis folks want to take everything south." [10]

Struggling with his illness, Dodge did not hurry to comply with the request. Two weeks later, Reed was after him again, repeating Durant's desire for a Dodge testimonial to the Platte Valley route, and explaining, "He said you knew more about it than any other man." [11]

That was true. And it was one of the main reasons why Durant wanted Dodge to become the Union Pacific's chief engineer. But, always the schemer, Durant now had a much livelier incentive. President Lincoln's obvious respect and friendliness for Dodge could be an important asset for the railroad company. Furthermore, relations between Durant and Peter Dey, the engineer already in his employ, were edgy. Dey was a competent professional, but he was devoted to Henry Farnam and blamed Durant for most of the troubles of the Mississippi & Missouri. He had grumbled to Dodge that he was afraid Durant had "eternally damned" [12] that unfortunate railroad. Dey, a dour, cautious man, deplored Durant's florid approach to life and the business of railroading. He had not tried to hide his distrust of the Union Pacific's vice-president. Durant was convinced that Dey would become increasingly hard to get along with. Besides, unlike Dodge, Dey had no important friends. Durant was quite willing to dispense with him if he could persuade Dodge to take his place.

At the end of September, Dodge had recovered sufficient health and strength to feel able to return to his command. But, in response to an urgent plea from Durant, he went first to New York. There, early in October, Durant offered him the job of chief engineer of the railroad, at a salary of $5,000 a year. Dodge asked for time to consider the proposal. Durant said he could have until the spring of 1864 to make up his mind.

Durant was behaving as if the Union Pacific, still ostensibly in the hands of the Board of Commissioners and not yet an independent company, were his to command. This was literally the case, though the commissioners didn't know it. In August of 1863, he had subscribed to $50,000 worth of U.P. stock, paying the required $5,000 down. This had been only the beginning of his outlay, though. By October, he had corralled subscribers for $2,177,000 worth of stock, enough to enable the Union Pacific to be incorporated, according to the terms of the law. But he had had to put up three-fourths of the down payment of $217,700 himself.

Under these circumstances, he naturally spoke with authority when he offered Dodge the chief engineer's post. When Dodge said he'd like time to think it over, Durant granted it. He did, however, press him to stop in Washington on the way back to the front and see if he couldn't nudge Lincoln into announcing where the initial point of the railroad was to be.

This had now become a matter of serious urgency for the Union Pacific's principal financial backer. During the summer, John C. Fremont, the stormy, long-haired explorer, soldier, and poet who had been the Republican's first candidate for President, and Samuel Hallett, an unprincipled railroad contractor from New York State, had acquired control of the Leavenworth, Pawnee & Western Railroad. Then, with what to Durant seemed outrageous effrontery, they had promptly renamed it Union Pacific Railway, Eastern Division. Only the use of "Railway" in place of "Railroad" saved it from being a complete steal of the older company's name. "Eastern Division" was added in the arrogant attempt to persuade the nation and casual investors that this, not the central branch, was going to be the chief connection between the Missouri and the main line of the Union Pacific at the 100th Meridian.

What's more, this upstart branch had broken ground for its track at Kansas City on September 7, 1863. Durant badly needed a pronouncement from Lincoln to restore the prestige of the central branch. But General Dodge refused to help him. He said he had already given the President all the engineering advice that he had sought or needed. He would not bother him again. Durant resolved to go to Washington and force the issue himself, if he could.

First, however, there was a meeting of fundamental importance that must be held in New York. On October 29 the stockholders of the Union Pacific Railroad gathered to vote the company into independent existence, free of the commissioners' supervision.

The original stockholders comprised 121 individuals and, curiously, Tiffany & Company, of New York, the nation's leading jewelry firm. Though there were no Vanderbilts or Astors on the roster, August Belmont, friend and agent of the Rothschilds, and one of the richest men in the United States, was there. The list also included Erastus Corning, a congressman and president of the New York Central Railroad, the largest American corporation of that day; William E. Dodge, the copper king; Moses H. Grinnell, a very wealthy shipowner; Leonard W. Jerome, millionaire broker and future grandfather of Sir Winston Churchill; Abiel A. Low, a leading China trader; young Thomas A. Scott, lately Assistant Secretary of War and already the leading developer of the Pennsylvania Railroad; Samuel Sloan, president of the Hudson River Railroad; Samuel J. Tilden, eminent railroad attorney and a forthcoming Democratic candidate for President; Moses Taylor, a New York banker who owned the controlling interest in the Delaware, Lackawanna & Western Railroad; and Thurlow Weed, New York newspaper editor and Republican boss. Several members of the Board of Commissioners of the Union Pacific, who at first had shown almost a unanimous impulse to avoid investing in the railroad, now bought shares. William B. Ogden, Cornelius Bushnell, and Ben Holladay, hedging against the U.P.'s threat to his stage lines, were among them.

The biggest stockholders, though certainly not the most distinguished, were Durant, Bushnell, and Col. George T. M. Davis, who had subscribed for 50 shares apiece. Davis had been one of Gen. Winfield Scott's aides in the Mexican War, and subsequently chief clerk in the War Department. He was now a leading supplier of railroad equipment.

The stockholders' first act of business, on October 29, 1863, was the election of directors. Several of the men tapped had not been asked if they'd mind being chosen, and promptly refused to serve. The following day, those directors who were left out of an original field of thirty, selected a slate of officers.

Gen. John A. Dix, a spartan, forthright man of sixty-four, who at the age of fourteen, being deceptively large, had joined the infantry and marched off to fight the British in the War of 1812, was elected president of the U.P. This was thought to be an effective bit of strategy. Dix was a major general on active duty. His uniform at once suggested that the government was closely identified with the railroad and that building it was a matter of military urgency. Besides, Dix was a very distinguished man. He had already been president of the Chicago & Rock Island Railroad, Postmaster of New York City, and Secretary of the Treasury. In the fall of 1863, he was commander of the Department of the East, with headquarters in New York City. This gave him little time for additional duties as president of the Union Pacific.

Durant controlled enough votes to have had any U.P. office he liked, but he wisely supported Dix's candidacy for the top job. Dix had national prestige and an untarnished reputation, both of which Durant lacked. Durant was content to become vice-president and general manager, the actual head of the railroad. He was also elected to the board of directors, and to membership on the executive and finance committees. John J. Cisco, a New York attorney who had lately become Assistant Secretary of the Treasury under Salmon P. Chase, was named treasurer of the U.P. Oddly, this choice did not raise cries in Congress about a conflict of interests. Henry Varnum Poor, recently resigned as first editor of the *American Railroad Journal,* and soon to found the celebrated annual *Poor's Manual of Railroads,* became secretary of the company.

With these officers chosen, the Union Pacific Railroad Company was formally in business.

Durant now revealed how thoroughly he had been preparing for this day, months before his relationship to the company's affairs had been made official. He reported that during the previous August he had, at his own expense, ordered Peter Dey to organize field parties of engineers and seek out the most favorable route for the railroad to follow from Omaha to Salt Lake City. There was no doubt that it would run through the Platte Valley as far as the junction of the North and South Platte Rivers. There was a great deal of doubt, however, about where it might cross the Rockies. This question involved the choice of a pass where the grades could be kept below 116 feet to the mile, where the rock-cutting and tunneling might be held to a minimum, and that led to open country in the direction of Utah's capital city.

Durant's orders to Dey, issued three months before the Union Pacific actually existed, had aroused immediate suspicion in that dour, round-faced little man. Dey already knew too well how Durant had operated before. He had undertaken Durant's latest commission, but it wasn't long before he was confiding his dubious feelings about it to his former assistant, Grenville Dodge.

Mr. Durant has got the whole thing in his hands [Dey reported], but he is managing it as he does everything else—a good deal spread and a good deal do-nothing. He considers it a big thing—the big thing of the age—and himself the father of it. Durant needs common sense more than anything else, and I have been so disgusted with his wild ideas that I have been disposed repeatedly to abandon the whole thing.[13]

Only two weeks before the U.P. directors' first meeting, Durant had hired James T. Hodge, a professional geologist, to join one of Dey's engineering parties. Hodge, who had already made geological surveys of several states, was to look for coal, iron ore, limestone, and other valuables in the vicinity of whatever route the railroad surveyors found best. Privately, Durant and Cornelius Bushnell had decided that if no coal was found on lands that would be included in the government's grant to the railroad, they would part company with the Union Pacific.

On October 30th, when the U.P. board met, Durant had nothing to report beyond the fact that he had started the surveys in August. None of his field parties had yet been heard from. The directors did him the courtesy of approving what he had done for the company before it existed. Then, with an air of rubbing hands in anticipation, they resolved that "as soon as the President fixed the eastern terminus, the company will proceed to grade the track, in anticipation of laying rails in the early spring." [14] So much for propaganda. The resolution would look good on paper. When printed and distributed, it would impress Congress. It might even spur some action at the White House.

But Durant, with customary impatience, could not bear to wait any longer for Lincoln to declare himself. He went to Washington in November, determined to get a decision from the President.

William O. Stoddard, Lincoln's youthful second-assistant secretary, whose unenviable job consisted largely of handling Mrs. Lincoln's correspondence and running errands for her, saw Durant just before his interview with Lincoln. He was an arresting sight.

Durant, wrote Stoddard afterward, was "one of the most remarkable-looking men I ever saw. He was tall, hawk-eyed, and could not stand still, but kept walking, walking, up and down the room. He was saying something, half to himself, half to me." [15]

What Durant was mumbling about, it developed, was the state of the gold market. He had sold short, and the price of gold was soaring. He was afraid he'd be wiped out. But he stopped worrying out loud when Secretary of the Interior Usher arrived to take him in to see Lincoln. Usher reported the encounter briefly:

Dr. Durant said, "Now, the natural place for this terminal point is at the mouth of the Platte River. But Omaha is the principal town in Nebraska. The wealth of the Territory is there, and the energies of the people radiate from there. I think they ought to be considered, and the best thing is to start it from Omaha."

I remember very well, Mr. Lincoln looked at the map and said, "I have got a quarter-section of land right across there, and if I fix it there, they will say that I have done it to benefit my land. But," he said, "I will fix it there anyhow." So that was the way it was done.[16]

On November 17, 1863, two days before he delivered his famous address at Gettysburg, Lincoln issued an executive order that attempted to state where the Union Pacific was to start. Unlike most of Lincoln's prose, this important fragment was confusing.

I . . . do hereby fix so much of the Western boundary of the State of Iowa as lies between the North and South boundaries of the United States Township, within which the City of Omaha is situated, as the point from which the line of railroad and telegraph . . . shall be constructed [17] [the order read].

Nobody was quite sure whether the President meant that the track should begin at Omaha or at Council Bluffs, opposite it, on the east bank of the Missouri. But Durant had no intention of starting a railroad to California by first building a long and costly bridge across one of the nation's major rivers. No matter what Lincoln had in mind, Durant chose to begin grading at Omaha.

It was there, on the mild afternoon of December 2, 1863, with the bare branches of the cottonwoods and willows in the river valley white as smoke in the wintry sunshine, that ground was broken for the Union Pacific. Most of the citizens of Council Bluffs and Omaha had assembled at the spot, with their mayors. Peter Dey was on hand to supervise the ceremony. He had been jogged by a sharp telegram from Durant a few days earlier: "You are behind time for so important an enterprise." [18] Augustus Kountze, the Omaha banker who had been made a director of the U.P., was among the special guests. But not one person was present who would be significant in the building of the railroad.

Single brass cannon on the opposing shores of the river thudded dully through the speeches by Lincoln's old friend Alvin Saunders, Governor of the Territory of Nebraska, and other local notables. Andrew J. Poppleton, who eventually became the Union Pacific's chief attorney, reminded his listeners that less than ten years before, when he had first reached there, nothing was to be seen west of the river but low hills and tall prairie grass. The wolves and the Omaha Indians had had the place largely to themselves. The postmaster of the cluster of huts that was then Omaha easily carried all incoming letters under his battered hat. "Today," said Poppleton, with parochial pride, "at least four thousand radiant faces gladden our streets." [19]

A handful of telegrams was read to the crowd and applauded. John Hay, one of Lincoln's secretaries, had gracefully conveyed the sentiments of the ailing President, still contending with a germ picked up at Gettysburg two weeks before. "The President regrets that his illness will prevent him from giving expression to the profound interest he feels in the success of a work so vast and beautiful as that which you are about to inaugurate," [20] Hay had wired.

There were suitable messages from Secretary of State Seward, Secretary of the Treasury Chase, and Secretary of the Interior Usher, from the mayor of New York, and from Brigham Young. A telegraphed announcement of the ground-breaking had been dispatched earlier in the day to Governor Stanford of California. Stanford, soon to leave office and devote himself entirely to the Central Pacific, responded with a flowery tribute:

California acknowledges with joy the greetings of her sister, Nebraska, and will prove her fraternal regard by her efforts to excel her sister in the rapidity with which, carrying the iron bands of Union, she seeks a sisterly embrace. Mountain and desert shall soon be overcome. [21]

That was Stanford's way of saying, "Watch out, here we come!" What most impressed the audience at Omaha, though, was the fact that a message had been flashed from there to Sacramento, and this ornate reply received, within the space of only five hours. Talk about wonders!

Thus, as night closed in on the river-bank scene and the rutted streets of the prairie town flickered in the light of hundreds of torches, the eastern end of the first transcontinental railroad made its feeble but hopeful start.

On the day after the festive ritual of breaking ground for the Union Pacific, General Dodge, with no knowledge of that event, was in a mood to quit the army. Thin, ailing again, and disconsolate, he wrote to his brother, Nathan, from Pulaski, Tennessee, where he was building a railroad for Grant from Nashville to Decatur, Alabama.

"I am troubled with neuralagy in the head," he complained. "It is very painful and keeps me worked down. I only weigh 126 pounds, rather light for a winter campaign. If my health does not improve, I shall resign from this campaign and take the position offered me on the Union Pacific Railroad." [22] But the mood and the ailment passed without Durant's being aware of how close he had come to winning his prolonged suit for the engineer's favor. And very soon the U.P.'s vice-president was absorbed in matters of more basic and immediate concern. For at noon on Monday, December 7th, the Thirty-eighth Congress convened.

The new members had scarcely got acquainted with their colleagues and with the labyrinthine corridors of the Capitol before a move was made in the Senate that altered the future strategy of both the railroad men and the senators who favored their aims. On December 22nd, Senator Henry B. Anthony, of Rhode Island, the urbane and charming editor of the Providence *Journal,* proposed that the Pacific Railroad Committee no longer be termed Select, which implied temporary status, but become a standing committee of the Senate. This seemed reasonable, since the railroad to the Pacific was expected to take fourteen years to build and would be a continuing concern of Congress until it was finished. The true motive behind Senator Anthony's proposal, however, was to remove bleary Senator McDougall from the chairmanship of the Pacific Railroad Committee, without being rough about it. McDougall was popular, but his growing ineptitude was obvious to all. He must be unseated from the Pacific Railroad Committee, his fellow-senators agreed, but they wished to do it gently. Changing the status of the committee from Select to Standing would automatically mean dissolving the old one and choosing a new roster. The senators present when Senator Anthony made his diplomatic suggestion unanimously endorsed it.

Nothing further was done about the matter that day, though. An hour or so later, Congress, unwilling to let a civil war interfere with its Christmas holidays, voted to adjourn for two weeks.

During the Christmas recess, Vice President Durant of the Union Pacific heard from his field parties. The reports contained news both heartening and ominous. Unseasonal blizzards had halted the work of two engineer groups in early November. Durant was left to ponder the practicality of operating a railroad in an area subject to snow blockade. He could not help taking heart, however, at the news of his geologist's reconnoitering. Once the early snow had melted, Hodge had found coal fields "of almost boundless extent, and of a quality well adapted to the use of locomotives" [23] on both sides of the Black Hills. He had also discovered a certain amount of iron ore in the vicinity.

Durant conveyed his engineers' reports to the U.P. directors. Then he settled down to some intensive sessions with those directors who formed the railroad's Committee to Memorialize Congress. This quaintly named group, whose purpose was to promote liberalizing amendments to the Railroad Act of 1862, had been chosen on the day of the first directors' meeting. It had its work cut out for it now.

CHAPTER FOUR

1864

INTERLUDE IN
WASHINGTON

Congress reconvened on January 6, 1864. On that day, Rhode Island's Senator Anthony was asked to nominate candidates for the new standing Pacific Railroad Committee. He had an imposing slate ready. It was headed by Senator Jacob M. Howard of Michigan, who had named the Republican party and helped organize it. Prominent among the proposed members were Senator John Sherman of Ohio, Senator James Harlan of Iowa, and Senator Edwin D. Morgan of New York. Feeling that California was owed a substitute for the scuttled Senator McDougall, Anthony had also proposed that its new senator, John Conness, be given a seat on the committee.

The Senate, with James McDougall present but probably not cognizant, since he often snored through debates with his head and arms sprawled across the top of his desk, approved the new committee membership without a dissenting vote. This action was in one respect a relief to the Central Pacific's officials. They had grown increasingly anxious at having to entrust McDougall with their legislative hopes in the Senate. But it also gave them a fresh worry. Would Senator Conness be as amenable to suggestions from the hard-core Republicans who ran the C.P. as Mc-Dougall had been? Both senators were Democrats, but McDougall was an amiable, compliant man who largely ignored political differences. Conness, on the other hand, was austere, pointedly abstemious, rather conceited, and inclined to be narrow in his outlook. He would resist any overt attempt to shape his opinions. It didn't seem at all likely that he would slip into the kind of hand-and-glove relationship that McDougall had had with Stanford and his business associates. For one thing, Stanford had roundly defeated Conness in the contest for the governorship of California in 1861. Then, when Conness afterward had been active in forming the local Union Administration party, an uneasy coalition of Republicans and so-called War Democrats, he had built into it a political machine that had slyly jilted Stanford out of being nominated for a second term as governor. Stanford hadn't seemed to mind much. He said he'd rather be president of the Central Pacific anyway. Still, the knowledge of what Conness had done to him while they were marching under a common political banner was not comforting.

However, Conness was a most effective advocate when he wanted to be. And he was a man who would work hard and doggedly for what he thought would benefit California. The Central Pacific hierarchy could only hope that he might be persuaded that whatever would help the railroad would help the state as well.

California also had three new representatives, its quota at that time, in the Thirty-eighth Congress. One of them was a particular joy to the men of the C.P. He was Cornelius Cole, forty-one, lately district attorney of Sacramento City and County. Cole was their devoted friend, a man who had helped them establish the Republican party in California and had been a member of the National Committee since the party's birth. He had also been a small stockholder in the railroad from the start, and was an enthusiastic promoter of it. Cole's fond spot in the hearts of the Central Pacific's officers was enhanced almost as soon as he took his seat in Congress. He was promptly chosen to become a member of the House Select Committee on the Pacific Railroad. This was astoundingly advantageous for them, they felt. And they were right, as it turned out.

Cole scrupulously sold his few shares of C.P. stock upon being appointed to his vital committee post, but that in no way diminished his zest for helping the railroad along. Stanford, Huntington, and their partners could feel confident that if Conness, on the Senate's Pacific Railroad

Committee, should make a wayward move, Cole, on the corresponding committee of the House, would do his utmost to counteract it.

"It's a pity Judah died," wrote California's former Representative Aaron A. Sargent to Cole, in commenting upon the latter's accession to the committee to which Sargent had belonged in the previous Congress. "He would be invaluable to you, as he was to me, in Pacific Railroad matters." [1] But Cornelius Cole soon demonstrated that he didn't need any assistance.

The renewed and reinvigorated campaign of the railroad builders to gain greater financial help from the Government opened in the Thirty-eighth Congress on February 24, 1864.

Senator Sherman was their instrument that day. The Union Pacific's Committee to Memorialize Congress had obviously been at work on him. And they were not the only ones, it appeared. Sherman told the Senate he was introducing a brand-new bill—not the one it had passed last March—to amend the Railroad Act of 1862. He said it had been prepared by "a committee representing the various interests of the different branches of the Pacific Railroad Company." [2] It was not really a bill so much as a petition to the Pacific Railroad Committee, Sherman explained. He stressed that he held no brief for its principles or its particulars, but he did think it ought to be sent along to the committee. The Senate agreed.

The "petition" of the railroaders was reported out of committee in mid-April. Such was the crush of war measures, however, that it didn't reach the floor until May 18th. Then at the outset of debate, Senator Howard, chairman of the Pacific Railroad Committee, announced that he and his colleagues had worked up something to take the place of "Mr. Sherman's bill." [3] What they now offered was a huge amendment to the Act of 1862— one that practically rewrote the original bill.

The chief items in this amendment fell short of the extreme liberality of the measure that was finally passed, a little more than a month later. Still, they have a certain evolutionary interest.

One novel proposition was that government aid bonds be abandoned altogether. Instead, the amendment suggested that the participating railroads be allowed to issue their own first-mortgage bonds, paying 6 per cent interest and maturing in thirty years. The proposed amounts were significant: $24,000 a mile for the easiest stretches, $48,000 a mile for the lofty, desiccated country between the major ranges, and $96,000 a mile across the Rockies and the Sierra Nevada. It was further stated that the government should pay the first year's interest on these bonds as a gift, and should guarantee interest on them for the following nineteen years, in case the companies should have trouble meeting the payments themselves. In return, the United States was to be given a deed of trust to the entire railroad system, to protect the bondholders. This section of the amendment added that the railroads could issue additional bonds, if they liked, so long as the guaranteed first-mortgage bonds kept their top priority.

No stockholder was to own more than 2,000 shares. This was simply restating the original limitation, however, for the amendment also proposed reducing the par value of Union Pacific shares from $1,000 to $100 apiece, to match the Central Pacific's.

The threat of forfeiture was removed from any participating railroad that might not be completed by July 1, 1876.

The railroads were to be allowed to use coal and iron deposits found within 20 miles of their routes, though the land grant of 6,400 acres to the mile was not changed.

A sensible effort had been made to relieve the builders from the necessity of buying only made-in-America iron at a time when the war caused it to be so scarce and so costly. Let's forget about this restriction for the next two years, the amendment proposed.

When the Senate began its arguments over the long amendment, Senator Lyman Trumbull at once said he thought there ought not to be any limit on the number of shares a stockholder could buy. It was going to be hard enough to sell the stock anyway, and presumably other railroads would be the heaviest purchasers. He wouldn't like to see them prevented from buying as much as they wanted.

If there were no limit on stock ownership, next thing you knew the Rothschilds or the Barings would have the Union Pacific in their pockets, warned Senator Charles Sumner. Nonsense, scoffed Senator Trumbull, the enterprise was much too big, even for them.

The argument seesawed. At first Trumbull's no-limit proposal passed. Conness, perhaps in a mood to show his independence of the Central Pacific owners, had voted against it. Stanford's letters had been just a bit too eager.

"Stanford (for railroad purposes) is hanging on to Conness with all his appendages," Aaron Sargent had written to Cole a short time before. And Sargent, an unreconciled Republican, was gloomy about how it would all end. "The Conness horde is the mean, dirty fringe of the old Democratic party," he declared. "It is contemptible in purpose and means but is firmly seated upon the abdicated throne of Republicanism. The election of John Conness made all these sequences inevitable." [4]

Conness' minor recalcitrance at this stage of the debate on amending railroad legislation was of no consequence, however. The matter was brought up again, and the Senate changed its collective mind. A limit on individual stock ownership was reimposed, but it was raised to 5,000 shares—$500,000 worth—per stockholder.

Then, a most curious little scene took place.

In the course of writing the lengthy amendment to the Act of 1862, members of the Pacific Railroad Committee had somehow eliminated a clause of the most crucial importance to the Central Pacific. Instead of the original wording that had permitted that railroad to build eastward indefinitely until it met the Union Pacific, the amendment carefully stated that it was to halt at the eastern border of California. This, of course, would cut the Central Pacific off from its most important source of potential revenue, the booming mining communities of Nevada. One can imagine how Huntington, hovering around Washington each week, had stormed about this to Conness and McDougall, demanding that they do something at once to remove the restriction.

What they did is simply mystifying.

On the morning of May 23rd, Senator McDougall urged the Senate to amend the offending section of the proposed law to give the Central Pacific the privilege of building 150 miles east of the Nevada border. There is no telling where this arbitrary figure came from. It certainly didn't originate with Huntington, for he later said that as soon as he heard about it, he had assumed it was some of Durant's work. He had, in fact, immediately challenged him on it. "I said to Mr. Union Pacific, when I saw it, I would take that out [of the law] as soon as I wanted it out," [5] Huntington recalled.

Yet the indisputable evidence of the *Congressional Globe* proves that it was Senator McDougall, supposedly the mouthpiece of the Central Pacific, who first publicly mentioned the 150-mile limitation. Furthermore, he told the Senate that day, "The representatives of the Union Pacific as well as of the Central Pacific Co. concur in this amendment, and I hope there will be no objection to it."

Senator Conness then said, "The amendment will merely restore a privilege that was in the original act." "Without limitation," [6] Senator McDougall was sharp enough to add.

This was true, and the best thing these senators could have done for the Central Pacific was to propose that the wording of the original act be restored. But they didn't. The 150-mile limit stayed in the amendment and was approved by the Senate. It was retained in the final version of the amendment, passed by both Houses.

The most curious aspect of the whole affair is that two years later, when Huntington had decided it was time to have the limit removed, Senator Conness told the Senate an extraordinary lie. He said the 150-mile limit hadn't been mentioned in Senate or House debates or conferences, but had been sneaked into the law by means of a base plot. "It was stolen in through the corruption of some parties and the clerk who eventually made up the report," Conness insisted. Yet any listening senator could have discovered this was balderdash by turning back only two years in his file of the *Congressional Globe*.

Then, with a boldness beyond comprehension, Conness elaborated on his story. "What I state cannot be contradicted," he said, "and the Senate and Congress ought to justify itself by a close inquiry as to who dared to make laws for the Congress of the United States." [7]

On May 23, 1864, however, when McDougall and Conness mysteriously introduced the 150-mile limit into the Senate's legislation amending the Railroad Act, it was accepted without further discussion.

There was only one more matter left for debate that day: whether or not the railroads should be allowed to buy iron abroad for the next two years. Senator Reverdy Johnson said they should. All the foundries in the Union were jammed with government orders. "It is utterly impracticable to get the iron here," he concluded. "It can be got from England—at a pretty high price, to be sure—but it cannot be obtained in the United States in any reasonable time." [8]

Senator Conness suggested that the privilege of importing the iron be granted only to the Central Pacific. Why? Because, he said, the cost of shipment and insurance from the Atlantic seaboard to California had gone from $8.90 a ton, before the war, to $34.05 a ton. The other branches of the Pacific Railroad had no such handicap as that. Nevertheless, the choice of the railroad builders should be to buy American iron or none, declared Senator Howard, chairman of the Pacific Railroad Committee. He emphasized that he was speaking for himself, not for the committee.

Still, the Senate decided to let that be the final word on the subject, as the original Railroad Act had intended.

Within minutes afterward, the proposed amendment to the Act of 1862 was passed, by a vote of 23 to 5.

The House of Representatives, meanwhile, had not been considering railroad legislation at all. Not since the day, back in March, when Representative Hiram Price of Iowa had introduced an amending bill. It had been read twice by a clerk, without comment from the floor, and sent along to the House's Select Committee on the Pacific Railroad. There it had remained ever since.

That committee, with thirteen members, was in the firm hands of Thaddeus Stevens, its chairman. Stevens was no longer in line for future benefits from vast purchases of iron rails. His own foundry had been burned to the ground by Confederate raiders the previous summer. Still, no man in Congress was more determined than he that the Pacific Railroad should be built.

The membership of Stevens' committee was noteworthy only for the presence of two men: Cornelius Cole of California, and a newcomer to Congress from Massachusetts, Representative Oakes Ames.

Cole, a tall, lean man with a solemn face and a full beard, which largely hid the floppy bow ties he liked to wear, had but one important friend in Washington at this time. That was Secretary of State Seward, in whose law office Cole, a native New Yorker, had learned his profession twenty years before. Cole was at first a stranger to all his colleagues on the Pacific Railroad Committee of the House. They soon found out, however, that he was the only one among them who had traveled through the country that the transcontinental railroad would cross. "I had made the journey over land on horseback and then again by stage, two years later," he once wrote. "This gave me the right-of-way, so to speak, in the committee." [9] It was to prove exceedingly useful to the Central Pacific.

Oakes Ames was, at sixty, one of the best-known industrialists in the nation and one of New England's wealthiest men. He and his brother Oliver were the leading U.S. manufacturers of shovels. Their grandfather, Capt. John Ames, had started the business, turning out trenching tools and a few flintlocks for General Washington's men. Their father, Oliver, had greatly expanded it. He was a really rugged individualist, a man of immense physical strength and exacting moral standards. It was his habit to inspect each new Ames shovel personally, and to break over his knees any that fell short of perfection. He once knocked down a horse that had made the mistake of biting him. His forthright approach to life had been transmitted to his sons, and especially to Oakes, whose integrity and dependability were widely renowned. In fact, some fellow-businessmen considered him almost a fanatic about keeping promises, even minor ones.

"Solid" was the word that invariably leapt to the mind of anyone first meeting Oakes Ames. He was the embodiment of his reputation. Over 6 feet tall and weighing more than 200 pounds, all muscle and bone, with a broad, square head that seemed to rest directly upon his massive shoulders, he had a granitic look. He was a teetotaler, too, but this had not dampened his popularity in that rather bibulous age. He was a kind, amiable man with no pretensions, liked by nearly everyone who knew him.

At the frequent meetings of the House's Select Committee on the Pacific Railroad during the winter and spring of 1864, it was not Oakes Ames, however, but Cornelius Cole who largely shaped the legislation that was being written there.

Cole, who lived to the age of 102, and could say before he died that he had voted in every Presidential election from Polk's to Coolidge's, never was reluctant to describe the unique role he had played in those committee sessions.

"Very commonly, the first question propounded by Mr. Stevens in committee was: 'Well, what does Mr. Cole say to that?' " he later wrote. And what Mr. Cole said, he also made clear, was what Collis Huntington had briefed him to say.

"Mr. Huntington was there [in Washington] all the while," he explained in a letter to the editor of the Los Angeles *Times* in 1890. "And I remember that it afforded me much pleasure to forward his wishes in reference to that legislation, particularly as he was an old personal and political friend, and because, moreover, my constituency were all in favor of the measures." [10] As it worked out, Cole elaborated elsewhere, "I was able to promote his wishes in connection with that great enterprise in almost every particular. This was done with alacrity and entirely to his satisfaction." [11]

Congressman Cole in 1864 was also being coached, in letters from Sacramento, by Judge E. B. Crocker, the Central Pacific's attorney and the oldest brother of Charles Crocker.

"The Gov. ought to give us $100,000 per mile in Govs. [bonds] for at least the portion over the Sierra Nevadas," Crocker wrote early in March, "and they ought not to retain any, for they are given to build the road with, and that object can only be accomplished by using them, and not storing them away in the Treasury Department." [12]

Small wonder, then, that when the House's proposed bill to amend the Railroad Act of 1862 emerged from committee, it went far beyond the Senate's concept of generosity. Chief among its benefactions was a section that, in effect, doubled the amount of money the railroads could obtain for construction. Section X of the bill provided that each company could issue a $1,000 bond for every one that the government provided. Company bonds were to bear the same interest and have the same term as the government's bonds. Furthermore, they were to supersede the latter and constitute a first mortgage on the property. (Dr. Durant's prescription, to the letter!) As in the original bill, the government was to pay 6 per cent interest on its aid bonds for thirty years, and not ask to be repaid either principal or interest till the end of that time.

Next in order of munificence came a doubled land grant—12,800 acres per mile now, with the use of coal and iron ore found there. This was painless largesse. The United States still possessed more than a billion acres of public land, 80 per cent of which hadn't even been surveyed. Most congressmen considered the country along the railroad route largely worthless anyhow. Why quibble about giving away a few million acres more?

There were other bonuses in the bill for the railroad builders: No limit on individual stock ownership. No longer any portion of government aid bonds to be withheld until the roads were finished. Two-thirds of the bonds due on any 20-mile section of track to be issued as soon as the grading was done, no matter whether that section hooked up to others or not.

The bill was first read to the House on the steamy night of June 16th. In a spell of moist, exasperating heat—"It is like Isthmus weather," [13] Representative Cole wrote to his wife—Congress was holding day and night sessions in order to adjourn as soon as possible. As a clerk droned through the particulars suggested by the Pacific Railroad Committee, at least one member of the House forgot the heat entirely. That was Representative Elihu B. Washburne of Illinois, who later called what he had just heard "the greatest legislative crime in history." [14]

Washburne, one of Lincoln's closest friends and General Grant's most devoted political patron, fancied himself as the only congressman in those desperate times who was guarding the public funds. He stood against the tumbling current of appropriations like a rocky island in a stream, and with about as much effect. Still, it was a bold spender indeed who could maintain his position without faltering before Washburne's stern, homely face, with its prowlike nose and set jaw. His crown of long, straight white hair appeared to stiffen with indignation as he stubbornly reminded the House, in the tones of a funeral oration, of its fiscal sins. Washburne cared nothing for personal popularity. And he was so independent that he insisted on spelling the family name with an "e" even though none of his four brothers, all prominent citizens as well, did so.

Washburne rallied one follower, Representative William S. Holman of Indiana. Together they figuratively ripped and tore the railroad bill and scattered its pieces. Holman began the attack. In a recent government report, he had found an estimate of what all this was going to cost the Treasury—$95,088,000—and he was appalled by it. He made no bones about the main cause of his indignation: Indiana would get little benefit from the building of a transcontinental railroad, yet its citizens would be taxed to raise that vast sum to pay for it. The figure he brandished was grossly exaggerated, but it suited his argument. He added that this sum didn't even include the value of the real-estate gift, "the most stupendous land grant in the history of mankind." [15] And who was going to benefit? Not the nation, surely, but the railroad corporations. He warned that "the patriotism of this thing does not weigh a feather in the estimation of these people." [16]

He drew a feeble protest from Representative John B. Steele of New York, a devoted friend of Collis Huntington's, who said he was slandering good and loyal men. Most of the members of the House merely sat and fanned themselves.

It was left for Washburne to bring righteous rage into the fray. He did so in a long and furious speech on the night of June 21st. And he long remembered the scene. It was "one of the most exciting I have ever witnessed," he recalled to the House in the course of a debate four years later.

"The galleries were packed with people interested in the measure, by lobbyists, male and female, and by shysters and adventurers hoping for something to 'turn up,' " he said. "Your gilded corridors were filled with lobbyists, who broke through all rules and made their way upon the floor and into the seats of members." [17]

His speech that night riddled nearly every provision in the new bill. But he concentrated his anger on Section X, dealing with the bond situation.

"I confess to a sort of admiration of the sublime audacity which parties must have to come here and ask Congress to enact such a provision into the law," he began, with heavy sarcasm. He proclaimed that Section X wiped out every safeguard for the government that had been provided in the original bill. There was no protection left for the huge sums it must spend to help the railroad-builders. And he wound up roaring.

"I pronounce this as the most monstrous and flagrant attempt to over-reach the Government and the people that can be found in all the legislative annals of the country." [18]

Representative Price of the Pacific Railroad Committee remarked that to hear Washburne rave, one would think that the committee had spent the last several months trying to devise ways to rob the Treasury and destroy the government. He patronizingly complimented Washburne for so stoutly defending the Treasury at a time "when there are so many contractors with their arms into it clear up to the shoulder." [19] But Washburne was guarding it against attack when there was none, said Price. He defied him to show where the new bill took one cent more from the Treasury than the old one did.

That, of course, was evading the issue. Washburne was far more concerned for the security of the government's aid bonds than alarmed at the cost of them. He was aroused not only because those bonds were to constitute a second mortgage. He was very suspicious of the men in control of the Union Pacific. All the really distinguished individuals who had been elected to its board of directors had resigned, or at least had no active part in its affairs, he claimed. "The real management," he charged, "is in the hands of a set of Wall Street stock-jobbers, who are using this great engine for their own private ends." [20]

Thaddeus Stevens then rumbled into the fight, his rounds of sarcasm causing frequent explosions of laughter. Referring to Washburne as "my friend, the detective," he jeered at him for finding so many "hobgoblins" in the bill.

"There is not a single thing asked for which is not in the original bill, except some little land," he declared. "And as to that land, I ask the gentleman what he is going to do with it, how he is going to feed the soldiers on it."

Stevens concluded his rebuttal with a realistic estimate of the revised bond situation.

"It is also charged, Mr. Speaker, that we allow this company to issue its own bonds and give a first mortgage," he said. "That is true. But that does not take a dollar from the government now. It does not weaken the Administration in carrying on this war and defraying its expenses. The only doubt is whether this road will bear two mortgages. It is very clear that unless the second mortgage is to be got in this way, the road will never be finished and will never earn a dollar."

As for the Union Pacific's management, Stevens said, "I believe the company is composed of pure men." Then, still in his bantering mood, he continued, "I will not say about the committee in that respect. I confess I have some little apprehension about my friend from Iowa [Mr. Price], because he makes so loud professions [laughter], but I believe this road is managed by pure men." [21]

Washburne was not appeased. "At the proper time," he said, he would move that all further consideration of the railroad bill be postponed until the next session of Congress.

This was a useless threat. On June 29th, remarking that the Senate's version of the proposed legislation disagreed with that of the House, Representative Cole asked for a joint conference to reconcile the differences. Elihu Washburne must have been absent, for there were no objections raised.

If Durant and Huntington had selected the committee of conference themselves, they couldn't have been more pleased with the choice of conferees. For the House, there were Stevens, Cole, and a newcomer named McClurg, from Missouri, unlikely to be difficult. For the Senate, there were Conness, Harlan, and LaFayette S. Foster of Connecticut, who could be counted on to be agreeable.

As might have been expected, the conferees had decided to forget the Senate bill altogether—except for one or two little items. The principal one was an amendment to increase the number of government directors on the Union Pacific's board from two to five, and to insist that at least one of them be a member of every important committee of the management. As Congress saw it, this was the best way for the government to keep an eye on "the set of Wall Street stock-jobbers." This uncomfortable chaperonage was gratefully escaped by the Central Pacific, which had its charter from California, not the United States.

At a final night session of the House of Representatives on July 1st, Thaddeus Stevens announced that a messenger had just brought him word that the Senate had already approved the changes agreed upon in the Senate-House conference on the railroad bill. He then asked a clerk to read the suggested changes to the members of the House. The clerk whisked through his reading, with no attempt to present a coherent revised text. His recital consisted entirely of such passages as this: "Page 5, line 6, strike out the word 'three' and in lieu thereof insert 'six.'" [22] It was assumed that interested members would follow him with a text of the House bill in front of them. Still, they could no sooner locate a revision than the clerk was halfway through the next one.

It is worth noting, however, that the provision limiting the Central Pacific to building only 150 miles east of the western edge of Nevada was read in full. Afterward, not one of California's representatives uttered a word of objection to it.

When the clerk had finished, Representative Washburne stood and said loudly, "I hope the chairman will consent to have the report printed, and let it go over until morning."

"No, sir," replied Stevens. "I do not know that we shall have a quorum here after tonight." He admitted that the revised bill contained "a great deal of verbiage," but he insisted that it boiled down to relatively few changes—"all in favor of the United States rather than the companies." He concluded politely, "If gentlemen wish information upon any other point, I will gladly give it."

Nobody had a question but Washburne. He repeated his: "Will the gentleman have the report printed, so that we may know what it is?"

"I do not know when a majority of the House will be found here again," retorted Stevens. In other words, no.

He then asked the House to vote on the conference report. The result gratified him: 80 to 13 in favor.

Washburne asked for a voice vote. It was refused. Stevens then briskly took up a new and, he hoped, diverting subject—a bill to bring fresh water into Washington from the Potomac by means of an aqueduct. But when the clerk had concluded reading that bill aloud, Representative Washburne was still worrying his bone of contention.

("The House," he said lugubriously, "has just voted away $96,000,000 of the public treasury, without even a vote of yeas and nays. I object.")

Representative Moorhead of Pennsylvania appealed to him to withdraw his objection.

"I insist upon my objection," Washburne angrily replied. "We have drank [sic] muddy water here for 10 years, and we can do so a little longer." [23]

But the perspiring House was in no mood to let the argument continue. It voted to adjourn at 10:45 P.M.

The next night, word came from the White House that Abraham Lincoln had approved the revised Railroad Act and signed it into law. Collis Huntington sent a jubilant telegram to Sacramento. Dr. Durant, too, had every reason to be content.

CHAPTER FIVE

1864

OPERATING ON
A SHOESTRING

During the first three months of 1864, while members of Congress argued or connived over liberalizing the Pacific Railroad Act, the track of the Central Pacific gradually grew 18 miles long. Occasionally, though most of the laborers itched to move on to the mines, it lengthened a half-mile in a day.

Twisting through the shaded town of Sacramento, through fringing orchards, past windmills lifting well water to irrigate the flourishing landscape, the C.P.'s rails curved to cross the long new bridge over the American River, then straightened for a beeline run northeastward to Roseville.

The line of the railroad climbed only 129 feet between the Sacramento waterfront and Roseville, 18 miles away. Beyond there, however, the terrain steepened rapidly, as the graders were already finding out.

Roseville was a meager fruit-growing settlement that had recently been named, in the delightfully casual way of pioneers, for the prettiest girl at a local picnic. The name hadn't yet become fixed in the public mind, though. Stage drivers still called the place Griders. The trainmen who were now about to supplant them called it Junction. This last was a natural choice. Here the Central Pacific intersected Samuel Brannan's little railroad, the California Central, which connected the farming center of Lincoln, 11 miles to the north, with the rich mining town of Folsom, 9 miles south. The crossing of the two railroads meant important business for both of them. In fact, Stanford and his associates were already scheming to acquire the California Central. In anticipation of that day, they had persuaded Brannan to get ready to narrow the gauge of his track from its original 5 feet to the 4 feet, 8½ inches of the Central Pacific. Then, after putting new trucks on his rolling stock, the trains of his railroad and theirs could run on each other's track. This would be mutually beneficial. Brannan planned to make the necessary adjustments as soon as the C.P. began operating.

The Central Pacific's track to Roseville was ready before the railroad had enough cars and locomotives to begin a regular schedule of train movements over it. The rolling stock was arriving from the East in bits and pieces. There had been incomplete deliveries and haphazard loading at the ports of embarkation. The iron frames and wheels of the cars usually weren't traveling on the same ships that brought the cut lumber for the car bodies. When, finally, all parts were at hand in Sacramento, assembling the cars was at first a slow and awkward process. The railroad's only machine shop had but two vises, a grindstone, and a stove, in a room 12 feet square. When more sophisticated tools and machinery began coming in from Philadelphia, C.P. carpenters built shafts for them out of the boxes in which they had arrived.

On the assembly schedule, platform cars (flatcars), for transporting rails and ties to the end of track, naturally came ahead of passenger cars. A compromise was a platform car with several rows of plank seats nailed crosswise on it. By mid-February, one of these improvised, open-air passenger cars was ready for the use of railroad officials and their friends. On the 18th, Stanford and Hopkins took a party of thirty, including C.P. directors and a gaggle of state senators and assemblymen, out to see what had already been accomplished and what remained to be done before the track could reach Newcastle Gap. The Gap was to mark the end of the railroad's first division. Newcastle is a hilltop town, 31 miles from Sacramento and nearly 1,000 feet higher. It was then bustling with the commerce stimulated by placer mining in adjacent Secret Ravine.

On the day of this small expedition, the rails had reached a distance of only 16 miles. Carriages were waiting at the end of the line, though, and in these the distinguished inspectors rode on to Newcastle and a bit beyond, being edified along the way by frequent stops where the graders were busiest. The magnitude of the job that the Central Pacific had undertaken revealed itself most clearly in the last 7 miles west of Newcastle. There, Lauren Upson, the editor of the *Sacramento Union*, reported, the cuts and fills were as great as one could find on any railroad in the nation. In that stretch, where the grade rose steadily at the rate of 105 feet to the mile, "the labor of ascending the mountains is fairly begun," [1] he wrote. There would be no steeper ascent anywhere in the crossing of the Sierra Nevada, he said.

One particularly awesome sample of the hard work in store was Bloomer Cut, just beyond Newcastle. This was a deep trough being gouged out of an enormous glacial drift of naturally cemented gravel, almost as hard as granite, that lay across the route the rails would take. It would require several months to do the job. When finished, this wedge-shaped slice in the tough mound of earth would be 63 feet deep and 800 feet long. Frequent blasts of black powder were just now beginning to bite out a furrow across the top of the mound. Charlie Crocker's laborers were refining the lines of the cut with their picks and shovels, carrying off the debris in one-horse dump carts and wheelbarrows.

After stepping out for a respectful look at the difficulties involved here, Stanford's guests on that mild February day in 1864 returned thankfully to their carriages and jogged back to Newcastle. There they were shown where the Central Pacific's passenger and freight depots and turntable would soon be built. It was explained to them that in order to carry the track across the Gap, beyond the depots, there would have to be an earth fill 1,000 feet long and up to 60 feet deep. This was a mammoth job for one-horse carts.

When the inspection party returned to Sacramento that night, Upson wrote enthusiastically of the day. The road was firm and level, he reported. Even the platform car that the guests had ridden on ran so smoothly that there was only a slight sway. Once passenger cars were ready, Upson confidently predicted, "a person could read almost as comfortably as in a rocking chair at home." [2]

Upson's unflagging enthusiasm for the Central Pacific was at least partially sustained by an annual handout from the railroad's board of directors. In 1863, he had been issued $2,000 worth of C.P. stock "for services." [3] In September, 1864, he would be given an additional $1,600 worth. [4]

Another member of the *Union's* staff, Noah Brooks, its Washington correspondent, was also to win a tangible favor from the Central Pacific's directors that summer. In June, 1864, Huntington would give him 10 shares of stock, in the course of distributing 310 in Washington and elsewhere. These gifts were all charged to the C.P.'s construction account.[5]

While the injunctions against using San Francisco's city and county funds to buy Central Pacific stock were still being fought in the courts, Stanford made another bid for the favor of the state Legislature. On March 19, 1864, the Central Pacific played host to nearly two-thirds of the lawmakers, their families, and friends, providing a gala railroad excursion to the end of track, then 22 miles out.

By now, two passenger cars, with room for sixty people in each, were ready. They were bright yellow on the outside and as sprightly as a Brussels carpet within. In fact, they looked as if they had been upholstered with precisely that material. The treat for the Legislature required a lot more rolling stock than these two proud new exhibits, however. The excursion train was made up with seven platform cars as well, topped with many rows of plank seats.

Cinders from the wood-burning locomotive must have been a constant menace to eyes and clothing. But the day was glorious, and Lauren Upson's account of it was lyrical and charming:

The locomotive Governor Stanford led the van, gay with star-spangled banners and other devices, and on the platform car next behind rode the Union Brass Band, with ten melodious and harmonious instruments of sound.

The start from Front Street was delayed till near half-past one o'clock by the constantly arriving throngs, but when the passenger cars had been comfortably packed, and the platform cars completely loaded with cone-shaped heaps of humanity, the locomotive hoarsely screamed, the band played "Wait for the Wagon," and the train moved sturdily off, amidst the cheers of a large concourse of non-participants and the mingled fluttering of handkerchiefs and banners from the train.

The weather was indubitably got up expressly for the occasion, regardless of expense. The sun shone brightly out from among fleecy clouds; the vivid green of the plains was bedecked here and there with bright patches of yellow flowers, just opening in the warmth of Spring-time, and the distant mountains looked darkly blue, and sharp in outline through the air cleansed by the late storm.

The time made by the train was, doubtless, excellent, though nobody seemed to think of noting it, and everybody was pleased with the smooth and steady motion of the train, which showed how well the new track had been laid.

The plain to the established but impalpable base of the Sierras was rapidly crossed, and the excursionists soon penetrated among beautifully rounded foothills, gemmed with groups of green trees—oaks, scrubby pines and buckeye clumps—with rocks picturesquely arranged in small cliffs, chasms, and grottoes, while through the little valleys brooklets meandered, albeit turbid with the inevitable reddish yellow soil of California.

Twenty-two miles were soon accomplished, bringing the train to the new granite quarries, where a halt was called and the cars in a twinkling were emptied. What all that multitude did at the quarry it would puzzle a whole battalion of item-mongers to tell. The children, of whom there were enough for a small regiment, scampered and tumbled about, wild with delight, gathering bouquets of wild flowers, only restrained by constant warnings against poison oak; matrons and maidens wandered off among trees and rocky knolls, according to their "own sweet will"; while grave legislators and solid men generally gathered around the quarry in groups, conversing learnedly and geologically. . . .

The quarry is directly by the side of the railroad, and the rock can be delivered at the Sacramento levee for only one dollar per ton. The company have, in fact, already contracted with a party in San Francisco to deliver several hundred tons immediately at that price.

Soon after the evacuation of the cars, it was discovered that a large stock of baskets had been piled upon the turf, each of which contained a dozen bottles with something in them. Also, that there was a bountiful bread and cheese accompaniment. . . .

Meantime the band, under the shade of a tree, uttered such notes that several of the ladies began to talk seriously about a "dance on the green," when suddenly the locomotive whistle blew the previous question, cutting off a debate, and the motion "all aboard" was carried without a division. The prudence of this motion was attested by a rain squall, apparently backing down from the Sierras, which had already scattered a few premonitory drops, but which the excursionists triumphantly ran away from on the return trip.

President Stanford and Contractor Crocker did the honors of the occasion with all that urbanity for which they are distinguished. The return trip was particularly jolly, "John Brown's Body" being duly commemorated on the platform cars, and the expedition reached the city without accident, and with colors flying, about five o'clock.[6]

Despite this brave show, the Central Pacific was fast running out of money. Three months before, its stockholders, who had subscribed to a total of 13,640 shares at $100 a share, had already paid in $863,140 of the amount they owed. But the railroad had spent more than $705,000 on construction and equipment up to that time. Since then, expenses had been growing at a speedier rate. There was an appalling drain on assets just to fight the legal battles forced upon the directors to try to obtain subsidies that had been voted but were bottled up by injunctions. Back in December, there had still been $225,000 worth of the Sacramento County bonds and $200,000 of Placer County bonds in the office safe. But those resources were constantly being dipped into. The company's convertible bonds and capital stock were marketable for only about half their par values. There were hardly any takers even at that discount. San Francisco's promised financial help seemed doomed to be frustrated. The state of California had yet to provide tangible assistance, despite the benign attitude of most of its legislators. Aid bonds from the U.S. government could not be collected until 40 miles of the railroad had been completed and approved.

It was of this gloomy period that Charles Crocker was speaking when he told one of historian H. H. Bancroft's reporters:

We could not borrow a dollar of money on the faith of the company. Mr. Stanford, Mr. Huntington, Mr. Hopkins, and myself had to give our personal obligations for the money necessary to carry us from month to month. There was not a bank that would lend the company a cent. They had no faith in it.

We bought the first fifty miles of iron on our own personal obligations. We procured from D. O. Mills, who was personally known to each of us, a paper testifying to our responsibility and our honor, as men and as merchants, and that whatever we agreed to do, he believed that we would faithfully adhere to. That stands to Mr. Mills' credit in the early history of the railroad. Mr. Huntington bought the iron and gave our personal obligations for it and put up the bonds of the company besides as security, and we entered into an agreement that we would personally be responsible for ten years, to pay the interest of those bonds, as individuals.

Those were the responsibilities we took, and if we had not done it, there would have been no railroad.[7]

As early as September, 1863, Crocker's expenses had begun running far ahead of the Central Pacific's ability to meet the terms of its contract with him. His contract for the first 18 miles had called for $250,000 in cash, which meant gold; $100,000 in company bonds; $50,000 in company stock. On September 12, 1863, he reminded the C.P. directors that, as they well

knew, "the company is largely in arrears to me upon the cash due me
under the contract, to wit, over $48,000, rendering it necessary for me
to have some securities upon which I can raise money to carry on the
work." He pointed out, further, that the cash value of the 100 bonds due
him didn't equal the amount of cash the company owed him. He asked
for the bonds anyhow. "Being well advised of the inability of the company to pay me the amount of the bill of extras at this time in cash, and
my needs being very urgent for money to carry on the work, I propose
to accept the bonds of the company at fifty cents on the dollar in payment thereof. . . ." [8]

The directors voted unanimously to accept this proposition.

In addition to his grave financial difficulties, Charlie Crocker now bore
the burden of most of the construction beyond Roseville. This had not
been intentional. When bids were solicited for the 13 miles of track-
building that lay between Roseville and Newcastle, there was noisy criticism of Crocker in certain quarters of Sacramento.

"There was a great hue and cry there that I was a favored contractor," [9]
he later recalled. The Central Pacific directors felt obliged to acknowledge
the uproar. They awarded Crocker only 2 miles of the road to build, but
they were the two hardest, just west of Newcastle. However, Cyrus Collins
& Brother, the contractors who had won the 2 miles nearest Roseville,
soon failed. Collins assigned his contract to Crocker. Moreover, a chaotic
labor condition quickly developed. Four contracting firms were all bidding
against one another for the services of a labor force that kept steadily
evaporating in the direction of the latest gold or silver discovery. Crocker
somehow held onto his men better than the others could. In consequence,
he was obliged to take over more and more of the work that his competitors had contracted to do.

Not that he really wished to avoid the increasing construction problems. "I had become thoroughly warmed up to the building of this road,"
he said years afterward. "My whole heart was in it. I was willing to do
anything to push it forward, and I took great risks in doing it." [10]

While Crocker struggled in the foothills, the Central Pacific slowly
added units to its rolling stock at Sacramento.

A week after the Legislature's blissful railroad picnic, the C.P.'s second
locomotive, Pacific, rolled out of the company's modest shop for a trial
run. It was a ton and a half heavier and a shade more powerful than the
Governor Stanford. Heralded as "the largest locomotive on the Coast," [11]

the Pacific and its tender weighed 47½ tons when stuffed with wood and water. Its four bright-red driving wheels were 5 feet in diameter. The pistons within its brass-encased, 16-inch cylinders had a 24-inch stroke. Pacific would be a workhorse indeed, but what a gay one! With a lavish spattering of brass trim, it was as gaudily decorated as a horse leading a rodeo parade. This profligate use of brass might dismay the fireman; it was his second duty to keep the metal burnished. But he'd be eternally proud of its shine. Even the engineer would cheerfully devote an occasional Sunday to help polish the brass.

The Pacific had been built by William Mason & Company, in Taunton, Massachusetts. It had then been taken apart for shipment and reassembled in Sacramento, like the Governor Stanford, which had come from Norris & Co.'s plant in Philadelphia. Though their costs seem remarkably small today, at the time of purchase they were considered to be outrageously high. Indeed, they were nearly 100 per cent higher than their prewar prices. The Central Pacific had paid $13,688.86 for the Governor Stanford, $15,196.22 for the Pacific. Those prices included the costs of shipping, insurance, and a government tax of 6 per cent.

On the day of its debut, March 25th, the Pacific pulled a tenderful of thrilled men and boys out across the American River bridge. It stopped there briefly at a trackside woodpile to refuel, ventured a mile or two farther into the country, and then backed home. That same evening, the Governor Stanford puffed into town from the granite quarry 22 miles away, with three carloads of stone. This was the Central Pacific's first freight train.

At 6:15 A.M. on April 25, 1864, the railroad began regular passenger service to Roseville. There were to be three trains a day in each direction. The two others were scheduled to depart early and late in the afternoon.

On that inaugural day, the first trains covered the 18 miles in 39 minutes upgrade and 33 minutes downgrade. This speed was more showy than could be expected every day. As the transcontinental railroad grew, both C.P. and U.P. passenger trains averaged about 22 miles an hour.

Central Pacific conductors and engineers set their watches by the public clock outside G. M. Parker's store, at 34 K Street. That dependable timepiece governed schedules through all the early years of the railroad's operations.

The small body of men who ran the first C.P. freight and passenger trains included almost no experienced railroaders. Most of the engineers and firemen had been recruited from sawmills, where they had tended the boilers. The conductors and brakemen had mostly been former stagecoach drivers. A few locomotive crews had slipped away from the Sacramento Valley Railroad to join up with the Central Pacific. They were impelled by the same sense of impending doom that drove the S.V.R.'s chief stockholders to battle the C.P. desperately with court action, pamphlets, and bought editorials. But, for the most part, Central Pacific trains were manned by enthusiastic novices. They applied themselves with far more than customary zeal. It was a common saying among them that anybody who lost his job on *this* railroad would have to travel 2,000 miles before he could find another one.

In its first week of operation, the Central Pacific carried 298 passengers and earned $354.25. Even this pittance was heartening to the owners. However small, it at least marked a reversal of the steady outflow of funds that had been taking place ever since the railroad was organized, nearly three years before.

The month of April, 1864, brought an even more stimulating turn in company affairs. It seemed to promise that the Central Pacific would soon have $1,500,000 in the treasury that was now so nearly empty. The California Legislature had finally agreed upon a way to help the railroad. It would not run the risk of investing state funds in it. It would not take the dubious course of making an outright gift of the taxpayers' money. Instead, the legislators voted to guarantee to pay the interest for twenty years on a million and a half of the Central Pacific's own 7 per cent bonds, with the understanding that the railroad would repay the state at the end of that time. The C.P. would have to find a market for those state-backed bonds before it could collect any fresh gold. That would undoubtedly be easy, though. With the backing of all California's resources, those particular C.P. bonds ought to sell at close to par. And so they did.

Briefly, the mood at Central Pacific headquarters was triumphant.

"You say you don't think we will get the aid we hope for from the State. *We have got it,*" Judge Crocker wrote exuberantly to Representative Cornelius Cole on April 27th. "We hope to be equally successful in Congress." [12]

Then there was a stunning setback. Hardly had the selling of the state-backed bonds begun when one of the many commercial opponents of the Central Pacific brought suit to test the constitutionality of the Legislature's action. This blocked further sales until the following January. Mark Hopkins had marketed only $27,000 worth of the bonds endorsed by the state treasurer when this promising new source of revenue was cut off.

Despite the jarring discouragement, Charlie Crocker kept his men on the grade. By the end of the first week in June, the Central Pacific had 31 miles of track and telegraph line. The road was open to Newcastle. On June 6th, daily trains began running between there and Sacramento.

Within a week afterward, the controversial Dutch Flat and Donner Lake Wagon Road was finished. Stanford and his partners had somehow scraped up $350,000 beyond the demands of railroad construction to build this important link between the eastward-moving track and the vast and tempting freight-wagon traffic running to and from Virginia City, Nevada.

"Teamsters can save three days in the round trip to Virginia City, and carry fully one-quarter more freight on account of light grades," Charles Crocker proclaimed in an opening advertisement in the *Union* on June 14th. He didn't need to specify the route over which his road was such a decided improvement; it was the only other route heavily used. It ran between Sacramento and Virginia City by way of Folsom, Placerville, Lake Tahoe, and Carson City. It closely approximated today's important automobile highway, U.S. Route 50. The Dutch Flat and Donner Lake road, on the other hand, took roughly the course of the famous U.S. 40 between the two points in its name. (Route 40 has now been supplanted by straighter, wider Interstate Route 80.) The "Dutch Flat Wagon Road," as it quickly came to be called, was a shorter, easier way to go from Sacramento to Nevada's Carson Valley than the Placerville stage road.

"Plenty of freight can always be procured at Newcastle, the terminus of the Central Pacific Railroad," Crocker's advertisement continued. Then it offered an attractive lure for immediate patronage. "Until further notice all teams going west without load can pass free of toll. All those taking loads at Newcastle can pass free up to July 1, 1864. Teamsters, try it and see for yourself."

The Dutch Flat Wagon Road was an immediate commercial success. It lacked the swank of the Placerville route, where constant sprinkling kept down the dust for elegantly varnished and upholstered Concord stages, drawn by six high-stepping horses under command of yellow-gloved drivers in straw hats and linen dusters. But it lured throngs of teamsters away from that route. And teams, like today's freight trains, were far more lucrative than passenger-carrying vehicles.

As the great cargo wagons forsook the Placerville route, which was served by the Sacramento Valley Railroad, the owners of that company were spurred to more savage efforts to defeat the Central Pacific. They promptly inspired the publication of a troublesome pamphlet, titled *The Great Dutch Flat Swindle!!* This scurrilous document was addressed "To the Board of Supervisors, Officers and People of San Francisco." It declared that the officers of the Central Pacific had no intention of building their railroad beyond Dutch Flat, despite all their talk of being part of a future transcontinental line. The new wagon road, the pamphlet shouted, was damning proof of their underhanded design.

The Central Pacific directors decided to fight fire with fire. They launched a little newspaper to make their scandal-refuting voices heard in San Francisco. With a grudgingly spared $5,000, in the spring of 1864, they started publishing the *Daily American Flag* in that city. It lasted from April, 1864, until September, 1867.

The intent of *The Great Dutch Flat Swindle!!* was to put an end forever to San Francisco's long-delayed effort to provide financial aid to the Central Pacific. It undoubtedly held up delivery of the San Francisco bonds for many extra months, and whittled down their final amount. But it could not prevent the Dutch Flat Wagon Road from doing a thriving business.

Timothy Hopkins, who was Mark Hopkins' adopted son, was only a youngster when the wagon road was opened, but he remembered it years later as having been "wide, well watered, and with a stream of prairie schooners and wagons passing over it in both directions." [13]

An interesting picture of its usual traffic can be derived from a glance at the schedule of tolls. Rates were not based directly on the tonnage rolling over the road, but they reflected it with fair accuracy. Charges depended on the number of animals required to pull a given vehicle. They ranged from $5, for a horse and buggy, to $17, for a ten-horse team. If more than ten horses, mules, or oxen were needed to haul a bulging wagon, the extra animals were charged $1 apiece. Rates were established for pack animals, for mounted horsemen, and for individual animals in loose herds of stock—50 cents apiece for horses and cows, 25 cents apiece for hogs and sheep.[14]

The stage lines flocked to the new railhead at Newcastle, and the stir of scores of wheels filled the dry mountain air with the red dust of July. A Central Pacific advertisement declared that Sacramento passengers boarding the early-morning train for Newcastle would find at the end of the line

Bloomer Cut, east of Newcastle, California, 63 feet deep and 800 feet long, was blasted out of naturally cemented conglomerate rock with only black powder. In use by S.P. today, westbound.

(Top left) *Theodore D. Judah at thirty-five. He was the Central Pacific's first chief engineer and a prime mover in launching the first transcontinental railroad.*

(Top right) *Leland Stanford, president of the Central Pacific and ex-governor of California, as he looked at the age of forty-five.*

(Bottom) *The Conness, first C.P. locomotive with six driving wheels, gives a new turntable a tryout near Newcastle, California, in 1865.*

(Right) *The C.P.'s Chinese could seldom be persuaded to stand still long enough for the slow cameras of the 1860s, so an artist depicted them.*

(Bottom) *This rare view of Chinese graders at work with shovels, picks, and dump carts was taken at Prospect Hill cut, on the Sierra's western slope.*

(Top) *Chinese were lowered in baskets to blast a path for the C.P. track around Cape Horn, 1,200 feet above the American River.*

(Left) *An eastbound Central Pacific train heads through Lost Camp Spur cut, 80 miles from Sacramento.*

stages for Auburn, Grass Valley, Nevada, San Juan, Forest City, Downieville, Illinois Town, Dutch Flat, Steamboat Springs, Virginia City, Forest Hill, Iowa Hill, and all intermediate towns. Passengers from any of these places, by taking stages to Newcastle, will arrive at Sacramento at 12 M., one hour before the departure of the San Francisco steamers.

The bustle on their wagon road and the regular movement of trains over their 31-mile track helped a bit to lift the low spirits of the Central Pacific's owners, so depressed by the weight of financial troubles. These activities brought in only a slender trickle of cash compared to the gushing outflow of expenses, but they were promising.

Then, in early July, came Huntington's heartening telegram from Washington announcing the huge benefits of the amended Pacific Railroad Act. This was a powerful stimulant, especially since one of the amendments provided that the Central Pacific could collect its first government-aid bonds at the end of 20 miles of completed track. The original bill had required 40 miles to be finished first.

However, this cheering news arrived at a time when the nation was close to despair. The tidings seemed almost as incongruous as a snicker at a funeral. At daybreak on June 3rd, Grant had launched a massive attack at Cold Harbor, in Virginia, and had lost 5,000 men in ten minutes. The Army of the Potomac had met a bewildering defeat. The spirited move against the Confederate citadel of Petersburg, farther south, had slumped into a dreary siege that showed no likelihood of being lifted for a long time. The people of the North dejectedly faced the prospect that the war, which had been thought to be nearly over, might drag on for many months or even years.

There was national disillusionment, and there was fresh alarm. During the first ten days of July, Confederate General Early came thundering up the Shenandoah Valley and pushed back the thin defending forces around Washington until his skirmishers were close enough to see the dome of the Capitol.

One congressman who hadn't yet left the city after adjournment was Representative Cornelius Cole. Now he wasn't sure that he would go. Writing to Mrs. Cole, who was tending her sick father in Trumansburg, New York, he said, "I don't at all like the idea of running away when rebel guns are pounding away at the very gates of the national capitol." Then, with a rather appealing little show of bravado, he added, "Mr. Rice [a congressman from Maine] and I are going out towards the front. I do not think we can be of any service but still if we can be we will." [15]

Matters looked even worse the next day, July 13th, when Cole wrote again. "If the capital falls *the Republic is gone*," he gloomily confided to Mrs. Cole, "and it will be of no use to me to go back to California to run for Congress again if there is no Congress to run for. Such is the view I am compelled to take of the matter, and I am going to stay by till the crisis is passed." [16]

Speculators in gold, of whom Lincoln had angrily said, "I wish every one of them had his *devilish* head shot off," [17] took advantage of the Union's spasm of fright to drive the price of that metal up to its highest point, 285. In practical terms, this meant that it then took $285 in greenbacks to buy $100 in gold; the paper dollar was worth little more than a third as much as the gold one.

At the time when Congress had just provided that the transcontinental railroad builders could issue their own first-mortgage bonds in amounts matching the government aid bonds for each mile of track, the premium on gold threatened to slash the impending rewards dismayingly. If Huntington at this moment had been forced to convert Central Pacific bonds into the gold that Crocker had to have to pay his workers in California, he would have realized only 35 cents on every dollar.

Only impending bankruptcy would have moved Huntington to market the company's bonds under such desperately bad conditions. The sole alternative, however, was to borrow more on his personal credit and that of his partners. This course was becoming increasingly difficult. The time was at hand when the work of construction would come almost to a stop. Charlie Crocker was in great distress. "I could not get any money," he said of that deplorable period. "They got all I had and all I could borrow." [18]

The financial, physical, and emotional strains on the coterie of Sacramento shopkeepers who had set out to build part of a transcontinental railroad were never more severe than now, in midsummer of 1864. One of the most remarkable and fortunate aspects of their relationship was the fact that it endured stress so well.

Unlike the Union Pacific, where personality clashes and rival intrigues dogged the progress of construction from the beginning, the Central Pacific moved forward without friction among those in control.

Crocker said that he and his colleagues worked so harmoniously because they were so anxious to succeed. "We were all ambitious," he declared, "and each one dropped into his place and filled it." [19]

There was more to it than that, however. From the outset, each of the five major stockholders and officials of the Central Pacific took hold of the portion of the work best suited to his natural abilities and tastes.

(Stanford tended political fences and was the railroad's suave front man in the home territory, where his reputation and connections as ex-Governor were most useful. (Charles Crocker's great energy, easy working relationship with his men, geniality, and persistence combined to make him an ideal leader of the construction work. Huntington, the wily trader, bold, supremely self-confident, nerveless, was the perfect member of this extraordinary team to do the major purchasing and arrange the financing. (E. B. Crocker was a skilled lawyer, with the prestige of having been a member of the State Supreme Court, even briefly. He loved dealing with the legal intricacies that wreathed and sometimes threatened to choke the building and operating of the railroad(Hopkins was the dedicated guardian of the corporate purse, devotedly absorbed always in "trying to make a dollar buy a dollar and five cents' worth." [20] His stewardship of the railroad's resources was so wholehearted that he even went around picking up nails and bolts that careless workmen had dropped or tossed aside.

Huntington's natural tendency to dominate any undertaking of which he was a part was nicely counterbalanced by the fact that, most of the time, he was 3,000 miles away from his partners. These men seemed to have little comradely feeling for one another. Yet they were bound together by a rare unanimity of interest and an even rarer mutual trust. Huntington sometimes wished that Stanford were a more assertive, shrewder man, but he confided his misgivings only to Hopkins.

The fact that each one of these men was involved financially to the utmost limit in the common enterprise would account for a certain amount of cohesion. But the very extravagance of this commitment might have been expected to lead to anguished differences of opinion. Yet it never did. There were minor disagreements, of course, but they were not permitted to bloom into feuds. To an amazing extent, the Big Four, as they came to be called—or the Big Five, whenever someone felt that Judge Crocker ought to be included—accepted the will of the majority, without resentment.)

In July, 1864, Stanford's special usefulness to the Central Pacific was emphasized by the practical effect of a crucial speech he made in Nevada. Many of the leading citizens of that Territory met at little Carson City, in the eastern shadow of the Sierra, on July 4th. They were gathered to make a second attempt to frame a state constitution. The first constitution had failed to be ratified.

Stanford had got wind of the fact that some of the delegates were anxious to write into this document a clause permitting the state to offer a bounty of $3 million to the California railroad that would first reach Nevada. Friends of the Sacramento Valley Railroad, which had never lost its foolish aspiration to build through to Carson City, were responsible for this movement. Friends of Stanford put him wise to it and arranged to have him invited to address the delegates at the constitutional convention.

Stanford arrived by stage and was graciously received. His speech was urbane but candid. He told the delegates that the offer of a bounty to the first railroad that could reach them from Western tidewater would do more harm than good. It would, he said, spread the entirely false impression that the Sacramento Valley Railroad was a serious rival of the Central Pacific. This, in turn, would intensify the uncertainties of the Eastern financial markets where the C.P. was already having a grim time trying to raise money to continue construction. Thus, if the Nevadans voted for this proposed measure, they would actually slow down the only railroad that had a reasonable chance of getting there from the West. Surely they didn't expect Congress to vote aid bonds and land grants to competing railroads!

When Stanford had finished, there was an informal question period. A delegate named Charles E. De Long, soon to lose by a narrow margin the first contest for Nevada's governorship, needled Stanford persistently. Finally, De Long asked him to tell the delegates precisely what he wished they'd do about this railroad matter.

Grant a subsidy to the Central Pacific, Stanford suggested. However, he'd rather get no help at all, he said, than have them vote for that proposed bounty. But, De Long protested, the delegates *wanted* to stir up competition between railroad companies.

"You can hardly expect to get two roads built across the mountains, Mr. De Long," Stanford testily remarked.

"We do not want more than one," De Long retorted, "but we want that as soon as possible." [21]

Stanford's frank and earnest plea had made a decisive impression, however. The delegates did not vote to give coin or bonds to the Central Pacific, but neither did they vote for the $3 million bounty. The measure was killed. A year later, during the first session of the Nevada State Legislature, De Long ruefully gave Stanford full credit for having slain it.

As the hot, dry summer of 1864 wore on, it looked as if Nevada were going to have to wait a long while to hear a locomotive whistle.

"I went on until we got tied up in suits and I had to stop," [22] Charles Crocker said.

There was one period when the company's treasury didn't have a penny in it for seventeen days in a row. Employees of the railroad were obliged to wait for their pay.

"I owed everybody that would trust me," declared Crocker, "and would have been very glad to have had them forgive me my debts, and take everything I had, even to the furniture of my family, and to have gone into the world and have started anew." [23]

Construction work was never altogether abandoned, but for several months in the fall of 1864 and the succeeding winter, progress was barely noticeable. The Central Pacific directors had resolved not to keep anybody on the job whom they couldn't pay regularly; if they could afford only one worker, they'd employ but one.

An individual whom Crocker took great care to keep on the payroll through those desolate months was James Harvey Strobridge, then thirty-seven years old, a Vermonter of Irish blood. Strobridge, who had helped build the Central Vermont Railway, had done a bit of grading for Crocker on the Sacramento waterfront, and some tracklaying out beyond Roseville. His portion of the work had not been extensive, but he had made a profound impression on Crocker because he applied himself with a kind of dedicated fury and drove his men hard. He was also a militant teetotaler, a rare bird indeed in the railroad camps of those days.

Strobridge was well over 6 feet tall, thin, agile, and tirelessly energetic. His profanity and temper were spectacular, but neighbors and friends thought these were but camouflage for a soft heart. He seemed mild enough at home. He even had a ready sense of humor, though it was usually expressed in sarcasm, as Huntington's was. And when intimates told Strobridge they couldn't understand why he had the reputation of being a wild man on the construction line, he seemed as surprised to hear it as they had been.

The secret of his renown as a terror at work is revealed at least partially in a recollection of Crocker's.

> I used to quarrel with Strobridge when I first went in. Said I, "Don't talk so to the men. They are human creatures. Don't talk so roughly to them." Said he, "You have got to do it, and you will come to it. You cannot talk to them as though you were talking to gentlemen, because they are not gentlemen. They are about as near brutes as they can get." I found out that it was true.[24]

Strobridge suffered a tragic injury in 1864. It happened at Bloomer Cut, where, impatient as always, he strode into a blasting area before all the charges had gone off. A delayed explosion cost him the sight of his right eye. For quite a long while afterward, he wore a patch to hide the eye's blankness. When he came to command an army of Chinese workmen, those who learned English invariably called him One-Eye Bossy Man. All of them came to resent his incessant push and fear his quick rages.

Crocker had already marked Strobridge as an ideal candidate to be his chief of staff in the tough mountain campaign that lay ahead—if, indeed, there was ever enough money to get on with the construction.

Meanwhile, if the Central Pacific directors couldn't build, they could at least operate the small railroad that they already had. Daily that was becoming a more absorbing and rewarding task. The public's appetite for "taking the cars," as a railroad journey was usually described, was whetted by tantalizing advertising copy. Here is a sample from one of the first ads. It was signed by Charlie Crocker, who was operating head of the railroad as well as its principal builder, but one suspects that Lauren Upson had been enlisted to write it:

> The road is constructed in the most substantial manner, and is provided with new first-class passenger cars, which run with a smoothness not excelled by any other road in the United States. It is laid among the foothills, affording delightful views of valley and mountain scenery. Travelers will find every convenience to promote their comfort. Persons taking the early morning train at Sacramento, on arrival at Newcastle, take the California Stage Co.'s coaches, and, traveling by the new Dutch Flat wagon road, will reach Virginia City in at least six hours less time than by any other route, and will also avoid the dangerous precipices which have so long been a terror to travelers. [Why pass up a chance to take a whack at the Placerville route?] They will also have an opportunity of viewing some of the most romantic mountain and lake scenery in the world, inhaling the cool breezes, perfumed by the fragrant pine and balsam, and seeing

grand forests of the towering firs and pines of California. The road borders
Donner Lake, a sheet of water of crystal purity, reflecting the snow-capped
summits of the surrounding Sierras, among which it lies embosomed, six
thousand feet above the level of the sea.[25]

It was flowery, but it was also true. The Central Pacific train and stage
traffic expanded gratifyingly in response to such blandishments. In fact,
by late fall the passenger and freight business of the railroad demanded
more rolling stock than could be supplied from ship and shop.

On November 10th, the C.P. directors made a deal with Sam Brannan
to relieve this situation. They bought half the locomotives and cars of the
California Central Railroad. The purchase included four engines, one
baggage car, four passenger cars, three boxcars, and twenty-three platform cars. Brannan must not have been pressed for funds at the time.
He accepted in payment C.P. stock and various bonds, all of which were
sadly depreciated at the moment. He did not get a cent of cash. The purchase price was $105,000, but if Brannan had been forced to convert the
paper he got into gold, he wouldn't have realized more than half of that.

The Central Pacific had the appearance of thriving. This was deceptive,
however. The income from operations was swelling encouragingly, but it
was paltry when compared to the sums needed to continue building track
up the west slope of the Sierra Nevada.

As the last days of 1864 slid by, the mood of the directors was one of
frustration and wishful thinking.

We have not been able to use our State aid Bonds yet [Judge Crocker told
Cornelius Cole in a letter written the day after Christmas], but we expect a
decision of the Supreme Court on them in a few days. Then we shall have a
million and a half to go on. With that we can press the work vigorously for
several months. We have not got the S.F. bonds yet, but another mandamus suit
is pending in the Sup. Court, which we think will be decided in a few weeks.

If we only had the Gov. bonds in hand, that would help our credit amazingly,
and crush out our enemies.[26]

They would have to wait five months more for those particular bonds.
(The President hadn't yet got around to appointing the three U.S. commissioners whose approval of the completed track must precede the
issuance of the bonds.) As for their enemies, there would never be an end
to them.

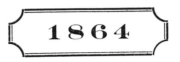

CHAPTER SIX

1864

SCOUTING FOR A
ROUTE WEST

W hile the leading men of the Central Pacific launched their railroad with the natural caution of small-town shopkeepers, Thomas Clark Durant set the Union Pacific project in motion with the flair of a ringmaster.

Durant believed that conspicuous consumption was a necessary ingredient of prestige. The way to make rich men eager to invest in his enterprise was to give it the look of affluence, he felt. He must always appear to be riding high, and so must his company. As soon as he was able, he would indulge himself in blooded horses, a lordly yacht, and parties that exuded extravagance. One of the earliest big businessmen to appreciate the usefulness of managed publicity, he would stage end-of-track excursions for newspapermen and politicians that would astonish the nation. He would deck the Union Pacific's New York headquarters, first at 13 William Street, but soon moved to 20 Nassau Street, with imported paintings, palms, statuary, and cages of canaries. (Durant shared a passion for those insistently vocal birds with another railroad executive of his day, Jim Fisk, the tubby scamp who was despoiling the Erie.)

In the first months of 1864, however, Durant's fondness for display was necessarily curbed. Most of the Union Pacific's uncomfortably limited funds had come from his own pocket and must be spent on getting the railroad under way. But he did not neglect appearances. The New York office, finished in handsome black walnut, had marble fireplaces, drawing-room furniture, and suitably elegant carpets from W. &. J. Sloane. Its overlord, the vice-president and general manager, presided in a velvet jacket, with a rope of gold securing the fat watch tucked in the lower left-hand pocket of his fancy vest.

Durant was something of a dandy. In a day when most men's clothes looked as if they had been made for larger physiques and then altered by someone who had never done it before, his suits and coats fitted conspicuously well. He favored rich materials and bright colors. He attracted attention on the street by wearing uncommon, low-crowned hats, and overcoats elaborately trimmed with fur. Even in his natural habitat, New York, he was a bird of striking plumage. In the drab setting of Washington, where he had to spend so much of his time during the first six months of 1864, he seemed even more dazzling.

In almost ludicrous contrast to this impressive Eastern façade, the actual work of building the Union Pacific Railroad began in the middle of a muddy street in Omaha in March, with Indian squaws helping out the few men who could be found to start the grading. There were fifteen husky women of the Omaha tribe in Contractor Carmichael's outfit. They earned 50 cents a day, and their lazy husbands hung around within sight of them, waiting to collect the wages.

Chief Engineer Peter Dey had already located the first few miles of the railroad's route himself. Webster Snyder, then superintendent of construction, and one of the few men close to Durant who truly admired him, had put 250 men and squaws to work along Dey's line. A crew of expert wood-cutters, imported from Illinois, was hunting for ties somewhere up the Missouri. Contracts had been let in the East for rails, locomotives, and freight cars. A letter that went out to Union Pacific stockholders in April, 1864, reported that the company had already spent, or was committed to spend, $800,000 on the railroad. The letter did not expose the awkward truth that this sum was several hundred thousand dollars more than the company possessed at that time.

One of the requirements of the Railroad Act of 1862 had been that a map of the first 100 miles of the Union Pacific's route should be filed with the Secretary of the Interior at the earliest feasible moment. After nearly two years, this hadn't yet been done. Now Durant demanded it in a hurry.

Moreover, he wanted the entire route of the railroad determined precisely as far as the California border and as soon as possible. It hadn't occurred to him that the Union Pacific track could meet that of the Central Pacific anywhere east of the California-Nevada line.

Accordingly, Peter Dey had been rounding up civil engineers he knew and could depend on, and who would work for $150 a month, which was all he could offer them. Samuel B. Reed, who had been Dey's assistant on two previous railroads, was his first choice. Reed was assigned to take a field party out to Salt Lake City and go carefully over the same ground that Brigham Young's son Joseph had been covering when a blizzard stopped his work the previous November. It was up to Reed to determine the best way for the future track to descend from western Wyoming's high plain to the Salt Lake Valley.

James A. Evans had been chosen to command a second group of surveyors. Evans' party was ordered to begin at Lodge Pole Creek, in the northeast corner of Colorado Territory, and complete B. B. Brayton's interrupted exploration of the Black Hills and Medicine Bow Mountains of Wyoming. Brayton's surveys had been cut short by a ferocious early winter storm in 1863. Evans was to finish them and locate the most suitable route across southern Wyoming to Green River, where he was to link up with Reed's line.

F. M. Case was given the task of investigating the passes back of Denver and determining, once and for all, whether the Union Pacific should turn in that direction, up the South Platte River, or swing northwest when it reached Lodge Pole Creek.

Ogden Edwards was assigned to the surveying job of greatest urgency, that of locating the line the track was to take for the first 100 miles west of Omaha.

By April 5th, Samuel B. Reed, bound for Salt Lake City, had jolted into Omaha at the end of a slow, tiresome stagecoach journey from Grinnell, Iowa, and was telling his wife all about it in a letter. Omaha, he wrote, was "full of people going to the gold fields, seeking their fortune or to escape the possibility of a draft." [1] But he had already met some prominent Mormons, and they had reassured him about the conditions he'd meet in their country.

One of Brigham Young's sons was in Omaha, waiting to meet a party of pilgrims from Europe, whom he would lead back to Salt Lake City in June. William H. Hooper, a recent delegate to Congress from Utah Territory, was with Young. Both men told Reed that Mormon leaders were deeply interested in the Union Pacific and anxious to help it along in every possible way. They also said he needn't worry about Indians where he was going. Mrs. Reed would be gratified to hear that.

Reed was detained in Omaha nearly a month. "Hundreds pass through here every day," he wrote Mrs. Reed, "old men, young men, the lame and the blind, with women and children, all going westward seeking the promised land." [2] As a result, "it is almost impossible to get a passage over the stage at any price."

He wasn't able to leave until the beginning of May. He got away then only by taking a steamer down the Missouri to Atchison, Kansas, and waiting his turn to board a westbound stage there.

What a long, tedious ride is before us [he complained to Mrs. Reed from Atchison]. Ten days and nights in a stage coach without room to move and the worst living on the continent: nothing to eat but bacon and hard bread. Fare has been raised to $200, and all baggage over 25 pounds will be charged one dollar per pound. My instruments and stationery will cost about $150 to transport them to Salt Lake. [3]

Reed finally reached his destination on May 20th. The trip had been even worse than he had anticipated. The stage route angled northwestward to Fort Kearny, Nebraska—named for the Mexican War hero Brig. Gen. Stephen Watts Kearny, but misspelled "Kearney" almost ever since. From there, it took a course approximating the future track of the Union Pacific. Reed's letter to his wife from Salt Lake City on May 21, 1864, provides a grim and graphic picture of what the journey was like before the railroad came:

Last evening, about five o'clock, we arrived here in this City of the Saints, tired and dirty after a thirteen days and nights ride in stage. I started from Atchison, Saturday the 7th, at five o'clock P.M., with nine passengers in the stage coach. No sleep Saturday night. Sunday's ride was over the hills of Kansas, no timber in sight except on the water courses and it was sparsely settled. Sunday night a severe storm of wind and rain, so severe that at 12 o'clock the driver was compelled to lay up until daylight. We thought ourselves fortunate in getting permission to sleep the balance of the night in the stable.

Monday morning we resumed our winding way westward over the dreary desolate hills of southern Nebraska with only here and there a solitary cabin, except the stage stations, which are built by the Overland Stage Co. The day was stormy and the roads muddy and at 2 o'clock in the night we were all glad to hear the driver say he could not go any further. We succeeded in getting a small space on the ranchman's floor, on which we slept until daylight, when we resumed our journey and reached the station (five miles) at 10 A.M. and got breakfast. After which we traveled slowly over or through the muddy roads and at daylight Wednesday we reached Fort Kearney, on the Platte River, distance from Atchison 253 miles and from Omaha 200 miles, all nearly played out. One lady in the party appears to stand the journey as well as the best of us.

Thursday we reach Cottonwood Springs, a watering place in the valley. Friday we are all sick from drinking alkali water. Saturday we reach Lathum, the station where the Denver and Pike's Peak passengers leave. Only Mr. Mathewson and myself left to go on west, so we had plenty of room. Sunday morning we entered the first gorge of the Rocky Mountains. All day we traversed the first chain of the mountains and then entered what was known as the Laramie Plains. Monday we crossed the plains and Tuesday we were on the summit of the second chain of mountains, which we crossed at what was called Bridger's pass.[4]

There, not far short of his destination, Samuel Reed's account of his rough journey to Salt Lake City ended. But he was pleased with what he found in Utah Territory. A week later, he wrote home to say, "I have never been in a town of this size in the United States where everything is kept in such perfect order as in this City of the Saints. No hogs or cattle allowed to run at large in the streets and every available nook of ground is made to bring forth fruit, vegetables or flowers for man's use." [5]

By the end of the first week in June, he and his men were hard at work at the mouth of Weber Canyon, near the present site of Ogden, 40 miles north of Brigham Young's capital. They formed a sizable expedition. There were "one four-mule and two two-mule teams, with tents, camp equipage, tools and instruments for the survey," Reed explained to his wife. "All told, teamsters, cook, engineering party and night guard, we are seventeen. The big dog makes eighteen." [6]

Reed had arranged for periodic mail pickups and deliveries by messenger from Salt Lake City. His few letters home in June were full of enthusiasm for the life he was leading.

"We breakfast quite frequently on the nicest trout, caught from the purest mountain water you ever saw," he told Mrs. Reed. "Our bed consists of Mother Earth and one good buffalo robe, one beaver robe, consisting of seven skins, for which I paid ten dollars, and my shawl, with boots, coats and pants for pillows. Sometimes we sleep in a tent and sometimes out in the open air." [7]

On June 12th, Reed's party was well up into Weber Canyon, and he was enthralled with his surroundings. "The scenery is magnificent," he wrote, "mountains composed of granite and gneiss towering four to five thousand feet almost perpendicular above us. The deep narrow gorge in which the river runs is only about 300 feet wide and is the wildest place you can imagine." [8] Eventually, the Union Pacific track was laid through this passage.

There were farms near, and the surveyors lived well. Reed carried an order from Mormon President Young to his people to supply the Union Pacific party with provisions whenever they sought to buy them. The engineer reported to his wife that his men were obtaining plenty of butter, eggs, milk, and fresh mutton. "We are in no danger of famine as long as we are in the settlements," [9] he assured her.

The going was getting rougher, though. High water delayed them. In their first three weeks they covered only 24 miles. As they climbed toward Wyoming, the nights grew colder. On June 18th there was a heavy frost and "ice as thick as a window glass in the dishes standing out last night." But the men were all thriving on the rugged life. "I can eat more at a meal than ever before in my life," Reed wrote, "and don't care how often the meals occur." [10]

It was now midsummer. Vice-president Durant and the other Union Pacific officials had just savored the upsurge of hope and confidence that followed Congress' passage of the bountifully amended Railroad Act of 1862. Very soon afterward, a distant scandal and murder provided them with an even more optimistic view of the future.

Durant, though fretful about the progress that the Central Pacific was making, had been far more concerned about the achievement of his rival in Kansas, the impudently named Union Pacific Railway, Eastern Division. On July 1st, Samuel Hallett, its builder, had sent out brash invitations to a large number of persons prominent in government and business. He offered them all free passage to Kansas from wherever they lived to ride on "the first 40 miles" of his railroad on August 18th. "The opening of this section," his invitations declared, "will give earnest to the people of the country that, within the time prescribed by law, the great highway will be built to San Francisco." [11]

The U.P. Railway, Eastern Division, had already provided the people of Leavenworth with a good deal of amusement. Its first locomotive had promptly run off the track and buried its nose in the Missouri River. But

Hallett's invitations were no laughing matter to Thomas C. Durant, who had nothing yet to show visitors to Omaha except some rather slipshod grading.

Actually, however, Hallett was lying. He did not have 40 miles of track laid. What he did have was so wretchedly constructed that the chief engineer of this railroad, O. A. Talcott, didn't want outsiders to see it, to say nothing of riding on it. Competent laborers had been even harder to find around Leavenworth than in Sacramento or Omaha. Talcott, a small man partially crippled by a stroke, felt his reputation threatened by shoddy workmanship that he had been powerless to improve. In desperation, he had written to President Lincoln. This railroad, he said, was too poorly constructed to merit the government subsidy. He urged Lincoln not to allow any aid bonds to be issued to its officials until the weaknesses of the road could be corrected.

Hallett was in Washington when he heard about it. At once, he sent a choleric telegram to his brother Tom, back in the railroad office at Leavenworth, telling him to fire Talcott and "kick him into the street" [12] if he made any demands. Tom Hallett, a burly man with a sadistic urge, did precisely that. Talcott swore revenge, and moodily waited for Samuel to return from Washington.

Samuel Hallett was home by the end of the month. Shortly after lunch on July 27, 1864, he was walking past a store on the main street of Wyandotte, Kansas, and had just spoken affably to the loungers in front of it, when Talcott stepped out of an adjacent alley and shot him in the back. While Hallett lay dying in the dust, Talcott flung himself onto a waiting horse and disappeared. He was never caught.

Col. Silas Seymour, brother of the controversial Governor Horatio Seymour of New York, and at this time chief engineer and superintendent of the Washington (D.C.) Aqueduct, was induced to take Talcott's place temporarily. The job didn't last long.

After Hallett's murder, John C. Fremont, the other principal owner of the U.P. Railway, Eastern Division, sold out. It was quite a while before Durant had to worry any more about this contender in the track-building sweepstakes. Seymour moved on to the employ of the Union Pacific Railroad. There, a good-looking, conceited man with the title of consulting engineer, though not well-qualified professionally for the job, he became a pawn of Durant's.

In August, 1864, Durant made the opening move in an elaborate game of shenanigans that he had been devising for many months. His goal from the start had been not only to control the Union Pacific but to make a fortune out of building it. Durant had no faith that the railroad would ever reward him well out of freight and passenger earnings. At least, he was much too impatient a man to wait for what seemed likely to be an exceedingly distant day indeed. He longed to cash in soon on those government aid bonds and the U.P.'s own first-mortgage bonds, now so enticingly placed almost within reach by the terms of the amended Pacific Railroad Act. He itched to realize a quick return on the millions of acres of land that would gradually become Union Pacific property as the track progressed westward.

It was obvious, though, that fattening on government bounty mustn't be done in the open. The intent of Congress in promising aid in bonds and land to help build a transcontinental railroad had clearly been to benefit the nation as a whole, not the builders in particular. Durant thought both ends could be accomplished, but the means must be subtle and legal. The U.P.'s government directors would be keeping an eye on him.

Early in 1864, he had begun contriving his scheme. It was not a lone effort. Cornelius Bushnell, an ex-grocer and railroad-builder from New Haven, now a U.P. director, was a fellow-conspirator. George Francis Train, a remarkably eccentric crony of Durant's, was their leg man in the initial maneuvering.

They started with the premise that the chief stockholders of the Union Pacific couldn't build the railroad at a fat profit made in the railroad's own name. They would have to disguise their identity. Most important, they would need to find a way to limit their financial responsibility. Ownership of shares in the Union Pacific at that time made each stockholder liable for its debts to the full extent of his personal property. If these men were to assume the great risks of constructing the road, they felt that they must have the protection of a company charter that would limit their liability to the amount of company stock they held.

Bushnell thought he had found a promising charter authorized by the state of Connecticut. But Train found a better one. It was the charter of the Pennsylvania Fiscal Agency, originally granted by the General Assembly of that state in November, 1859. What a document it was! It entitled its holders to engage in just about any commercial enterprise they fancied, except banking, and it limited their responsibility to the value of the shares for which they had subscribed.

How George Francis Train had found out about it is not clear, for the Pennsylvania Fiscal Agency existed in name only. Its owners, after paying in the 5 per cent of stock subscriptions that had made them a going concern, had not done anything else of note. Yet Train appeared at the door of the agency's office in Philadelphia on March 2, 1864, and offered to buy its charter. He explained that Thomas C. Durant, whom these men had never heard of, wanted it for a contracting company to build the Union Pacific. The chief stockholders of the Pennsylvania Fiscal Agency said it was a deal. The following day they sold their charter for $25,000, which more than repaid them for what it had cost them. Two of the former owners, in turn, said they'd like to put some money in Durant's enterprise. Train said it could easily be arranged.

The next thing was to get the name of the Pennsylvania Fiscal Agency changed. Train took care of that, he said later, by distributing $500 here and there among the members of the General Assembly. When he told a Philadelphia newspaperman what he had done, the fellow snorted and said he could have arranged the whole matter for $50.

In any event, on March 26, 1864, the General Assembly conferred a flossy new name, of Train's devising, upon the former Pennsylvania Fiscal Agency. It was now the Credit Mobilier of America.

For a few months, the charter was tucked away among Durant's papers while he and Bushnell did what they could in Washington to help persuade congressmen to liberalize the Railroad Act. Even when the bountiful amendments had been safely passed, Durant was not yet ready to unveil the Credit Mobilier. According to his elaborate plot, two other moves must come first. To start with, an ostensibly bona-fide independent contractor should be found, who would undertake to build the road and then, rather promptly, falter for lack of funds. Then Durant, Bushnell, and a few cronies would step forward and agree to underwrite the contract. They would soon discover that the financial responsibilities they had assumed were too vast, and that they could not entice any other capitalists to share them. Then, and only then, would Durant and his gang assign the contract to the Credit Mobilier, where the financial liability was comfortably limited and the attraction to speculators was thereby much enhanced.

Durant seemed to feel that this devious plot must govern his moves to get the assets of the Union Pacific into his hands and those of his helpers. The essence of the plot was that each move after the first must seem forced upon the plotters by circumstance.

With his customary instinct for the dramatic, Durant began the unfolding of his scheme at that fashionable capital of speculative enterprise, Saratoga Springs, at the height of the 1864 season. Here, early in August, he persuaded Herbert M. Hoxie, a minor-league Republican politician from Des Moines, Iowa, to be his straw man—the contractor who would ostensibly make the winning bid to build the U.P., then shortly "fail."

How Durant happened to select Hoxie is a mystery. The two men had known each other, but only casually, since 1860, when they met in Chicago at the Republican National Convention that nominated Lincoln. Dodge, whose acquaintance with Durant went back several years before then, probably introduced them. Hoxie was an old friend of Dodge, and the two had come to Chicago together, as members of the Iowa delegation at the Convention. Durant was there, along with Dix, Sheffield, Farnam, and other leading railroad men, to crusade for a strong Pacific Railroad plank in the Republican platform.

Hoxie had had some small experience as a contractor, and he had made it plain that he was anxious to promote railroads. But "he was a man of no means," [13] as Oliver Ames, who was to succeed General Dix as president of the Union Pacific, later said. Right now, in the summer of 1864, he was earning a modest living as operator of a freight ferry on the Missouri at Omaha.

What led him to agree to play the initial role in Durant's drama of subterfuge is less obscure than Durant's reason for choosing him for the part. Hoxie obviously expected to make money. After the two had come to terms, Hoxie wrote Dodge, "I have just returned from Saratoga, New York, where I went to see T. C. Durant. He's going to push the Pacific railroad and wanted me to enter his service. I partly declined for political reasons; still I shall have a connection with him and may make something out of it." [14]

Hoxie was less than candid. His "connection" with Durant was no less than an agreement to front for him in his intrigue to acquire as much as possible of the future property of the Union Pacific.

A proposal signed by Hoxie had been made officially to the railroad at New York City on August 8, 1864. It was the only bid submitted. The signature read, "H. M. Hoxie, by H. C. Crane, Attorney." [15] This was fitting enough. Crane was Durant's attorney, and he and Durant had drawn up the extraordinary document before Hoxie had ever heard of it.

The audacious terms on which Thomas Clark Durant, in the guise of "H. M. Hoxie," proposed to build the first 100 miles of railroad and telegraph for the Union Pacific began with a price of $50,000 a mile. It was stated, curiously and without explanation, that no bridge on the line was to cost more than $85,000. The document further declared that the cost of all stations, water tanks, machine shops, roundhouses, and other necessary structures should not exceed $500,000. If the charges for iron rails rose to more than $130 a ton, delivered at Omaha, the Union Pacific was to pay the excess cost.

The proposal then went into fine detail as to how "Hoxie" was to be paid. The terms called for $5,000 a mile in cash, and the balance in securities: U.P. first-mortgage, government-aid, and land-grant bonds. The railroad was to mortgage the lands it received, for not more than $16,000 a mile, and the subsequent bonds were to yield 7 per cent interest.

It was recognized in the document that none of these classes of bonds could be issued until 20 miles of track had been completed and approved by the government commissioners, as required by the amended Railroad Act. But the Hoxie proposal had a suggestion for getting around that. Let the railroad at once issue certificates, paying 6 per cent interest, that could be exchanged for the bonds when the latter could legally be issued. Certificates for the first-mortgage and government-aid bonds would be accepted at 80 per cent of their par value; those for the land-grant bonds at 70 per cent of par.

If the Union Pacific would agree to these remarkable propositions, "Hoxie" avowed, "I will . . . subscribe, or cause to be subscribed, to the capital stock of your company, five hundred thousand dollars." [16]

The proposal was promptly accepted in a letter signed by George T. M. Davis, for the special committee of the Union Pacific's board of directors that had been chosen to let the construction contract. Then, on September 23rd, it was formally ratified by the full committee: Dix, Bushnell, and Davis.

So far, so good. Within ten days, "Hoxie" was emboldened to make a further proposition. Why not let him build the road all the way to the 100th Meridian? This would more than double the amount of track covered by the first proposal, and in return he would subscribe, "or cause to be subscribed," an additional $500,000 to Union Pacific stock.

The Dix-Bushnell-Davis committee accepted this offer the day it was made, October 4, 1864.[17]

Three days later, without explanation, Hoxie abruptly assigned his enlarged contract to Durant and his associates. These men, in return, agreed to provide $1,600,000 to guarantee the completion of the Hoxie contract. Durant signed up for the largest single portion: $600,000. All the men made a down payment of 25 per cent at once.

The second act of the guileful melodrama had now been played, according to plan. The third, and last, was deliberately postponed until the following March.

The Hoxie contract was the immediate cause of the Union Pacific's losing its first chief engineer, Peter Dey. Trouble had been brewing almost from the moment Dey accepted the job, in December, 1863. The Hoxie contract proved to be his final incentive for leaving.

At the beginning of summer in 1864, Dey had sent Durant his estimate of what the first 100 miles of road would cost. He had made what he considered liberal allowance for the exorbitant prices of labor and materials, and he still believed the job could be done for $30,000 a mile.

Not long after Dey's estimate arrived in New York, a henchman of Durant's unexpectedly appeared in Omaha. He was John E. Henry, one of the Union Pacific's directors. Henry brought verbal orders from Durant that Dey was to increase his estimates very considerably. The explanation was that the directors had heard that the Platte Valley was subject to serious flooding. They believed there should be many miles of heavy embankments to protect the track out there.

Dey said this was nonsense. But he agreed to refigure his original estimate to include the cost of those entirely unnecessary embankments. With great distaste, he forwarded the new estimate to New York. It now calculated the cost at about $50,000 a mile.

A fresh indignity, soon after, was the arrival of Col. Silas Seymour, Durant's "consulting engineer," from New York. Seymour looked over the direct route that Dey had laid out for the track to follow from Omaha to the Platte Valley, and said the grades were too steep. He hunted around the local terrain for a while and then suggested a wide loop to the south and west, which would add 9 miles to the length of the railroad. Dey was furious. He rejected the criticism of his grades as wholly unwarranted, and made no secret of his suspicion that lengthening the track was simply a means of bilking the government out of additional bonds. He would have no part of it. Seymour listened to him with an air of tolerant disdain, and then boarded an eastbound stagecoach.

Unknown to Dey, that very same month, Durant had made another effort to enlist General Dodge to take the chief engineer's place. This time, Durant felt rather sure of himself. Dodge had been shot in the head during the Battle of Atlanta, back in mid-August. He had been unconscious for two days, and had had to be invalided home in September. By October, when he was able to travel, he let Durant persuade him to come to New York for talks. But Durant wasted his breath and train fare. Dodge, with a devotion to duty that the U.P. official found mystifying, was determined to return to military service until the war was over.

In November, Dey was sent a copy of the Hoxie contract. He read it in indignation and disbelief. Its terms of $50,000 a mile were obviously based on his second estimate, the one he had been forced to pad to suit Durant.

Dey brooded over his situation for nearly a month, torn between his fondness for "the best position in my profession this country has ever offered to any man" [18] and the affront to his reputation and personal honor. On December 7th he made up his mind. He sent his resignation to General Dix, president of the Union Pacific, to take effect on December 30th, just a year after he had so enthusiastically begun the job. Officially, he explained, "My reasons for this step are simply that I do not approve of the contract made with Mr. Hoxie for building the first hundred miles from Omaha west, and I do not care to have my name so connected with the railroad that I shall appear to endorse this contract." [19]

On the same day, he sent a personal letter to General Dix, his longtime employer, that more fully revealed his feelings. "My views of the Pacific Railroad are perhaps peculiar," he wrote bitterly. "I look upon its managers as trustees of the bounty of Congress." [20] And if construction contracts as bloated as Hoxie's were to be tolerated, by the time the Union Pacific had reached the mountains, its securities would be worthless. "You are doubtless uninformed how disproportionate the amount to be paid is to the work contracted for," [21] he added, trying to excuse Dix for his apparent lapse in having approved the Hoxie document.

Dix didn't reply for more than two months, and his eventual answer was lame. He was offhand about Dey's resignation, and said it was too bad they couldn't talk things over in person. But, really, the directors had thought the Hoxie contract was the best they could get. Besides, "the arrangements for the first hundred miles had the approval of the Government directors." [22]

That, indeed, was true. But the approval hadn't been cordial. The full slate of five government directors, demanded by the revised Railroad Act, had not been appointed until October, 1864. At their first meeting, they were confronted with the accomplished fact of the Hoxie contract.

"We then condemned it," eventually testified Charles T. Sherman, one of the government directors chosen to take office in 1864. Why? Because "the price was too large, too extravagant. It was $50,000 a mile, but it should not have cost the half of that." [23]

"We condemned it," Sherman explained to the congressional committee that finally investigated the affairs of the Credit Mobilier.

But, under the circumstances, considering that it was made while the war was still existing, considering the high price of labor, and the want of means to transport iron and other materials to Omaha—except up the Missouri River, which was an uncertain way—and considering the consequently enhanced cost of materials, we concluded that we would simply protest against the contract in our report to the Secretary of the Interior, and let it go.[24]

They did protest, but it was a mild statement of objection, and it didn't reach the Secretary of the Interior until July, 1865.

Meanwhile, T. C. Durant had had his way. And, with the stubbornly scrupulous Peter Dey now out of his path, he seemed likely to continue to do so.

CHAPTER SEVEN

1865

ENLISTING HELP
FROM CHINA

Eighteen sixty-five began as the happiest new year the founders of the Central Pacific had faced since they organized their railroad. On the very first day, after a span of six months so devoid of funds that construction had nearly come to a stop, they learned that there would soon be $1,500,000 in the till.

The State Supreme Court had at last decided that California could constitutionally honor a pledge that its Legislature had made to the Central Pacific long before. The state was now permitted to guarantee to pay the interest (7 per cent) for the next twenty years on 1,500 of the railroad's $1,000 bonds. The bonds previously had been about as popular as Confederate money. Now a million and a half dollars' worth of them, with the state treasurer's endorsement, could be sold as promptly as desired, and at a price close to par.

The C.P. made a bold bid for action within a week of the Supreme Court's decision. On January 7, 1865, J. H. Strobridge, the able, arrogant young Vermonter whom Charles Crocker had placed in command of his field forces, advertised in newspapers and handbills in post offices throughout the state that the railroad wanted 5,000 laborers immediately

—"for constant and permanent work." This excited readers who yearned to see the Central Pacific advance briskly eastward. But the offer did not attract an eager horde of applicants.

There were idle men available, too. The editor of the Sacramento *Union* said there were a good many, and urged them to seek jobs on the railroad at once. He added the sarcastic suggestion that the "enterprising cutthroats" who had lately been frightening his community by bold hold-ups "can get better pay for their labor by working by the month in the mountains than by robbing Sacramentans at the alley corners these hard times at a dollar and a half per head." [1]

But neither idle workingman nor cutthroat seemed inspired to help build the Central Pacific. Crocker heard repeated rumors that the Sacramento Valley Railroad, Wells, Fargo & Co., and the stage lines on the Placerville road were paying men *not* to work for the C.P. The largest force that Strobridge had on his rolls at any time during the next two or three months was 800. And that was never for long. Immediately after each pay day, he invariably lost a hundred or two—some of them drunken and wayward, others already on their way to those alluring mines in Nevada. The loss was slowly made up as the next pay day approached.

Strobridge, driving his small force of graders and tracklayers up the long, bony ridge that led toward far-off Donner Summit, was running into other labor trouble. His Irishmen had assessed the value of the man-power shortage and found it enticing. They were asking for more money.

The Central Pacific's officials were exasperated and indignant. The workers' demand was bluntly refused, and many of them quit.

Charles Crocker was the first to suggest a way out of the railroad's dilemma. It was a solution peculiarly embarrassing for Stanford. Crocker said they ought to hire Chinese, those widely despised immigrants who had originally flooded into the Golden Hills, as they called California, to pick over the rubble of mines after the white men had extracted the prime ore. Those who had not returned in discouragement to China had become cooks, waiters, houseboys, laundrymen, vegetable peddlers. Un-skilled white laborers and servants, mostly Irish, regarded the Chinese with distaste and resentment as usurpers. But many an employer knew the placid, patient diligence of these Orientals and savored it. Besides, they could be hired for less than whites.

Anti-Chinese sentiment was strong among all classes of voters in California, however. The principal men of the Central Pacific, with the exception of Collis Huntington, shared it. Their private opinions might be relatively easy to change, but the whole state, unfortunately, knew Stanford's views on the subject. When he became Governor on January 10, 1862, he had referred to the local Chinese in his inaugural address as the "dregs" of Asia, a "degraded" people, and had said it would give him great pleasure to back the Legislature in any constitutional move to prevent any more of them from entering the country. He had reaffirmed these sentiments in his annual message to the legislators a year later. Now, after a lapse of only two years, he was faced with the need to reverse himself completely. This was not an unprecedented problem for a politician, however. Stanford, after the initial shock, found that he could accommodate himself quite comfortably to an about-face that was so obviously to his financial advantage.

The chief objecter to the move was Strobridge.

This "smart, pushing Irishman," as a friendly observer called him, said to Crocker, "I will not boss Chinese. I will not be responsible for work done on the road by Chinese labor. From what I've seen of them, they're not fit laborers anyway. I don't think they could build a railroad." [2] He added that the problem of trying to feed them the weird things they liked to eat would alone be a plaguey nuisance.

Because Strobridge was far too valuable to the Central Pacific to antagonize, especially at this delicate juncture, Crocker briefly let the matter drop. There soon came a day, though, when Strobridge began to see the Chinese in a very different light.

On this occasion, Crocker was out on the line with him. The two men stood conversing at the edge of an excavation for the roadbed east of Newcastle. A delegation of workers approached and threatened to leave the job unless they got a raise. Before Strobridge could explode, Crocker quickly turned to him and said, "Why don't you go over to Auburn and get some Chinamen and put them to work?" [3]

The effect on the petitioners was dramatic. Their bravado collapsed. Their spokesman said plaintively that if only the railroad wouldn't hire Chinamen, they'd go back to work and say no more about wages. It was easy then for Strobridge to comply, but the incident left a sharp impression on his thoughts. Harassed by his inability to find even a fourth as many white laborers as he had advertised for, incensed because most of the men working for him were unreliable and given to going on sprees after every pay day, Strobridge in a short time was fully ready to try Crocker's suggestion.

He began by hiring fifty Chinese from the vicinity. At first, he restricted them to the simplest work, filling dump carts. The white laborers were so resentful of their presence that they avoided all contact with the new-comers. "They wouldn't work within a hundred rods of them," [4] said Crocker.

It was at this time that a friend of Crocker's stopped beside the grading to chat with an Irishman who was resting on his pick. He asked the work-man how his wages compared with those of the Chinese. The man ex-plained that he and the other whites got $35 a month and board, while the Chinese were paid $30 and boarded themselves. Crocker's friend, who later told him the story, then commented that he thought the Irishmen on the job had the better deal.

"Yes," the other agreed. Then, with a bitter glance at the nearest Chinese, he added, "But if it wasn't for them damned nagurs we could get $50 and not do half the work." [5]

The Chinese proved so tractable and quick to learn that Strobridge soon had them driving the carts as well as loading them. Next, though doubtful that they were physically capable of really hard work, he handed them picks and tried them out on the softer excavations. The results were most gratifying.

Strobridge now began eagerly to hire more Chinese, fifty at a time. According to random notes left by Timothy Hopkins, Mark's adopted son, there were before long as many Chinese as Irishmen working for the Central Pacific. It was then, Hopkins related, that many of the Irishmen talked openly of banding together and driving all the Chinese off the job for good. They held a meeting to plan their attack. But Strobridge and Crocker followed with a summons to another meeting, and there delivered an ultimatum. Since we can't get anywhere near enough white labor to build this railroad, they told the crowd, we were forced to hire Chinamen. If you can't get along with them, we have only one alternative: we'll let you go and hire nobody but them.

"This argument prevailed," wrote Hopkins, "and no more trouble was experienced during the progress of the road." [6]

Before long, the Irishmen had become sufficiently used to their inoffen-sive companions to be willing to hammer rock drills while the others held them steady. Strobridge at first thought the short, slender Chinese too frail to swing the heavy hammers themselves. He quickly found he was wrong.

Crocker later explained how the Chinese steadily won their hearts.

"Wherever we put them, we found them good," he said, "and they worked themselves into our favor to such an extent that if we found we were in a hurry for a job of work, it was better to put Chinese on at once."[7]

The trouble was that by mid-March, 1865, the local Chinese labor market was rapidly running out. It was then that Crocker, taking a deep breath, asked a San Francisco labor contractor named Koopmanschap, who had useful connections at Canton, to hire men for him in China— "all he could bring, up to 2,000."[8] Koopmanschap said he'd do his best, and sent off agents on the next ship.

March of 1865 was a significant month in the history of the Central Pacific for other reasons as well. On its third day, Congress passed a brief but very important amendment to the already liberally amended Pacific Railroad Act. All companies engaged in constructing the transcontinental railroad and its branches were now permitted to issue their first-mortgage bonds, in the amounts the law allowed per mile, "to the extent of one hundred miles in advance of a continuous completed line of construction." This was a practical measure to provide funds for starting work at once on the bridges, and especially the tunnels, that lay well beyond the advancing graders.

Obtaining cash in advance for the costly job of digging tunnels was far more urgent for the Central Pacific than for the Union Pacific. The C.P. had nine tunnels to blast and cut out of granite before it could cross the summit of the Sierra Nevada, only 70 miles way. The U.P. wouldn't reach its first tunnel until it was 680 miles west of Omaha.

Government aid bonds could not be issued except on 20-mile sections of the railroads that were all ready for use and approved by the U.S. commissioners. Congressmen had agreed that it was imposing an unfair financial hardship on the companies to force them to wait until they had received each consignment of government bonds before they could sell comparable amounts of their own bonds.

Judge Crocker gave full credit for the passage of this most welcome amendment to the Central Pacific's old friend and helpmate, California's Representative Cornelius Cole. Cole, in his advantageous position as a member of the House's Pacific Railroad Committee and in his persistent eagerness to be of service to the C.P., had doubtless been set at this latest task by Collis Huntington. Huntington was on hand in Washington when the amendment passed, Cole noted in a letter to his wife.

Writing to Cole soon afterward, Judge Crocker said, in part, "I must congratulate you on your success in getting through Congress some of the most important measures for Cal., especially that bill for the Pacific. It has removed the great obstacles we found to our progress, and we can now go on with confidence." [9]

The month of March brought, too, a stirring reminder that even as the Central Pacific's construction effort was gaining in vigor, muscle was being added to its operating strength. On March 16th, the big freight locomotive Conness, with six scarlet driving wheels, 4 feet in diameter, and a body festive with gleaming brass and liberally applied colors, huffed out across the American River bridge on its trial run. Its tender bulged with as many joyriders as could find places on the wood stacked there.

Named in honor of California's junior U.S. senator,[10] in whom Stanford and his colleagues hoped to rouse more enthusiasm for the C.P. than he had yet shown, this dashing "railroad giant" [11] weighed 50 tons when provisioned with water and fuel. It was hailed as the heaviest and most powerful locomotive on the West Coast. In fact, it was considered too strong to haul passenger cars safely.

"She is designed for drawing freight up the heaviest grade of the road, which is 105 feet to the mile," [12] wrote a *Union* reporter, not hesitating to apply a feminine pronoun to a locomotive with a masculine name. He added that the Conness would be able to pull eighteen loaded cars up such a grade, and that was six more than any other C.P. engine could haul up it. On a level track, the impressive newcomer was said to be capable of pulling eighty-nine full cars—if only the railroad had that many.

The Conness had been built at the famous Mason works in Taunton, Massachusetts, in 1864, had been disassembled and shipped around the Horn in a sailing vessel, had arrived in late November, been put together in the railroad's growing shops, and was now ready to go to work. On its first day in the sunshine, it ran to Arcade Creek and back, and was said to be functioning perfectly.

Out beyond Newcastle Gap, where the swelling force of graders was confronting harder rock, blasting powder was now being consumed at an astonishing rate. An urgent call for more was telegraphed to Huntington. It brought him into a memorable clash with Edwin M. Stanton, Lincoln's almost obsessively dedicated Secretary of War. After bitter disappointment with the shoddy outcome of many a war contract, Stanton had grown to regard manufacturers, builders, and businessmen in general with contempt. They were, he believed, mere conscienceless profiteers. Whenever they sought him out, he listened to them with virulent suspicion. For the most part, he avoided them altogether.

Into this hostile atmosphere strode Collis Huntington with a request for a permit to ship 5,000 kegs of black powder to California, at a time when the needs of Grant's and Sherman's armies for this commodity were uppermost in Stanton's troubled thoughts.

"What for?" growled Stanton.

"I want it to use in building the Pacific road and to sell to my customers," Huntington replied. He added that he had been selling powder in California for years and had been supplying miners as well as meeting the railroad's needs.

"Stanton looked up like a hog, as he was," Huntington recalled later, "and said, 'What you have been doing for the last three or four years is nothing to me. I shall not give you any permit.'"

Huntington bitingly retorted that there was certainly one thing the Secretary couldn't do for him, and that was treat him like a gentleman, for he was incapable of it. He then stalked off to see the President.

To Lincoln, he repeated his request, but foxily refrained from mentioning his jarring encounter with Stanton. Instead, he asked the President if he would kindly give him a note to the Secretary of War, requesting him to oblige Huntington.

The railroad builder used to enjoy telling what followed:

"'Well,' replied Mr. Lincoln, 'that seems proper to me. Yes, that is very proper,' and then he wrote on a card, which I have preserved, 'Mr. Stanton: Mr. Huntington requests permission to send 5,000 kegs of powder from Boston to California. Unless you know of some good reason why this should not be done, you will please give him the necessary permit.'"

Holding the Presidential sanction in reserve in case of trouble, Huntington then boldly bypassed Stanton.

"I put the card in my pocket, and said nothing—although I have since regretted not telling Lincoln that his Secretary was a hog. I did not return to Stanton, but telegraphed an order to Newhall of Boston: 'Ship me 5,000 kegs of powder, and put it aboard the steamer. I will pay you for the powder, and for any damage you may hold me responsible.' The powder was sold, shipped, and paid for, without Mr. Stanton's permit and, as far as I know, without his knowledge." [13]

As April opened, Sacramento's citizens joyously reddened the night sky with the light of huge bonfires to celebrate the fall of Richmond. Only twelve days later, the town was in shocked mourning at the incredible news of the President's assassination. Early on Saturday morning, April 15th, the tragic bulletin announcing Lincoln's death reached the local telegraph office. By afternoon, most of the stores and homes of Sacramento wore black. The afternoon passenger train from Newcastle crept into the station with long streamers of black crepe draped above and below its windows from end to end.

But the heartfelt grief and horror at Lincoln's brutal, senseless death could not long subdue the nation's relief and delight that the long war had ended. Businessmen were soon assuring one another that the surge of prosperity and expansion that would now follow would astonish the world.

Writing to Cornelius Cole in a mood of jubilant confidence, Judge Crocker had only one regret about the war's termination.

I at one time thought it would be a good plan for U.S. to send us about 5,000 rebel prisoners, and let us set them at work building R.R., but I suppose they will all be let loose now.

At least, there were many compensations.

We have now about 2,000 men at work with about 300 wagons and carts [he reported], and I can assure you they are moving the earth and rock rapidly. . . . You will be astonished when you come back to see the amt. of work we have done.

A large part of our force are Chinese, and they prove nearly equal to white men in the amount of labor they perform and are far more reliable. No danger of strikes among them. . . .

We want to get a body of 2,500 trained laborers, and keep them steadily at work until the road is built clear across the continent, or until we meet them coming from the other side.

I tell you, Cole, we are in dead earnest about this R.R., and you take 6 or 8 men in real earnest, and if they have any brains and industry, they will accomplish something.[14]

He said they were laying track so rapidly that they expected to complete 55 miles by fall, and by winter reach Dutch Flat, 10 miles farther on. "Then a bold push for the summit in the summer of 1866." The Judge concluded, "All this requires money and we are spending it rapidly." [15]

Surprisingly, he did not mention, in this connection, that the long-awaited San Francisco bonds were at last in the railroad's possession. On April 5th, the State Supreme Court had decided that the supervisors of San Francisco must delay no longer in releasing them to the Central Pacific. The bonds were delivered within a week of the Court's decision.

The financial benefit to the railroad was only half as great now, though, as had been originally intended. The citizens of San Francisco in 1863 had voted to buy $600,000 worth of C.P. stock. But the wary supervisors balked, because, under the state laws of the time, every stockholder in a corporation was liable for its debts. The men who controlled the fiscal affairs of San Francisco had no confidence that the Central Pacific would ever be built. On the contrary, if San Francisco bought C.P. stock, it might very well wind up being responsible for most of the debts of a bankrupt railroad. So the supervisors voted instead to present the Central Pacific with an outright gift of $400,000 worth of the bonds of the city and county of San Francisco. The directors of the railroad had reluctantly accepted the compromise. But then they had been obliged to take the matter into court to pry the bonds loose. As a result, in two years they had spent $100,000 in legal fees to acquire a $400,000 gift.

Still, $300,000 was never more welcome to them than right now. And on the heels of this tidy present came a much greater sum. On May 13th, Huntington telegraphed Stanford from New York: "I received yesterday twelve hundred and fifty-eight thousand dollars ($1,258,000) United States bonds for account of Central Pacific Railroad of California." [16]

Because of the fact that gold remained the medium of exchange in the Far West all the while the Central Pacific was being built, the company repeatedly went through the galling experience of having its bounty from the Government shrink by a sizable percentage in the necessary process of being converted into gold. Gold remained at a stiff premium throughout those years. For example, the initial consignment of $1,258,000 in U.S. bonds, which arrived in mid-May, 1865, was worth at the time only $953,030.30 in gold. And the persistent attrition of exchange down the years was such that the total government aid turned out to be nearly $7 million less in coin than it had appeared to be on paper and on the Treasury records.

The first batch of U.S. bonds received by the Central Pacific applied to the 31 miles of track that had been completed the previous year. Though no more rails had been laid till this spring, construction trains were now able to push into Auburn, 5 miles beyond Newcastle.

By June 10th, the track was at Clipper Gap, a lumber settlement, 43 miles east of Sacramento and 1,751 feet above sea level.

"The boom of the powder blast is continually heard," reported the Auburn *Stars & Stripes*. "Frowning embankments rise as if by magic. High trestle bridges spring up in a week." [17]

These trestles were consuming hundreds of thousands of feet of lumber. Most of it had been cut in coastal forests of the Northwest and brought to the sites by schooner and flatcar. C.P. lumbermen, however, were already beginning to hack away at huge trees much closer at hand, giant red firs not far ahead of the graders. From now on, the railroad would rely on timber adjacent to its route for ties, bridges, trestles, freight sheds, and stations.

The forested ridge up which the Central Pacific was slowly climbing was by no means an unbroken back of rock, but, rather, like an enormous fossil spine. The track must wind around successive vertebrae and cross gaps between them. The builders at first had intended filling these gaps— even the deepest—with earth bridges. That, however, proved to be frequently impractical. Soil in many places covered the ridge to a depth of only a foot or two. Scraping up enough dirt to make heaps from 50 to 100 feet high and several hundred feet long was out of the question in such thin-skinned territory. It was decided early in 1865 to build trestles there instead. Later, when the railroad was finished, earth from more plentiful sources could be hauled in by train, and then the trestles would be replaced by fills.

Several of these trestles, beginning at Newcastle, had now been built. They stood like transfixed centipedes straddling the gaps in the ridge, their massive, multiple pairs of legs, immense pines from Puget Sound forests, planted at 16-foot intervals, their feet braced in masonry. "Bents," the engineers called those sturdy timber limbs, and they were laced together and steadied by rows of horizontal beams. The track was laid along the backs of the multi-legged structures. Secure though they were, they had a spindly look, as if the weight of a locomotive and cars might make them swaybacked. And the ravines lay shudderingly far below. The trestle at Deep Gulch, for example, was 100 feet high at its center, and 500 feet long.

By the end of July, Koopmanschap's first cargoes of Chinese laborers from the fields around Canton had arrived in San Francisco and been shipped forward by river boat and train to the grading beyond Clipper Gap. Strobridge's force soon doubled to 4,000, and by early fall it would at last reach the number he had called for in vain the previous January.

A sea captain named Thomas H. King, who in time brought thousands of Chinese to California in various vessels, eventually told a congressional investigating committee what these human cargoes for the Central Pacific were like.[18] The men, he said, were recruited mainly from two agricultural districts, Sinong and Sinwai, that lay close to the great city of Canton. Unfortunately, natives from those districts seemed to have a traditional antagonism for each other as dire as that of feuding American mountaineers. They had to be kept apart as carefully as possible, but identities were occasionally mistaken. When that happened, there were maimings or killings on shipboard.

The Chinese recruited by agents of San Francisco labor contractors were largely ignorant (but far from stupid) farm boys, fully half of them in their early twenties and very few as old as thirty. They came aboard with a scattering of interpreters. Through the latter, Captain King learned the typical terms on which they had agreed to go to work in America. Invariably, the contractor advanced passage money—$40 by steamship, $25 to $35 by sailing vessel—with the assurance that it would be repaid, with interest sometimes as high as 5 per cent a month, out of wages earned overseas. In the contract, the family or friends of each laborer underwrote those terms. The seal of some petty Chinese official legalized the bargain.

Winter, when there was little work for these young men on their home farms, was the best time to collect them in large numbers, said Captain King. Since it was not their custom to bathe during the winter, however, they were usually filthy and lice-ridden when they embarked. Some even attempted to come aboard while ill with smallpox or venereal disease, but they were usually caught and prevented from sailing.

The bewildered travelers were packed in like bags of produce. On the Pacific Mail Steamship Line, especially, the captain testified, they were stowed on the upper deck, contrary to maritime law, as well as on the two lower ones. This way, Pacific Mail vessels usually carried 20 to 30 per cent more passengers than they were legally entitled to do.

On board, the jam-packed Chinese often sickened from inactivity, more food than they were used to, and the unfamiliar motion of the sea. When not ailing, they smoked incessantly, and gambled with such passion that most of them landed at San Francisco considerably deeper in debt than when they had set sail.

The voyage across the Pacific took thirty-five to forty days by steamer, longer under sail. At its end, the bewildered farm boys from Sinong and Sinwai often met a cruel reception. Though they were quickly taken under the wing of San Francisco's celebrated Six Companies—leading Chinese firms that controlled the commercial life of Chinatown and served in a multiple capacity as banks, hiring halls, clubs, stores, and reception centers for the immigrants—they usually first had to run a gantlet of white hoodlums. This riffraff of the city's streets expressed in violence the subdued resentment felt by many of the more restrained citizens.

After the Chinese had stoically submitted to patting and pawing by customs officials in search of hidden opium, they hauled their few belongings to waiting wagons and set off for Chinatown. It was then, more often than not, that the torment began.

An indignant observer, Reverend O. Gibson, left a vivid account of a typical hoodlum attack:

These Chinamen, with their shaven crown and braided cue [sic], their flowing sleeves, their peculiar trousers, their discordant language, and their utter helplessness, seem to offer especial attractions for the practice of those peculiar amenities of life for which the San Francisco hoodlum is notorious. They follow the Chinaman through the streets, howling and screaming after him to frighten him. They catch hold of his cue, and pull him from the wagon. They throw brickbats and missiles at him, and so, often, these poor heathen . . . reach their quarter of this Christian city covered with wounds and bruises and blood, received at the hands of parties whom Chinamen suppose to be fair representatives of this boasted Christian civilization. Sometimes the police have made a show of protecting the Chinamen, but too frequently the effort has been a heartless one, and the hoodlums have well understood their liberties under our sacred guardians of law and order.[19]

Matters grew so bad, in fact, that as the Central Pacific brought in more and more thousands of Chinese in the following few years, compassionate citizens of San Francisco formed a Chinese Protective Society, and met each immigrant ship with special police to guard the arrivals.

In midsummer, 1865, the Central Pacific had to learn how to feed, house, train, and pay its exotic new employees, most of whom knew not one word of English.

The problem of housing was easily solved by the use of tents. The weather was hot and dry. These Chinese farmhands were used to spending their days outdoors and sharing crowded quarters at night. "In a little tent, ten by twelve feet, a half dozen or more Chinamen . . . find abundant accommodations for eating and sleeping," [20] wrote one visitor to the C.P. construction sites.

The matters of food and pay were intertwined. Probably on the advice of men from the Six Companies, which gave the immigrants shelter and briefings on the life they faced before they boarded river boats for Sacramento, the Chinese laborers formed themselves into gangs of twelve to twenty men, each with a head man and a cook. The head man, who invariably could understand and speak a little English, worked alongside the gang, but on pay day he collected the gang's wages in a lump sum. He then deducted what was owed to the labor contractor, distributed the remainder to the individuals, and kept all the records. Each cook was paid by the railroad, but the members of each gang shared equally in the cost of cooking utensils and of their food, which consisted largely of imported items obtained periodically from Chinatown merchants in San Francisco.

To Strobridge's white workmen, who were content with an unvarying fare of boiled beef and potatoes, beans, bread, butter, and coffee, the Chinese diet must have seemed outlandish. It was astonishing in variety and strange in detail. It included oysters, cuttlefish, exotic finned fish and abalone meat, oriental fruits and vegetables, bamboo sprouts, seaweed, and mushrooms. What seemed even more curious to the C.P.'s Irishmen was the fact that every one of these foods came dried, requiring the addition of water to regain its flavor and bulk. In addition, the Chinese ate rice, salted cabbage, vermicelli, bacon, and sweet crackers. They drank nothing but tea, and oceans of it, flavored with a kind of molasses sugar. They cooked nearly all their food in peanut oil. The only fresh meats they had were pork, a prime favorite, and, for the frequent Chinese feast days, chicken. The pigs and poultry were invariably slaughtered in camp on Sundays.

Training these farm boys to the wholly unfamiliar jobs of railroad construction proved a lot simpler than had been anticipated. At first, the head men of the gangs translated instructions. Before long, though, large numbers of the workmen had picked up enough English to get along without interpreters. For the most part, the Chinese learned by observation. Once having been shown what to do and how to do it, they needed little further guidance.

They quickly set an example for their Irish co-workers in diligence, steadiness, and clean living. "They are . . . ready to begin work the moment they hear the signal, and labor steadily and honestly on till [*sic*] admonished that the working hours are ended," wrote A. W. Loomis, a minister who came to observe them and to talk with officials of the railroad about them. "They have no storytelling; they have no sentinel set to watch while his companions enjoy their pipes, and to pass the word when the 'boss' comes in sight. Not having acquired a taste for whiskey, they have few fights, and no 'blue Mondays.' " [21]

Most of the Chinese took daily sponge baths in warm water, washed their clothes frequently, and, by dint of their devotion to tea, were far less often ill than the white workmen. The water they drank in their tea had been boiled and thus purified. On the other hand, the water the Irishmen drank was gulped down just as it came from its source. Too often, it was contaminated and made them sick.

With Strobridge's army vigorously reinforced by a couple of thousand recruits from across the Pacific, the red dust of that unusually dry summer swirled high above the lofty conifers that shaded the work.

The powder that Huntington had slipped past Stanton's vigilance had now arrived in Sacramento. So much of it was being forwarded to the front to blast a path for the track and raise even more dust, that Charles Crocker had a "spark-proof" [22] car built to transport it. The car had iron sides. The edges of its doors were lined with India rubber. Its roof was tin. This roof, unlike the wooden roofs of the regular freight cars, could not catch fire from locomotive sparks, and, being tin, would easily give way in case of an accidental explosion. Thus the force of the blast would harmlessly shoot upward instead of outward.

The powder car was part of an impressive outpouring of new rolling stock from the railroad's workshops at E and Sixth Streets in Sacramento. There were twenty-four fresh boxcars, too, each provided with two pairs of interchangeable doors—solid for ordinary freight, iron-grated ones for livestock. And there was a curious hybrid, a baggage-passenger car. The Central Pacific's freight conductors had reported that every time a freight train pulled out of a station, there were always a few people who wanted to climb aboard. Either they had just missed the last passenger train or were in too much of a hurry to wait for the next. Invariably, they had been accommodated in the baggage car, but had been obliged to stand for the length of their journey. The railroad's officers had decided to cater to these clients who ignored passenger schedules. They had built a 35-foot baggage car—longer than usual—and partitioned off one end of it. Back of the partition were seats for twenty passengers. Henceforth, the company announced, there would be one of these cars on every freight.

The Central Pacific now had a total of 113 cars, only six of them for passengers alone, and a half-dozen locomotives. Its car builders still obtained their wheels and ironwork from the East. Enough for seventy more flatcars and thirty boxcars were on order at this moment. But they no longer got the woodwork from there. They were now using California lumber and completing the cars themselves.

The railroad's swelling business fully justified this expansion of its rolling stock. Operating revenues must have made the principal owners congratulate themselves on having had the courage to tackle railroading. The C.P.'s monthly income during 1865 rose from $11,040 in January to $22,939 in May. It leapt $10,000 higher in June, and by October it would soar to $65,925.

Up the brown Sacramento River at the end of August sailed a party of distinguished Easterners who were winding up a sightseeing journey of several months. They had now come to view this extraordinary railroad that aimed to climb over the Sierra Nevada. The most important person in the group was little Schuyler Colfax, Speaker of the U.S. House of Representatives, who in a few years would be Grant's first Vice President. Colfax, a teetotaler who chain-smoked cigars and regarded life with such a persistently pleased expression that he had earned the nickname "Smiler," was a six-term Republican congressman from Indiana. Before he entered politics, he had been a printer and editor. With him now were three prominent newspapermen, the first arrivals of a pilgrimage of journalists that would continue for the next four years. Their senior member was William Bross, the full-bearded, rather fierce-looking editor of the Chicago *Tribune* and lieutenant governor of Illinois. His companions of the press were slim, dapper Albert D. Richardson, of the New York *Tribune,* who had been Horace Greeley's most distinguished correspondent during the late war, and Samuel Bowles, tall, nervously energetic, quick-tempered editor of the Springfield (Massachusetts) *Republican.* Richardson and Bowles were both adventure-loving, outstandingly able writers in their thirties.

At Sacramento, after suitable honors, Stanford and Charles Crocker proudly escorted the visitors into the Central Pacific's newest yellow passenger car, and off they went on a jolly ride to the end of track. There was champagne available for those who enjoyed it.

Out at the grading, Richardson found a sight that fascinated him. He later wrote of Strobridge's men at work:

> They were a great army laying siege to Nature in her strongest citadel. The rugged mountains looked like stupendous ant-hills. They swarmed with Celestials, shoveling, wheeling, carting, drilling and blasting rocks and earth, while their dull, moony eyes stared out from under immense basket-hats, like umbrellas. At several dining-camps we saw hundreds sitting on the ground, eating soft boiled rice with chop-sticks as fast as terrestrials could with soup-ladles.[23]

At Illinoistown, which the track was fast approaching, Stanford honored the Speaker of the House by changing the name of the community to Colfax. The Speaker was most appreciative.

On horseback, the party then moved up the line of grading toward the mining settlement of Gold Run. Not far beyond Colfax, they rounded the spectacular point of Cape Horn, a nearly perpendicular promontory that pitched southward at an angle of 75 degrees toward the slate-green North Fork of the American River, 1,400 feet below the line of the railroad. Here Strobridge had had to lower Chinese from the top of the cliff in wicker baskets to chip out holes for the initial charges of powder. By now repeated blasts had blown away enough rock to form a secure ledge for the track around the face of Cape Horn. The view was both grand and chilling.

At Gold Run, 63 miles east of Sacramento, Speaker Colfax and his companions climbed into a six-horse coach and set out for the summit of the Sierra, still 42 miles farther on.

Reported Bert Richardson:

> Our day's ride was up a graded winding road [the Dutch Flat & Donner Lake Wagon Road], commanding an endless sweep of dense forest and grand mountain, among graceful tamaracks, gigantic pines and pyramidal firs. We reached the summit two hours after dark, when its wild, gloomy grandeur is far more impressive than by day. It is boundless mountain piled on mountain—unbroken granite, bare, verdureless, cold and gray.
>
> Through the biting night air [at 7,000 feet above sea level] we were whirled down the eastern slope for three miles to Donner Lake, blue, shining, and sprinkled with stars, while from the wooded hill beyond glared an Indian fire like a great fiendish eyeball.[24]

Richardson was wrong about the origin of that distant campfire. The wretched, sub-human Digger Indians, who lived mainly on grasshoppers, had fled those forests years ago. The flames that flared into view on the north slope of Donner Peak as Richardson gazed upward had been lighted by Central Pacific surveyors.

Next day, the travelers from the East climbed up to talk with the surveyors, "among the precipitous ledges." That night, in one of the parlors at Lake House, where the Colfax party was staying, Richardson was captivated by the spectacle of the Central Pacific's builders in an informal conference.

The candles lighted up a curious picture [he wrote]. The carpet was covered with maps, profiles and diagrams, held down at the edges by candlesticks to keep them from rolling up. On their knees were president, directors and surveyors, creeping from one map to another, and earnestly discussing the plans of their magnificent enterprise. . . . Outside the night wind moaned and shrieked, as if the Mountain Spirit resented this invasion of his ancient domain.[25]

The final details of the route over the summit were being fixed. This was urgent business. Seven of the thirteen tunnels that the Central Pacific was going to have to blast out before it met the Union Pacific would be clustered in a stretch of 2 miles at the top of the long climb from Sacramento. All tunnels were to be wide enough to accommodate two tracks. "We are confident a double track will be needed in a few years to do the business of the road," [26] declared Stanford.

The biggest tunnel, right at the summit and within a few hundred feet of Donner Pass, was going to be 1,659 feet long, 26 feet wide, 20 feet high, and would lie as much as 124 feet beneath the surface of the granite cliff through which it would run. That job, it was anticipated, would take at least a year and a half to finish. It must be begun at the earliest possible moment.

In mid-October, Chief Engineer Montague started three shifts of Chinese, under experienced white foremen, at each end of the formidable Summit Tunnel. There they began driving rock drills into the stubborn faces of granite and exploding the first powder charges. It was intended that work would go on around the clock until the great task was done.

Also in mid-October, Leland Stanford wrote a long report of progress to President Andrew Johnson and Secretary of the Interior James Harlan. The track had reached Colfax, 55 miles from Sacramento, on September

1st, he reported. The company now had 5,000 men and more than 600 teams at work. It expected to have 6,000 laborers on the job before the end of the year.

However, he pointed out, the huge expenditures necessary to purchase rails, timber, and rolling stock, to build bridges and trestles in advance of the grading, to start work on the tunnels that lay ahead, had forced the Central Pacific to spend $4 million more than it would get in government-aid bonds for some time to come. Do what you can, he said—only in more diplomatic words—to make sure nothing holds up the delivery of those bonds when they have been earned.

Two weeks later, the three government commissioners appointed to examine the progress of the Central Pacific reported to Washington that they had looked over the 23 miles of track between Newcastle and Colfax and found them satisfactory in every way. The government now owed the Central Pacific $1,104,000 more.

That was far short of what was currently needed, though. Charles Crocker, with the full responsibility of pushing construction and operating the railroad, was terribly worried. He was getting relatively little gold from the Central Pacific—five-eighths of what was owed him. The rest of his bill was being settled in C.P. stock, at the rate of $2 worth of stock for every $1 of indebtedness. Crocker was personally extended to the limit, and he felt unbearably lonely in his predicament.

At this juncture, his associates rallied to his side, as he had probably been fairly sure they would. True, they were not legally his partners in Charles Crocker & Co., but there was no doubt that they all would stand or fall together.

"Go on! We will stand by you," [27] Stanford assured him, speaking confidently for the others as well as himself. And so they did, while Crocker took in masses of Central Pacific stock in lieu of cash, acquiring vastly more of it than his associates, who were not openly involved in constructing the railroad. But so completely were their futures and their fortunes interwoven by now that Stanford, Huntington, and Hopkins seem not to have fretted about the temporary imbalance in Crocker's stock holdings. In due time, they would all work out a satisfactory legal device for divvying up the shares.

CHAPTER EIGHT

1865

THE U.P. GETS OFF
TO A SLOW START

For a distance of 18 miles west of Omaha, the countryside is a plateau, from 200 to 300 feet higher than the bottom lands of the Missouri River and from 75 to 100 feet higher than the vast Platte Valley, on its western edge. This tableland is folded into broad billows, with three small water courses flowing southward down their troughs. The line that Peter Dey had proposed for the Union Pacific would have sliced straight through these waves of richly fertile farmland, reaching the natural highway of the Platte Valley in the fewest possible miles. This was the best line. However, it involved a steep climb for the first 3 miles out of Omaha, and a costly and time-consuming sequence of cuts and fills until the mouth of the little Elkhorn River was crossed. Where the Elkhorn entered the Platte Valley, the Union Pacific would begin an incredibly gentle but steady westward rise for 500 miles, its route ascending from 5 to 20 feet per mile, an almost imperceptible gradient.

Vice-President Durant, in his anxious search for funds with which to begin building the railroad and lining his pockets, had sent his compliant consulting engineer, Col. Silas Seymour, to Omaha the previous fall to lengthen and lighten the initial portion of Dey's conservative route. His purpose was to collect, right at the start, more bonds and more land from the government than were truly justified.

Seymour "discovered" an alternative that Dey had previously rejected. That was that if the U.P. route were to run south from Omaha for a few miles before swinging west, it could follow generally much easier grades between its starting point and the Platte Valley. This change, soon tabbed the "ox-bow route," would add 9 miles to the length of track needed to reach the valley. Durant looked at it this way: 9 extra miles would entitle the Union Pacific to an additional $144,000 in government subsidy bonds and permit it to market an extra $144,000 worth of its own first-mortgage bonds, to say nothing of acquiring added land grants. Furthermore, since Seymour's miles would be simpler to build than the ones Dey favored, the margin of profit on them would be higher, and more quickly acquired.

Durant was well pleased with this scheme. But Peter Dey, his integrity outraged and his pride hurt, promptly resigned from the company. The doctor did not express regrets.

Durant knew that the Railroad Act required the President of the United States to approve any changes in route after it had been accepted by the Interior Department, as Dey's line had been. He realized he needed more distinguished and less biased sanction than Seymour's to win the President's approval. It occurred to him that Jesse L. Williams might possibly provide it. Williams, a rather stern-eyed man with a close-cropped dark beard, his face deeply wrinkled from long seasons of working in the sun, was one of the newly appointed government directors of the Union Pacific. He was also an eminent engineer. He had spent more than thirty of his fifty-seven years building canals and railroads. Furthermore, as soon as President Lincoln had named Williams to the U.P. directorate, in October, 1864, the four other government directors had dispatched him to Nebraska to look over the route and examine the progress of the railroad. Durant now took the risk of asking him for his formal opinion of Seymour's proposition.

On January 2, 1865, Williams responded. There was nothing wrong with the change, he said, *provided* the new route was as good as Seymour made it out to be. Personally, he didn't know. He hadn't looked over that particular ground last October.

The matter was referred to Washington, where it remained unresolved for months.

Meanwhile, Durant and the four gentlemen who had underwritten the

Hoxie contract with him decided abruptly in March that their individual financial risks in that partnership could no longer be borne. So they told Hoxie to transfer the contract, which was still in his name, to the Credit Mobilier of America. Durant and his chums were the Credit Mobilier's principal stockholders; Durant was its president.

Assuming the Hoxie contract was a move carefully timed. On March 3rd, Congress had amended the Pacific Railroad Act to permit participating roads to market their first-mortgage and land-grant bonds on 100 miles of route in advance. This seemed to promise a substantial supply of cash with which to start construction. On March 15th, Durant called the signals, and Hoxie turned over to the Credit Mobilier his contract to build the first 247 miles of the Union Pacific. (He had done no work under the contract, anyway.) In return he was promised $5,000 in cash and $10,000 worth of U.P. stock. He may have received the cash, but four years later he was still waiting for the stock. In the meantime, he at least had a job. In the spring of 1865, Durant made him the U.P.'s Master of Transportation. This meant he was in charge of receiving and forwarding all construction materials, which at last were beginning to trickle into Omaha. Hoxie did very well at it, and in later years became a railroad vice-president himself—on the Missouri Pacific.

As soon as the Credit Mobilier was in legal possession of the contract to build the Union Pacific, Durant, in his alternate role of executive vice-president of the railroad, confidently moved to market the bonds that Congress had declared he could now sell. He received a jolting setback. When the bonds went on sale, there were almost no buyers. Jay Cooke & Co. of Philadelphia, the nation's best-known banking house of that day, disposed of a piddling number, and then the market dried up. Cooke's firm, moreover, refused to lend the railroad a cent. Agreeing to try to sell the bonds was as far as it cared to go.

Durant turned to his Washington contacts for help and advice. It was soon forthcoming. In May, the new Secretary of the Interior, former Senator James Harlan, introduced him to John Pondir, a New York broker, who Harlan thought would prove to be helpful. On the same day, according to Pondir's later, windy testimony, Secretary of the Treasury Chase also did his bit to get the Union Pacific underway. He wrote Pondir and urged him to do all he could to raise money for the railroad.

Pondir claimed that within a few days afterward he provided Durant and his colleagues with a million dollars. He then tried to launch a scheme to persuade every important New York bank to lend 5 per cent of its capital to the Union Pacific. Several bankers hedged by saying that if he could first win over Charles H. Russell of the Bank of Commerce, they might support his radical plan. Russell balked at the terms of Pondir's proposal. He did, however, lend the railroad a million dollars. With $2 million of working capital now in hand, the Union Pacific seemed likely to be able to lay some track. In fact, declared Pondir, he understood that the U.P.'s President Dix had said that as long as they had Pondir with them, they'd finish the road by 1876, which was when the law said it must be done.

Two million dollars didn't last long, though. Durant had to buy great quantities of rails and ties, materials for the initial railroad buildings, machinery and tools, and a long list of rolling stock to replace the first U.P. locomotives and cars, which he'd been forced to sell for quick cash the previous fall. He also had to finance engineering field parties and round up a much larger labor force than ever before. Freight charges were exorbitant. Delivery routes were awkward in the extreme, and frustratingly slow.

By midsummer, Durant was running out of money again. Finally, he and Cornelius Bushnell were obliged to turn to a potential source of funds that they were most reluctant to approach, the cautious financiers of Boston. Enlisting their help—if, indeed, that were possible—would be bound to bring about a degree of restriction on Durant's swashbuckling management that he would not welcome. Nevertheless, that was a risk he now felt forced to take.

In August, Congressman Oakes Ames of Massachusetts, the shovel manufacturer and one of New England's wealthiest men, responded to Durant's and Bushnell's persuasion. He and his brother, Oliver, together bought $1 million worth of Credit Mobilier stock. In addition, Oakes Ames lent the Union Pacific nearly $600,000. Such was his standing in Boston's financial community that his example led several other wealthy men to follow him. Altogether, "the Boston crowd," as the Ameses and their closest associates came to be called within the Union Pacific organization, provided the railroad with a total of $2,500,000 in fresh capital that fall.

Oakes Ames' crucial decision to help the enterprise was not impulsive, any more than any other move he ever made. He was as deliberate in thought as he was in speech. He had been considering this action for many months.

On January 20, 1865, Mrs. Oakes Ames wrote in her diary, "Today Mr. Lincoln sent for Oakes to come to the White House. He went immediately after dinner and talked with the President until after midnight." [1]

What they had talked about, her husband explained to her when he got home, was the Union Pacific Railroad.

"Ames, you take hold of this," President Lincoln had said, according to the congressman's domestic report. "If the subsidies provided are not enough to build the road, ask double, and you shall have it. The road must be built, and you are the man to do it. Take hold of it yourself. By building the Union Pacific, you will become the remembered man of your generation." [2]

Durant and Huntington had already asked, in effect, for double subsidies, and got them. Representative Ames, a 6-foot, monolithic figure of a man, whom Lincoln admiringly called "the broad-shouldered Ames," [3] had not yet taken a financial interest in the U.P. at this time. He knew altogether too much about it, for he was a member of the Pacific Railroad Committee of the House. Lincoln's appeal moved him, however, for he was earnestly public-spirited as well as rich. Besides, he admitted later, the thought of having posterity identify his name with the building of the Union Pacific was a most agreeable one.

Ames promised Lincoln that he would give his suggestion careful consideration, but the President did not live to see his appeal take effect. Even Lincoln might have had misgivings at the thought of the instinctively forthright Ameses in harness with the innately tricky Durant, whose "New York crowd" began disagreeing with the "Boston crowd" almost at once. The relationship between the two factions was little better than an uneasy truce at any time during the building of the Union Pacific. Occasionally, it disintegrated into warfare. Durant was solely interested in making as great a profit as he could from the construction contracts, and never mind what became of the railroad later. The Ameses were by no means disinterested in profit, but they wanted to build a good railroad, too, one that would be a lucrative investment for long years to come.

On the construction front, very little happened during the first six months of 1865, mostly because of lack of funds, partly because of the uncertainty about route. At the beginning of the year, about 20 miles of grading had been finished. Most of it was out in the Platte Valley, beyond the Elkhorn, where the going was easy and there was no doubt about the line. Durant stopped all further work until the controversy over the route should be settled.

By the time Seymour's "ox-bow" proposal had filtered through official channels to the White House for approval, Lincoln was dead. President Andrew Johnson was much more inclined to suspect railroad builders' motives than Lincoln had been. Johnson wouldn't endorse the altered route until he had sent out an impartial government expert, Brig. Gen. James H. Simpson, U.S. Corps of Engineers, to look it over carefully. The matter was to drag on for months.

Durant, ever impatient, would wait no longer. In April, 1865, he managed to persuade the five government directors of the U.P. to approve the change of route. Then, with the recklessness that often marked his actions when his footing was least secure, he ordered the railroad built with the ox bow in it. (When Simpson turned in his verdict, late in the fall, it was qualified approval only, contingent upon the making of certain basic changes in Seymour's plan. The changes were never made. Nearly forty years afterward, under E. H. Harriman, the Union Pacific reverted to Dey's original route out of Omaha. Until that was done, and Seymour's ox bow eliminated, all U.P. distances on the main line between Omaha and Cheyenne were 9 miles greater than they are today.)

One of Durant's first actions after deciding to go ahead with Seymour's ox bow in the spring of 1865 was to send three engineering parties into the field. One was ordered to make a final location of the line from the 100th Meridian to the Black Hills of Wyoming. Another was to hunt for a better crossing of the Black Hills than any found in 1864. The last was to try to find a more southerly route between the Black Hills and Salt Lake City than the one tentatively selected the year before. The men in charge of the Union Pacific still hankered to have their line go through Denver, if a practical way could be found.

Samuel B. Reed was to head the third group, further exploring country that had already become generally familiar to him in 1864. On April 20th he arrived at Omaha from the east, "after three days and nights in the stage coach, nearly worn out for want of rest and sleep." [4] It had taken that long, over the nearly bottomless Iowa roads, to cover the hundred miles or so from the end of the nearest railroad. Many of the Union Pacific's supplies would have to travel the same, deplorable route during the next year and a half.

"At Fort Des Moines," Reed wrote to his wife, "I heard of the death of President Lincoln. We draped our coach in mourning, and at most of the [stage] stations were the first to inform the people of the great assassination that had been committed in Washington." [5]

General Dodge, who had been engaged all winter in a campaign against the Indians of the plains, journeyed with his staff to Springfield, Illinois, for Lincoln's funeral. Shortly after their return, on May 3rd, Dodge wrote to his brother, Nathan, from St. Louis, "I expect to be allowed to leave the service before long and take office of chief engineer of the U.P.R.R. Durant is shipping here 50 miles of iron, five locomotives, and 80 cars. It looks like work. Hoxie is here attending to the reshipping up river." [6]

Already, though, rumors were reaching St. Louis that the Indians were again gathering in strength out on the plains. With fresh fighting in prospect, Dodge was given command of all U.S. troops in Nebraska, Kansas, Colorado, Utah, and Dakota Territory, and ordered to take to the field.

Before starting out, he received a protesting letter from Durant. The doctor reminded him of his promise to resign from the Army as soon as the war was over. Why hadn't he done so? A salary of $10,000 a year and stock in the Credit Mobilier were awaiting him, said Durant, and the U.P. needed him badly.

Dodge's reply was brief but emphatic. As long as the Indians were on the warpath, nobody was going to be able to build the Union Pacific, he said. His army duty obviously had to come first. Durant and the U.P. directors reluctantly agreed, and assured Dodge that their offer would be kept open until he was free to accept it.

In May, another engineer, D. H. Ainsworth, formerly Reed's assistant on the old Mississippi & Missouri R.R., joined the Union Pacific organization that was slowly taking shape. Durant had hired him by mail "to take charge of the company's engineering," Ainsworth wrote. But when the engineer got to Omaha, on May 14th, he found instead that he was little more than a disbursing agent, "the ever accessible dog to be kicked whenever anything went wrong." [7]

Within five days of Ainsworth's arrival, Indians swooped closer to the Missouri River settlements than they had come before. On May 19th, between Leavenworth, Kansas, and Fort Kearny, Nebraska, a war party of twenty-five ambushed a small group of Dodge's soldiers, who happened to be unarmed. Two of them were killed, the rest brutally wounded and left to die. The next morning, the same warriors attacked a crowded stagecoach, inbound for Atchison. They chased it for miles, making it bristle with arrows before the rifles of the men riding on top drove them off.

As an incidental result of the raids, the Speaker of the House of Representatives, Schuyler Colfax, was stalled at the start of his summer-long stagecoach journey to the Far West. Colfax and the three celebrated newspapermen who were with him—William Bross, of the Chicago *Tribune;* Bert Richardson, of the New York *Tribune;* and Samuel Bowles, of the Springfield *Republican*—were obliged to wait for a military escort before leaving Atchison.

On the morning of May 21st, up trotted a squad of cavalrymen, sent by Gen. Patrick E. Connor, and the Colfax expedition got underway again. The men rode without stopping for sleep until they reached Fort Kearny, on the Platte, but saw no Indians—only the ruins of barns and homes they had burned.

The prominent travelers now caught up with long white wagon trains, crossing the green ocean of prairie with goods and people bound for the growing communities of Colorado, Montana, and Utah. The trains were huddling together for greater protection. As the teams creaked onward, covering 12 to 15 miles a day, prairie hens and plover fled through the tall grass that stretched to meet the sky in every direction. Larks climbed singing toward the cloud puffs floating languidly above Nebraska Territory.

Bowles gazed around him in admiration, and declared that since a fine, hard stage road was created merely by driving over this plain, building a railroad across it would be "baby work." For 500 miles or more, he said, "there is scarcely more required than to scrape a place in the soft soil for sleepers and ties and iron." [8] Yet not a mile of the Union Pacific had yet been built.

It was a shame, Bowles wrote—to a national audience, for his paper was very widely read—that the U.P. wasn't already running as far as the Rockies. What if fuel for locomotives was scarce on these treeless expanses? Suppose it did have to be hauled for hundreds of miles? That was not an insuperable problem. Besides, he added prophetically, "we shall soon learn to make steam from petroleum." [9]

Bowles knew nothing of the men who formed the Union Pacific Railroad Company, he admitted. Probably they were better known in Wall Street than anywhere else. But from what he had heard about them along the way, he was convinced that they had neither the will nor the power to do the job of building a railroad to California. And what an opportunity awaited them! It was anticipated that 200 million pounds of freight would be moving westward from the Missouri this year. Already, in the first two months of fine weather, 10,000 teams and 50,000 head of cattle had crossed the plains toward Colorado, Montana, and Utah.

Bowles found no sign of life in the Union Pacific until he reached Salt Lake City. On the way, in Wyoming, the Colfax party had once more come alarmingly close to Indians. They rode into an area where every ranch within 50 miles had just been robbed of its horses. The next day their cavalry escort, sweeping forward to scout the countryside ahead of the Colfax stagecoach, drove off a band of Indians in the act of attacking a Mormon wagon train almost within sight of the Speaker. That night, the travelers passed a stage station. Next morning, they learned that it had been raided soon after they went by. Its horses had been driven off, their herders killed, and a guard of infantrymen badly mauled.

At Salt Lake City, Colfax and his newspaper friends came upon Sam Reed and his engineering group. Bowles wrote disparagingly of them. They were, he said, "on a straggling hunt for the best route through the Rocky Mountains," but "seemed to have no proper leadership, and no clear purpose, and in fact confessed that the company had no chief engineer worthy the name or position." [10]

Reed was stirred up at the rumored approach of other visitors, said to be coming along behind Colfax. "There is a committee from Congress on their way out here to investigate the affairs of the Overland Stage Co. and Indian difficulties," he wrote to his wife on June 4th. "I don't wish them any harm, but hope they may be corraled by the Indians and kept, as others have been, defending themselves for days without food. They would, no doubt, realize some of the difficulties of traveling on the plains and make a report that would insure a more effectual protection of the business of this country." [11]

There were but two congressional investigators on their way West. Still, they were a weighty pair. One of them was Senator James R. Doolittle of Wisconsin, the big-framed, emotional chairman of the Senate's Committee on Indian Affairs and possessor of one of the loudest voices on Capitol Hill. The other was Senator Lafayette S. Foster of Connecticut,

(Top left) *Samuel B. Reed, the Union Pacific's superintendent of construction, at the time the railroad-building at last had begun to achieve a brisk tempo.*

(Top right) *Representative Oakes Ames, the U.P.'s chief financial backer from 1865 until his death, looked as solid and imposing as his credit rating.*

(Bottom) *General John S. Casement, commander of the roistering ex-soldiers who comprised most of the Union Pacific's graders and tracklayers, in 1867.*

(Top left) *Brand-new U.P. locomotive No. 23, standing beside a typical Nebraska station of the time, was built and delivered to the railroad during 1866.*

(Bottom left) *This drawing of U.P. trackbuilding in western Nebraska caught the elements of action, supply, and protection as no photograph of the time could have done.*

(Top right) *U.P. tracklayers perform for guests at the 100th Meridian party. Ancient inked arrow points to T. C. Durant, the railroad's executive vice-president.*

(Bottom right) *A group of U.P. graders eating from a chuck wagon beside the South Platte in 1867. Beyond is the herd that kept them in beef.*

U.P.

U.P.

(Top) *Rare photo of the 100th Meridian Expedition, October 22–26, 1866. Seated, General Dodge is first, Sidney Dillon third, and T. C. Durant fifth from left.* (Bottom) *Prairie fires were once a common sight in Nebraska in the fall. Durant had one set deliberately to thrill guests of his 100th Meridian Expedition.*

an unobtrusive little man who nevertheless had been elected president pro tempore of the Senate upon Andrew Johnson's sudden elevation from that job, and was thus acting Vice-President of the United States.

Their mission, which would take all summer and part of the fall, was to find out if the Indians could be restrained by means other than fighting. They were the forerunners of a parade of hopeful emissaries who would intermittently endeavor, during the next three years, to settle this problem by treaties rather than punitive expeditions. President Johnson and a shrill group of Eastern congressmen were ready to believe that the Army was at least as much to blame for hostilities as the Indians were, if not more so.

It was July before the watchdogs that Congress had tethered within the Union Pacific organization—the five government directors—growled over the terms of the Hoxie contract, now the property of the Credit Mobilier. The agreed price of $50,000 a mile had seemed very high to them at the time the contract was signed, they reported, seven months too late, to Secretary of the Interior Harlan. Now that the war was over, with prices expected to drop rapidly, the labor supply to increase greatly, and government bonds to gain in value, the Hoxie contract looked downright extravagant to the government directors. Only the stringencies of the dark times of 1864 could have justified it, they said—those and the fact that the U.P. must get 100 miles of track built by July 1, 1866, or lose its charter.

But their growl became little more than a mutter. After complaining of how the "large profits to contractors and capitalists" would inflate the cost of building the railroad, they concluded weakly, "We trust, however, that more moderate profits and free competition will be the rule in all future contracts." [12]

At least, their report continued, the Union Pacific now expected to build 50 miles of track by December. This was bold prophecy indeed. The government directors' report was dated July 8th. The Union Pacific didn't lay its first rail until July 10th.

The most reliable ferry at Omaha crossed the shifting Missouri about a mile above the town. It was there, in order to make it easier to receive cargoes from the East, that track-building began. The passenger and freight stations were located toward the north end of Omaha's waterfront of that day, at Seventh and Chicago Streets.

Eleven days later, the Omaha *Weekly Republican* reported with enthusiasm that "the Major General Sherman is puffing and dashing away continuously on the first mile of the railroad, aiding that national enterprise by carrying ties, iron, etc." [13] The Union Pacific's first locomotive that didn't have to be sold for cash had been named for Sherman—very properly, since no one in government circles was a more devoted friend of the railroad than he. Its second was named for Sherman's deeply mourned comrade, the late Maj. Gen. James B. McPherson, who had been killed at the Battle of Atlanta.

Both engines had been delivered to St. Joseph on flatcars, over the Horrible St. Joe, and then brought up the Missouri on steamboats, at a cost of nearly a thousand dollars apiece for just that short, uncertain voyage. Big boats could navigate as far upstream as Omaha only in the late spring and early summer, usually for no more than three months of the year. By midsummer the Missouri had normally dwindled until it was too shallow for them there. Thereafter, the chief reliance of the Union Pacific for delivery of materials purchased in the East was a combination of the Chicago & North Western R.R., for as far as it went across Iowa, and ox teams. The U.P.'s first stationary engine for its Omaha shops was hauled by oxen for the last 100 miles of its journey.

The bulk of the railroad's initial supply of rails had traveled to Omaha from Pittsburgh on a steamboat, the *Elkhorn*, and two barges, *Hero* and *Heroine*, which Durant had had built there for the purpose. This little fleet made the trip by way of the Ohio, Mississippi, and Missouri Rivers.

The Union Pacific was using lighter rails—50 pounds per yard—for its main line than the Central Pacific had decided it must have in the Sierra. The track on the U.P.'s sidings was lighter still, weighing only 45 pounds to the yard.

Bridge timbers, ties, and locomotive firewood were being cut far up the Missouri and floated down to Omaha on huge rafts. Only about one-sixth of the ties were of oak or cedar, and thus sufficiently durable to go into the track just as they were. The rest were of cottonwood, which deteriorated rapidly without protective treatment. The cottonwood ties had to be impregnated with zinc, by a process called burnetizing—named for its originator, Burnet, an Englishman. At Omaha, they were loaded, 250 at a time, into an iron chamber 100 feet long and 5 feet in diameter. With a steam-driven pump, a vacuum was first created in the chamber, emptying all the pores in the wood. Then, under pressure, the ties were flooded with a zinc solution, which permeated their pores. When dry, the burnetized ties looked metallic, were almost as heavy as metal, and were good for several years' service. They were not ideal, but they would have to suffice until the railroad reached its first timberland, in the Black Hills. There was nothing else available in sufficient abundance to make practical ties.

The pace of the Union Pacific's construction was almost unbelievably slow at first. It took eleven days to lay the first mile of track, even though the grade had long been ready. By August 3rd, nearly a month after track-laying began, the road stretched only a mile and a half. Part of the trouble lay in the distressingly languid delivery of materials. Mostly, however, it stemmed from the usual lack of money.

On July 1st, about 1,000 men were working for the railroad, but not happily. They had received no wages for two months, and on June 29th, with more than $100,000 owed them and no pay day in prospect, John Henry notified Durant that he expected the work would soon have to stop altogether. The $2 million obtained in May was nearly gone. Durant somehow met the crisis, however, and the Union Pacific dawdled on until durably vitalized by the funds that the Ameses and their friends provided, beginning in August.

From then on, the roadbuilders began to show evidence of their mettle. By September 25th they had completed 11 miles of track. By early November they had added 5½ miles more. In celebration, Durant staged his first excursion for distinguished visitors. His small audience included one very eminent and admiring guest, General Sherman.

Sherman had been appointed commander of the military division of the Missouri, which encompassed nearly all troops between the Atlantic and Pacific Coasts, on June 27th. By mid-July he had set up his headquarters at St. Louis, but, being a restless man, he was soon off inspecting his vast realm. His persistent and eager interest in the building of the Union Pacific was well known. Shrewdly, Durant, also aware of Sherman's high regard for Dodge, invited him to come to Omaha on his travels and see how the U.P. was getting along.

On a mild November day, Durant had two flatcars hitched to the locomotive that bore Sherman's name, and took the general and twenty other guests out to the end of the track. Sherman, as capable of being charming and gracious as he was of becoming explosively profane and tyrannical, was at his cordial best that day, even though he had nothing to sit on but a nail keg.

Despite the fact that there were only two dozen people present, there were, inevitably, speeches made. Sherman was more amused than impressed. He wrote of the occasion in his *Memoirs:*

When the orators spoke so confidently of the determination to build two thousand miles of railway across the plains, mountains, and desert, devoid of timber, with no population, but on the contrary raided by the bold and bloody Sioux and Cheyennes, who had almost successfully defied our power for half a century, I was disposed to treat it jocularly. . . .

"This is a great enterprise," he told his fellow-excursionists that day in November, 1865, "but I hardly expect to live to see it completed." [14]

The "bold and bloody Sioux and Cheyennes" had fully engaged the attention of Sherman's friend and favored subordinate, General Dodge, since early in the year. Dodge opened his 1865 campaign in "the worst winter I ever saw on the Plains." His most useful troops, ironically, were five regiments of ex-Confederates and a battalion of Pawnees. The former, who called themselves "galvanized Yankees," [16] had chosen to enlist in the Union Army to fight Indians rather than enter prison camps. The Pawnees, christened Pawnee Scouts, were natural enemies of the Sioux and Cheyennes. They were formed into a military unit by Frank North, a quiet, gentlemanly young clerk and interpreter with a paradoxical aptitude for fighting. North's Pawnees provided their own mounts, but wore bits and pieces of cavalry uniforms most of the time, so that friendly troops wouldn't mistake them for hostile Indians. In battle, though, even in winter, they often tore off their encumbering clothes and fought as naked as their ancestors.

"My troops marched from the Arkansas to the Yellowstone, and fought many battles," [17] Dodge declared. They were not allowed a clean-cut victory, however. In the late-summer Battle of Tongue River, in southeastern Montana, when General Connor's men and the Pawnee Scouts nearly obliterated their opponents, the Pawnees got out of hand and indulged in what Dodge called "some promiscuous scalping." [18]

A sharp reaction from Washington was not long in coming. General Grant telegraphed Dodge to close up the campaign, persuade the Indians to meet him at Fort Laramie, and make peace with them. Dodge balked. He said he needed only three months more to put an end to the Indian troubles forever. Grant replied that President Johnson was up in arms, and pressing him so hard that he couldn't permit Dodge to have his way.

"This was a fatal mistake," Dodge wrote in his *Personal Recollections,* "and gave the Indians the idea that they were the victors instead of ourselves."

Parleying at Fort Laramie brought only a brief lull in the Indian wars, as Dodge had anticipated. However, his campaigning in 1865 produced one important and unexpected benefit for the Union Pacific.

On his way back from the Powder River region in mid-September, Dodge took advantage of his geographical position to inspect the Black Hills minutely, from Fort Laramie southward. The U.P. engineers had kept him fully informed of the results of their various surveys, and he knew they had not yet found a truly advantageous crossing of this low but abrupt spur of the Rockies.

While his main column ambled down the eastern base of the range, day after day, Dodge repeatedly took a half-dozen troopers and a guide and rode up to the summit, following it persistently while he hunted for a likely pass. It was understood that if his exploring party should run into trouble, it would notify the troop train by smoke signals.

One day, about noon, Dodge's guide discovered that a rather large body of Indians had stealthily slipped in between them and the distant train. It quickly became evident that the warriors intended to cut Dodge and his men off. The General ordered signal fires lighted at various intervals as he and his escort worked their way hastily toward a ridge that appeared to lead down to the plain. But the troop train plodded on unheedingly. Dodge's men were able to keep their stalkers from closing in, for their Winchesters had greater range and more accuracy than the Indians' older rifles. Still, as the afternoon waned, the riders on the ridge were getting distinctly uneasy.

At last, the far-off troopers noticed the smoke, or heard the firing, and responded in strength. At the first shots from their rear, the Indians fled.

Dodge stared in fascination at the slope down which they had galloped.

"Boys," he said excitedly, "if we save our scalps, I believe we've found a pass through which the Union Pacific can go." [19]

So it eventually proved to be, for the slope continued at a consistently low angle all the way back to the open plain. There was a single tree at its base, and Dodge made a note of it, the configuration of the surroundings, and the general location.

Prudently, perhaps with the thought that it was always good to have an ace in the hole when dealing with Durant, Dodge kept his discovery to himself.

When the Union Pacific's field parties of engineers reported to the board of directors on their accomplishments for 1865, they wrote that Indian marauding and threats had prevented them from getting a sizable portion of their intended work done. The engineers still had found no route across the Black Hills that didn't encompass 116-foot grades, and far too many miles of them. They hadn't discovered any better line for the railroad to take in Colorado and Utah than they had earlier selected across southern Wyoming. It looked as if Denver would have to be bypassed.

The consensus of all concerned was: keep trying. As the government directors told Secretary Harlan, let's not be content with merely practicable routes; let's find the very best ones.

Colonel Seymour came into New York from Omaha on October 28th, with the report that 20 miles of track were then laid, and enough rails were on hand to build 50 miles more. Track-building was proceeding at the rate of half a mile a day. (By year's end, the U.P. was 40 miles long.) A roundhouse and station buildings of brick and stone were rising in front of Omaha, he said. Grading was nearly complete for 100 miles. All necessary bridges for the first 30 miles were about ready. Around 30,000 ties had been delivered, and were going through the burnetizing process at the rate of 1,000 to 1,200 a day.

Seymour also declared that the roadbed up the Platte Valley as far as Fort Kearny, and probably for 200 miles beyond, could be prepared for the track faster than the rails could be laid.

After listening to him, the government directors cheerily sent word to the Secretary of the Interior that they now had confidence that there would be 100 miles of the Union Pacific in use by the following July. They felt sure that the railroad's charter would be saved.

CHAPTER NINE

COMING TO GRIPS
WITH THE SIERRA

As the Central Pacific's construction forces flung themselves into the huge tasks of 1866, their achievements had already won commendation from one of the nation's leading railroad engineers, George E. Gray. Gray had been the first chief engineer of the New York Central Railroad. In 1865, Stanford had commissioned him, a veteran of forty-eight, to look over what young Sam Montague, only twenty-nine, had already accomplished as Judah's successor, and learn how he planned to surmount the Sierra. Gray was gratifyingly pleased with it all. His report went to the President and the Secretary of the Interior. A key paragraph was reproduced in the Sacramento *Union* on January 8, 1866:

From the examination I have made, having traveled the distance on horseback or on foot, I feel confident that your railroad can be constructed over the Sierra Nevada, with the laboring force you will probably be able to command in California, within two years from next Spring, and at a cost not exceeding the Mountain work on the Baltimore and Ohio, Pennsylvania Central, New York and Erie, and Hudson River Railroads. In fact, it is quite a remarkable feature of your route that so elevated a mountain range can be surmounted with such comparatively light grades and curves, and at a cost which will favorably compare with other important railroads, long in successful operation.

Stanford had promptly hired Gray to remain as consulting engineer. This situation may well have nettled the highly capable Montague. He was a self-confident young man, impatient with supervision. And he obviously was gifted. He had even won James Strobridge's approval, rarely granted to engineers. Montague soon found, however, that he had nothing to fear from Gray. Their working relationship proved to be most agreeable.

However favorably the Central Pacific might be regarded in engineering circles, Collis Huntington wasn't entirely pleased with it. Complaining to Hopkins at this time that Crocker wasn't consulting them about the hardware he was buying, Huntington wrote angrily, "If it had not been for you and I, my opinion is that the Central Pacific would have gone to the Devil before this." [1]

The railroad's customers were not universally happy with it, either. The Nevada (California) *Transcript* had recently sputtered that goods carried by the railroad from Sacramento to Colfax, and thence by wagon to Nevada City, were frequently damaged en route. The *Transcript* preferred to assume that the battering had not taken place in the wagons. It added, with a special sense of injury, that three barrels of whiskey that had recently started out from Sacramento had never arrived at all.

The Grass Valley *National* was even more outspokenly critical.

Enormous prices are charged for freight and it is slow in coming. . . . The only benefits so far experienced from this road are higher freights, not only in Winter but in Summer, than our merchants have ever paid before [declared one of its editorials]. The embankments are so miserably built that they give way under the soaking rains of this climate, and long delays are occasioned. . . .[2]

The rains were indeed raising havoc. The winter of 1865–66 was turning out to be the wettest in many years. On the higher levels, heavy snows had already driven out the crews of Chinese whom Montague had set to work on the tunnels the previous fall. Farther down the western slope of the Sierra, the grading was fast becoming a morass. The red soil was thick and spongy. It soon formed a vast, mucky trap for vehicles. Wagons and carts had to be abandoned. Hundreds of pack animals were mobilized to carry food, powder, tools, and even grain and hay to the soggy construction camps beyond the end of track. A stagecoach bound for Virginia City became so mired in the soupy street at Gold Run that it was left there for six weeks. Its passengers took to saddle horses to complete their journey.

Construction costs rocketed as downpour followed downpour. Making matters even more doleful, heavy landslides spread tons of mud and boulders across the completed track. Six of them blocked the road beyond Auburn for more than a week in January. A cave-in near Dutch Flat in March buried and killed one of the railroad's Chinese workers.

Once again, there were rumblings of labor trouble among the white workmen. One moist pay day, when, as usual, portly Charlie Crocker was jogging from camp to camp on a burdened sorrel horse, his leather saddle-bags sagging with gold coin with which to settle accounts, he saw a group of men who had thrown down their picks and gathered in an earnest huddle. Strobridge happened to be at hand. Crocker said to him, with a nod at the somewhat distant cluster of laborers, "There is something breeding there."

"They're getting up a strike," replied Strobridge grimly.

"Let me handle them," said Crocker.

"The only way to do was to rule them with an iron hand," he explained long afterward, when reminiscing about construction days on the Central Pacific.

By the time I got pretty near through paying [the other workers] . . . Strobridge said, "There, they are coming. Now get ready."

As soon as they got close up, I turned around and said, "Strobridge, I think you had better reduce wages on this cut. We are paying a little more than we ought to. There is no reason why we should pay more on this cut and that tunnel than on the other work. You had better reduce them about 25 cents a day."

The men heard this, and they stopped and chattered together awhile. Finally, one of them stepped forward and said, "We thought, sir, that we ought to have our wages raised a little on this tunnel. The tunnel is very wet, and the cut is wet."

"Well," said I, "I have just been telling Strobridge that you are getting too much, and he had better reduce it."

"Yes, sir," said he, "I heard it. But, Your Honor, I think you better not reduce it. We thought we ought to get an advance, but you ought not to reduce it, certainly."

"Well, Strobridge," said I. "What do you think? Can we afford to pay them that wage?"

"Oh," said he, "I wouldn't make a fuss over it. We had better let them go on at the same figure."

"All right," said I. And they went on, satisfied with what we had been paying them.[3]

Hardly satisfied, of course, but at least submissive—and that's the way Crocker and Strobridge wanted to keep them.

At length, the woes of that drenching winter were largely over, and the hot spring sunlight began to dry out the line of grading. Strobridge threw 10,000 Chinese, officered by white foremen, into a full-scale attack on the granite ridge that the track was to climb. This was quite probably the largest labor force employed by any company in the United States at the time. It drained California's farms and ranches of every able-bodied horse and mule that could be spared. More than 1,200 of them were working for the railroad. The daily requirements of Strobridge's army taxed the output of every foundry and machine shop, wagonmaker and harness shop, sawmill and blacksmith shop within dozens of miles.

Strobridge, who used to say, "Men generally earn their money when they work for me," [4] lived close to the line of march. The Chinese were especially aware of his imminent presence, for they dreaded to see him stalking toward them with his usual stern air, a black eyepatch lending a piratical note to his appearance. In fact, one white foreman used occasionally to spur his Chinese to frantic activity by clapping a hand over his right eye and striding about like Strobridge, implying that Himself was about to arrive on the scene.

Sunday was the only day when the incessant labor was interrupted. Then the Irish laborers mostly slept or played games. The Chinese slaughtered chickens and pigs for subsequent meals, mended, laundered, and noisily gambled. There was never any drunkenness, for liquor was forbidden in camp, and forcibly ejected if it came within reach. Timothy Hopkins once quoted Strobridge as saying, "We and pick handles were King." [5] If a liquor vender ventured near a railroad camp with a wagonload of whiskey, he was first ordered to move on. If he lingered, a strong-arm squad of Strobridge's soon descended upon the wagon, removed the bungs from the barrels, and poured all the whiskey onto the ground.

Charlie Crocker, the overlord of the Central Pacific's construction effort, was often on the line. He pioneered the "piggy-back" freight technique of today by having his buggy placed aboard a flatcar in Sacramento and carried to the end of track whenever he was on an inspection trip. Sometimes his own horses made the trip with the buggy. More often, the wagon traveled alone as far as the rails went. Then any spare team was hitched to it to enable Crocker to explore the line of grading.

The railroad company had long since been forced to apply to sources other than the San Francisco labor contractor Koopmanschap for fresh contingents of Chinese workers. Additional agents, named Sisson and and Wallace, at first separately and then as partners in a new firm, were commissioned to bring in all they could persuade to leave the fields around Canton. The business of importing Chinese to work on the railroad was becoming such an attractively lucrative enterprise that one of Charles Crocker's brothers, Clark, acquired a partnership in Sisson, Walker & Co. at this time.

Even with an all-out effort, however, the Central Pacific was unable to attract more than 10,000 Chinese laborers during 1866, though it yearned for 15,000. It also was desperately in need of more powder.

The supply of powder now came from young mills in Santa Cruz, California. The railroad had largely freed itself from dependence on Eastern sources. But the Santa Cruz mills couldn't keep up with the fantastic rate of explosions along the route of the graders and tunnel-diggers. Blasting often consumed 400 kegs of powder a day, at a cost of $4 a keg. The rock was so hard that in some places the powder charges simply blew back out of the holes that had been drilled for them, as if fired from a cannon.

Breaking up masses of rock that lay in the way of the graders was not the only task for powder, either. It took from two to ten kegs to shatter single tree stumps that lay rooted in the roadbed. When, in later years, an inquiring congressional investigator from the East expressed incredulity at this fact, Lewis M. Clement, who was Montague's chief assistant during the building of the railroad, tersely explained why it was true.

"Those are not *Yankee* forests," said Clement, "but forests with trees four, six, and eight feet in diameter." [6] The trees were also often 100 to 150 feet tall.

Clement explained that a path 100 feet wide had to be cleared through the woods for the advancing railroad. Sometimes, when trees more than 100 feet tall stood at the fringe of the clearing, they, too, had to be cut down, lest some future gale or lightning bolt send them crashing across the track.

Gangs of 300 men to the mile, most of them Chinese, not only cut down all trees in the 100-foot strip that straddled the surveyed line; they had to remove every stump in a central path from 20 to 25 feet wide. That was the embankment line. It would form the base of the track.

So expensive was this tree-felling and grubbing of gargantuan stumps that its cost alone rose as high as $5,000 a mile in heavily forested sections.

When the Central Pacific's secretary, Edward H. Miller, Jr., first learned of the costly grubbing, he deplored it to Chief Engineer Montague.

"It seems to me to be going to an enormous expense for nothing," [7] he said.

Montague explained that if the stumps were left in the embankment, they would eventually rot. The roadbed would then slump, and the track would be dangerously undermined. The stumps had to be removed, whatever the cost.

Because the railroad's powder supply was exasperatingly scanty in the vigorous spring of 1866, Crocker and Strobridge decided to experiment with a bit of nitroglycerin. It was then brand-new—commonly spelled as two words and given a final "e." Its reputation as an extraordinary explosive had filtered to the United States from Europe. Relatively few people here knew anything about its properties, however.

A little of it was obtained for the Central Pacific, tried, and found to work spectacularly well. But as hopes rapidly rose that here lay the means of greatly speeding up completion of the railroad's tunnels, the happy vision was shattered by two distant calamities.

On April 16th, at 1:13½ P.M. (so precisely did the shocked city note the time), a sizable part of downtown San Francisco appeared to jump and fly apart. People and buildings staggered under the impact of a giant concussion, which instantly filled an area of many blocks with a whirlwind of dust, debris, shredded glass, and fragments of bodies. Opposite the Wells, Fargo office, at the northwest corner of California and Montgomery Streets, where the explosion had occurred, a man's bloody arm came hurtling through a third-story window.

"The consternation which seized on the passers-by in the vicinity of Wells, Fargo & Co. was terrible," reported the *Alta California*. "Men, women, children, horsemen, pedestrians, dray and express teams without drivers, came charging pell-mell down the street in inextricable confusion." [8]

When the panic had subsided, police and firemen found that a dozen people had been killed, many more injured, and the entire rear end of the Wells, Fargo building blown out. The cause of the disaster had been the explosion of a damaged box of nitroglycerin. It had been one of two dumped in the courtyard behind the express company's office when the consignee had refused to accept them from the steamship line that had brought them to the city.

Endeavoring to reconstruct the events that led immediately to the tragedy, investigators learned that a freight clerk from the steamship company had had lunch that day with a clerk from Wells, Fargo. They had eaten at the Union Club, on the floor above the express company's offices. After lunch, they had gone down the back stairs to the courtyard, evidently intending to examine the damaged boxes, which were nearly 15 feet long and 2½ feet high. It was believed that the men either had kicked one of the boxes or had tried to turn it over and dropped it. Whatever they had done to cause the explosion, they were blown to pieces by it. The oddest aspect of the appalling accident was that the second box of nitroglycerin had survived the blast. Nervous city officials ordered it to be placed on a barge and anchored out in the middle of the bay.

The Sacramento *Union*, reported the dreadful news from San Francisco. It then made a rather casual editorial comment:

This article of nitro glycerine has been used in blasting on the Central Pacific Railroad and is stated to be much more powerful than gun-powder, explosion taking place so quickly that effects are produced downwards as well as laterally and upwards.[9]

The *Union* was far from calm the following day, however. By then, it had discovered that only a week before, three boxes of nitroglycerin, consigned to the Central Pacific, had arrived in Sacramento and been left in the freight sheds of the riverboat line *for ten hours* without anyone's knowing that they were extremely dangerous.

The quantity contained in these boxes was enough, of course—had they been roughly handled—to have produced terrible destruction of life and property [wrote the thoroughly aroused editor]. They were shipped at San Francisco as ordinary freight, without any word of caution being given to the officers of the boat. It is true they were marked "nitro glycerine," but as nobody knew what that meant, no special caution was observed.[10]

The *Union* cried for rigid enforcement of the laws regulating the transportation of explosives.

The very next day, April 21st, the newspaper had an even greater horror to report than the recent one in San Francisco. Word of it had just arrived by steamer from Panama. Three days before the ill-fated clerks had gone down the back stairs to their sudden death behind Wells, Fargo & Co., the ship *European,* at her dock in Aspinwall, Panama, had violently disintegrated. The explosion killed fifty people, including the captain and other officers of the vessel, and ripped to shreds some 400 feet of the pier. The *European* had been carrying "blasting oil" in her hold.

The reaction to the two castastrophes was widespread and panicky. "Nitro glycerine," the *Union* said, "is the calamitous sensation of the day." [11]

In San Francisco, wrote B. W. Brooks to Cornelius Cole the day after the big blast there, the explosion "spread horror and dismay throughout the community. . . . I think it will spoil the market for that article [nitroglycerin]. I think no one would undertake to transport it to the interior." [12]

In New York, the mayor ordered seizure of every container of the explosive that could be found within the city or on any ship in the harbor. Police discovered hundreds of pounds of it. The whole lot was warily transported to a powder magazine, and future public sales of nitroglycerin were forbidden. An Ohio colonel who had shipped to California the consignment that exploded in San Francisco was arrested.

The furor was loud in Sacramento, too, and the Central Pacific abruptly abandoned efforts to import this frightening new explosive.

Far east of Sacramento, in the eventful month of April, 1866, three C.P. exploring parties were plodding across Nevada. They had just begun for Montague a thorough investigation of potential routes for the railroad between the Big Bend of the Truckee, 30 miles east of present-day Reno, and the Salt Lake Valley, 500 miles beyond.

At that time, a scanner of maps who was unfamiliar with the terrain of Nevada would doubtless have supposed that the best place to build a railroad would be across the center of the state, through the rich, populous mining towns of Austin and Virginia City. The stages traveled that way. The single telegraph line was strung there. Almost the entire population of Nevada lived there.

But a dozen or more mountain ranges, slanting from northeast to southwest, lay like skeleton fingers across this broad and dusty territory, as if to deny it to a railroad track. There was little doubt in the minds of Central Pacific engineers that it would be impractical to build the road in this direction, where its progress would be a forbidding, costly series of upgrades and downgrades. Still, it must be seriously reconnoitered and not dismissed without careful investigation. So some surveyors were sent that way. Others moved northeastward up the valley of the little Humboldt River, which bubbled out of the ground near Humboldt Wells, 329 miles east of the Big Bend of the Truckee, ran southwestward as far as the Humboldt Sink, and there disappeared into a vast, dirty white waste of alkali and salt.

"The Humboldt route would be more easily built," declared Samuel Bowles, after he had visited Nevada—but not that part of it—a year before, "and goes through a naturally better country as to wood, water, and fertility of soil. It is generally conceded to be the true natural roadway across the Continent. The emigration has always taken it." [13]

During the months of favorable weather in 1866, Butler Ives, of Montague's staff, made a more thorough exploration of the Humboldt Valley than had ever been made before. Then, from Humboldt Wells, he tried two approaches to Salt Lake City. One angled southeastward across the Great American Desert and around the bottom of the lake to the Mormon capital. When he had surveyed this barren route, he returned to the Wells and set off in a northeasterly direction. He rounded the north end of the low Ombe Range, skirted the top edge of the Desert, crossed the Promontory Range through an easy pass, swung around the north shore of Great Salt Lake, across Bear River, and thence moved southward along the base of the lofty Wasatch Range to Weber Canyon. His reports would be in the hands of the Central Pacific's board of directors by snowfall.

Meanwhile, those harassed gentlemen were shoveling more money than ever into the mighty effort to climb to the summit of the Sierra Nevada.

Chief Engineer Montague wrote:

The obstacles with which we have had to contend have been great. The country over which the track has been laid is rugged and rocky, upon a steep mountain side, and up by deep ravines, requiring a continued succession of deep cuts and high embankments, many of which had to be protected by heavy stone walls, and requiring large and long culverts of stone to pass the torrents of water which fall in the mountains. The material has been almost entirely rock, much of it being the hardest kind.[14]

One of those culverts Montague referred to was described with awe by a visiting reporter as being "a noble piece of solid masonry, 28 feet in height and 54 feet in breadth." [15]

From their soggy, dejected start in the deep muds of winter, Strobridge's 10,000 men built only 39 miles of railroad that year. But, said Sam Montague when he reviewed the painful progress made during 1866, those 39 miles were "conceded by all to be the most difficult ever yet surmounted by any railroad in the United States, if not in Europe." [16] They cost more than $8 million to build.

In a dogged endeavor to meet these drastically increased expenditures, Collis Huntington, 3,000 miles away, was having what he called "a laborious year." Yet he endured it with more aplomb than perhaps any of his associates might have done. "I never worried," he said. "I did what I had to do without apprehension of tomorrow."

Recalling the financial ordeal of that year, he said, "I have gone to sleep at night in New York when I had a million and a half dollars to be paid by three o'clock on the following day, without knowing where the money was coming from, and slept soundly."

His quest for additional funds was nevertheless a restless one.

I spent four days of the week in Washington [he told an interviewer] including Sunday, two days in New York, and one in Boston. This called for four nights of riding. . . . I endeavored to obtain funds from men . . . whom I had known for years. I spent months in trying to induce capitalists to enter the company, but they thought it a great risk and would not take the chances.[17]

However, some of them were at least willing to take a chance on Huntington himself and on his partners. He declared that at one time he owed William E. Dodge & Co. $3,250,000, but prided himself on the fact that he had never had to pay more than 7 per cent interest per year on any amount that he borrowed for the Central Pacific.

Despite Huntington's implication that he remained calm and confident throughout this harrowing year, when the Central Pacific's costs rose so sharply and its debts steadily mounted, there is evidence that he and his associates were at least uneasy about the railroad's future. In May, Charles Crocker & Co. formerly asked the C.P. board of directors thereafter to be paid in stock at the rate of 30 cents on the dollar, instead of 50 cents, which had been the previous rate. Since the "& Co." of Crocker's firm actually, though not openly, consisted of Stanford, Huntington, E. B.

Crocker, and Hopkins, this move meant that they all felt their risk was greater than ever, and they considered themselves entitled to larger blocks of stock in consequence. As they were C.P. directors as well as Charles Crocker's silent partners, they naturally granted his request. They were justified, too. Subsequent opinion has judged that at this time a share of Central Pacific stock, despite its fanciful par value of $100, was worth less than 10 cents. No outsider would buy any.

At this depressing, debt-ridden moment in the Central Pacific's affairs, with the heaviest construction work only just begun, the principal owners of the railroad deliberately schemed to increase their burdens.

The agent of their scheme, Collis Huntington, was now in Washington, exerting all possible influences to persuade the Thirty-ninth Congress to remove the clause in the Pacific Railroad Act that forbade the Central Pacific to build more than 150 miles east of the California-Nevada line. That point still lay roughly 200 miles ahead of the graders, and sometimes seemed unobtainable. But if C.P. stock was ever to be worth more than 10 cents a share, the railroad must somehow reach the rich Salt Lake Valley and tap its lucrative business. That essential goal spurred Huntington and his associates to incur even greater risks than they already ran.

In Washington, Huntington was an energetic lobbyist, but his personal campaign had to stop at the doors of the legislative chambers. In the Senate, he had the energetic help of John Conness, who indignantly told his fellow senators that, in the first place, the 150-mile limitation that held the Central Pacific in leash had got into law through trickery. (This, as has been shown, was not true.) He urged the prompt removal of the restriction.

Senator Henry Wilson of Massachusetts rebutted with a letter of protest from the Union Pacific's president, Gen. John A. Dix. The general pointed out that his railroad was then in the delicate midst of negotiations to obtain loans of $20 million from bankers in France, Germany, and England, on the strength of its future prospects. If Congress were now to allow the Central Pacific to push east as far as it could go, the result would be "in the highest degree prejudicial to this company [Union Pacific] and dangerous to the great enterprise it is engaged in." [18]

Dix added that such a move would be especially unfair because there was little likelihood anyway that the Central Pacific could ever build beyond the eastern border of its own state before the Union Pacific met it.

Then rose that masterful orator, Senator William M. Stewart of Nevada, who in the previous four years had earned $500,000 in fees as lawyer for various litigants in Comstock Lode disputes. Stewart was an old friend of the Central Pacific owners and a vigorous proponent of the railroad itself. Huntington once called him "one of the best men that ever went to Congress from the Pacific Coast." [19] In a speech of savage sarcasm, Stewart now attacked Dix and all his associates as men of dubious probity, and deplored the arrogance of their assumption that the Union Pacific had "a vested right to build all the way to California." [20]

On June 19th the controversy was decided. A majority of senators sided with the Central Pacific. The vote was 20-12 in favor of lifting the 150-mile restriction.

In the House, which hadn't prepared a bill of its own on the subject, Thaddeus Stevens, chairman of the Pacific Railroad Committee, did very well for the Central Pacific in the absence of Cornelius Cole. On June 26th, the representatives obligingly followed Stevens' lead and voted, 98-36, to approve the Senate bill.

Collis Huntington sat in the visitors' gallery during the final arguments and the voting. He studied the scene through a favorite spyglass. It was one that he had often used to advantage when he was an eager young trader, freshly arrived in San Francisco, watching for incoming ships in order to get the jump on other bargainers for the goods on board.

When the voting was over and the House rose, Huntington was accosted in a corridor by Representative John B. Alley of Massachusetts. Alley, as determined a friend of the Union Pacific as Cornelius Cole had been of the Central Pacific, was seething at the removal of the 150-mile limit to the C.P.'s progress.

"There must have been great corruption and much money used in passing that bill," he said angrily.

Huntington looked down at him with contempt, and scorched him with some of his sharpest sarcasm. As he told the story afterward, he said, "Well, Mr. Alley, I'm surprised to hear you speak in that way of your associates here. I am very much surprised. But I will be frank with you, and tell you that I brought over half a million dollars with the intention of using every dollar of it, if necessary, to pass this bill. [Alley, presumably, couldn't have known that this would have been wildly beyond the current resources of the Central Pacific, even if its officials had been tempted to try bribery.] I got a large majority of members, that I knew were in favor of it, without the use of one dollar. We still had our means and wanted to get every vote. So I went into the gallery and examined the face of every man—and I am a good judge of faces. I examined them carefully through my glass. I saw but one man who I thought would sell his vote—and you know devilish well I didn't try it on *you!*" [21]

Eight days later the Central Pacific helped celebrate the Fourth of July in Sacramento by entering Charles and E. B. Crocker, Mark Hopkins, and a vivid series of floats in the local parade. The officers rode in a carriage at the head of the line. From it, Judge Crocker waved the shovel with which Stanford had turned the first earth for the railroad, three and a half years before. Behind came a string of seven horse-drawn carts, crammed with Chinese. In their wake, over the C.P. track, rolled a locomotive and tender, a flatcar, a passenger car, and a freight car—all separate, crowded with railroad employees, and pulled by big teams of mules. Large banners on the flatcar read, "Pacific Railroad Laborers. Ho for Salt Lake, 1870!" [22]

In New York, the immediate result of the amended railroad legislation was to ignite a burst of flamboyance in Thomas C. Durant. He told the press that the Union Pacific would need 60,000 tons of rails and a million ties within the next six months. He also distributed circulars to that effect. This move created a sensation in the iron industry, but it had little foundation in fact. It revealed Durant, once more, as far more of a showman than a businessman. Inevitably, his injudicious bid for publicity sent the nation's leading ironmakers into a huddle. They came out of it in happy agreement to raise the price of rails. They figured that if the Union Pacific was going to buy 60,000 tons of rails, the Central Pacific would want about as many more, to say nothing of the needs of the feeder lines that were to join the Union Pacific at the 100th Meridian or beyond.

In this adverse climate for purchasing, needlessly induced by Durant's lack of prudence, Collis Huntington must have raged privately at his rival. But he soon managed to ruin the effect of Durant's heady statements with a little well-placed subversion.

Col. George T. M. Davis, chief among the manufacturers' agents, called on Huntington with an order book soon after Durant had scattered his circulars around the country. The colonel asked how many tons of rails the Central Pacific would need during the rest of 1866.

"Don't talk to me, Davis," said Huntington, "for I am mad. I have 15,000 tons of rails on the way to California, and if they don't lay all those rails this year, I will have to get rid of those we have left on hand."

Davis was taken aback, but countered by quoting Durant's intention to lay 60,000 tons that year.

"You know he will do nothing of the kind," retorted Huntington. "The Kansas people [Union Pacific Railway, Eastern Division] are growling— they won't want a rail. Sioux City won't start to build until the Cedar [Rapids] road is secured. The Central branch is not organized and will not begin."

Davis retreated, and passed Huntington's deflating remarks along to the ironmakers. They decided not to advance the price of rails after all.

Huntington waited two weeks for Davis's report to get around. Then, swiftly and quietly, he acted.

"I ordered 10,000 tons from the Cambria, 10,000 from the Bethlehem, 10,000 from the Simonton, and scattered orders among various other makers till I had secured 66,000 tons," he said at a later time. "Not a boy in my office knew that I wanted rails. I telegraphed all my orders at once, and every one of them was accepted by telegram within an hour."[23]

After this typical coup, Huntington proceeded to take similar advantage of a leading shipping agent, E. B. Sutton.

"As these rails would require a large number of ships for transportation," he explained afterward, "the next question was how to secure the vessels at satisfactory rates."

First, he said, he told Sutton, "I want to get a good ship, one that will be steady and safe. You go out and give me a list of what you can find."

Sutton called on him a few days later, with the names of several vessels and their rates.

"Too high," declared Huntington. "I can't take one of those. I am in no hurry, for ships are coming in all along."

Sutton eventually returned with a list of twenty-three ships, some of which were on their way to Liverpool, where they would have to discharge their present cargoes.

"I noted down the vessels as we were talking," Huntington recalled, "and suddenly said, 'I will take them.' "

"Take them?" asked Sutton. "Take what?"

"I will take those ships," said Huntington, "if they are A-1."

"I can't let you have all of them," Sutton protested. "I thought you wanted only one. I will have to have two or three of them myself."

"Not of these, you won't!" retorted Huntington.

"I secured them," he related smugly, "and these vessels took out some

45,000 tons of rails. Mr. Sutton afterward said that these ships would have cost me at least $10 a ton more had he known that all of them were wanted—a clear gain of $450,000 for my company." [24]

Huntington by now had an old henchman helping him out in Washington. Cornelius Cole had been elected to succeed the alcoholic Senator McDougall when the latter's term ended. That would be in the following January, but Cole was already in the nation's capital in the summer of 1866. His premature presence there must have been somewhat irritating to McDougall in his more lucid moments, and evidently irked California's other senator, John Conness.

Senator-elect Cole wrote to his wife that Conness was "manifesting indifference as to my whereabouts. I fear I shall not be able to get along with him smoothly." [25]

Even though Cole as yet had no official status, he was already scurrying about on Central Pacific errands. On August 6th he confided to Mrs. Cole that he *must* see Secretary of the Treasury Hugh McCulloch "about those railroad bonds," [26] but that McCulloch's assistant was irksomely vague as to when the Secretary would return to town.

Extracting government-aid bonds from the Treasury when they were due was a continuing trial to the men of the Central Pacific. Years afterward, Charlie Crocker was still complaining about the bureaucratic lethargy they had encountered.

They were always behind in delivering them. There was not a clerk—there was not anybody—that did anything there but must be paid for it. He had his salary, but that was nothing. He simply would not do anything except somebody came to him and said, "Here, hurry that up and you shall have $50 or $100," according to the character of the matter. . . .

They did not move till they were "greased." Then they would slide. Everything was pigeonholed, and when it got into a pigeonhole, there had to be money used to get it out. I have often said that I would never have anything more to do with anything that had to be managed in the Government style.[27]

Because of the painfully slow pace of construction as the railroad climbed the steepening slope toward Cisco, which was nearly 6,000 feet above the sea, government aid became a dribble. During the entire year of 1866, the C.P. collected only $1,600,000 worth of bonds from the U.S. Treasury. When they had been converted into gold—always a necessity for the Central Pacific—they brought almost $500,000 less. It was ironic that as the cost of building the road rose and the mileage dwindled, because of the difficulties encountered, the government's financial help tapered off.

But, now that there were no longer any legal limits to the distance they could go, if they could make it, the C.P.'s work forces were pushed ahead with a bold disregard for the high cost of hurry.

Montague remarked that heavy rock excavations that should have taken eighteen months to complete, if they were to be done economically, were finished in four or five, "of course requiring a greatly increased outlay of money to accomplish it." [28]

Stanford explained that he and his partners spent their money with the greatest economy "except in the matter of speed, and then we never hesitated to make a sacrifice." [29]

By mid-August, graders were at work night and day. The night shifts, despite the awkwardness of laboring by the light of lanterns and bonfires, accomplished most. Everybody agreed it was because the men were so much more comfortable after dark. The daylight hours were "hot enough just about now to give a thick beefsteak a decent broil," [30] reported the Dutch Flat *Enquirer*.

As fast as men could be released from the grade west of Cisco, they were sent forward to start excavating the series of twelve tunnels that the track must thread between there and the Nevada state line. Cisco, 92 miles from Sacramento, would become the terminus of the track in 1866, and remain so until November, 1867. It would take that long to bore holes through all the granite barriers that blocked its progress eastward from there.

Engineer John R. Gilliss indicated where the excavating was to be done, and he laid out the work for the Chinese in compulsive haste. For example, he said, he once hiked 2 miles along dark cliffs and through murky woods after sundown to stake out the east end of Tunnel No. 12 by the light of a bonfire. By nine o'clock that evening, the first shift was at work there.

At the tunnel faces, gangs of thirty to forty Chinese worked in three eight-hour relays, under white foremen who divided each day into two twelve-hour tours of duty. With blasting powder, hammer, drill, and chisel, the men hacked their way into the rock at the excruciatingly slow rate of one foot every twenty-four hours.

On August 27th Sam Montague ordered a new tactic for work on

Tunnel No. 6 at the summit of the route. The Summit Tunnel, as it was usually called, was to be 1,659 feet long, far longer than any other on the railroad. Montague now set gangs to sinking a shaft at its center. The shaft would be 8 feet by 12, and nearly 73 feet deep. As soon as it was finished, horizontal excavating could proceed from the middle toward both ends, as well as from both ends toward the middle.

At first, the shaft deepened at the rate of a foot a day. After 30 feet, the pace slowed, mostly because of time consumed in hoisting rock debris to the surface by means of a hand derrick. The job wouldn't be completed until December 19th.

Meanwhile, at Grizzly Hill, 77 miles east of Sacramento, the railroad's first tunnel, 498 feet long, had been finished. Seven miles farther on, at Emigrant Gap, the considerably smaller Tunnel No. 2 was completed on September 21st. There were no major obstacles remaining in the way of the track's steady movement toward Cisco.

Shacks for laborers, and warehouses for materials, were already rising along the Truckee River, 20 miles beyond the summit, as crews of Crocker's carpenters prepared for the forward leap that would occur when the first heavy snow fell.

Learning of this, the editor of Virginia City's *Territorial Enterprise* was greatly cheered. "What a joyful day it will be," he exclaimed in print, "when the shrill whistle of the locomotive shall be heard as the train of cars from across the mountains shall go rattling down the Truckee. And that day is not two years distant." [31]

Supply trains labored up the western slope of the Sierra in a steady, shrill procession. "A 116-foot grade, with a dozen heavily loaded freight cars, is no sardine," commented the Dutch Fat *Enquirer*. "It makes the fur fly, but they manage to do it somehow." [32] At the end of the rails, the trains disgorged their cargoes onto wagons bound eastward, and puffed and shrieked down the mountain for more.

One spectator who viewed this bustle ruefully was Ben Holladay, the swashbuckling stage-line tycoon, who lurched upon the scene from the East in mid-November, in the most elaborate horse-drawn vehicle anybody had ever seen. It was an outsize, bulletproof coach, containing a kitchen, dining room, and bedroom. Holladay had had it built especially for this trip, on which he and a doctor friend had set out to see how his potential competitors were getting along.

The stage king and the doctor had traveled from New York to Iowa by train. At the end of the track in Iowa, still many miles short of its goal, Council Bluffs, they had switched to stagecoach. After being ferried across the Missouri, they had boarded the Union Pacific at Omaha. They had ridden on U.P. cars as far as the rails extended, which was well beyond Fort Kearny. There Holladay's unique equipage was waiting. They had then crossed 1,500 miles of plain and mountain in it. Once, as an experiment, they drove 400 miles in forty consecutive hours. When they rocked into Alta, California, they brought to Central Pacific officials the chilling news that the U.P. was coming toward them like a prairie fire. After its years of inactivity, it had sprung to life with spectacular vigor. The travelers reported that in one recent span of only thirty days, it had laid 65 miles of track.

When this news was passed along to the editor of the *Union,* he found one rather bleak solace; "The building of one mile of road anywhere between Newcastle and Cisco involves more labor and expense than the construction of 20 miles on the level prairie," [33] he wrote.

On November 27th a heartening telegram arrived at the Central Pacific's Sacramento offices from the little Sierra town of Alta:

Track will be laid tonight within 4,500 feet of Cisco depot. Ties will be distributed tonight and track laid tomorrow. Can run passengers to Cisco Thursday [November 29th]. Snow at Crystal Lake this morning 8 inches deep and 12 inches at Cisco. Temp. 28. Montague.[34]

The C.P. thought it was ready for snow. A month earlier, its workshops had produced a monster plow, which was a fascinating novelty to the citizens of Sacramento. It ran on a pair of trucks, like other railroad cars, but they were entirely hidden under its bizarre superstructure. The plow was 10 feet wide, 11 feet high, and 30 feet long. Its rear was square and sheer, like one end of a huge box. Its front resembled a big wooden wedge, laid on its side, with iron plates reinforcing the forward edge, which slanted down nearly to the rails. A few feet back from this edge, a sharp iron prow rose out of the broad wooden slope, like a ship breasting a wave. The intention was that the wedge should scoop up drifts like a spade, and that the prow would then part them as a vessel parts sea foam. Snow would be tossed to both sides of the track as far as 60 feet, railroadmen said.

Ninety miles to the east, and nearly 6,000 feet higher, the super-plow would soon have its work cut out for it.

The Sacramento Valley had again been soaked with rains that had fallen earlier and lasted longer than usual. The total rainfall to date now topped the previous record, which had produced the worst floods in local history, in 1861–62. As each moisture-heavy storm swept in from the Pacific, its drops turned to flakes when it approached the upper regions of the Sierra. There was more than a foot of snow on the level at Cisco in late November, when Strobridge's tracklayers spiked down the last rail beside the station. Californians who had migrated from New England were reminded that C.P. trains now climbed to a point only 315 feet lower than the summit of Mount Washington in New Hampshire, which was usually snowbound by now.

A foot of snow was but a mild prelude to the fantastic fall that would bury the Sierra in the approaching winter. Still, it spurred Charlie Crocker into carrying out promptly the strategic move planned earlier for out-flanking the white blockade in his path. As soon as Cisco was firmly estab-lished as the end of track for the season, Crocker sent 1,000 men across the summit and 30 miles beyond it, down the Truckee Valley. Another thousand soon followed. They established themselves well below the snow line, and started to make grade back toward Donner Pass. After them labored a long line of wagons, loaded with materials and provisions. The supply line, over the Dutch Flat and Donner Lake Wagon Road, grew increasingly choked with snow. The traffic was so heavy, however, that men and animals managed to break their way through the drifts, with few interruptions, throughout the long succession of blizzards that made that winter terrible for the railroad builders.

The strangest cargo that traveled to the summit just before the snows began was a stripped locomotive, the old Sacramento, which had been the first steam engine in California. It once had hauled trains for the Sacramento Valley Railroad. Now it was destined to become a hoisting engine, mounted above the shaft being sunk in the middle of the Summit Tunnel. A house 50 feet square had been built to receive it. The structure was big enough to allow room, as well, for forges, fuel, tools, and other supplies that would need to be right at hand when drifts smothered the ridge through which the tunnel was being dug.

The Sacramento was a small Hinkley engine with four driving wheels. In its home city, before the trip up the mountain began, the locomotive's stack, cab, and everything else that could safely be dispensed with were removed to lighten the load. Then it was hauled up the track to Gold Run.

There, its wheels were removed, and, with the aid of traveling jacks, it was eased onto a long, low logging wagon. The wagon had wheels 2 feet wide, built to prevent its becoming mired during the rainy season. Once the engine's torso had been bolted and braced in place, ten yoke of oxen were hitched to the wagon, and a traumatic journey began.

"The black picked goose," [35] as the railroad's chief wagonmaster called his special charge, made the trip without jarring a valve. But its crawling advance along the busy mountain road produced panic and wreckage wherever it moved. It loomed through the trees like some strange idol in a pagan procession. A half-mile east of Dutch Flat, the sight of it sent an approaching ten-mule freight team into hysterics. Bucking and kicking, they broke harness and tug chains, and bolted for the woods.

From there on, similar mishaps occurred daily. Mules and horses of all ages became unnerved when they spied the Sacramento. Even seasoned stagecoach horses balked at it. The damage to passing vehicles grew awesome in amount. Teamsters' complaints to the Central Pacific management mounted in volume and tone. Finally, word was passed to all freighters to keep in mind about where the terrifying spectacle might be met. They were urged to blindfold their teams just before they reached the "goose," and lead them past it. The Sacramento's own accompanying teamsters helped out the passersby whenever they were needed.

This worked perfectly, except for the occasional stranger trotting along in a buggy, unaware of what lay ahead. If he was able to get past the Sacramento without his horse's kicking the dashboard to splinters, he was lucky.

On the road's twisting downgrades, the dismembered locomotive was kept from pitching headlong onto its straining mules, or tipping sideways, by lashing it to big pine trees with heavy logging chains and tackle, and lowering it a few feet at a time.

After six weeks of tortured progress, the Sacramento reached the summit. There it was hauled up into its house and placed on a bed of huge timbers at the top of the tunnel shaft. At last, the anemic hand derrick and its scanty wooden buckets could be abandoned for muscular steam power, geared to a 6-foot drum, and big buckets of boiler plate. Rock debris could now be removed at a brisker rate, speeding the shaft to completion.

The bottom was reached on December 19th. At once, gangs were lowered to start burrowing east and west from the center chamber, by the light of oil lanterns and candles. Crocker and his associates decided that they needed more experienced men for this tunneling work. They sent an emissary to Virginia City, to lure some of the best Cornish miners out of the ground with the assurance of higher wages in the Sierra.

The Cornishmen came to the summit of Donner Pass. Instead of giving them exclusive charge of excavating the tunnel from its center toward its ends, though, Crocker faced the miners in one direction and a gang of Chinese in the other.

"The Chinese, without fail, always outmeasured the Cornish miners," recalled Charles Crocker. "That is to say, they would cut more rock in a week than the Cornish miners did. And there it was hard work, steady pounding on the rock, bone-labor." [36]

The race became so obviously one-sided that the Cornishmen quit. "They swore they would not work with Chinamen anyhow," said Crocker. From then on, "the Chinamen had possession of the whole work." [37]

Outside, the snow was piling ever deeper. At twelve tunnels, men had bored far enough into the rock to be out of reach of the weather. As drifts mounted at the tunnel entrances, however, they had to burrow through them to get from their log shacks to the day's work, and to provide channels for getting rid of the rubble that was accumulating. The Chinese who spent that fearsome winter at the top of the Sierra lived like a hardy breed of moles.

Before the worst troubles descended upon the summit, Central Pacific employees were in tedious difficulties much closer to the Sacramento plain.

"And still it rains," mourned the *Union's* editor on December 27th.

The roads become sloughs, through which stage horses stagger, or in which they break down altogether. Railroad men, who have been busily solving the problem of travel through mountain snow, suddenly find themselves, though successful above, baffled below by an enemy not particularly feared. The rain washes and the swollen streams sap the high embankments over which the locomotive has ascended to the region of snow.

On the following day, Cisco reported the worst storm in a decade. The story ended ominously. "The railroad can be put in order in 10 days," it stated.

Bulletins on the storms so comfortably remote put the editor of the *Union* in a lyric reverie, seasoned with memories of his Eastern youth:

Within five hours ride of Sacramento, where roses still bloom in the gardens and the air is balmy as the breath of Spring, snow has fallen to a depth of three feet on a level, and the sleigh-bells are making music along white highways, fenced with spire-like pines. One can breakfast here in the valley, where ice is chiefly known as an imported luxury for cooling drinks on sultry days . . . ; dine where frozen lakes tempt the graceful skater, where cutters and buffalo robes and bells offer the swift and rollicking fascination of New England sport . . . ; and sup in time to see the curtain rise at the theater in Sacramento on the same evening. The locomotive makes this concentration of the seasons—this transition from Spring flowers to Wintry delights—on the same day, a possibility. Each puffing engine that rolls away from the green cottonwoods on the levee is armed with a snow plow. And this suggests the beginning of that battle of the railroad men with the white storms of the Sierra which the ravens have croaked into defeat before the first onset has been sounded.[38]

As it turned out, the ravens, unfortunately, knew what they were croaking about. The Central Pacific's greatest ordeal had begun.

CHAPTER TEN

THE U.P. SPRINGS
TO LIFE

Like a jogging distance runner suddenly awakening to a threat of being overtaken, the Union Pacific spurted ahead in 1866 and began moving at high speed. The increase in miles of track laid that year was astonishing. From groundbreaking, in 1863, to the last day of 1865, the railroad's total advance had measured only 40 miles. In 1866, its track leapt forward more than six times that far.

In the course of the first five months of 1866, the cast of principals in the drama of the Union Pacific's construction was rounded out by the arrival on the scene of the last three key figures. In February, Brig. Gen. John Stephen Casement and his brother Daniel, of Painesville, Ohio, signed an agreement to lay track for the railroad. In May, Maj. Gen. Grenville Dodge at last took the job that Durant had so persistently offered him. He became, at thirty-five, the U.P.'s chief engineer. In June, Congress rewarded Collis Huntington's efforts and lifted the legal barrier that otherwise would have penned up the Central Pacific in the middle of northern Nevada. This liberating move was an imperative challenge to the Union Pacific to get going. It was ready. The Ameses and their friends seemed likely to be able to provide a steady supply of money for the effort. The work itself, finally, was in thoroughly capable hands.

The Casement brothers, an acquaintance said, were "a pair of the biggest little men you every saw—about as large as twelve-year-old boys, but requiring larger hats." [1] Their admiring workmen generally called them Jack and Dan, except to their faces. The general, barely 5 feet 4 but heavily muscled and tough, was full-bearded and looked like a Romanoff. His manner was often gruff, and he carried a big ivory-handled Colt in his belt. He rode his horse with an unrelaxingly stiff back and a combative look. On the other hand, his letters to his wife reveal him to have been an ardent, considerate, warmhearted man. He had a large capacity for leadership, repeatedly evidenced by the performance of his troops during the Civil War, in which he served from start to finish. "His look and command held them as firmly as the silken sashes that bound together the Greeks at the pass of Thermopylae," [2] resoundingly declared Gen. John M. Schofield, speaking of Casement's outstanding help to him during the Atlanta campaign in 1864.

Jack Casement, who became thirty-seven years old in January, 1866, took to the field that spring with a mixed but predominantly Irish force of former Union and Confederate soldiers, muleskinners, disillusioned miners, adventurers, newly arrived immigrants, runaway sons from Eastern families, fed-up farmers, gamblers, and problem drinkers. He quickly whipped them into the semblance of a military outfit. Indeed, that is what they had to resemble, not only to build track with precision and efficiency but to defend themselves and their droves of accompanying livestock against the persistent threat of Indian attack. They were not in the least deterred by danger. The fact that they might have to battle Indians on the job was, as General Sherman remarked, more of an inducement than a discouragement to these men. They worked and fought with discipline. Afterward, they relaxed with an explosive abandon that made their passage notorious even in the uninhibited annals of the West.

Dan Casement was slighter and younger than Jack, and smooth-faced. He was "five feet nothing," [3] according to his brother-in-law, E. C. Lockwood, but unusually imaginative and clever. Dan was the business manager of the Casement brothers' partnership. He was also in charge of logistics. The general relied on Dan to make certain than no awkward pauses for supplies developed at the construction front. The brothers' relationship was unusually close. The general summed it up years later as he stood beside his long-time partner's coffin. "Poor Dan," he mourned. "I have my hands, but I feel that I have lost my head." [4]

The parents of the Casement brothers had come from the Isle of Man, in the Irish Sea. Their American-born sons had been given only a partial grade-school education, and then were put to work to help support the large family when they were barely in their teens. Jack and Dan had been building track for various Midwestern railroads since they were in their early twenties.

On February 6, 1866, they submitted their first business proposal to T. C. Durant. They offered "to lay and fill the track on the Union Pacific Railroad for Seven Hundred and Fifty Dollars per mile." [5] They agreed to do this at as fast a pace as the company desired. However, perhaps for want of confidence in the flow of supplies up the Missouri and across the Iowa prairie, they stipulated that the top speed for tracklaying should not exceed a mile a day. The result, they promised, would be "good and workmanlike." [6] They'd start as soon as they were asked, and keep at it as long as the U.P. wished. The railroad was to furnish materials, transportation, and all motive power needed. The Casements would, of course, feed and shelter their own men, as well as any railroad employees on special duty with them.

Two days later, Durant sent them a favorable answer from New York. Though he wrote as if the Union Pacific were hiring them, their contract was actually with the Credit Mobilier, of which Durant was president.

Winter had the supply lines in a tight grip at the time this initial bargain between the Casements and Durant was concluded. Dan Casement soon journeyed to Omaha, though, to begin preparations that would enable the general to lead his construction force forward as soon as spring arrived. An essential part of the preliminaries was the building of a boarding train, with crude kitchen, mess cars, and bunk cars. This rolling headquarters would enable the tracklayers to eat and sleep within a few feet of each day's work. It would guarantee a minimum of lost time, a maximum of personnel control.

As the train began to take shape, Grenville Dodge, at Fort Leavenworth, was in the throes of making a final decision about Durant's long-standing job offer. He had told Durant many times that he would accept it when he was free to do so. Now that he was on the verge of quitting the Army, he was having troubled thoughts about the wisdom of his commitment.

If I go on the U.P.R.R. as Chief Engineer [he had written to his brother, Nathan, on January 26th], I am tied up and have got to work all day and night, and I am afraid I might have trouble with Durant, though that doesn't enter into my decision. . . .

The U.P.R.R. would pay me well [he continued], but the vexation, trouble, and continual hindrance one continually meets with in building railroads, especially when we are subject to the whims of the money market to get along, is terrible, and I cannot always last with my brain and nerves strained to their utmost tension all the time. However, I have got to decide in a short time, for as soon as the river opens in the spring, I am going to leave the Army.[7]

Early in March, he notified his brother that he was going to meet Durant somewhere within a few weeks and settle the nagging issue between them.

On April 24th Dodge had a rendezvous with Durant at St. Joseph, the main river port for transshipping rail-borne cargoes bound for the Union Pacific. Dodge told him that he was ready to become the railroad's chief engineer, but only on condition that he be given absolute authority in the field. Probably with Dey's unhappy experience in mind, Dodge insisted that, so long as he got results that satisfied the company, there must be no interference from New York. He told Durant that the railroad builders were going into "a country without law, where might is right," [8] and that the only way he could command respect and obedience was to have the active support of his superiors. Durant seemed to accept the ultimatum. He said he had talked about Dodge with both Grant and Sherman. They had assured him that if Dodge became the U.P.'s chief engineer, he'd have their complete support. When could he take charge of the work? Dodge said he'd be in Omaha around the first of May.

The new field commander of the Union Pacific arrived at his Omaha headquarters for the first time on May 6th. He had had his thirty-fifth birthday only three weeks before, but he looked considerably older than that. His dark beard was already veined with gray hairs. His narrow, haggard face was furrowed with lines that war wounds and anxieties had left there. His eyes still showed a shadow of pain. Short, square, soft-spoken, careless in dress, Dodge was not an imposing figure. His reputation made up for that. His feats of military railroad-building for Grant and Sherman were among the popular tales of the war, and alone assured him the immediate respect of his associates. They quickly found, besides, that his renown was backed by thorough professional knowledge, firm self-confidence, and a fondness for vigorous action.

Dodge's first move was to pull the uncoordinated parts of the Union Pacific organization together. Each department had previously been receiving independent orders from New York and sending back separate reports. Dodge now officially established Sam Reed as superintendent of construction, Webster Snyder as head of transportation, and H. M. Hoxie as chief freight handler. The Casements were under Reed's jurisdiction. All department heads henceforth took their orders from the chief engineer.

Next, Dodge asked Gen. Philip St. George Cooke to provide troops to protect his engineering field parties and track builders from Indians, in case they broke loose again this summer. Cooke, a fusty, aging Virginia cavalryman who had remained loyal to the Union while his headstrong son-in-law, Jeb Stuart, rode off to glory with the South, now commanded the newly created military department of the Platte. He was willing enough to oblige Dodge, but his readiness to furnish escorts was naturally predicated upon the supply of troops that the War Department allowed him. It wasn't a liberal supply. Cooke had about 2,500 soldiers with whom to police 1,000 miles of frontier. Dodge quickly decided that he'd have to arm most of his own men, too. He proceeded to do so.

The Casements had moved out from Omaha to the line of grading in the Platte Valley. They had mustered impressive strength: 1,000 men and 100 teams. The tracklayers numbered only 250. The rest were graders and teamsters, herdsmen and cooks. The men wore parts of faded blue and gray uniforms, checkered shirts, brightly colored neckerchiefs, leather boots, with their trouser legs tucked into them, and a weird assortment of civilian and military hats to shield them from the sun. They unvaryingly ate beef and bread, pie and coffee, drank as much raw whiskey as they could find, and went happily unwashed between streams, which were infrequent.

Their boarding train was finished, and already stood at the end of track. Its four principal cars were each 85 feet long. Ceiling racks in them held a total of a thousand rifles. One entire car and half of the next formed a mess hall. A kitchen and an office occupied the remainder of the second mess car. Then came two bunk cars. The bunks ran lengthwise, three tiers high. There was a corridor down the center of both cars. Additional bunk cars were built later. They never accommodated more than relatively

few members of the Casements' forces, however. Most of the men preferred to sleep in tents, for better air, more room, and for the same reason
that often drove soldiers at the crumbling adobe Army post on the plains
to bed down in blankets on their parade grounds—to escape vermin.

E. C. Lockwood, a lad in his late teens, slept on top of one of the bunk
cars. "To tell the truth," he once wrote, "we were troubled by 'cooties,' and
a companion and myself escaped them by making our bed between two
skylights on the roof." [9] A tailor in the Casement outfit created a canvas
shelter for the boys out of an old piece of tent cloth. It hung on a pole
that stretched between the skylights, and as they lay under it on their
blankets, it cleared their faces by only 2 feet. When a storm came up in
the night, as it frequently did on the Nebraska prairie during the stifling
summer, they buttoned their canvas to rows of brass fasteners they had
mounted along the near edges of the roof.

Those notorious "Platte storms" that struck in the darkness were terrify-
ingly violent. William Henry Jackson, the pioneer Western photographer,
a disappointed young man of twenty-three who had joined a westbound
wagon train that summer to forget the girl who had jilted him in Vermont,
wrote a vivid description of one in his diary:

> It came down raging and howling like a madman, tearing and pulling away
> at the [wagon] sheets as though it meant to vent its fury upon us personally.
> It rocked and shook us and started some of the wagons on their wheels. Ours
> was broadside to the storm and we had serious apprehensions that we should
> be capsized. After a short spat of hail, the rain came down steady torrents—
> the roaring thunder and the flashing lightning were incessant, reverberating
> through the heavens with an awful majesty of sound and lighting up every-
> thing with the brilliancy of day. The storm did not last long, but its force and
> fury were indescribable. The rain came right through the wagon sheets, but we
> hauled a buffalo robe over our heads and so kept dry all night.[10]

General Casement's men encountered a number of these strident storms
their first two months out, and then were granted a reprieve in the form
of a drought.

Several boxcars, mostly provision storehouses, filled out the Casement
boarding train. The camp butchers hung quarters of beef in one of them,
after periodic slaughters among the 500 cattle that ambled along in the
wake of the tracklayers. Another car had been converted into a bakery—

"Better bread one never ate," [11] Lockwood testified. Next to it was a car bulging with sacks of flour and sugar. Beyond that stood a carload of oats for the horses.

Long strings of mixed freight cars, laden with ties, rails, track fastenings, spikes, firewood for locomotives, provisions to replenish the tracklayers' stocks, and supplies for the graders, working miles ahead, arrived from Omaha on a regular schedule and nosed up behind the boarding train. There they were unloaded onto the plain, and the empty cars were hauled away to pick up another cargo. The boarding train was then pushed back a few hundred yards. Ties were flung into waiting carts for horses to pull to the line of completed grading, well in advance of the tracklayers. Rails were carried forward on little open-work flatcars, also horse-drawn, that rolled along the track to its advancing end. When emptied, they could easily be lifted off the track to make way for the next load moving up to the front.

Supplies for the graders were shifted to prairie wagons and started toward their distant destinations. Bridge frames, their members cut to size in Omaha, were transferred to flatbed wagons here and forwarded to the bridgebuilders, who, when there were streams to be spanned, usually worked at least 20 miles ahead of the trackmen.

The volume of wagon traffic from the end of track forward to the bulk of the construction force, which labored far in advance of the tracklayers, soon became enormous. At the peak of the railroad's building activity, 10,000 horses were working for the U.P., nearly one for every man.

The Union Pacific's construction army stretched over a vast distance. Way out in front, the surveyors, often hundreds of miles ahead of the graders, moved in groups of from eighteen to twenty-two. They consisted of civil engineers, rodmen, flagmen, chainmen, axmen, and teamsters. When the party had to carry its own meat supply, there were herders as well, for the beef traveled on the hoof until it was needed for the table. In good game country, hunters took the place of herders.

Each group of surveyors was given a military escort of at least ten men, and sometimes as many as a company. Every morning, the troops, usually cavalrymen, spread out to the highest knolls in the vicinity and there maintained a day-long vigil against surprise attack. The figures in this pattern moved forward together as many as 12 miles a day while the engineers were making a preliminary survey. The pace slowed to 3 or

4 miles a day on a final location of the line in open country. It rarely
exceeded a mile a day when work of the latter sort was being done in the
mountains.

The presence of the troops was comforting to the surveyors. "Their
campfires burn brightly after nightfall," one of them wrote in his diary,
"and the solemn tread of the sentinel, with bright gleaming carbine,
assures one if, in the still hours of night, we are attacked, the enemy will
receive a warm reception." [12]

In spite of these military precautions, though, "the parties were often
attacked, their chief or some of their men killed or wounded, and their
stock run off," [13] General Dodge reported. At times, surveyors who survived attack angrily attributed their losses to their escorts, who had
carelessly attracted the Indians' attention by shooting at game or blowing
bugles. A cavalry officer retorted that the basic trouble was not noise but
the fact that "you can't surround three Indians with one soldier." [14]

The railroad's main construction corps—graders, bridgebuilders, station
builders—ranged in number from a few hundred at the start to several
thousand as the U.P. rapidly increased its forward speed. This largest
contingent of the work force was generally scattered over the surveyed
route for as far as 100 miles ahead of the tracklayers. The bridgebuilders
had the railroad's only semblance of construction machinery—hand-
operated derricks, mounted on flatcars—to help them. The graders had
plows, scrapers, dump carts, wheelbarrows, picks, and shovels.

The Army shielded these men, too, though in a less intimate way than
it protected the surveyors. Mounted patrols rode along the line of grading,
and frequently camped within sight of graders' tents, but their function
was more that of a reconnoitering force than that of a close guard. The
railroadmen were armed and, since most of them had been soldiers on one
side or the other during the Civil War, knew how to use their weapons.
Where they worked together in large groups, neither they nor the screen-
ing troops had much to worry about. Indians preferred to attack small
parties, especially when they were spread thin or isolated. Surveyors and
tie-cutters were in the greatest peril.

General Casement's men marched at the rear of the U.P.'s army of railroad builders. Behind them, as they left a completed track beneath their
steadily moving feet, the supply trains grew in number and length.

Four of the Union Pacific's first five locomotives were named for Civil
War heroes: Generals Sherman, McPherson, and Sheridan, and Admiral

Farragut. (Oddly, none was ever named for Grant, an oversight that one would have expected Dodge to remedy.) After these came a brief flurry of geographical names—Idaho, Omaha, Osceola, Manchester, Colorado, Denver. Then the transportation department appeared to run out of inspiration. It merely gave numbers to all the engines that followed. The railroad acquired twenty-five locomotives during 1866. Twenty of them did all the hauling involved in building track as far as North Platte, the first winter headquarters in the field, then 290 miles from Omaha by rail. All of the Union Pacific's early locomotives ranged in weight from 25 to 35 tons. They were from the best U.S. works, in Taunton and Springfield, Massachusetts, Trenton and Paterson, New Jersey.

Their fuel was mostly cottonwood, cut into 6-foot lengths for the tender and then chopped by the fireman into chunks that would fit his firebox. Much of it was so green that locomotive crews used to swear that it sprouted after it landed on the fire. With fuel such as this, the problem of getting up enough steam to do their work was a tormenting and continuous one for every locomotive engineer and fireman.

The Union Pacific accumulated more than 250 freight cars in the course of that year. The early work trains had no cabooses, however. If they ran into rain or snow on a journey, the brakemen took cover beneath a big tarpaulin on a flatcar at the rear. Under the urgent pressure of forwarding materials and supplies to the front, the railroad made no effort to cater to the traveling public. If one felt obliged to take a trip on the U.P., one could sit on a board ledge nailed against the inner walls of a boxcar, or ride on a pile of railroad iron or ties on a flatcar. The fare was the same for either type of accommodation.

The railroad's first carbuilders were more eager than expert. The boxcars and coaches they knocked together often sagged in the middle and had to wear iron trusses. Some of the coaches, lighted by candles and heated by wood stoves, strayed so far from standard dimensions that couplings had to be lengthened a link or two to allow for varying platform heights. In addition, planks occasionally had to be laid down to enable passengers to climb or descend from one car to the next. After the carpenters developed greater skill at their craft and were allowed more time in which to do it, they produced what were called "first-class passenger cars." Then the early, gravid-looking coaches were converted into smokers. Railroadmen invariably referred to these as "sow belly" coaches.[15]

Herbert Hoxie had telegraphed Dodge, soon after the young general assumed his U.P. command, that river boats were at last becoming plentiful at St. Joseph. He wired that he was shipping iron up to Omaha as fast as it arrived from the East on the Horrible St. Joe. He was also forwarding disassembled locomotives and a few Eastern-built cars.

The fate of these shipments was always uncertain. One boatload of rails went to the bottom when the *City of Memphis* burst her boilers and sank. Another disappeared with the *Ontario,* which ripped open its hull on a submerged tree and drowned. The fluid mud that formed the unpredictable Missouri hid a forest of snags and sandbars. Pilots were never quite sure where the channel lay. Nearly every voyage was marked by a boat's running aground at least once, and usually several times. When this happened, passengers and cargoes were first shifted in the effort to work the keel free. If that failed, as it generally did, long poles were extended from each side of the vessel and, manipulated by donkey engines, used to force it back out of its mucky trap, as a man in a rowboat would wield an oar for the same purpose. Sometimes a foundered steamer could not be budged, and had to be left to its fate. The passengers were then taken off in small boats. Workmen on scows came around later to cut through the high side of the hull and rescue as much of the cargo as they could move. Then the gutted derelict would slump ever lower in the dark-brown river until perhaps only one forlorn, sharply canted paddle wheel remained visible above the turbid current.

Despite the erosion of such accidents, the stream of construction materials flowing toward Omaha swelled steadily as summer began. As soon as the Iowa prairie had dried and hardened, a supply line of teams, reaching from the westward-moving end of the Chicago & North Western R.R. to Council Bluffs, more than made up for cargoes lost in the Missouri. Rafts brought down tall heaps of ties cut along the river banks for 150 miles north. Tugs labored upstream with scows nearly hidden under other great piles of them, gathered as far as 60 miles south. Both steamboats and wagons also carried military and commercial freight to Omaha for the U.P.'s overworked trains to haul. The Army quartermaster at Omaha notified Dodge on May 29th that he had 2 million pounds of supplies waiting to be forwarded by rail as far west as the track went.

By this time, the Casements' men, swinging sledges to the cadence of work songs, were already surpassing the top speed for tracklaying that had been set in their contract. Hezekiah Bissell, of the U.P.'s engineering

staff, told of the lures used to urge them on. At first, he said, Jack Casement had offered the men a pound of tobacco apiece if they would lay
a mile of track in a single day. They easily won that prize. Dan Casement
then proposed to pay them half-time extra for any day in which they
managed to spike down a mile and a half of track. This was a much more
lusty stimulus than free tobacco. The men stepped up their pace with no
apparent strain. Soon they were being offered, and were often earning,
double pay for laying 2 miles of track in a day.[16]

The amended Pacific Railroad Act required the U.P. to have its first
100 miles in operation by July 1st or forfeit its charter. General Casement's
army, every man doing one specified job only and keeping out of everybody else's way, swung past the 100th milepost early in June. They were
now moving across table-flat grassland, bleaching in the sun, with almost
nothing to vary the blank look of the horizon except a meandering line of
cottonwoods and willows, from 5 to 8 miles south. Those trees marked the
course of the broad, shallow Platte. The tracklayers were just beginning
to hit their stride. Later in the summer they would add 65 miles to the
length of the Union Pacific in one month.

Railroad stations were being built about every 20 miles. "Each depot,"
reported the engineer in charge of this work, "has now a town attached,
giving all an opportunity to purchase and settle at very reasonable rates." [17]
The railroad was offering its lots for from $25 to $250 each. It asked a
down payment of one-third in cash, and gave the buyer one or two years
to pay the balance. The purchase contract obligated him to plant shade
trees on his property within a year from the time he bought it.

By mid-July, Samuel Reed was writing his wife that the U.P. was really
going to keep the government commissioners hopping that summer, inspecting each 20-mile section of track as it was finished. The three commissioners then were Dr. William M. White, a former congressman from
Connecticut; Brig. Gen. James H. Simpson; and Maj. Gen. Samuel R.
Curtis.

They were riding up and down the line in an ornate railroad car with
a lugubrious history. It had been intended to be the private car of the
President of the United States. Lincoln was in office when it was being
built, but when it was finished, he refused to ride in it. Perhaps that was
because a few newspapers hostile to his Administration had derided the
vehicle as an unseemly extravagance. The car, beyond question, was
elaborate. It was finished entirely in black walnut, upholstered in dark

green plush, and contained almost as much silk as a queen's boudoir—billowy pale-green curtains at the windows and a profusion of crimson folds overhead, gathered into a rosette in the center of the ceiling.

Lincoln was undoubtedly obeying a characteristic instinct in rejecting this gaudy railway carriage, but fate soon placed him in it against his will. After his assassination, his body was borne on its slow, ceremonial journey to Springfield, Illinois, in this car. Its bright adornments were replaced by ample yards of black cloth and silver fringe for the sad occasion. Afterward, the car was returned to a railroad shop in Alexandria, Virginia. There it stood forlornly on its unconventional four sets of trucks for several months, until T. C. Durant bought it to ride about in on the Union Pacific track. He was not afraid of ghosts, and, with its original trappings restored, it was as appropriate a setting for Durant as it had been unsuitable for Old Abe. However, in 1866, the Union Pacific acquired an even more elaborate private car for the use of its directors. Durant then turned the so-called "Lincoln car," with two of its four pairs of trucks removed, over to the government commissioners. In it, they were now happily earning their $10 a day and 10 cents a mile for inspecting 20-mile sections of the U.P. when completed.

In August of 1866, Jack Casement's men met their first Indians. It was in the vicinity of Grand Island, more than 150 miles from Omaha. Though the warriors were Sioux, they seemed friendly. There were only eighteen of them, but one was a renowned tribal leader, Chief Spotted Tail. He was a prime favorite of the U.S. Bureau of Indian Affairs, because he was considered to be a moderate, anxious to keep his young braves out of trouble.

Spotted Tail and his band had a half-breed interpreter with them as they splashed across the Platte and rode through the tall, tawny prairie grass to the boarding train. The interpreter explained that they had come simply to watch the white men lay track. A Casement foreman greeted them cordially. Then, as his tracklayers pounded past, he explained each action of theirs to the visitors. Finally, he led his unexpected guests through the boarding cars. He took particular pains to show them the hundreds of rifles on the ceiling racks.

"I was following them," E. C. Lockwood afterward recalled, "and noticed one Indian put his hand out of a window and measure the thickness of the wall of the car. As he looked to another Indian, I could imagine hearing him say, 'I wonder if a bullet could go through.'" [18]

Somebody then suggested that the Sioux demonstrate their marksmanship with bow and arrow. Lockwood stood up a shovel in the sand about 6o feet off, and all Indians but the chief took turns shooting at it. Sixteen sent their arrows through the hole in the handle. The last man's arrow struck the handle just below the hole, and knocked over the shovel. His companions were disgusted with him.

The Sioux seemed so interested in the locomotive that a race was proposed. The engine was uncoupled from the train. The Indians mounted their ponies. Spotted Tail was persuaded, after considerable reluctance, to ride in the engine cab, and the contest began. At first, the horsemen easily outdistanced the locomotive, and whooped their satisfaction. But the engine steadily gained. When it surged past the ponies, the engineer opened his whistle wide. The unfamiliar shriek so startled the riders that they all swung to the off side of their ponies, holding on with their arms around the animal's necks and one leg over the saddle—a defensive battle maneuver.

It was now lunchtime, and the Casement foreman invited the Indians to sit down and eat with his tracklayers. The Sioux refused to touch a bite until the white men had begun, presumably for fear the food might be poisoned. They then grabbed at beef and bread with ravenous enthusiasm. When they could hold no more, they prepared to leave.

At this moment, the rare camaraderie of the day was shattered. Through his interpreter, Spotted Tail demanded that he and his men be given all the flour and beef they could carry. Their host said he didn't mind how much food they ate there, but they couldn't take the larder with them. The chief grew angry. "He threatened," according to Lockwood, "to come over some night with three thousand warriors and clean us out."

"You tell him what I'm saying," shouted the foreman to the interpreter. Then, reported young Lockwood, he flourished a fist under Spotted Tail's nose and swore "a string of oaths such as I never heard before."

The chief seemed unshaken. He made no reply, but swung onto his pony and led his band off at a gallop.

"That was the last we ever saw of them—they had seen the guns," [19] wrote Lockwood. "However, fearing they might return, we doubled our night patrol for some weeks."

Not long afterward, the tracklayers advanced into country of a subtly changed character. Sand hills angled up from the south toward the line of railroad grading, and brought the horizon closer on the north. General

Dodge one day was making a periodic inspection of the work at the front. Indians suddenly boiled out of the southern hills, 10 miles behind him, and captured a solitary freight train, temporarily stalled for lack of steampower. They set fire to the cars and were about to leave the scene, with the train crew as prisoners. At this juncture, Dodge, summoned by the frantic telegraph operator at a station within distant view of the blazing train, came racing back down the track on a one-car special with twenty volunteer riflemen. As soon as the train could be halted, the general and his men hit the ground and deployed as skirmishers. As they commenced firing, the Indians promptly abandoned their badly frightened captives and turned their ponies toward the hills at a dead run.

This happened under a fierce August sun, in a period of prolonged drought.

"We are nearly burned up with the heat and choked with the dust," Sam Reed wrote to his family on August 18th. "No rain since the first of July." [20] There was not much news, he continued, but General Sherman was in Omaha with his staff, bound for the mountains.

Sherman's chief concern that summer was that impetuous frontiersmen would take up arms somewhere in the enormous realm of his military responsibility and precipitate another Indian war, on the scale of the previous year's.

"I would like the frontier States to be somewhat prepared by organized volunteer companies to help us in case of a general combination of Indians, which is not unlikely," he had recently confided by letter to the Governor of Kansas, "but it will not do to let the people of any one locality draw us all into such a war." [21]

Sherman was on his way to inspect the principal outposts of his vast command, the Division of the Missouri, and spread this cautious doctrine along the route. His brother, Senator John Sherman, was going to travel with him as far as Denver, and then return to the East alone.

The Sioux had already killed a few whites along the Powder and Tongue Rivers, in Montana, within recent weeks. But General Sherman, despite his mercurial temper and impatient disposition, was wary of retaliating with his present strength.

We are in no condition to punish the Indians this year [he wrote from Omaha to Gen. John A. Rawlins, the Army's chief of staff, on August 17th]. Our troops are barely able to hold the long thin lines that are traveled by daily stages and small parties of emigrants. By next year this railroad [the U.P.] will enable us to put a regiment of cavalry at Ft. Laramie, which can punish the Indians, who are evidently disposed to contest our right to make roads leading to Montana.[22]

The reason the Sioux were so disposed was that they had a treaty with the United States that guaranteed part of that region to them exclusively. Once gold had been discovered there, however, the government was powerless to hold back the swarm of goldseekers that headed into Montana. When they yelled for protection, the Army began to build a string of forts along the Bozeman Trail. The Indians' resentment of this treaty violation was rising toward an explosion in December of 1866.

Sherman had ordered up a regiment of Negro troops from Arkansas to reinforce General Cooke's command, he told Rawlins, but they were now quarantined with cholera at St. Louis. Cooke would just have to do the best he could with what forces he had until the following spring.

Cooke, already apprised of this bleak situation, had thought the best way to make up for his own lack of reinforcement was to deprive potentially hostile Indians of their chief source of arms. On July 31st he had issued a general order to all Indian agents within the territory of his Department of the Platte to stop selling weapons and ammunition. In addition, he gave his post commanders orders to "take vigilant and decisive measures" [23] to see to it that nobody either sold or gave guns or cartridges to any Indian, hostile or friendly.

The agents, most of whom were "political party adventurers and speculators, without conscience or principles," [24] as Secretary of the Navy Welles observed, almost unanimously defied Cooke's order. They were licensed by the Department of Interior's Bureau of Indian Affairs. They insisted that the Army had no right to tell them what they could or couldn't do. With perilous irresponsibility, they continued to peddle arms to all Indians whom they considered peaceful. This was in accordance with the bureau's policy that its wards should be allowed weapons with which to hunt game and keep themselves alive. The Army indignantly protested that any warrior was capable of pretending to be friendly long enough to acquire a rifle and cartridges. Besides, the military declared, Indians were quite able to shoot all the game they needed with bows and arrows.

The dangerous cleavage between Indian agents and military men in the territories merely reflected a longstanding struggle in Washington. The War Department had been obliged to turn over the administration of Indian relations to the Department of the Interior in 1849. Practically ever since, it had been trying to regain its lost control. Each time the question came up again for a vote in Congress, the Interior Department was sustained, though usually by a slim margin. Now that the Army was in open conflict with many tribesmen on the Plains and in the foothills of the Rockies, the opposing policy of the Bureau of Indian Affairs became seriously subversive. This was the only war in American history, as someone has remarked, in which the War Department's active enemy was given aid and comfort by the Interior Department.

From the Army's point of view, the situation would soon grow worse. In July, 1866, James Harlan resigned as Secretary of the Interior, in disagreement with President Johnson. In September his place would be taken by Orville Hickman Browning, a deeply religious humanitarian from Illinois, with a paradoxical fondness for florid clothes. Browning disliked and distrusted General Grant, and his hostile, suspicious attitude came to embrace the entire Army, Grenville Dodge, and the Union Pacific. Browning took very seriously his official guardianship of the American Indian.

General Sherman regarded with equal earnestness his responsibility to protect white settlers, travelers, and railroad builders from Indian attack. On August 17th he was about to set forth from Omaha to find out for himself what needed to be done to accomplish that mission. He had already had a reunion, he wrote General Rawlins that morning, with "our friend General Dodge," who, as usual, "was possessed of every possible piece of information that is desirable." Sherman was full of admiration at what Dodge had already accomplished for the Union Pacific. Its progress, he declared, "surpasses everything in the way of rapid construction I have ever known." [25]

Dodge had told Sherman that he then had enough rails and ties on hand to build 100 miles of track beyond the present end of the line. That, he said, was the way he intended to maintain the situation, with always enough material available to build 100 miles of railroad in spite of any interruption in supply.

Tracklaying parties are so organized [Sherman explained to Rawlins], that he [Dodge] intends to go right along, and doubts not that he will reach a point on the North Fork of the Platte, two miles above the junction, this fall. There he proposes to cross by a bridge the North Fork of the Platte and follow the valley of the South Fork up as far as Julesburg, or Fort Sedgwick, by April of next year. This will be a great achievement, but perfectly feasible when we see what has been done. . . .

I am perfectly satisfied that this road is in excellent hands, and I propose to give them all the protection and encouragement we can.[26]

The next morning, General Dodge placed a special train at Sherman's disposal and rode with him and his staff to the end of track, then 190 miles west of Omaha. There they found Jack Casement's men spiking down rails within a short distance of Fort Kearny, where the American flag hung limp in the August heat above a square stockade nearly 5 miles south of the railroad, on the opposite side of the Platte. Sherman was not impressed by the perils that the U.P.'s construction forces reputedly faced. "As usual," he wrote to the Chief of Staff on August 21st, "I find the size of Indian stampedes and stories diminishes as I approach their location." On the other hand, "there is a general apprehension of danger, though no one seems to have a definite idea of whence it is to come. I have met a few straggling parties of Indians who seemed to be pure beggars, and, poor devils, more to be pitied than dreaded." [27]

By the end of August, Sherman was at Fort Laramie, at the north end of Wyoming's Black Hills, having a parley with a few of the older Sioux and Arapaho chieftains. Through an interpreter, they agreed with him that there should be no more bloodshed between their race and his. However, they pointed out, their young men were rash and hot-tempered, hard to restrain.

"Well, then," Sherman said sharply to the interpreter, his anger igniting, "tell the rascals, so are *my* young men. And if another white man is scalped in all this region, it will be *impossible* to hold *mine* in." [28]

The meeting ended peaceably enough, though, and left Sherman in a compassionate mood. Writing about the Indians to General Rawlins on August 31st, from Fort Laramie, he said:

All the Sioux have been driven west from Minnesota and the Missouri River, and the mountain region of Montana, Colorado, and Utah is being settled up with gold miners and ranchers, so that poor Indian finds himself hemmed in. The Indian agents over on the Missouri tell him to come over here for hunting, and from here he is turned to some other quarter, and so the poor devil naturally wriggles against his doom.[29]

Sherman had set out on this tour of inspection with the suspicion that Indian alarms were mostly manufactured by frontier settlers with surplus produce on their hands. If their outcries succeeded in summoning troops to their aid, they could then sell them grain, corn, milk, livestock, vegetables, fruit, and wood at inflated prices.

That fall, he returned to his headquarters at St. Louis with his suspicion grown into a conviction. He wrote his brother John on October 20th:

I got back all safe and well the day before yesterday, having met no trouble whatever, notwithstanding the many rumors of Indian troubles. These are all mysterious, and only accountable on the supposition that our people out West are resolved on trouble for the sake of the profit resulting from military occupation.[30]

Bloodcurdling news from Wyoming would soon force him to change his mind.

On December 21st, near Fort Phil Kearny, on the upper reaches of the North Platte, an overeager cavalry officer named Capt. W. J. Fetterman led eighty-one men into an Indian ambush. More than 2,000 waiting Sioux, Arapahoes, and Cheyennes overwhelmed the soldiers, killing them all and then indulging in an orgy of mutilation.

This horror, taking place only 60 miles north of the projected track, U.P. rekindled in a flash the Army's war with the Plains Indians. It led inevitably to the sequence of clashes between railroadmen and Indians that would make the year to come the most tragic in Union Pacific history.

While General Sherman was enjoying his disarming inspection of the Indian country in 1866, however, the immediate future of the railroad seemed bright indeed.

Durant was savoring the prospect to the full. His horses, declared the New York *Tribune's* slim, fastidious roving correspondent, Albert D. Richardson, were

the envy of Central Park, and his yacht was the admiration of the New York Yacht Club. I have seen him entertain a party of ladies and gentlemen upon it, down the bay, through an entire afternoon, as if he had not a care in the world beyond the comfort of his guests; and at one o'clock say nonchalantly, "Well, goodbye, I must go ashore; I have a million of dollars to pay before three o'clock. Have your sail out, and don't return till you get ready."

Meanwhile, he was working like a galley slave. Sometimes he was hardly in bed for a week; again he would spend nights and Sundays upon the yacht for the quiet and the cool air. Narcotics and stimulants were avoided that he might keep his brain clear. He plunged into the controversies in the Company with characteristic energy, and I fancy there were times when he could not have told whether the next turn of the wheel would leave him worth a few millions or a few millions worse than nothing.[31]

In September, having turned away from the fascinating spectacle of Durant, Bert Richardson looked in on Omaha's expanding economy. He found Nebraska's capital city, with its white state house crowning a mile-long slope down to the chocolate Missouri, "the liveliest city in the United States." [32] He admired the immense brick carshop that the Union Pacific had built, and the adjacent locomotive roundhouse and machine shops. He was told that several hundred new buildings had been put up in the city during the past summer. The sidewalks were teeming with discharged soldiers, disappointed gold miners, farmers peddling their crops, gamblers, Pawnees. New streets were being graded. The U.P., he heard, was spending locally about $250,000 a month.

Richardson, solemn in dress and looks but a genial companion over wine and cigars, rode out to the end of the rails, then 240 miles west. He traveled in elegance with the government commissioners. He was struck by the fact that one section of the track was perfectly straight for 40 miles —"a good place for studying perspective." [33] Most of all, he felt grateful, having previously made the trip to Fort Kearny seven times by wagon or stagecoach, that the railroad was there to travel on at last, straight or crooked.

The reporter and his companions enlivened their trip by shooting at antelope from the car windows. Richardson marveled at the speed with which Casement's army was lengthening the track. What impressed him most about his visit, however, was George Francis Train. That curious crony of Durant's, a promoter, lobbyist, and kind of court jester for the Union Pacific, looked as if he might be a professional magician. He was a tall, dark, wiry man with pointed beard, extravagantly curly hair, and a large, sharp nose. Having given the Credit Mobilier its flossy name, Train had now created a companion enterprise and christened it Credit Foncier. Its purpose was to deal in real estate, to create cities along the line of the Union Pacific. Nebraska's Territorial Legislature had granted the Credit Foncier a charter that, as Richardson drily remarked, gave it "nearly every power imaginable, save that of reconstructing the late rebel States." [34]

Already it was putting up cottages at Omaha, and especially at Columbus, 100 miles out along the U.P. track, which Train vowed would someday become the new capital of the United States.

Train, a fey creature of stupendous schemes, talked torrents about them and left Richardson's ears ringing with his enthusiasm. The newspaperman shook his head over this man "who might have built the Pyramids, or been confined in a straight jacket for eccentricities." [35] Even Train recognized himself as somewhat excessive in everything. However, he confided to Richardson, now that he was making money, people no longer considered him crazy.

In September the summer's long drought was broken. On the twenty-third, Sam Reed worriedly wrote his wife that "unless the rain ceases soon, we cannot get to the end of the line." [36] This concerned him all the more because he had just had unsettling news from Train. Durant was planning a party. The track would soon reach that long-significant geographical position, the 100th Meridian, 247 miles west of Omaha. Durant felt a swelling need to celebrate.

Train had told Reed that the event was planned to take place sometime in October. "I hope that there will be but few in the party," [37] Reed confessed to his wife. He had little patience with any inspection that wasn't essential.

Reed should have known Durant better. This was going to be the most elaborate affair that any American railroad had ever held to commemorate a stint of tracklaying, if Durant could make it so. He had begun, grandly enough, by inviting President Andrew Johnson and his whole Cabinet, every member of Congress, all foreign diplomatic representatives in Washington, top Army and Navy officers, and leading railroad officials and financiers from the East and Midwest.

Durant's buckshot approach didn't bring down quite the bag of guests he had hoped for. Still, he had some impressive trophies among the two hundred finally assembled at Omaha on October 22nd. In the gathering were a future President of the United States, Representative Rutherford B. Hayes, of Ohio, and a late President's son, Robert T. Lincoln. Also on hand were that powerful and vindictive senator, Benjamin F. Wade of Ohio, and Senator James W. Patterson of New Hampshire, as well as a covey of representatives. Scotland's Earl of Airlie, with a jaunty feather in his tam-o-shanter and Dundreary whiskers adorning his cheeks, and France's tall, long-bearded Marquis de Chambrun, a Lafayette descendant in a derby, gave the inspection party a rare social tone. Domestic bigwigs included George M. Pullman, who had provided "a magnificent train of Palace Sleeping Cars" [38] for most of the guests to ride in over the C. B. & Q.; Joseph Medill, publisher of the Chicago *Tribune*; and John Crerar, one of that city's wealthiest manufacturers. Five members of the Union Pacific's board of directors, headed by Durant, were present. They included Sidney Dillon of New York, newly elected to the board but already a notably successful developer of railroads. Dillon, a large, well-tailored man of fifty-four, whose gravely handsome face was framed by flourishing sideburns, was by far the most distinguished-looking executive involved in the building of the first transcontinental railroad.

Most of the guests who had come from the East had traveled on three different railroads to reach Chicago, and ridden on two more to get from there to St. Joseph. When they reached the Missouri, they boarded the *Denver* and the *Colorado*, two of the river's biggest steamers, for one of the most festive and overfed voyages ever made from St. Joseph to Omaha.

At Omaha, on only two days' advance notice from Durant, General Dodge had rounded up enough Army tents, blankets, and bedding to assure the visitors three comfortable nights on the prairie. However, Durant's shopping list for the expedition also included a welcoming banquet and ball; buffalo, antelope, ponies, and guides for a hunt; an encampment of picturesque but friendly Indians; and an abundance of game to eat.[39]

Those travelers who were not dyspeptic by the time they had finished their banquet at the Herndon House on October 22nd must have flinched before the meals served to them on the rail journey that began the next morning. Dodge later wrote that "what game we had not killed, we invented." [40]

Dodge, the Casements, Webster Snyder, and Hoxie ran the show for Durant. Reed, with probably small regret, escaped the party he had deplored by taking to his bed with typhoid fever, the frequent scourge of those less sanitary days.

For window dressing, Durant had urged Dodge to set up as many locomotives as possible, and arrange them conspicuously. Two pulled the nine-car excursion train over the grades to the Platte Valley. From there on, the eight-wheeler Idaho, trimmed with flags, mottoes, and a pair of antlers, easily hauled the railroad's guests out to the end of the line and back. The engine's pace was deliberately indolent, to enable the travelers to see whatever there was to see.

The U.P.'s splendid new directors' car, built for it in the Pittsburgh, Fort Wayne, and Chicago R.R. shops, rode at the rear of the train. This had been reserved for members of Congress and other distinguished guests. Ahead of it was the Lincoln car, which Durant had selected for himself, family, and close friends. Four of the railroad's entire stock of five first-class passenger cars were included in the train. A mail car had been converted into a bar car. There was a "cooking car," as Colonel Seymour called it, and, farthest front, a car for baggage and supplies.

Dodge had arranged with that highly valued aide of his '65 campaign, Major North, to assemble fifty or sixty of his most dependable Pawnee warriors at Columbus. There the travelers spent the first night out, occupying a huge circular encampment brightly lighted by torches and bonfires. The Pawnees staged a war dance after supper. Then, with Dodge leading them, they sneaked back into the sleeping camp at three o'clock the next morning and put on a mock raid. This was almost too sensational. Dodge had to make a hasty round of the tent circle, assuring panicky guests that it was all in fun.[41]

The next day, the excursion train traveled as far as Willow Island, across the Platte from Fort McPherson, 279 miles west of Omaha. At the start, the cars halted long enough for their passengers to watch Pawnees whoop into a sham fight with other Pawnees, dressed as Sioux, beside the little Loup River. Late in the afternoon, the train stopped again, this time for group photographs near an ornate "100th Meridian" milepost, which Dodge had had set up.

That night, after some vaudeville acts and band music, the Union Pacific's exhausted guests were ready to go straight to bed. They felt secure from Indian attack, for across the river burned the campfires of a company of solders sent out from the fort especially to spend the night within reassuring view of the excursionists.

On the morning of the third day, October 25th, Durant offered his guests the choice of a buffalo-or-antelope hunt or a ride to the very end of the rails, 10 miles beyond, to watch Jack Casement's fast-moving Irishmen lay track. Both groups enjoyed themselves thoroughly, and after a long day in the crisp air were even eager for one more game dinner that night. A band concert and fireworks followed.

The train headed back for Omaha the following day, stopping only for wood and water and to permit its riders to make a fascinated inspection of the vast prairie-dog colony near Fort Kearny.

Durant saved his final dazzler for nightfall, just before the returning train curved eastward out of the Platte Valley toward the Missouri. There, with a gesture worthy of Louis XV, he had arranged in advance to have the prairie set afire—at a safe distance, of course. The line of leaping flames lighted the sky for 20 miles as the cars approached from the west.

Nobody who took this trip ever forgot it, and the Union Pacific garnered an immense amount of publicity as a result. "It must have cost a great deal of money," General Dodge wrote, but the stunt paid off. "The result of the trip was the negotiation of some of our bonds." [42]

There was an intangible result of far greater significance.

One year ago, the great Union Pacific Railroad was regarded as a myth [wrote Colonel Seymour to *The New York Times*], and the men engaged in and controlling it, as a set of stock-jobbing Wall-street speculators. Today, it is known and felt to be a power and a reality; and Mr. Durant and his associates are believed to be in earnest, and fully capable of carrying out to successful completion the mammoth work which they have undertaken. [43]

The Union Pacific's first president, Gen. John Adams Dix, wouldn't be around to see the job completed, though. In the fall of 1866, he was confronted with a dilemma. Contentedly settled in the incongruous government position of Naval Officer of the Port of New York, and presiding as the U.P.'s figurehead as well, Dix was suddenly offered the appointment of United States Minister to the Court of Napoleon III.

While he was thinking it over, Oakes Ames dropped in to tell him that the railroad's directors unanimously urged him to take the appointment, and keep his U.P. job, too. In fact, Dix recalled, "he added, with a distinctness I have never forgotten, that it was their wish to have me remain in France to the end of Mr. Johnson's administration." [44] His representing the railroad as well as the United States would help make the U.P. favorably known abroad, Ames had declared. This would be most useful if foreign loans were sought.

General Dix was persuaded, though somewhat regretfully. With a sigh at having to give up his naval sinecure, he sailed for France on November 24th. Oakes Ames' brother, Oliver, was named acting president of the Union Pacific.

A dilemma somewhat similar to Dix's had faced General Dodge that same month. The nation's biennial Election Day was November 6th. One of its unexpected results was Dodge's election to the House of Representatives from Iowa. He had been nominated in the spring by Republican war veterans in his district, but had paid so little attention to the campaign that he even forgot about Election Day. He was first reminded of it, far out in the field with surveyors, by the telegraphed news of his victory.

His subsequent service to Iowa's Fifth Congressional District was rather less than dedicated. Though the Congress to which he had been elected convened for the first time on March 4, 1867, the tormenting problems that the Union Pacific encountered that year kept Dodge away from Washington from the end of March until December 2nd, when the second session began.

By late fall of 1866 the U.P. surveyors' reports were all in.

James Evans had proved beyond question that Dodge's accidentally discovered divide between Lone Tree and Crow Creeks was by far the best place for the railroad to cross Wyoming's Black Hills. Along that amiable ridge, the sedimentary rock of the plains met the eroding granite of the mountain range at practically the same altitude. The slope could be climbed at a rate of rise no greater than 90 feet to the mile. Everywhere else that Evans and his men had looked along the east base of the Black Hills, in the course of three years of hunting, they had found discrepancies in height between plain and mountain that ranged from 500 feet to as much as 1,500 feet in a mile. Now that this blessed ridge had been found, a barrier that had loomed menacingly in the minds of the U.P. planners from the start of their enterprise shrank suddenly to proportions that were not frightening at all.

Dodge emphatically recommended that the Evans Pass route, as he called it, with agreeable modesty, be chosen the official Union Pacific route between Nebraska and the Laramie Plains of Wyoming. The railroad's directors obliged him by vote on November 23rd.

Percy Browne's explorations in the Rockies back of Denver had persisted until a furious early September snowstorm drove him out. He reported, and Dodge agreed, that there was no possible railroad route through the Front Range that could compare with the "shorter, cheaper, better grades" [45] already selected in Wyoming. Denver was definitely not to lie on the Union Pacific's main line. It would be reached by a branch track, leaving the main line at a point 112 miles north—the site of the future city of Cheyenne.

L. L. Hills had located the route the railroad would take westward from the fork in the Platte, along the north side of the South Platte, to the mouth of Lodge Pole Creek, near Julesburg, Colorado.

When a blizzard chased Browne out of the Rockies, Dodge assigned him to selecting a line for 105 miles up Lodge Pole Creek to connect with Evans' route over the Black Hills. The Lodge Pole provided a natural pathway almost straight west between the diverging courses of the South and North Platte Rivers.

From the California-Nevada border, on November 3rd, Thomas Bates wrote that though it would not be impossible for the Union Pacific to run through Salt Lake City and then northwestward across 42 miles of salt desert, it would be far better for it to go around the head of Great Salt Lake and then west to Humboldt Wells. From there on to California, the obvious route, he said, would be that of the Humboldt and Truckee Rivers.

It began to look as if Salt Lake City, as well as Denver, might have to be reached by a branch line.

After snow and cold had made further field work unfeasible, one small group of U.P. surveyors settled down, at Dodge's orders, to share "a comfortable log house" with their livestock for the winter at Dale Creek, Wyoming. This place was on the westward slope of the Black Hills, nearly 8,000 feet above sea level. Dodge had told the men to run trial lines across the Laramie Plains on good days, but most of the time they were to observe and record the vagaries of the weather. Dodge wanted to know what the Union Pacific would be up against when it began operating trains over the Black Hills in winter.

He couldn't have chosen a better time for this test. The winter of 1866–67 turned out to be terrible.

At the beginning of November, the triangle of land that lay in the fork of the Platte, 290 miles from Omaha, had no inhabitants but prairie dogs. Three weeks later, the burgeoning town of North Platte stood there, with a population of 1,000 people. The railroad entered it across a low, pile-trestle bridge, more than a third of a mile long, over the reedy North Platte River, where whooping cranes gathered in spring.

Here the Casements soon established their first winter headquarters in the field—prefabricated warehouse, bunkhouse, mess hall, and general store. The various sections of these buildings were all numbered, thus making it an easy matter to take them apart and put them together again when it was time to move to a new location. Almost all of North Platte was prefabricated, in fact. In turn, it formed parts of a series of temporary towns that expanded and contracted along the way as the Union Pacific's track pushed on toward its meeting with the Central Pacific's.

The lure of accumulated cash and youthful high spirits attracted whiskey peddlers, saloonkeepers, gamblers, prostitutes, and confidence men to these places in droves. With their encouragement, General Casement's army spent its leisure hours in such an orgiastic manner that the temporary towns quickly came to be called "hells on wheels."

North Platte was the first of these ephemeral communities. In the winter of 1866–67 it did its best to be the most sinful. Its merry population began to gather in November, for the extremely severe weather that was to follow had already made its approach felt. There had been a blizzard in the vicinity on November 13th.

"When the day broke," wrote Arthur N. Ferguson, a solemn young law student from Omaha who was working with a U.P. surveying outfit a few miles west of North Platte,

I raised my head above the blankets and discovered that we were covered with snow—snow on our bedding, snow inside the tent in places a foot or so deep—while outside the energies of the Storm King were unabated. When we rose, which was late, on account of the intense cold, our camp presented a scene of desolation. Three tents were completely blown to the ground, the stock sheeted with snow. And the men hovering around a fire which they had built on the floor of the cook's quarters. Here the men were grouped together, standing with their feet in the water which the heat of the fire had causd, their eyes red and swollen by smoke, and their every energy bent upon securing what little warmth it was possible to get.[46]

The next morning, the South Platte was nearly frozen over, and track-layers and graders were retreating toward North Platte. "I think the line will be almost deserted in a few days," Arthur Ferguson wrote in his journal that cold day, "as winter has about commenced in earnest." [47]

There was a brief return to mild temperatures after this, but tracklaying for 1866 stopped altogether in December. By Christmas, the rails stretched to O'Fallons Bluffs, a pioneer landmark 305 miles west of Omaha, where low sand hills shouldered up against the roadbed from the north. The Casements' men had built 265 miles of railroad in nine months. In one spectacular month, they had laid 65 miles of track. In a single day, they had set a new record by spiking down 3 miles of rails.

CHAPTER ELEVEN

ORDEAL IN THE SNOW

One of the Central Pacific's tunnel-builders was an engineer with a rare eye for beauty. Despite the savage storms that assaulted the Sierra in the first four months of 1867, making of railroad construction a formidable daily battle with weather as well as with stubborn rock, John R. Gilliss found there were occasional moments of tranquil glory.

Such moments might come during one of those infrequent nights when the wind was not roaring through Donner Pass, hiding everything beyond an arm's length with flying snow. Then "the scene was strangely beautiful," wrote Engineer Gilliss. He had viewed it from the wagon road that was the supply line of Crocker's army, 500 or 600 feet below the Chinese gangs hacking through the granite roots of Crested Peak.

The tall firs [he recalled], though drooping under their heavy burdens, pointed to the mountains that overhung them, where the fires that lit seven tunnels shone like stars on their snowy sides. The only sound that came down to break the stillness of the winter night was the sharp ring of hammer on steel, or the heavy reports of the blasts.[1]

Moments like these seldom occurred.

One member of the engineering crew that worked through that harrowing winter with the tunnel gangs kept a thorough record of its weather changes. There were forty-four storms. They varied from a squall that dusted the landscape with a quarter-inch of snow to a fantastic blizzard that lasted thirteen days.

The biggest storm of all began at two o'clock in the afternoon of February 18th. Snow fell without interruption until ten o'clock in the evening of February 22nd. By then, the fresh fall had added 6 feet to the previous level. Though the snowflakes now petered out for a time, the wind did not. It raged on for the next five days, heaping up huge drifts. It blew so violently that it tore heavy branches from the pines, and filled the air with such a turmoil of snow that it was impossible for men and animals to face it.

The engineers lived in rough wooden quarters at the eastern end of Donner Pass, where the cleft in the mountain walls was narrowest. There was a big warehouse within 30 feet of their upper windows, yet it often disappeared completely behind torrents of snowflakes.

Three of these men, with their backs to the pummeling gale, stumbled through the Pass toward their shelter one evening during this storm. Screaming wind shut out all other sounds. Pelting snow made it difficult for the men to open their eyes. Though always close together, they were but vaguely aware of one another. Two of them finally found the way to their door, but for several anxious minutes afterward the third man failed to follow. Just as they were bundling up again to begin a search for him, the door was flung open, and he collapsed at their feet. "In a short, straight path between two walls of rock," John Gilliss wrote, "he had lost his way and thought his last hour had come." [2]

After five days of unrelenting gale, a new mass of damp air moved in from the Pacific. Snow began falling again, and persisted until March 2nd, when the historic blizzard finally blew itself out. It had added 10 feet to the level of the snow pack. It had raised drifts so high that at the eastern approach to the Summit Tunnel, the Chinese had to lengthen their snow tunnel 50 feet in order to get to work inside the mountain.

Though the winter's forty-four storms varied widely in force and duration, their pattern was invariable. They began with a drop in the barometer reading and the onset of a strong wind from the southwest, filling the sky with hurrying cloud masses. The temperature at the start was usually around 20 degrees above zero. As a rule, it slowly rose during the course of the storm, until, at the end, it was 32. The finale was normally wet and heavy. Often the snow turned to freezing rain. Then the wind whipped around to the east, scattering the clouds and lowering the temperature drastically. After one storm it fell close to zero.

There were snowstorms across the crest of the Sierra every month from November, 1866, through May, 1867. The average depth of snow on the level was 5 feet in December. It rose to 8 feet in January, 10 in February, 12½ in March, and 13 in April. The winter's total snowfall in that region was 44 feet, 7¾ inches. Even in June, the snow was still 3 feet deep in Donner Pass.

The Chinese lived almost entirely out of sight of the sky that winter. Their shacks were largely buried in snow. They walked to and from work through snow tunnels. They endured long, gruelling shifts underground in a dim, dank world of smoky lights, ear-ringing explosions, and choking dust.

Twenty of them were killed in a single snowslide, a swift, silent burial of their house and themselves in it. Many other individuals, from time to time, simply disappeared, caught in small avalanches that no one else had happened to see when they occurred. Their frozen bodies were found in the spring, often upright in the melting drifts, with shovels or picks still gripped in their hands.

In one of the workmen's camps, snow covered the crude houses entirely. The men inside had first to dig their way to the roof, then cut steps from there to the surface of the drift. The blockade lasted for a couple of weeks, and for part of that time these men had nothing left to eat but cornmeal and tea. "Had it lasted a week longer," declared one of them, "we would have been compelled to eat horse meat, for there were 200 men or more in this camp." [3]

The dwellings had been so hastily constructed that snow sifted through wide cracks in the walls every time the wind blew. One of the engineers said that whenever he returned to his shack, he had to shovel it out before he could enter.

Slides were frequent. The men were working along steep slopes that faced generally northeast. Since the storm winds invariably blew from the southwest, they formed great, overhanging brows of snow above the men and their camps. Often, these brows collapsed of their own increasing weight at the wet conclusion of a storm and slumped into the valley, like icebergs crumbling from a glacier's edge.

The snow tunnels through which the Chinese commuted developed into a remarkable labyrinth. The arched corridors in many places were wide enough to allow two-horse sleds to move through them freely. Some of the tunnels were 200 feet long, and led to dumps where the sleds could deposit broken rock from the constant blasting. The ceilings tended to settle as more snow fell on top of the drifts, but additional headroom was casually scooped out as it was needed.

At the approach of spring, some of the men were set to burrowing through the snow for another purpose. Work had been begun the previous fall on the foundation of an enormous retaining wall that would support an earth fill to be heaped across the ravine between Tunnels Nos. 7 and 8. Strobridge now had men start a couple of hundred feet down the ravine and dig several snow tunnels in toward the unfinished foundation, which lay under drifts 50 feet deep. Some of the tunnels were used to haul out quarried rock, which needed to be cut before it could help form the foundation wall. At the inner end of the main tunnel, a lofty, wide cave was hollowed out of the snow bank. There, stone masons began to build a culvert, 5 feet high and 4 feet wide, to carry a small stream through the future wall and embankment. When the culvert was finished, 25 to 30 feet of snow still hung above the masons' heads.

Along the Dutch Flat & Donner Lake Wagon Road, that exhausting and perilous winter, the teamsters who brought up supplies from the end of track and kept materials moving to the graders east of the snows had the toughest struggle with the weather. They and their unfortunate oxen, flinching under the pistol-shot snaps of bull whips, were usually out breaking a path through the steadily rising snow from beginning to end of every storm. Often gales and driven flakes immediately hid whatever progress they had made, but the men persisted with amazing vigor and courage.

At first on snowshoes, the teamsters floundered up to their shoulders in some fresh falls of snow. Later, they took to skis, which they called "Norwegian snowshoes," and were able to get about more readily.

Their oxen were far less lucky. The poor beasts would wallow in the deep, light snow until so exhausted that they fell, coughing and gasping. The men gave them scant time to rest, but spurred them back to work by twisting their tails until they bellowed with pain and scrambled to their feet. Engineer Gilliss, a man with a softer heart than the teamsters', noted thankfully that several oxen had had their tails twisted clean off, and thus were free forevermore from this agonizing treatment.

West of the Summit, while snow choked the railroad's lifeline beyond the end of track at Cisco, the storms did drastic damage. About 2 miles below Cisco stood a trestle 100 feet high. On a slope above it lay a small lake. The rains of the previous fall had raised the lake to its brim before winter set in. As the year 1867 began, an unusually heavy snowstorm put an intolerable strain on the dam at the foot of the lake. It suddenly collapsed. A thunderous surge of water rushed down the ravine beneath the dam and carried away the whole center section of the trestle.

The bridge had to be repaired as fast as possible. But snow lay 15 feet deep in the woods. Loggers and oxen fought their way through it and hauled in huge trees. Swarms of lumbermen whipsawed them into shape for company carpenters. By February 4th, trains were crossing the trestle once more, with heavy loads of rails and track hardware for the 3,000 track-builders 40 miles away on the Truckee.

It was at this time that the Central Pacific's high command made the costly but unavoidable decision to put a roof over the entire length of track that led through the deepest part of the snow belt. Though the expense, testified Arthur Brown, superintendent of bridges and buildings, "was almost appalling, and unprecedented in railroad construction, yet there seemed to be no alternative." [4]

Vice-President Huntington was especially pained by the inescapable new financial burden. "It costs a fearful amount of money to pay all the bills," he protested to Hopkins. "I sometimes think," he added, "I would change my place for any other in this world." [5]

Nevertheless, work began in the summer of 1867 on a line of snowsheds that eventually covered a total of 37 miles of Central Pacific track, subjecting locomotive engineers to "railroading in a barn," as one of them disgustedly called it.

During the summer of 1867, carpenters roofed about 5 miles of sheds. The construction was not continuous, except on one stretch of half a mile. The rest was spotted along the line below and above Cisco wherever the track ran through a deep cut. It was in such places that the railroad had had the most trouble getting through during the winter.

Early in 1867, dismayed by the slow progress their tunnel crews were making through granite walls by blasting with gunpowder, Crocker and

Strobridge decided to risk using nitroglycerin again. This time, however, they brought in the separate ingredients—glycerin and nitric and sulphuric acids—and hired James Howden, a Scottish chemist, to mix them where they were to be used. Mr. Howden's brew, widely feared at first by the workmen, was a yellow liquid, light and oily. He made up a fresh batch each day, and estimated that it cost only 75 cents a pound.

Engineer Gilliss reported that the new explosive was eight times as powerful as powder. By February 9th it was in use in all four headings of the Summit Tunnel. At once, though the gangs of Chinese were not increased in size, there was a noticeable spurt in the pace of tunneling. With gunpowder, the men had averaged only a bit more than a foot of progress a day in the headings, and 2½ feet in clearing out the rock that remained in the bottoms. With nitroglycerin, they speeded up to nearly 2 feet a day in the headings, and more than 4 feet in the bottoms.

It was immediately obvious that there were other advantages to nitroglycerin. It worked best in holes only an inch and a quarter in diameter. Powder had required 2½-inch holes, and more of them. After a nitroglycerin blast, a tunnel cleared of smoke faster than when powder was exploded in it. In wet rock, where gunpowder was useless, the remarkable new "blasting oil" worked like a charm. Furthermore, rock debris from its explosions was usually so fine that it didn't need further breaking up. Powder didn't do as thorough a job.

The usual blasting procedure was to drill holes 15 to 18 inches deep, and pour nitroglycerin into them until they were nearly full. If the rock was dry, each hole was plugged with a wad of hay, peppered with powder. One end of the fuse was nested in the powder and held in place with sand. In wet rock, a tin cartridge about 4 inches long, filled with powder, stoppered each holeful of nitroglycerin. A waterproof fuse protruded from the can.

As the Chinese grew more accustomed to handling Mr. Howden's daily concoction, they lost their fear of it and became careless. As an inevitable result, wrote one of the engineers, "many an honest John went to China feet first." [6]

Before the Summit Tunnel was finished, late in November, 1867, there had been two especially drastic accidents. "Those would have happened with powder," [7] John Gilliss calmly observed. But Charlie Crocker had had enough. "Bury that stuff," [8] he ordered.

A little had been used to pep up work on Tunnel No. 8, but almost all of it had been exploded in excavating the Summit Tunnel. After that was ready, the Central Pacific never used another drop of nitroglycerin.

At dawn on May 17th, Brig. Gen. James F. Rusling, of the Army's Quartermaster Department, swung aboard a C.P. train at Sacramento, bound for the mountains and beyond. Rusling was nearing the end of a year-long field trip, in which he had been inspecting every Army post in the Far West. The day was hot and humid.

There was an appreciable change in the air as the cars "plunged into the foothills." By noon, when they reached Cisco, the chill was no longer refreshing. "We were shivering in winter garments," wrote the general.

The railroad, so far as it went, had impressed him greatly. He and his companions were surprised that it was so well built, and awed by its "audacity."

"Some of its grades were over a hundred feet to the mile," Rusling observed, "and in many places it literally springs into the air, over immense trestle-work bridges or along the dizzy edges of precipices that seem fraught with peril and destruction." [9]

The general and his party were rather relieved to reach Cisco safe and sound, and to be able to sit down to a hot dinner. Outside, snow still reached to the eaves of the hotel.

Cisco, a cluster of shabby frame buildings, was only a few months old and had a raw look. It was throbbing with business, however. Here the Overland Mail met the daily passenger train from Sacramento, and left shortly afterward for Virginia City and points east. Most supplies for Nevada's chief mining towns now traveled this way, being transferred from freight cars to wagons at Cisco. Everything needed by the thousands of C.P. employees down the Truckee valley came through here.

After dinner on May 17th, General Rusling and staff climbed into stage-coaches—"mountain mud-wagons," he called them—and headed up the road toward Donner Pass. The sloppy highway at the start was free of snow, but the surrounding countryside was not. The stages lurched along between slowly melting snow banks 6 to 8 feet high. Soon the footing became a mixture of slush, mud, and ice. The travelers were obliged to change to sleighs. "Then came a long and dreary pull . . . for several miles, till we got well across the summit of the Sierras," wrote the general. Though amazed that the snow level was still so high, Rusling remembered that a man in San Francisco had told him that when he had taken this route late in the previous December, even the tops of the telegraph poles had been buried in drifts.

Near the Summit, the Chinese seemed to be everywhere one looked. Rusling was told that 5,000 were at work on the tunnels and approaching grades. He noted that those he saw had their pigtails coiled around their heads, not dangling as they did in San Francisco. Also, except for the blue cotton blouses that all Chinese seemed to wear, they were dressed like any American laborers. Rusling talked to a few of their foremen, whom the engineers called "China herders." "All spoke well of the almond-eyed strangers," he reported, "and praised them especially for their docility and intelligence." [10] That docility would shortly prove to be subject to change.

By June, Crocker and Strobridge had summoned back to the Summit their forces that had been building grade along the Truckee during the winter. Since April, the company's agents had been filtering through the towns of Central California and scouring the entire mining region in search of more Chinese laborers. They marshaled hordes of newcomers from across the Pacific. The Grass Valley *Union* declared that at this rate there would soon be "at least 20,000 of these prospective unbleached American citizens scratching gravel on the great national highway." [11] The grating tone of the *Union* was mild compared to the angry note of anti-Chinese feeling being voiced in San Francisco and in the State Legislature.

The Central Pacific, ignoring the widespread antagonism toward its labor policy, did try to get 20,000 Chinese that season, but fell considerably short of its goal. Still, by mid-June, there were nearly 14,000 at work on the line of grading that lay between Cisco and the Nevada border, 128 miles east of Sacramento. In some places, even this late in the year, 10 to 12 feet of snow had to be shoveled from the route before the men could get at the bare earth with their picks and shovels.

In the last week of June, Crocker and Strobridge were given a shocking surprise. Two thousand Chinese, engaged on the most critical part of the work, the tunnels, went on strike. Placards in their own language suddenly appeared in camp one Saturday morning. At dawn on the following Monday, the tunnel drillers failed to report for work. Their spokesmen asked the Central Pacific for more money and shorter hours. Henceforth, the Chinese wanted $40 a month, instead of $30. They wanted the work day in the open limited to ten hours, and that in the tunnels reduced to eight. It was the company's policy to keep its men on the job outdoors from dawn till sunset, no matter how many hours were entailed. As for the tunnel workers, they were supposed to have eight-hour shifts. Obviously, their foremen had been keeping careless track of time.

An ugly glimpse beneath the ostensibly placid surface of the Central Pacific's labor relations was provided in one additional protest of the strikers. They denied, reported the Sacramento *Union,* "the right of the overseers of the company to either whip them or restrain them from leaving the road when they desire to seek other employment." [12]

Charles Crocker, a few years later, told a congressional committee how he met the unexpected challenge of a Chinese strike. In the first place, he said, he and his associates were convinced that agents of the Union Pacific had incited the trouble—"to keep us in the mountains while they were building the road over the plains." [13] But they could never prove it.

Even on strike, however, the behavior of the Chinese had won Crocker's approval.

If there had been that number of white laborers . . . in a strike, there would have been murder and drunkenness and disorder of all kinds. It would have been impossible to have controlled them. But this strike of the Chinese was just like Sunday all along the work. These men stayed in their camps. That is, they would come out and walk around, but not a word was said; nothing was done. No violence was perpetrated along the whole line.

As a week of idleness wore on, Crocker cut off the men's provisions and stopped the butchers from killing pigs and chickens for them.

"I then went up there and made them a little war speech," he said, "and told them they could not control the works, that no one made laws there but me."

He then laid down his terms: They could stay out until the following Monday, if they liked, and all would be forgiven. But if they weren't back at work at six o'clock that morning, they would be fined the total cost of keeping their foremen and all the horses idle for a week.

"On Monday morning at six o'clock, the whole country swarmed with them," concluded Crocker, with relish, "and we never had so many working before or since as we had on that day." [14]

They never tried striking again.

By this time, Collis Huntington's long, lonely quest for funds to keep the Central Pacific going had ceased to be a one-man campaign. He had at last enlisted important helpers.

They were two young Vermonters, Harvey Fisk and Alfrederick Hatch, who, with a small amount of borrowed money, had opened a bond house in New York City in March, 1862, and had made a blazing success of it. At first, they sold nothing but government bonds. In this, they soon out-distanced all competitors in the Northeast. During the melancholy days of 1864, when Grant's armies seemed unable to secure victory, the firm of Fisk & Hatch managed to obtain so much fresh money for the uncertain Union cause that Southern sympathizers wrote the partners letters threatening their lives if they persisted. The brokers' response was to deck their offices at 5 Nassau Street with red, white, and blue bunting, inside and out, and push government issues harder than ever. By the end of the war, they were famous in the financial communities of the United States.

In 1867, Huntington asked Fisk & Hatch, first, to take over the marketing of the Central Pacific's subsidy bonds, and next, to handle the sale of the railroad's own first-mortgage bonds. They readily agreed to do both. They had already begun to perform comparable services for the Union Pacific, and had an enthusiastic interest in speeding the completion of the first railroad line to the Pacific.

Fisk and Hatch and Huntington were a chummy triumvirate from the start. Whether or not it was based upon a mutual appreciation of their common Yankee shrewdness and enterprise, the business relationship of these men was extraordinarily trusting. They worked together for many years thereafter, and never was there a written contract among them. The bond-house partners repeatedly assured Huntington, in person, that they would obtain whatever funds he needed for his expanding railroad system, and they never failed him. Whenever a special negotiation was begun, Fisk wrote a brief memo about it on a little slip of blue paper, then both he and Huntington penciled their initials at the end. That was the sole record of their agreement.

On this tenuous basis, Fisk & Hatch eventually marketed $27,855,000 worth of government-aid bonds for the Central Pacific, and $53,000,000 worth of the railroad's own bonds. The brokers also helped popularize C.P. stock. To promote these endeavors, they hired one of the earliest financial publicity men, an able ex-newspaperman named Richard T. Colburn. According to his friend Albert D. Richardson, the New York

(Right) *This C.P. plow was 10 feet wide, 11 feet high, and 30 feet long. Sometimes even twelve locomotives couldn't budge it through drifts.*

(Bottom) *Bridging the gap in the Central Pacific's supply line while the Sierra tunnels were being built involved an endless chain of freight wagons.*

S.P.

SOC. OF CALIF. PIONEERS

S.P.

S.P.

(Top left) *A Chinese tea carrier, bringing refreshment to his fellow workers in discarded powder kegs, outside the east portal of Tunnel No. 8 in 1867.*

(Middle left) *This freight is coming around a bend at Emigrant Gap, Calif. Charlie Crocker's carriage is riding on one of the flatcars. The view is eastward.*

(Above) *Cisco, 92 miles east of Sacramento, was the end of the C.P. line from November, 1866, to November, 1867, while Sierra tunnels were under construction.*

(Bottom left) *Snowsheds at Summit Station, on the Central Pacific, in the fall of 1867. Here they were made wide enough to cover double tracks.*

(Left) *An artist's view of winter "railroading in a barn" in the loftiest regions of the Central Pacific's route after the snowsheds were finished.*

(Below) *A Central Pacific train pulls in beside the main Sacramento freight depot in 1868. Here the C.P. track met the S.V.R.R.'s, taken over in 1865.*

Tribune's star reporter, Colburn skillfully "sent forth upon the wings of the press fact after fact showing the greatness of the work and the value and safety of the security." [15]

Some of these winged facts curved back like boomerangs. Before long, the California Legislature was receiving petitions from indignant voters in three counties through which the C.P. track passed. If the Central Pacific was making as much money and had as brilliant prospects as the Fisk & Hatch pamphlets proclaimed, the petitioners said, then its freight rates and passenger fares were "exorbitant, oppressive, and out of all due proportion to the services rendered and expenses incurred by the railroad company." They demanded that the Legislature pass a law fixing the rates at one-third of what was being charged. Fortunately for the Central Pacific, nothing came of the petitions.

Colburn's paeans in praise of "9% annual interest in gold, paid semi-annually," [16] even though they offended some passengers and shippers, attracted investors to the company's first-mortgage bonds.

Early in June, the owners of the Central Pacific were sufficiently heartened to take first steps toward empire-building. They acquired the right to extend their track westward to San Francisco, by buying up at small cost the franchise of the Western Pacific Railroad (not related to the present road of that name).

Meanwhile, Engineer Butler Ives was leading a survey party of sixteen on a mission to fix the preliminary location of the Central Pacific track from the California-Nevada line to Weber Canyon, Utah, just east of Ogden.

"We pass through an Indian country all the way," he wrote to his brother on June 8th, "though I anticipate no trouble with them, for we are well armed with Spencer and Henry rifles, and are all pretty good travelers when there are any *hostile Indians behind*." [17]

By the end of August they were at Ogden. Ives was able to report that from the source of the Humboldt River eastward, he and his men had run "250 miles of preliminary R.R. line on one of the routes I explored last year, skirting the north end of the Great Desert & the north end of Salt Lake to the Wahsatch [*sic*] Mts." They had accomplished this in only six weeks, "about the quickest R.R. work on record this side of the mountains." [18]

At Ogden, Ives found orders from Chief Engineer Montague, telling him to continue his surveys to Fort Bridger, Wyoming. Knowing that Ives would be encountering some of General Dodge's engineers, working westward, Montague followed up his instructions with a warning:

Do not give the U.P.R.R. folks any information about our line between Humboldt Wells and Weber, or of the results of your examinations east of there.

Let them get the idea if possible that we are going to build to Ft. Bridger, and as this season will close our work in the Sierras, we can build to Salt Lake by Jan. 1st 1870 at the furthest—probably a year sooner. I think they will probably propose some terms for agreeing upon a meeting point soon—but if they do not, we shall meet them as far east as we can.[19]

The government was already assuming that the rails would meet at Fort Bridger. So the Secretary of the Interior had told the House of Representatives on February 14, 1867. His reasoning was based on the fact that at that point, "78 295/1000 miles east of Salt Lake City," the converging railroads would be entitled to exactly even amounts of financial aid from the U.S. Treasury. This official opinion had a clerical tidiness, but it was unrealistic to suppose that the Union Pacific would be content to end its line in the wilderness, within such short reach of the lucrative goal of the Salt Lake Valley.

In January, 1867, Chief Engineer Montague had warned his superiors that pushing construction in defiance of winter's obstacles, as they were then just beginning to do, was certain to increase the cost of the job at least 50 per cent. He said they had better ask themselves right away whether they could stand the drain or not, or if it were even worth while to do so.

Stanford and his associates had chosen to risk ruin in order to keep the track moving forward. By August, in fact, Strobridge had 20 miles of grading done along the Truckee and had begun to lay track on it. A locomotive and ten cars, whose parts had been carried over the mountains on teams, along with the rails, were being set up there.

By October, however, after nearly an additional year of sharply rising costs and fewer than 40 extra miles of track to show for them, the Central Pacific's officers began to feel fiscally anemic.

"We had mortgaged the road, and issued bonds 100 miles in advance of construction," said Stanford, much later. "They were all consumed, together with the county aid and all the aid that we received." [20]

Once more, he and his cronies wondered if they could possibly keep going. Huntington, even with the important assistance of Fisk & Hatch, wasn't yet finding sufficient funds for them in the East.

It was then that they decided the only way left to bring in fresh capital was to make room for additional partners in their tightly held enterprise. The device they chose was one that railroad promoters commonly used: a construction company that would acquire the railroad's assets in return for building it. This they already had, to a limited degree, in Charles Crocker & Co. But Crocker's associates were tired of being silent partners in a firm whose acquisitions of Central Pacific stock were all in Crocker's name. They did not distrust Charlie, but the arrangement was clumsy and irksome. They wanted openly to be partners in a new firm whose assets would be legally and unmistakably shared by them all to the extent of their respective investments in it. Only this sort of arrangement, too, would attract additional investors, whose cash they so badly needed.

Accordingly, on October 28, 1867, the chief stockholders of the Central Pacific organized the Contract and Finance Company. It failed in its original purpose, though.

"We did not succeed in any quarter in interesting others," Stanford later said, "and finally gave it up." [21]

"Then," he continued, "I think each of us subscribed for a fifth; Mr. Hopkins, Mr. Huntington, Charles Crocker, E. B. Crocker, and myself." [22] In so doing, though they had to incur greater personal indebtedness than ever before, they laid the foundations of their fortunes.

Charles Crocker was elected president of the Contract and Finance Co. Then, to make everything tidy, he turned over to its treasury all the Central Pacific stock that he had acquired up till then in part payment for the construction done by Charles Crocker & Co. Except on paper, though, there was no change made in the working arrangements that had existed from the beginning among the five men who now owned the Contract and Finance Co. Charlie Crocker continued to be generalissimo of the Central Pacific's army of builders until the troops reached Promontory Summit. After that goal was attained, the original Crocker shares of C.P. stock were divided equally among all the owners of the Contract and Finance Co., Stanford testified, and the construction company was dissolved.

Two months before the birth of the Contract and Finance Co., daylight first shone through the Summit Tunnel. On August 29, 1867, the headings met. There was much rock still to be removed from the bottoms. Nevertheless, it was a moment for rejoicing. "Many predicted it would require three years to accomplish what has been done in one," [23] the Sacramento *Union* proudly declared.

By early morning of November 30th, not only was the tunnel finished, but the track was laid through it. At a point within the tunnel, the Central Pacific reached its highest altitude, 7,042 feet above the sea, the top of its 105-mile climb from Sacramento.

The *Union* was jubilant. "Thus has been completed the most difficult portion of the Company's labors." True. "As compared to what have been encountered," the editorial continued, "the rest of the route to Salt Lake has no obstacles worth mentioning." [24] Untrue.

On Saturday morning, December 7th, members of the Legislature and of the Sacramento Pioneers, state officers, and a considerable number of their womenfolk set out on a railroad excursion to the Summit. It turned out to have almost as many ludicrous aspects as an early film comedy.

The excursion train, a long one, was pulled by two locomotives, the Idaho and the Tamaroo. It was made up of ten passenger cars, one flatcar, and two baggage cars—one for serving food, the other for dispensing drinks. Most of the men favored the latter. The ladies and their escorts sat in the last two coaches. There were 700 to 800 invited guests. The party, which began as soon as the train moved out of Sacramento, at 7 A.M., was a merry one as far as Emigrant Gap.

There, after making a brief stop, the Idaho and Tamaroo started up so convulsively that the front platform was torn off one of the passenger cars. At the exact moment, a man was crossing from that car to the one ahead. He was left clinging to the rear railing of the forward car, while his legs bumped over the snowy ties. Shouts from onlookers brought the train to a halt before the dangler was badly injured. "His hurts were limited to a strained ankle," [25] a reporter wrote. The damaged car was removed from the train, and a new one substituted.

After that, tipsy contentment reigned until the excursionists reached the Summit. Snow was falling there. It almost entirely hid the noble view of Donner Lake that the railroad's guests had been expecting to enjoy. However, almost to a man, the legislators and state officers rejoiced to see what many of them hadn't seen in years, not since they had left their old homes in the East. They promptly got into a rousing snow fight, "much to the demoralization of high-crowned hats and immaculate shirt collars." [26]

When this frenzy had spent itself, and everybody had eaten enough lunch to sober him, the more venturesome guests tramped down the track toward Nevada to inspect an unfinished tunnel. But by three o'clock, everybody was cold and ready to go home.

Another engine, the Yuba, then backed through the Summit Tunnel and hooked onto the tail end of the train. Off it started, with the usual jerk, but it didn't get far. When the cars were entirely within the Summit Tunnel, they abruptly stopped. In a very few minutes, dense smoke from the wood-burning locomotive nearly suffocated the passengers. A panicky rumor spread that several of the forward cars had been derailed. A few of the calmer people said that was nonsense; the railroad officials had simply chosen this vivid way of showing their guests that the tunnel was long enough to engulf the entire train.

There was imminent danger of real panic, though, until, to everyone's vast relief, the cars began to move forward again after about fifteen distracting minutes. When the smoke had cleared out of the coaches, an official explanation was passed through the train that someone unknown had pulled the connecting pin between the third and fourth cars in the tunnel. The train had separated at that point, and the Yuba had surged ahead a short distance with only three cars in tow. But it had quickly stopped and gone back for the rest.

As the true story of the stall was being disseminated, a passenger named A. P. Smith suddenly leaped to his feet and shouted that someone had stolen his gold watch and chain. Those who heard him promptly decided that pickpockets had staged the incident in the tunnel. His fellow-passengers felt hastily for their own watches and wallets. No other property was missing, but in the general search two men were exposed as having crashed the party at Cisco on the way up. With frontier directness, they were accused of being pickpockets, and were forced to submit to a search. A. P. Smith's watch and chain were not found on either of them. But the crowd was in no mood to apologize. The conductor was summoned and the situation explained to him. He ordered the train stopped, and told the two suspects to get off. They slunk away into the snowy dusk, several miles from the nearest station.

At Yuba Pass, on the homeward run, the fireman of the locomotive stepped out onto one of the engine's footboards in order to oil a valve. The footboard was coated with ice. The fireman slipped and fell off into a drift beside the track. Fortunately, the engineer saw him disappear, and hastily tooted for brakes to be applied. Brakemen sprang to their wheels in every car, and soon the train screeched to a halt. The fireman came running back to his cab. He had landed in deep snow and hadn't been hurt.

At Colfax, in another abrupt forward lunge from a standing stop, the front platform was ripped off the last car of the train. The train crew simply reversed the car on a nearby turntable and hitched the sound end to the rest of the train. Both cars whose platforms had given way had come to the Central Pacific from the California Central R.R., which the C.P. had finally acquired altogether in September.

It was late in the evening of December 7th before the excursionists got back to Sacramento after their eventful day, tired but generally pleased. Not pleased, reported the *Union,* were the poor ladies, who "had kept to their cars for 15 hours, on account of the stormy weather." With Victorian understatement, it declared that they "were much fatigued." [27]

Six days later, John R. Brown, the diary-keeping freight clerk at Cisco station, hitched a ride to the Summit on a construction train to see the biggest tunnel for himself. When he got there, he walked through it. The day was lovely, he recorded.

There were few lovely days thereafter until late the following spring. On December 16th, Brown noted that it was "snowing quite hard" at Cisco. This meant worse weather up the line. His diary entry on the following day was more emphatic. "Snowing very hard," he wrote. On December 18th, it "snowed all night. This A.M. it is 3½ feet deep on a level and still snowing as hard as ever." [28]

This winter was beginning to be as rough as the one before it.

Charles Crocker was not taking any chances of having a snow blockade interrupt the course of construction east of the Summit. The Union Pacific was now reported nearly halfway to Salt Lake, which, if true, meant that it had built 500 miles of track since 1865. Crocker's thousands of hard-working Chinese had completed only 39 miles in 1867—15 west of the Summit, 24 between there and the Nevada line.

The Central Pacific's total mileage was about 131, but it was not continuous. The track ran unbroken from Sacramento to a point 2½ miles east of the Summit Tunnel. There it ended, at unfinished Tunnel No. 12. Beyond, down the northeast slopes of the mountains that rimmed the south shore of Donner Lake, there was a gap of 7 miles. At a camp called

Cold Stream, the track began again, and stretched 24 miles from there to the Nevada border.

Crocker's men were going to have to take giant steps forward in 1868. Below the snow belt on the east side of the Sierra, railroad-building must proceed through the winter without a hitch. The men had to have construction trains to help them. There was only one way to transport locomotives and freight cars eastward from the Summit—the way the "black picked goose" had traveled a year earlier.

In a taut race with oncoming storms, Crocker sent two stripped-down steam engines from Sacramento to the end of the line. With them rode the trucks and ironwork for ten flatcars. At the east end of the Summit Valley, these were transferred from trains to ox-drawn sleds, chained securely, and hauled down the twisting wagon road past Donner Lake till they met the track once more. There the engines regained their wheels and smokestacks, and the cars were assembled. Two dozen sawmills had cropped up along the Truckee. The necessary lumber for these cars and many more was cut and waiting.

The first locomotives and cars were at work on the eastern side of the mountains before December was over. Behind them came enough rails and track hardware to build 40 miles of railroad. A third engine followed, so big that it had to be carried over the snow on a huge raft of logs, for no sled could cope with it. Finally, the makings of thirty more cars were dispatched over the same laborious route, fast becoming too deeply drifted to use. Soon, a winter every bit as wild as that of 1866–67 put a stop to this traffic.

On December 6th, the *Virginia City* (Nevada) *Enterprise* had revealed that the railroad builders were saying they could close the 7-mile gap in the track "in two weeks, if the weather holds good." [29]

It didn't.

CHAPTER TWELVE

1867

YEAR   OF   TRAGEDY

While Strobridge's Chinese burrowed through the winter of 1866–67 under mountains of snow in the Sierra Nevada, the most severe weather in many years spread across the United States.

In Wyoming, frostbitten soldiers limping to the relief of Fort Phil Kearny, whose depleted garrison was in a highly nervous state of siege after the Fetterman massacre, wallowed in "fantastic drifts." [1] The temperature there was 40 degrees below zero.

In New York City, the East River froze solid, immobilizing the nation's biggest port and delighting skaters. In Chicago, firemen stared in angry frustration at blazes they could not quench because water congealed in their hose lines.

At Omaha, the Missouri's ice lid grew 16 inches thick. This was the winter's only boon to the Union Pacific. The ice was strong enough to support trains. As soon as the Chicago & North Western's track reached Council Bluffs and the first locomotive coughed into town on the frosty night of January 17th, a spur was slung across the bottomland and over the ice to Omaha. The rails rested on bridge stringers and low pilings. This link was a crude and temporary expedient, but it broke the winter's usual blockade of freight movements from the East to the Union Pacific.

North Platte was the forward base for the U.P.'s next advance. All winter long, battling through a succession of heavy snows, train crews hauled materials and supplies from Omaha out to the Casements' prefabricated warehouses there. A burst of track-building was anticipated as soon as frost left the ground, presumably in March.

General Dodge had set his sights high. He was aiming to push the Union Pacific as far as Fort Sanders, Wyoming Territory, in 1867. That outpost on the Laramie River, in a broad trough between the Black Hills and the Medicine Bow Mountains, was 288 miles beyond North Platte. To get there, Jack Casement's men would first lay track along the South Platte as far as Julesburg. There, after barely setting their feet inside the northeast corner of Colorado Territory, they would swing up Lodge Pole Creek for 105 miles, through far western Nebraska and southeastern Wyoming. Curving westward from the Lodge Pole, they would cross Crow Creek and climb the felicitous divide between that stream and Lone Tree Creek. They would surmount the summit of Wyoming's Black Hills at an altitude of 8,242 feet. (The Union Pacific's highest point was to top the Central Pacific's by 1,200 feet.) From there, the graders and track-layers would ease down the western slope of the Black Hills, cross Dale Creek, where a major job awaited the railroad's bridge-builders, and descend to the high Laramie Plains. At this point, they would curve almost straight north through the valley between the paralleling Black Hills and Medicine Bow Mountains. A third of their way up that wide valley, the Laramie River would cross their path. There they expected to drive the last spikes of the season.

Dodge made a point of keeping his old commander, General Sherman, in touch with his plans and progress by frequent letters. When Dodge revealed the U.P.'s goal for 1867, Sherman responded admiringly, "It is almost a miracle to grasp your purpose to finish to Fort Sanders this year, but you have done so much that I mistrust my own judgment and accept yours." [2]

There was also the problem of Indians to consider.

"I hope you will have troops to give us ample protection," Dodge wrote to Sherman from Council Bluffs on January 14th. "We are going to be short of labor, and any lack of military protection, when Indians are at war, would render it almost impossible to keep men on the line." [3]

He was in sympathy with Sherman's plan to send expeditions once more into the Republican River Valley of Kansas and up the Powder River in Montana, striking at the centers of Indian strength. He realized that these strategic moves were likely to draw raiders away from the Platte and his railroad builders. But would the U.P.'s construction forces understand that the absence of troops was really part of a scheme to protect them?

"What you and I know is going to be hard to make a lot of Irishmen believe," declared Dodge. "They want to see occasionally a soldier to give them confidence, and that is all we need to get labor on the line." [4] He urged Sherman to provide General Cooke with at least 5,000 men to guard the Union Pacific's workers and lines of communication. Altogether, there really ought to be 10,000 soldiers west of the Missouri, Dodge advised. "And I hope the Government will not do by you as they did by me," he added, "get you well after the Indians, just ready to punish them, and then under the hue and cry of wrongs, cruelty, etc., stop you." [5]

Sherman replied by return mail from St. Louis. "I regard this road of yours as the solution of the Indian question, and of the Mormon affairs," he wrote on January 16th, "and therefore give you all that I possibly can." [6] It wasn't going to be easy. Every officer in his command was exaggerating his own troubles and asking for reinforcements. The government's police-state treatment of the defeated South distressed Sherman, too. That consumed troops that he could put to far better use on the Plains.

I am disposed to find fault that our soldiers are now tied up in the Southern states [he declared], but in the light they are now regarded, it would be impolitic and imprudent of me to say so publicly. All I can do is to keep General Grant well informed, so that he may distribute his army to the best advantage of the whole country. [7]

Sherman soon afterward notified Dodge that he was replacing General Cooke with Gen. Christopher C. Augur, a much younger and more vigorous commander for the Department of the Platte. Augur would be fighting Indians, off and on, for the next eighteen years. Sherman assured Dodge:

You will lose nothing by the change, for I will make it incumbent on the military to give you earnest attention for the protection of your road. You have General Hancock on the south of you [in Kansas], and Augur with you—two of the best officers, and they shall have every man that I can get and spare. [8]

While generals discussed their future protection, the men of Jack Casement's idle army were devoting themselves wholeheartedly to frivolity and sin at North Platte, one of the few places where that miserable winter was being enjoyed.

The town had sprung into existence in December. In a period of only three weeks, starting from blank prairie, it had acquired a large frame hotel, the portable settlement that was the Casements' headquarters and storage area, a frame depot "of the usual beautiful design," [9] the outlines of a forty-locomotive roundhouse of brick, and a towering water tank, heated by a stove, as they all were. Other buildings, of a more temporary character, sheltered saloons, gambling places, brothels, boardinghouses, barbershops, and stores. They had been assembled so fast that there were now a thousand of them. North Platte soon bulged with 5,000 inhabitants. Most of them were U.P. construction workers, freely spending what was left of the previous season's wages in blithe assurance of being hired again in the approaching spring. The town seethed, too, with teamsters, emigrants bound for Salt Lake City and California, travelers waiting for Denver stages, and goldseekers killing time until the weather was right for them to set out for Montana and Idaho. Soldiers rode in from Omaha on freights loaded with military supplies for the next summer's campaigns. The goods were stacked under sailcloth on the fringe of town. Their guardians headed for the nearest bar. There were shooting sprees nearly every night, and the railroad's low line of telegraph poles that ran past North Platte frequently served as gallows. Wolves and coyotes howled on the outskirts of this lurid carnival, but their mournful comments were seldom heard above the gay din of the community.

Henry M. Stanley, then a fledgling British journalist who did not yet know of David Livingstone's existence, arrived there that spring. Stanley, a dark, sullen-looking little man of twenty-six, with a strong streak of prudishness, found its sights and scenes both shocking and fascinating. He wrote:

Every gambler in the Union seems to have steered his course for North Platte, and every known game under the sun is played here. The days of Pike's Peak and California are revived. Every house is a saloon, and every saloon is a gambling den. Revolvers are in great requisition. Beardless youths imitate to the life the peculiar swagger of the devil-may-care bull whacker and blackleg, and here, for the first time, they try their hands at the "Mexican monte," "high-low-jack," "strap," "rouge-et-noir," "three-card monte," and that satanic game, "chuck-a-luck," and lose their all.

"Try again, my buck. Nothing like 'sperience. You are cuttin' your high teeth now. By-and-by you will be a pioneer." Such are the encouraging words shouted to an unfortunate young man by the sympathizing bystanders.

On account of the immense freighting done to Idaho, Montana, Utah, Dakota, and Colorado, hundreds of bull whackers walk about, and turn the one street into a perfect Babel. Old gamblers who revelled in the glorious days of "flush times" in the gold districts declare that this town outstrips all yet.[10]

The furious winter had repeatedly isolated North Platte and obliged its reveling citizens to make the most of the diversions they had accumulated. A blizzard in mid-February halted all traffic on the Union Pacific and the Chicago & North Western for more than a week. Another, in the middle of March, buried most of Nebraska and Iowa for ten days.

The Missouri was frozen deep as late as March 25th, Samuel Reed reported to his wife. "I have six locomotives on the east side of the river," he wrote that day, from Omaha, "and would not hesitate to cross them on the ice if we needed their services on this side immediately." [11] As it was, however, the U.P. couldn't yet send the locomotives it had available in the direction it wanted them to go.

We are still laboring hard to clear the track [Reed wrote home on March 27th], Erastus has just wired me the following from Grand Island: "We are out of luck in this country, wind blowing and snow drifting worse than ever, half men either blind or frozen, looks bad." . . . There is an immense quantity of snow on the plains and in the mountains. I expect very high water and we may lose some bridges.[12]

Reed's foreboding was fully substantiated. While he was in the midst of assigning the season's grading work for as far west as 25 miles beyond Julesburg, a drastic spring thaw set in. Soon the Platte was vastly swollen and trying to sweep the winter's ice debris out of its path. Its tributaries were writhing in similar efforts.

The long bridge at North Platte held, and its approaches as well. At Columbus, where the U.P. track crossed the Loup River, the 1,500-foot bridge resisted a tremendous crush of ice and water, but the railroad embankment was ripped away for more than a mile on both sides of it. Between Kearny and North Platte, the track was undermined in many places. East of Grand Island, an ice jam in the Platte forced the turbulent river out of its channel altogether. It raced northward, cut a half-mile swath through the Union Pacific's roadbed, ran wild for 20 miles on the wrong side of the track, then swung back again toward its normal course. In returning, it once more tore its way through grading, ties, and rails, bending some of the new iron double and littering the valley with the line's wreckage. From 4 to 6 miles of embankment near Shell Creek melted away, leaving a braid of track lying aimlessly on the muddy plain. Where the fuming Elkhorn rushed to join the Platte, another mile of the Union Pacific disappeared.

A prolonged spell of heavy rain hurried the melting of the deep snow blanket and greatly increased the destructiveness of the floods.

"The Missouri is coming over its Banks and rising all the time," wrote Jack Casement, lonely and homesick in Omaha, to his wife on April 13th. "Miles of Road is washed away in the Platte Valey so that we cannot get over the Road for a few days even if it stops Raining. We are all in a heap generally . . ." [13]

By April 20th, parts of the track in Omaha had disappeared under water. The following morning, a Sunday, the muddy grounds around the car shops churned with teams, hastily mobilized to rescue the massive heaps of cut timber piled there.

The flood crested on April 22nd. On April 25th, Superintendent Reed wrote his wife that he had a large force of workmen repairing the track, and a train had passed over the entire length of it for the first time in ten days. But a great deal of work remained to be done before the railroad could be considered to be in proper order again, he said.

Reed moaned that not a bit of new grading or tracklaying had yet been possible to accomplish. "Before the break, there was a prospect of rushing ahead more rapidly than last year," he wrote wistfully. "It gives me the blues to think that our road, which was in such good shape, should be at this season of the year so badly cut up." [14]

However, his battalions of repairmen were fast making up for the misfortune. On April 27th, he was able to report that trains once more were running on schedule. Four heavily burdened freights had left for the construction front the previous morning.

At this most unsuitable moment, T. C. Durant arrived from New York, accompanied by the U.P.'s Acting President Oliver Ames, Director John Duff, and Springer Harbaugh, one of the government directors. The last three comprised a committee whose purpose was to take formal acceptance of the railroad, as far as completed, from the Credit Mobilier. There couldn't have been a less desirable time for them to look it over.

Sam Reed sent the little steamer *Elkhorn* across the subsiding Missouri to meet them, and wrote a hasty note home to reinforce his courage. "Doctor Durant and party are just landing," he told his wife on April 27th. ". . . I do not feel any trembling in my boots. Let what will, come. I have a clear conscience because I know that I have done my whole duty for him and the company he represents." [15]

The committee rode out to O'Fallons Bluffs and back, with General Dodge escorting them. They were gratifyingly appreciative of Reed's unhappy position and told him they were "well pleased" [16] with the road. Oliver Ames was appalled, however, to discover what Nebraska looked like west of Fort Kearny. One Eastern traveler that summer called it "a miserable waste," and feared it always would be. Ames told Duff that if it were up to him alone, he wouldn't take *all* the land along the railroad as a gift. For a quarter, he vowed, he'd even ask the U.P.'s board of directors to refuse the government's land grants.

This disillusioned reaction to the western Nebraska of those days was common. Indignant as Peter Dey had been at the exorbitance of the so-called Hoxie contract that Durant had concocted for building the railroad's first 247 miles, he had been able to understand Durant's point of view.

At that time [Dey wrote to a friend some years later], it was generally believed that two hundred miles west of the Missouri River was the limit of arable lands, except where irrigation was available, and it was thought the entire country, on account of the absence of rain, would ever remain a desert. There can be but little doubt that the motive influencing Mr. Durant, if not his associates, was to realize from the contract for construction all the profit possible, and turn the property over to the government to operate, under the conviction that it could never earn its expenses.[17]

Durant made no secret of this attitude among his associates.[He believed the Union Pacific should be built just well enough to pass government inspection, and no better. His only chance for profit, and theirs, he believed, lay in the difference between what it actually cost the Credit Mobilier to build the road and what it was able to charge the Union Pacific for the work. Thus, his steadfast aim was to cheapen the construction as much as he dared, and lengthen the mileage, if possible, wherever the work was light but the bond subsidy heavy. Once the job was done, he intended to sell all his shares in the U.P. and let somebody else worry about running the railroad. ⌐

The Ameses and the friends whose capital they had enlisted in the enterprise did not agree with this attitude at all. They expected to make money on the construction contracts, of course—at least 20 per cent profit, Oakes Ames later declared—but they felt that their best opportunity for gain lay in the future, long-term operation of a well-built railroad. For this worthier point of view, Durant openly called them "damn fools." [18]

It was an ironic fact, however, that much as he desired fast, cheap construction, Durant was so impractical, so bent on doing everything with reckless flourish, that he was largely defeating his own ends.

"He was the most extravagant man I ever knew in my life," [19] declared John M. S. Williams, of Boston, a director of the Credit Mobilier at this time and one of the rich, frugal New Englanders whom the Ames brothers had brought into the organization with them.

"I never saw such a man as Durant," an old Missouri River steamboat captain once said, recalling his improvident ways.

He made a contract with me for transporting supplies to Omaha, amounting to a million and a half dollars, and he actually signed that contract without ever reading it. He just glanced at it and said, "Well, Captain, I suppose this is all right," and wrote his name at the bottom.[20]

In truth, Durant was paying far too high a price for the cheap sort of railroad he wanted. The "Boston crowd" believed it could get a better road for less money. It had begun a campaign to oust Durant and his "New York crowd" from control of the Credit Mobilier and let veteran railroad builders Sidney Dillon and John Duff manage the company instead.

Durant knew, of course, what was afoot. He was fighting back. Ever since the Union Pacific had reached its 247th milepost, the Credit Mobilier had been obliged to continue building it without a contract. The reason: Durant wouldn't let one be consummated. Whenever a new proposal was drawn up, at the old rate of $50,000 a mile, and submitted to the U.P. directors, Durant brought legal proceedings against the board to prevent its putting the contract into effect. He couldn't very well expose his suit as pure obstructionism, which it was, so he chose to base his opposition on the argument that each new contract proposal was too costly and would be unjust to U.P. stockholders. This was utter hypocrisy, for Durant himself had set the price of $50,000 a mile in the original construction contract. He wouldn't think of taking the work for less. Yet in his injunction suits, he several times declared for the record that the actual cost of building and equipping the Union Pacific through Nebraska's prairie was no more than $27,500 a mile. This was evidently a true figure, and one that his opponents must have squirmed at having revealed. Since they knew he was as anxious as they to garner a rich profit in this territory where the going was easy, they at first were exasperatedly puzzled over his motive for exposing the profit margin in the law courts. Later, they judged, probably with accuracy, that he was farsightedly preparing his own defense in case the government ever investigated the Credit Mobilier. His immediate aim, though, was to frustrate the "Boston crowd" into abandoning its battle to kick him out of Credit Mobilier control.

This, then, was the background for the thoughts of Durant and the U.P.'s official examining committee as they arrived in Omaha on April 27th. In consequence, they spent a morose and uncomfortable time together as they looked over the 305 miles of track completed.

While Oliver Ames was endeavoring to overcome his distaste and doubt regarding the territory that the Casements' tracklayers were now penetrating, General Dodge confided to him a disenchantment of his own. "Durant is in the way," [21] he declared, as if Ames didn't have poignant reasons for agreeing with him. Despite the assurance of a free hand that the erratic U.P. vice-president had given Dodge at St. Joseph the previous April, Durant had lately shown an obstinate tendency to meddle with the chief engineer's plans and orders. Dodge asked Ames for official support. Ames gave it with gusto.

As for the committee of inspection, it was not able to depart for the East without a flare-up of its disagreement with Durant. Reed reported to his wife on May 6th:

They broke up in a row and no one knows what will be the end. No work has been let west of the fourth hundred [miles] and will not be until they come to some agreement in New York.

This fight places me in a very unpleasant situation and I have a mind to resign my position, but shall remain a few days until I hear from New York. The Doctor is very jealous of every one and I think dare not let any more work until he goes East.[22]

Durant, after staying three days longer than the others, departed from Omaha on May 9th, leaving a greatly relieved Reed and Dodge behind him. The builders of the railroad were glad to get on with their great task, content to let distant directors battle over profits and control.

Dodge had sent engineers on their way to Wyoming before April ended. Some were to make a final location of the route from the Laramie River westward to Salt Lake City. Others were to put finishing touches on the line over the Black Hills. Before May was more than a few days old, General Casement had pushed his graders out for 100 miles beyond North Platte. Hundreds of tracklayers were stretching the rails toward Julesburg, 82 miles west, at an increasing pace.

It was fortunate that Dan Casement had accumulated a huge stockpile of materials at North Platte. The supply line from the East was still semi-crippled by the severe winter and its after-effects. There was Indian trouble coming, too.

Stagecoaches in western Nebraska were rushed and mauled. Colorado ranches were stripped of horses, mules, and cattle. Indian raids on travelers were so fierce across Wyoming that stage traffic between Denver and Salt Lake City was halted altogether for two weeks. Telegraph lines, which the Indians called "talking wires" and suspected of blabbing whenever they rode under them, were ripped down by the mile. Some of the repairmen trying to restore service were shot down from the tops of poles by bucks who crawled up through the rank grass and fired at them from underneath.

The Union Pacific was hit successive blows. On May 25th, warriors sprang out of the tall weeds and killed and scalped all but one man in a section gang of six who were puttering with the track near Overton, Nebraska, 70 miles east of North Platte. The survivor managed to run away and hide in the prairie grass. On the same day, more than 100 miles westward, a war party pounced on scattered groups of graders, killing four, wounding one, and racing off with several dozen horses. They also came hooting down toward the Casements' boarding train.

General Dodge, who was at the front that afternoon, derived a certain gray satisfaction from the fact that the three government commissioners happened to be there, too, and saw the brief brawl that swirled within sight of the cars. The Indians swept in upon a grading outfit doing some patchwork just ahead of the tracklayers. Although the graders had stacked rifles near at hand, the attack materialized so swiftly that it panicked them. They dropped their shovels and picks and sprinted for the protection of the train. The raiders cut loose the stock tethered nearby, and thundered off as fast as they had come.

The commissioners present, who were there to inspect the 40 miles of track that the Casements' men had added to the railroad in the past month, were Maj. Gen. Francis P. Blair, Jr., who had replaced the late Gen. S. R. Curtis; Brig. Gen. J. H. Simpson; and Dr. W. M. White. "They showed their grit by running to my car for arms to aid in the fight," [23] Dodge wrote of the occasion. But there was no fight to aid by then. The enemy had vanished.

Dodge stormed out to berate the graders for violating his basic order to all hands in case of attack: "Don't run." Then he stalked back to his official visitors and angrily exclaimed, "We've got to clean the damn Indians out or give up building the Union Pacific Railroad. The government may take its choice." [24] The shock of the raid and the multiple other losses of the day, which he had already learned about by telegraph, had shaken him out of his usual calm.

The day's results were not wholly adverse, though. "We did not fail to benefit from this experience," Dodge once pointed out, "for, on returning to the East, the Commission dwelt earnestly on the necessity of our being protected." [25]

When casualty reports and alarms poured in upon him from the Plains immediately afterward, General Sherman decided to take to the field as fast as he could get there. By June 6th, he was at Julesburg, and sent the following telegram to Governor A. C. Hunt, of Colorado Territory.

I am here now and General Augur is across the Platte on the line of the Union Pacific. The Indians are everywhere. Ranchers should gather at stage stations. Stages should bunch up and travel together at irregular times. I have six companies of cavalry and General Custer is coming up from the Smoky Hill Route.[26]

Sherman was in a mood for battle. "The more we can kill this year," he wrote at the time, "the less will have to be killed the next war, for the more I see of these Indians the more convinced I am that they all have to be killed or be maintained as a species of paupers." [27] His adversaries repeatedly eluded him, however.

Throughout the rest of the summer, one full regiment of infantry, parts of two others, four companies of cavalry, and four companies of Pawnee scouts were assigned to guarding the U.P., from its westernmost surveyors to its trains as far east as Kearny. (Their value as a shield was enhanced by the fact that most of the infantrymen carried Springfield rifles that had just been converted from muzzle-loaders to breech-loaders, thus making them simpler, more dependable, and more accurate weapons. The cavalry-men were even better armed, with new repeating rifles.)

Just before the initial Indian attacks of that summer, General Dodge was notified by telegram that Durant had been ousted from his post in the Credit Mobilier. Sidney Dillon was its new head. On May 25th, Oliver Ames followed up the telegram with a letter of explanation:

The ejectment of Durant from Presidency of Credit Mobilier has raised the very devil in that amiable gent, and he has come down upon us with injunctions, and proposes to visit us with every form of legal document to keep us honest. . . . I cannot understand such a change as has come over the Doctor—the man of all others who has from the beginning stolen whenever he had the chance, and who is today, we think, holding stock, and a large portion of his stock, on fictitious claims and trumped-up accounts. He is now in open hostility to the road and any orders he may give you, or any parties under you, should be entirely disregarded.[28]

Nothing could have pleased Dodge more than to be told he could ignore Durant. He at once wrote to Sidney Dillon, urging him to put more graders along the Lodge Pole as quickly as possible. Otherwise, he feared, the Indians would burn the ties distributed there. The few grading outfits in the vicinity had already been raided. The armed surveyors staking out the grading and bridges on the Lodge Pole line spent their days in apprehension, despite the near presence of their military escort, and at night lay awake listening uneasily to the coyotes and wolves.

On June 14th General Dodge received a shocking telegram. L. L. Hills, the engineer who had completed the final location of the U.P. line from North Platte to the present site of Cheyenne the previous year, had been killed by a band of Arapahoes.

Hills had been leading a group of ten surveyors, guarded by six troopers from the Second Cavalry. As they worked eastward from the crossing of Crow Creek, on June 12th, tidying up details of the railroad's route, Hills and a tie inspector had carelessly become separated from the others by about a mile. Suddenly, a column of Indian horsemen streamed out of a thicketed ravine and cut these two men off. While the majority of the raiders pushed Hills' command into a defensive stand, the rest tore after the engineer and the tie inspector, who rode in opposite directions.

The warriors soon broke off the attack and disappeared. Five hours later, searching troops found Hills' body, with nineteen arrows and five bullet wounds in it. They also came upon the tie inspector, severely wounded but able to crawl. He had been knocked off his horse by a hurled lance, and then trampled by the frantic animal before it could free itself from the reins.

A month later, General Dodge and the entire engineering staff of the Union Pacific mourned an even more jolting loss. The Sioux had slaughtered Percy Browne, whose warm personality and notable ability had made him one of the most popular men on the railroad.

Browne was near Rock Creek, Wyoming, at the north end of the Laramie Plains, in the course of locating the best line between Fort Sanders and Green River. He had already lost a few men of his original group in a raid three weeks earlier, but had brought the dead in to Fort Sanders and bravely set out again with reinforcements. At noon on July 23rd, a large Sioux war party surprised him and eight escorting cavalrymen in a deep, twisting dry stream. The nine white men, forcing their horses to lie down, formed a ring on top of a nearby knoll and fought off repeated charges for hours. At twilight, the Indians stampeded the party's horses and, in the course of the rush, shot Browne in the abdomen. Then they seemed to tire of the fighting and vanished. The stricken man, in desperate pain and aware that he had almost no chance of surviving, tried to persuade the soldiers to escape in the darkness without him. Instead, they made a stretcher out of their rifles and a blanket or two and carried him 15 miles through the sagebrush to the nearest stage station. There he died.

The bitter news reached Dodge when he was least able to accept it stoically. He was ailing and harassed. His old wounds were giving him a great deal of pain. The U.P.'s consulting engineer, Colonel Seymour, was giving him even more mental anguish. Seymour was such a poor railroad engineer that he seriously thought rails should be laid on longitudinal ties, and that wooden bridges were superior to iron ones, but, as Durant's favorite, he could not be ignored.

Dodge had just arrived at Fort Sanders, with an important official visitor and old friend, Gen. John A. Rawlins, Grant's profane but puritanical chief of staff. Rawlins was consumptive, and, at Grant's and Sherman's urging, had accepted an invitation from Dodge to spend the summer with him on horseback in the high mountain air. They had celebrated the birth of Cheyenne on July 4th, and were now on a wide reconnaissance that would take them as far as Salt Lake City and the upper Wasatch Mountains before they returned. They had with them nearly 300 cavalrymen, to be distributed along the way for the protection of the U.P. engineering parties in Wyoming.

Colonel Seymour, always an irritant to Dodge, had appeared at Cheyenne just as they were leaving, and had asked to go part way with them. At once, he proceeded to become infuriating. "Seymour is here for mischief and trouble—only finds fault," Dodge wrote his wife. "I hope to get rid of him at Bridger Pass." [29] The consulting engineer had begun tampering with James Evans' admirable ninety-foot gradient to the summit of the Black Hills. Durant was behind this activity, Dodge had no doubt. However, having in mind Oliver Ames' firm command, earlier in the season, to pay no attention to Durant's orders or wishes, Dodge felt certain that Seymour had no other backers of weight. Nevertheless, he was acutely uneasy about him.

Dodge spilled his grievances to Sidney Dillon in a doleful letter written on July 27th.

Trouble never comes single [*sic*]. Have but just gotten Hills' work straightened out and now poor Brown [Dodge always ignored the final "e"], the best and most promising of all and my reliance for work west, is killed, and I must push out to his party. I am suffering everything but death from my rides—how long I can stand it God only knows. Add to this the fact that I have nothing but grief along with me and you can imagine my humor. . . .

Indians on the plains have been very bad for two weeks. They have been attacking everything and everybody.

Gen. Rawlins has been of great aid to me. I believe he takes more interest in the road than Seymour, who seems not to care a damn whether the Indians get the road or not so long as he can play gentleman and have a big company to foot his bills. He will be my everlasting bitter enemy for I have taken occasion to give him some pretty strong licks at his actions. He cares about as much for our interests as we do for Japan and will sell any or all of us if he can better Seymour. . . . He . . . will do what he can to change lines and cause delay—and you must all be careful about what you allow him to do—better hear from me on changes before you make any, as he would not hesitate to delay you if it suited his purpose. . . .

Sick as I am, I believe I shall get through to Salt Lake if Indians do not kill off all my party. It takes the nerve out of them losing so many. . . .

The whole thing is now on the shoulders of Evans and myself. Seymour would not take a party out if the road had to stop—told me yesterday that he did not think it policy to push parties out during Indian troubles; said there would be plenty of time next year, when the fact is every cut must be worked this winter and the light work all done for forty miles west of here this fall.[30]

Dodge had to leave Seymour behind to concoct whatever mischief occurred to him. The chief engineer was obliged to hurry on westward. He must reorganize Browne's badly shaken group. He must find out how Tom Bates and his men were making out with the line from Green River east. He must make a final decision about the crossing of the Wasatch Range. (Before the summer was over, Seymour managed to make $90,000 worth of alterations in Evans' line, only to have them abandoned in the fall, when Dodge, Evans, and Reed together convinced the U.P.'s board of directors that the changes were not only pointless but actually harmful.)

Dodge was several hundred miles west of the scene when the Indians made their most lurid raid on the railroad that year. On the night of August 6th, near Plum Creek station, 59 miles east of North Platte, a band of Cheyennes wrecked, looted, and burned a freight train. At the same time, they killed seven U.P. employees and scalped another, whose story is one of the strangest in the railroad's history.

Generals Custer and Hancock had been trying to force the Cheyennes out of action altogether by a headlong campaign through their home territory of Kansas, but the Indians had escaped northward into Nebraska to harry the U.P. The party that derailed the freight 4 miles from Plum Creek station, where an ancient north-south trail crossed the railroad track, had only just seen their first train. In wonder, they had watched it from a distant ridge to the south, and after it had moved out of sight, they rode down to find out what kind of trail it had left on the prairie. When they discovered the track, it didn't take them long to figure out a way in which they might capture the next train that came along. They found some loose ties beside the rails, heaped them up, and lashed them to the track with telegraph wire, obtained by ripping down the nearest section of line. It was the sudden break in the railroad's telegraphic communications that attracted the Indians' first victims to the spot. They arrived about dusk.

Six repairmen came clicking up the rails on a handcar. Along with tools and wire, they had Spencer carbines aboard, but they had no chance to use them. As they neared the obstacle on the tracks, the impatient Cheyennes rose yelling from the prairie grass. The repairmen, their attention so suddenly distracted, didn't notice the stacked ties ahead. The handcar hit the barrier hard and flung its passengers to the ground. The Indians sprang upon them and quickly killed all but one.

William Thompson, a rugged young Englishman with long blond hair, broke away and started to run. A warrior dashed after him on horseback, fired at close range, and wounded him in the right arm. This didn't stop Thompson, so the Indian wheeled and clouted him with the butt of his rifle. Thompson collapsed. He was barely conscious, but pretended to be dead when the Indian twisted one hand around a hank of his hair and hurriedly scalped him. Through a haze of blood and agonizing pain, Thompson saw his scalp slip from the Indian's belt as he rode away. He crawled to retrieve it and then slumped forward in the grass, in severe shock, while the Indians set a trap for bigger game.

Experimenting with the tools that had been scattered when the handcar smashed into the barrier, the Cheyennes found they could pry spikes out of ties. Soon they had loosened a pair of rails, bent them upward, and twisted them. For good measure, they lashed a heap of ties to the upended rails.

The prairie was now dark. Thompson was becoming lucid enough to consider how he might steal away. Suddenly, a locomotive's headlight flashed into view in the east. A freight train was approaching. Three miles behind it came another.

Many of the Indians jumped onto their ponies and rode off to find out what the mysterious lights were. When they reached the first train, they turned and galloped alongside it, firing and yelling. The engineer and fireman, knowing that many a U.P. train had managed to outrun such pursuers, worked frantically to get all possible speed out of their engine. Gradually, the train pulled ahead of the horsemen. By now, it was going too fast to be stopped in time when the engineer sighted the obstacle on the track. In a screeching slide, the locomotive struck the barrier, leapt off the rails, and fell on one side, pulling the tender and first five cars into a crashing heap behind it.

The waiting Indians surged over the wreckage. They located the men in the cab, both badly hurt, and hauled them out to be killed. Then the warriors began furiously ripping open packing cases spilled from the broken cars, and setting fire to everything they didn't want. They tossed their victims' bodies onto the flames.

In the deep shadows at the back end of the train, the conductor and three other crewmen crept out of the caboose, where they had been riding at the time of the crash, and ran back to halt and board the following train. This they succeeded in doing, though the last man declared he had been chased most of the way. Once the survivors of the wreck were aboard the second train, the engineer started backing it at urgent speed. When he had retreated to Plum Creek station, 4 miles east, he telegraphed the news of the attack eastward, then continued to belt along in that direction.

Meanwhile, the marauding Cheyennes had discovered a barrel of whiskey among the plundered freight and were fast getting drunk. They had decked themselves in bonnets and velvets found in the wreckage. They had cut the feet off leather boots unearthed there, and were wearing the uppers as leggings. Some had fastened bolts of calico and muslin to their ponies' tails and tied ribbons to their manes. All were galloping erratically around the bonfires in boozy ecstasy.

Thompson peered blearily through the tall grass at this bacchanalia until, as the horsemen began to take soggy tumbles and lie where they fell, he realized it was time to make a break. Still clutching his scalp, he crawled away until it seemed safe to rise and hobble eastward down the dark track. Before dawn, he found his way to Plum Creek station, where he was taken care of until a rescue party arrived.

Thompson was carried back to Omaha on the floor of a boxcar, where he lay, as if dead, under a sheet. Beside him, in a pail of water, rode his salvaged scalp. He had the forlorn hope that if he kept it moist, someone would be able to restore it to his head.

It was rumored in Omaha that Dr. R. C. Moore, who treated him as soon as he arrived, might graft the scalp—9 inches wide, 7 inches long— back on Thompson's skull. Moore's case report reveals that he didn't even make the attempt. Thompson, being a young, vigorous man, eventually recovered and even went back to work for the railroad. (Quixotically, he had his useless scalp tanned, like an animal's hide, and in time mailed it to Dr. Moore for a souvenir. Eventually, it was given to the Omaha Public Library. There it still is today, ninety-five years after the Cheyenne dropped it, under a bell jar on a bookcase in the Boys' and Girls' Department. Youngsters are invariably fascinated by it.)

In spite of snow and floods at the start of the 1867 construction season, General Casement's tracklayers had covered the 65 miles between O'Fallons and Julesburg by June 25th. In early August, though somewhat rattled and slowed by Indian raids, they were many miles beyond Julesburg, up the Lodge Pole.

A correspondent for the Cincinnati *Gazette* watched them tramp past, and marveled at their speed and efficiency. He had counted strings of as many as eighty freight cars, loaded with materials, lined up on sidings to their rear. He had explored the boarding train and watched, fascinated, as supplies were moved up to the end of the rails, shifted to carts and horse-drawn rail cars, and rapidly transmuted into finished track.

He found the rhythmic progress of the tracklayers symbolic. As each pair of rails was swung off its low car and laid in place on the ties, by five men to a side, "the chief of the squad calls out 'Down,' " he wrote, "in a tone that equals the 'Forward' to any army. Every 30 seconds there came that brave 'Down,' 'Down,' on either side the track. They were the pendulum beats of a mighty era; they marked the time of the march and its regulation beat." [31]

Most of North Platte had been dismantled, shipped to Julesburg, and reassembled there before July had passed. The new "hell on wheels" was hotter and bigger than the first.

"Julesburg continues to grow with magic rapidity," Samuel Reed wrote his wife from there on July 30th. "Vice and crime stalk unblushingly in the mid-day sun." [32]

Henry M. Stanley arrived in mid-August, and was amazed at the sights he saw on his first evening stroll around town.

I walked on till I came to a dance-house, bearing the euphonious title of "King of the Hills," gorgeously decorated and brilliantly lighted. Coming suddenly from the dimly lighted street to the kerosene lighted restaurant, I was almost blinded by the glare and stunned by the clatter. The ground floor was as crowded as it could well be, and all were talking loud and fast, and mostly every one seemed bent on debauchery and dissipation.

The women appeared to be the most reckless, and the men seemed nothing loth to enter a whirlpool of sin. . . . These women are expensive articles, and come in for a large share of the money wasted. In broad daylight they may be seen gliding through the sandy streets in Black Crook dresses, carrying fancy derringers slung to their waists, with which tools they are dangerously expert. Should they get into a fuss, western chivalry will not allow them to be abused by any man whom they may have robbed.

At night, new aspects are presented in this city of premature growth. Watch-fires gleam over the sealike expanse of ground outside of the city, while inside soldiers, herdsmen, teamsters, women, railroad men, are dancing, singing or gambling. I verily believe that there are men here who would murder a fellow-creature for five dollars. Nay, there are men who have already done it, and who stalk abroad in daylight unwhipped of justice. Not a day passes but a dead body is found somewhere in the vicinity with pockets rifled of their contents. But the people generally are strangely indifferent to what is going on.

The only sure preventive of these murderous scenes is martial law [the British journalist concluded], or the ready strong arm of the vigilantes.[33]

A clique of gamblers decided to seize control of Julesburg and refuse to pay the Union Pacific for the lots they occupied. Dodge's land agent telegraphed him the news. The general immediately wired Jack Casement, telling him to take as big a force as he needed and go down and clean up the town. "This was fun for Casement," Dodge later commented, explaining that he hadn't learned what followed until he was on his way back from his western reconnaissance that fall. When he finally asked Casement for an accounting, the latter said, "When we get to Julesburg, I'll show you." Once there, Dodge recalled, "he took me up on a hill where there was quite a burial ground, and he said, 'General, they all died in their boots, and Julesburg has been quiet ever since.'" [34]

Dodge was told later that General Casement had armed 200 tracklayers and ridden into town down the Lodge Pole. The little general had first called a parley with the leaders of the revolt. They refused to obey his orders. At this point, said Dodge, Casement ordered his men to fire, "not caring whom he hit." He quickly had Julesburg in his grasp. Before he left, the surviving rebels were begging to be allowed to occupy quarters there and pay for them in full.

"They learned a lesson that lasted for some time," [35] wrote Dodge. It didn't last so very long, at that. Many of the same crowd tried defying the railroad once more when it got to Laramie.

By the midle of August, the Union Pacific was advertising in Denver papers that it was ready to start selling lots in Cheyenne, then only a little over a month old. The influx of settlers had begun earlier. On July 15th, Dodge had written his wife from Cheyenne that

people are already flocking here and, like Julesburg, at first it will be a second hell. I have got Gen. Augur to throw his protecting arm over it to keep them from owning town and all. They are coming from all quarters and all expect to make a fortune. . . . From the town site, which is a huge table land bounding Crow Creek, you can see the snow-capped Rocky Mountains for a distance of 100 miles. . . .

Government alone will build up here a large town, as it is to be the depot for all posts north and south and also the distributing point for all points in Colorado. During this winter our trains will stop here and the travel west will here leave; can take stage and other transportation. We shall also build a large workshop, machine shops, round houses, etc., and finally I hope here to meet you on my return from the mountains. I want you to see this country before you go to Washington.[36]

The Fortieth Congress, to which Dodge had been elected, through no effort or desire of his own, had been in session since March, and, as the general later confessed, "my constituents thought I should be there." However, he said, "I felt it was my duty to be out upon the work, thinking I could do more good than I could in Washington." [37] He didn't intend to arrive in the capital until December, at the start of the second session.

Dodge and Rawlins, with their large escort, were out on their 1,400-mile ride through Wyoming and eastern Utah for more than two months. An important companion during the initial part of the trip was Jacob Blickensderfer, Jr., a distinguished civil engineer from Ohio, who had been appointed by President Johnson to determine for the government and the railroad precisely where the Union Pacific's route encountered the east base of the Rockies. This point was of the utmost importance to the railroad-builders, of course. There, the U.S. bond subsidy granted them by the Pacific Railway Act would leap from $16,000 a mile to $48,000 a mile. It would remain at that attractive level for 150 miles beyond, and then slack off only to $32,000 a mile for all the rest of the way to wherever the U.P. met the C.P.

Blickensderfer determined by instrument that the east base of the Rockies began a trifle more than 6 miles west of Cheyenne. The 150-mile section of route on which the U.P. could draw its maximum subsidy would stretch from there to the second crossing of the North Platte, not far from the river's origin. This was technically the most mountainous portion of the Union Pacific's line. In actuality, however, except for the climb over Evans' Pass, which wasn't strenuous, the bulk of the territory lay in the high Laramie Plains, where railroad-building would be almost as cheap and easy as it had been in the Platte Valley. The chance for profit on the work was bright indeed. There was a striking difference between the minor difficulties the U.P. would encounter there and the great and costly ones with which the Central Pacific had to contend in its own 150-mile section of most mountainous country.

On their westward journey across the Laramie Plains, General Dodge and his fellow-travelers were moving through terrain that was only sketchily mapped, whose landmarks often bore no names, and they enjoyed the rare and exhilarating experience of christening geographical features as they rode by.

On the eastern edge of the Bitter Creek region, the travelers came upon Thomas Bates and his despairing band of surveyors, close to death from thirst. They had lost most of their horses to Indian raiders. Dodge arranged to restore and replenish this party, left it an escort, and pushed on to Fort Bridger, in southwestern Wyoming.

There, late in August, the U.P.'s chief engineer found a significant letter from Oliver Ames awaiting him. It was written from Ames' home, in North Easton, Massachusetts, and dated August 15th.

We had a special meeting last week, and gave out a contract to my brother, Mr. Oakes Ames, to construct the road 667 miles beyond the 100th Meridian. This takes the road on 914 miles beyond Omaha and, according to your last report, within 110 miles of Salt Lake. This contract has no provision to favor Durant or any other individual, and will be managed very much as the road construction is now being managed, only we hope to every year have additional economies carried into the construction and by better line and better management make the road a paying institution.[38]

The Ames contract, as it was always called thereafter, anticipated a total expenditure of nearly $48 million. The charge for construction per mile would vary from $42,000 to $96,000, according to its location. Those figures included a price of not less than $7,500 a mile for stations and other essential buildings, rolling stock, machinery, water tanks, turntables, switches, and side tracks. Applying, as it did, to 667 miles of route, it was the biggest construction contract in American railroad history up to that time. Some friends of Oakes Ames thought, as one of them said, that it was also "the wildest contract ever made by a civilized man." [39]

It seemed wild when viewed superficially as one individual's assumption of enormous financial risk. There were aspects of it, however, that made it a much less hazardous proposition. In the first place, the Ames contract was written to start from the 247th milepost, where the Hoxie contract had run out. Therefore, it applied to 138 miles of track already completed beyond that point by the Credit Mobilier. Since those miles, as Durant had already testified in his injunction suits, had cost no more than $27,500 apiece, the Ames contract assured an immediate, large profit to the builders.

Besides, Oakes Ames and his closest associates had agreed from the beginning that the potential profits of the new contract, as well as its risks, must be shared with all the stockholders of the Credit Mobilier, practically all of whom were also stockholders of the Union Pacific. The only question to be resolved at the time Ames signed the contract, in August, was just how this arrangement could be made to satisfy the major stockholders concerned. More particularly, the question was: How could Durant and his friends be made to cooperate? The Ameses would have been greatly relieved to be rid of them altogether. This was impossible because of the amount of stock they controlled. Nevertheless, as late as mid-September, Oliver Ames was still hoping to remove Durant from the U.P.'s governing circle.

I do not think we should do right to put Durant in as a director [he wrote to Henry McComb, one of Durant's chief cohorts, on September 17th], unless he withdraws his injunction suits and submits to the will of the majority. He cannot hurt us half so badly out of the direction as he can in, and there is no pleasure, peace, safety, or comfort with him unless he agrees to abide the decision of the majority, as the rest of us do.[40]

The Ames faction attempted to drop Durant from the U.P. directorate at the annual meeting of stockholders, October 2nd. After a sharp fight, the effort failed.

In order to keep the work at the construction front going full blast while this top-echelon conflict raged, the contestants were content for a time to let Oakes Ames have the construction contract in his own name. He was the only one among them whose credit was equal to the task and whose integrity was accepted by all. His position of lonely financial vulnerability lasted only two months, however. By October 15th, all the details for sharing the profits and hazards had been worked out. On that date, Oakes Ames assigned his contract to seven trustees—Oliver Ames, Thomas C. Durant, John B. Alley, Sidney Dillon, Cornelius S. Bushnell, Henry S. McComb, and Benjamin E. Bates. They were to carry out its terms as trustees for the stockholders of the Credit Mobilier (who, almost to the last man, were also stockholders in the Union Pacific). They were to be held harmless by that corporation in case of liability, loss, or damage incurred in the process.

To make sure that they would have as tight control of the Union Pacific during the life of the contract as they had of the Credit Mobilier, the trustees stipulated that every stockholder in the Credit Mobilier must promptly grant them authority in writing to vote six-tenths of his present shares of U.P. stock, and of any he might later acquire, as they pleased. If he refused, he was to be denied his part of any benefits accruing from the Ames contract and be bought out.

Four of the trustees—Ames, Alley, Dillon, and Bates—represented the viewpoint of the "Boston crowd," and had strength enough behind them to insist on a clause in the contract that required all seven trustees to abide by any decision to which four of them agreed. The Ames faction felt pretty certain of being able to prevail over Durant, Bushnell, and Mc-Comb (though Bates' vote could not be counted on with certainty). Moreover, they saw to it that the terms of the trusteeship required that if any one of them refused to abide by majority rule or was caught cheating, he was immediately to lose his position and all future benefits from the Credit Mobilier. Durant could not have rejoiced at this arrangement, but it was the best he could get. He never again became an officer of the Credit Mobilier, but he retained his vice-presidency and directorship of the Union Pacific, for what they were worth to him, until the railroad was finished.

Nearly all stockholders in the Credit Mobilier hurried to give the trustees of the Ames contract the endorsement they demanded. The only holdout of note was Gen. John Adams Dix, U.S. Minister to France, who owned no Credit Mobilier stock but was the possessor of a number of original Union Pacific shares. The trustees were anxious to control those shares. Dix said afterward that he couldn't stomach the terms of the Ames contract; he thought them "unjust" [41] to the government and the people of the United States. So after arranging, from Paris, to sell his U.P. stock back to the company for $50,000, he resigned as president of the railroad. In November, 1867, Oliver Ames, who had been acting president for a year, was elected to take Dix's place.

Out on the construction front, Sam Reed heard about the doings in New York with considerable misgiving. "Seven men have been chosen by the company to control the building the coming season," he reported to his wife from Julesburg on October 21st, "and I fear that business will be seven times more complicated than heretofore." [42]

Throughout the fall of 1867 there were 3,500 graders at work on the line between Julesburg and Evans' Pass. The Casements had swelled their tracklaying force to 450. From the 440th mile on, by orders from New York, they had been spiking down heavier rails—56 pounds to the yard instead of the original 50—and linking the ends with fish-plate joints instead of the earlier, less suitable "chairs." Three hundred men were running the Union Pacific's trains, of which there was now an impressive stable. The company's rolling stock consisted of fifty-three locomotives, 1,100 freight cars, ten passenger cars, five baggage cars, and sixty hand-cars. There were 350 mechanics and carpenters at work in the big new shops at Omaha and North Platte. Together they could turn out twenty cars a week and make all of the railroad's mechanical repairs.

Things were going so well in October that Sam Reed had written, "For once I am not driven to death by work. My bridges are built a long way ahead of the track." [43]

Indian attacks on the railroad builders had petered out gradually as the summer waned and President Johnson's Peace Commission progressed from parley to parley with tribal chieftains. General Sherman had been appointed to it in August, and by the end of September was convinced that it would not accomplish much. Furthermore, he found himself entirely out of agreement with Senator John B. Henderson of Missouri, chairman of the Senate's Committee on Indian Affairs.

We have now been near two months on the Indian Commission [Sherman wrote his brother, the Senator, from St. Louis on September 28th], and I can pretty closely judge the result. It cannot be complete or final, because it will take years to do all the law requires, and I suppose the pressure will force Congress to do something conclusive this winter. According to existing treaties with Indians, they have a right to wander and hunt across all the railroads toward the West, and Henderson thinks we had no right to locate roads through without a prior assent, and by the payment of damages. Whether right or wrong, those roads will be built, and everybody knows that Congress, after granting the charters and fixing the routes, cannot now back out and surrender the country to a few bands of roving Indians.[44]

In any event, the commissioners were planning to meet more tribes the following spring, at Fort Laramie. Maybe something would be settled then.

As October began, many of the grading outfits strung out below Crow Creek had finished their work and were shifting to the Laramie Plains. Arthur Ferguson's engineering group moved along behind, while Ferguson admired the approach to Cheyenne and, 31 miles beyond, the summit of the Black Hills. "This region is well adapted for a railroad," he noted in his diary, "it being a long valley of heavy, though gradual, ascent, and at the western extremity the Black Hills can be dimly seen, like some hazy cloud looming up in the distance." [45]

On October 5th Ferguson's party was camped 35 miles west of the summit, on the Big Laramie River. So were Generals Dodge and Rawlins, with escort, on their homeward way from Salt Lake City. The generals had had a cordial meeting with Brigham Young, who still expected the Union Pacific to run through his capital, though Dodge was secretly sure it wouldn't. They had also explored the Wasatch Mountains, assured themselves that a line through Echo and Weber Canyons would be the best route into the valley from Wyoming, and had even taken a hasty look at the approaches to the Snake River in southeastern Idaho. Dodge had in mind the possibility of the Union Pacific's eventually using part of the valley of the Snake to get to Idaho, Oregon, and Washington.

By mid-November, the Union Pacific's track was at Cheyenne. By the end of the year it would be nearly at the top of Evans' Pass. Dodge had already christened the railroad's highest point Sherman Summit. The late winter, the spring's destructive floods, the Indian raids of summer had prevented Dodge and his organization from realizing their goal of building as far as Fort Sanders, but they had not fallen far short of it. The total mileage for 1867 would be 245 instead of the anticipated 288. The chief engineer felt confident his men would more than make up the difference in 1868.

The exodus from Julesburg had begun long before Cheyenne preempted its position as the forward base for construction. The first train to reach Cheyenne after the track did, on November 13th, was made up entirely of flatcars, heaped high with numbered sections of dismantled buildings. As the train creaked in beside the hangers-on at Cheyenne station, a brakeman mockingly called out, "Gentlemen, here's Julesburg." There was little left behind but a large pile of tin cans, bottles, and rubbish. In a few hours, Julesburg's buildings were set up beside Crow Creek, and Cheyenne began burgeoning with arrivals bent on a winter of sensual indulgence.

On November 14th everyone in town celebrated the railroad's arrival. Sidney Dillon and Jack Casement were on hand to make short speeches in response to the crowd's demands. Afterward, in McDaniel's Museum, which featured more than one kind of entertainment, the little general hopped up on the long bar and jovially sat there, dangling his feet, while treating his men to Tom and Jerrys. The walls were plastered with crude slogans, among them "The Iron Horse Snorts Defiance at the Rocky Mountains" and "Get Out Ox Train You Make Me Laugh."

In Washington, at noon on Monday, December 2, 1867, the second session of the notorious Fortieth Congress began. Its consuming interest was an effort to punish President Johnson for perpetuating Lincoln's conciliatory attitude toward the defeated South. The new representative from Iowa's Fifth Congressional District, Gen. Grenville Dodge, was on hand for a roll call for only the second time in the thirteen months since his election. His presence would be but slightly felt. The Department of the Interior had considerately provided him with a special office and telegraph facilities, so he could keep in constant touch with his division engineers out West. He spent a good deal of time in that office, making only one speech on the floor of the House, and that in defense of the Union Pacific, during the following six months.

Dodge drew a seat in the next-to-the-last row on the west side of the House of Representatives. Four seats to his right sat a veteran representative from Wisconsin, Cadwalader C. Washburn, a rich man and former major general of volunteers in the late war, who was a loud-voiced, self-styled champion of the people. He and his even more vociferous brother, Representative Elihu B. Washburne of Illinois, were on their feet, talking, more often and at greater length than any other members of the House. Any American voter with a legitimate grievance knew that he merely needed to reveal it to either of these gentlemen to have it clamorously aired in Congress. They vied with each other in defending the Constitution and protecting the U.S. Treasury from raids by special interests.

They vehemently dedicated themselves to trying to safeguard the taxpayer's dollar. Some of their colleagues resented or snickered at these alertly suspicious congressmen, who appeared at times to assume that they alone were acting in the public interest, but if ever such men were needed, it was in the Fortieth Congress.

Diagonally across the House chamber from Dodge and C. C. Washburn, Representative Oakes Ames stolidly occupied a seat in the front row. From there he occasionally introduced a bill of local importance to his loyal constituents in eastern Massachusetts, but rarely took part in debate and never made a speech. He was serving his third term in Congress. He would be reelected twice more.

On December 9th, when the second session of the Fortieth Congress was only a week old, Representative C. C. Washburn introduced a bill of apparently casual significance that lighted a slow-burning fuse of events leading eventually to a spectacular explosion. The bill aimed to reduce freight rates and passenger fares on the Union Pacific and Central Pacific Railroads, declaring that they must not be permitted to exceed double the rates charged on railroads east of the Mississippi and north of the latitude of St. Louis.

The Clerk of the House read Washburn's bill twice through aloud. The House then voted to send it to the Committee on the Pacific Railroad. This procedure was entirely routine. There was no debate at the time.

However, historians have generally agreed that it was the introduction of the Washburn bill that persuaded Oakes Ames to embark upon unwise and questionable negotiations in the month of December, 1867. They led in the course of five years to one of the noisiest political uproars of the nineteenth century, the Credit Mobilier Scandal. The scandal would tar the Republican party for four Presidential campaigns, bring public humiliation upon Ames, and hasten his death.

CHAPTER THIRTEEN

PICKING UP SPEED
IN NEVADA

Charlie Crocker's New Year's resolution for 1868 was "a mile of track for every working day." [1] It seemed an incredible goal, wholly unlikely to be realized, but there was desperate pressure on him to attain it.

The Central Pacific had now been under construction for five years. Yet the product of those years was only 131 miles of track, and they were not continuous. A gap of 7 miles still broke the line on the eastern slope of the Sierra, not far below the Summit.

So far, building the roadbed alone had cost more than $22 million. Rolling stock, stations, shops, roundhouses, warehouses, and essential equipment had added $10 million to the bill. This meant an average cost of $245,600 a mile—dismayingly higher than the maximum government subsidy, $48,000 a mile. A lot of first-mortgage bonds, land-grant bonds, and shares of C.P. stock would have to be sold to make up the difference.

If the builders had not been in a frantic hurry to meet the Union Pacific at Salt Lake, expenses needn't have been nearly so great. J. H. Strobridge, Crocker's chief-of-staff, later declared that if the Central Pacific could have been built at a relaxed pace, selecting the most advantageous times for purchasing and shipping, and the most favorable seasons for working, it would have cost at least 70 per cent less than it did. Instead, from midsummer of 1866 onward, it was constructed, as Strobridge said, "without regard to any outlay that would hasten its completion." [2]

The steep cost of speed was afterward detailed by Lewis M. Clement, Chief Engineer Montague's principal assistant. By 1868, he said, the price of rails had risen to $91.70 a ton at the Eastern rolling mills. To get the rails to Sacramento dependably, and as fast as possible, it was necessary to send them by steamer and by the shortest route, conveying them across the Isthmus of Panama by train. Yet, using the Isthmus route cost a fearful amount in freight charges—as much as $51.97 a ton. The rates were also exorbitant for rolling stock. Freight costs on one locomotive sent by way of Panama were $8,100—almost as much as the engine itself cost. Even these fancy expenses were enlarged before the shipments reached their ultimate destination. At San Francisco, ocean cargoes had to be transferred to river schooners for the trip to Sacramento. At Sacramento, the schooners' loads were shifted to trains. In the winter of 1867–68, as during the one before, the trains carried them only as far as they could push their way through the snow, often no farther than Cisco. From there, the essential materials from the East had to travel by sled and log raft until they were down below the snow line on the Truckee River. At the Truckee, they got back on the track, now lengthening eastward at increasing speed.

Unseasonal demand and grave difficulties in delivery enormously inflated the prices of such homely items as barley and oats and hay, for the Central Pacific's droves of work horses. Barley and oats soared to from $200 to $280 a ton. Hay cost as much as $120 a ton, and was often not recognizable as such.

Strobridge told of once meeting a farmer with "a stack of rough stuff, willows, wiregrass, tules, and weeds." He asked the man, who did not associate him with the C.P., what he intended to do with this motley load.

"Oh," the farmer replied, "I am going to take it up to the railroad camp. If hay is high, I'll sell it for hay. If wood is high, I'll sell it for wood." [3]

Crocker had transferred nearly 5,000 men to the Truckee before winter seriously obstructed his supply line across the mountains. He left only enough of his work force in the high country to complete Tunnels Nos. 12 and 13, above Donner Lake. There, Chinese gangs worked and lived like moles, as they had the previous year.

This winter was as rugged as its predecessor. Snow had fallen at Cisco as early as September 14, 1867. By December, it seemed to be coming down continuously. John R. Brown, the freight agent at Cisco, a young man whose heart was with a girl in Sacramento and who longed to flee from accumulating drifts and railroad cargoes, kept a diary that recorded little else but bad weather during the following six months.

Down the tumbling stream that flowed eastward past the crude settlement of Truckee—named for a benevolent local Indian chief who had greeted his first white visitors with that word, the Piute equivalent of "O.K."—Strobridge was busily setting up an organzation to make good Crocker's boast to construct more than 300 miles of track during 1868.

He no longer anticipated trouble from the weather. Beginning at Truckee, 5,825 feet above sea level, where the snow was seldom more than 3 feet deep, the railroad's route for 35 miles followed the little river's gentle, zigzag descent of 35 to 40 feet per mile to the Truckee Meadows, 1,329 feet below. There, snow was infrequent, and rarely amounted to more than 6 inches at any time.

For a few days early in January, however, Strobridge anxiously wondered if he had been wrong in assuming that the weather would be on his side. An unexpectedly severe storm swept across the Sierra's crest and spread heavy snow far inland. It dumped 2 feet on the Truckee Meadows, and in the plunging temperatures that followed, the storm tapered off into a freezing fog, which coated everything with thick frost.

This dismal climatic caper was a brief one, fortunately. Very soon there was nothing worse than mud to delay the railroaders.

Strobridge now lived at the front, as the end of track was called. He had persuaded his wife to join him, and they had set up housekeeping in a slightly embellished boxcar. It had three small rooms, windows, a narrow, recessed porch in the middle of the right side, and a ventilator in the roof. Mrs. Strobridge must have had a special genius for decorating. When a West Coast newspaperman first saw her crude menage on wheels, he declared that it was "a home that would not discredit San Francisco." [4] Attached to it were other windowed boxcars, several of them with tin chimneys. These headquarters cars contained a telegraph office, a camp kitchen, a store, and sleeping quarters for Strobridge's staff. They remained coupled together and were shifted to a new siding every few days as the track persistently lengthened. During the building of the railroad, Strobridge put in a siding about every 10 miles.

At the outset of 1868, the Chinese laborers and their Irish foremen lived in huts and sheds in Truckee, and rode to each day's work on construction trains. Spring arrives early on the east slopes of the Sierra, however, and it was not long before communities of tents blossomed along the line of grading. From then on, the easily moved tent cities rarely settled anywhere for more than a couple of nights.

On the outskirts of every encampment, the horses and mules were staked out at night, with rows of carts and wagons walling them in. Portable blacksmith and harness shops were essential parts of this assemblage.

Each workday began with a shrill signal from a locomotive whistle at dawn, and closed with a similar, prolonged hoot at sunset. The tactics of construction were intricate, but were soon refined into a smooth flow of materials and a strict division of labor that resulted in astonishing progress.

The graders and bridge builders worked many miles in advance of the tracklayers, of course. For the latter, a supply train moved up from the nearest distribution point—at this time, Truckee—during each night, scheduled to arrive at the end of track just before dawn. It was loaded with ties, rails, spikes, fish joints (iron plates, shaped vaguely like fish, for bolting rail ends together), bolts and nuts, telegraph poles, and wire. After the train had been pushed as far forward as it could go, these materials were thrown off onto the ground beside the cars, and the emptied train was hauled away. Workmen drew on the trackside piles of supplies all day long. Ties were carried forward in wagons, rails on little low flatcars—mere frames on wheels—drawn by horses over the track as it grew.

While the tracklayers were busy with their mission, telegraph crews were distributing poles alongside by wagon, nailing crossbars in place, digging holes, erecting the poles in them, unreeling wire and stringing it. They ran a daily race with the track men, determined that it would be possible each night to telegraph the day's accomplishment from the very end of the rail.[5] In one respect, these men were well ahead of their rivals. There was no break in their line from Sacramento, whereas the track builders must return to the mountains and close a 7-mile gap, as soon as the snow would let them.

By mid-April, 1868, Strobridge moved a large number of his Chinese back into the still snowbound region above Donner Lake and set them to digging out the surveyed line where the unfinished link in the track must be forged as soon as possible. Snow had drifted and frozen there to depths of from 10 to 30 feet. The cuts that had been blasted out the previous year between Tunnels Nos. 8 and 10 were buried under snow mounds 20 to 60 feet high. For 15 miles west of the Summit, the track leading up from Cisco lay far beneath the crusty surface of snow so firmly impacted that plows made no impression on it. Thousands of men had to clear that 15-mile stretch of track and the 7-mile gap east of it, with blasting powder as well as picks and shovels, before two major construction tasks could begin. The first, in order of urgency, was to make the track continuous from Sacramento to its eastern end, now rapidly approaching the Truckee Meadows. The second task, though less pressing, was of far greater magnitude. That was the building of snow sheds over most of the line that lay within the belt of heaviest snowfall.

Arthur Brown, the thirty-eight-year-old Scot who was the C.P.'s diligent superintendent of bridges and buildings, threw 2,500 men into this last endeavor as soon as the west end of the line was clear of the past winter's snow. He kept six trains constantly busy bringing them timber and spikes and bolts. All the sawmills within reach were overburdened trying to meet Brown's demands for beams for his sheds and bridges and Strobridge's constant need for more ties. Finally, Brown was obliged to resort to tree trunks, stripped of bark, and hewn timber to piece out his inadequate supply of sawed lumber.

The labor market was also strained to accommodate Brown's requisitions. As a result, wages climbed. Brown had to pay carpenters $4 a day, a startling rate at the time, and ordinary laborers from $2.50 to $3. These men were mostly Irish. Crocker kept the majority of his Chinese under Strobridge's command, pushing the railroad itself eastward at an ever faster pace.

Experience during the winter of 1867–68, when only about 5 miles of sheds had been in use, had shown that large expanses of deep snow on a steep slope had an inexorable downhill movement, like that of a glacier, only much faster. The heaviest timber snapped under the strain of trying to resist it. Though only about 250 feet of snow sheds had succumbed to this sort of attack already, Brown and his superiors decided that action must be taken at once to protect the 32 miles of sheds that were to be built during 1868 and 1869. It was essential to prevent side pressure on them.

Two pieces of strategy foiled the crawling snow fields. First, in intermittent stretches adding up to 4 miles, huge retaining walls were built upslope from the track, the walls being strengthened on the downside by heaps of boulders. These walls, it was later found, acted like dams in the path of the snow flow, forcing it over their tops when it became too deep to halt. It was then that the second strategic action took effect. Downslope, the roofs of the sheds were built at a slant to match that of the hillside. Once the accumulating, slowly moving snow had brimmed the retaining walls, it slid on over the roofs of the sheds instead of pushing the sheds out of its way.

Brown's men covered 18 miles of track with snow sheds during 1868. By the time the first big storms of the following winter blustered in, C.P. train crews were "railroading in a barn" almost continuously for 9 miles west of the Summit and 4 miles east of it. Elsewhere, they passed through wooden tunnels wherever snowslides or especially deep drifting had occurred during the winter of 1867–68. A total of 2 miles of sheds protected double tracks, at stations.

This construction work had proceeded under a nagging handicap. In addition to unloading their own supply trains, the builders had had to spend a third of their time getting themselves and their materials out of the way of freights moving to and from Strobridge's forces in Nevada.

The traffic through the ranks of the shed-builders was heavy. As soon as the track was open all the way from Sacramento to the Truckee Meadows, Crocker sent fifty carloads of supplies a day to Strobridge. The cars were divided into five trains, each hauled by two locomotives, and, of course, they came rattling back over the Sierra as soon as they had been emptied.

Every 2 miles of new track, recorded the English traveler W. A. Bell, who watched the hurly-burly with fascination that spring, consumed 500 tons of rails, ties, and track hardware.

While the snow-lined gap in the track above Donner Lake was being closed at top speed, Strobridge's railroad builders along the Truckee were thundering down toward a point on the western edge of the lush Truckee Meadows, where the wild grass grew 2 to 3 feet high. Here, westbound pioneers used to fatten their lean horses and cattle before pushing over the Sierra to their journeys' ends in the late spring. N. C. Lake had built a bridge across the Truckee at a place where the wagon trains had formerly forded the little river. This spot was now called Lake's Crossing.

Central Pacific officials, some months earlier, had chosen Lake's Crossing as the ideal place to locate a station to serve the free-spending communities of tiny Carson City, the state capital, and, especially, of Virginia

City. Carson City was more than 25 miles south, and rich Virginia City, on its lofty perch in the mountains, about 18 miles south of Lake's Crossing, but this was the point on the C.P. route that would be nearest to them.

Charles Crocker had obtained from Lake a deed to 40 acres of land surrounding the Crossing. He had the tract laid out in town lots and, when his map was duly filed with the proper authorities, in May, 1868, christened the place Reno. There's a story that the name of Maj. Gen. Jesse Lee Reno, a Union Army hero killed at the Battle of South Mountain in September, 1862, had been written on a slip and placed in a hat with a handful of other possibilities. A few classically minded Nevadans had suggested christening Crocker's town Argenta, in deference to the state's chief product at the time, but that was saved for another community along the line. Reno was the name drawn out of the hat, supposedly by Crocker himself. One Nevada newspaper noted thankfully that the railroad officials had omitted the common appendage "City," which, it said, was usually no better than a joke anyway.

Reno sprang to life in a dazzling hurry. Its lots went on public sale May 9th, and at the auction some of them brought as much as $1,000 apiece. Within a few days 200 crude stores and dwellings were sprouting on the lots.

Immediately, Carson City was jealous. Three days after the sale, the Carson *Daily Appeal* warned its readers, "Reno has just sprung up full feathered and lively. Carson must make the best of its natural advantages and not let the new city on the Truckee run away with the capital one of these days." [6]

The month of May was merry indeed in Reno, as the lot-buyers began putting up their shops and houses, expecting daily to see the end of track come sliding in from the west. An early history sourly commented:

Saloons were the first places of business to be opened, and by far the best patronized. For a few weeks, men had nothing to do but to see to it that these "necessary evils" did not fail for lack of an occasional two-bit piece, and it is hardly necessary to remark that they attended to this duty with a zeal worthy of a better cause. [7]

The C.P. officials had decided to confront the Union Pacific with completed grading, and perhaps a section of track in place on it, by the time Casement's men began nosing down into Salt Lake Valley from the east.

To implement that strategy, the Central Pacific had already filed with the Secretary of the Interior the plans and profiles for its proposed route from Humboldt Wells, Nevada, to Monument Point, at the northwest corner of Great Salt Lake. In a few months, it would file a sequel, extending the C.P. line all the way to Echo Summit, Utah, 69 miles east of Ogden. That would precipitate trouble in Washington and with the U.P., but it was half a year away.

At present, the Central Pacific's rails were more than 500 miles west of Echo Summit. The Pacific Railroad Act forbade the builders to draw subsidies on work done more than 300 miles ahead of their continuous track. Yet the C.P. officials now decided that it was so important to get grade built in Utah that they could dispense with subsidies on it until the track was near enough to justify them. The Utah grading must begin at once.

With this purpose, Stanford and Consulting Engineer Gray set out for Salt Lake City the first week in June to make the necessary arrangements with Brigham Young. Without Young's approval, there would be no Mormon help for the Central Pacific, or any other company.

On June 9th Stanford sent distasteful news back to Hopkins. He reported that the Union Pacific's Colonel Seymour and Sam Reed were already in Salt Lake City. Moreover, they were on cozy terms with Young, and Stanford at first felt forlorn.

He had reason to be depressed. Reed had written home triumphantly on June 7th that

Governor Stanford and Mr. Gray . . . are very much disappointed to learn that we are so advanced with our end of the work. They are trying to contract with Brigham Young to do their work west of this place, but he answers that he has all he can do at present to complete the work taken from me; after that is completed he will make contracts with them if they want to. In the meantime our road will be finished one or two hundred miles west of this city.[8]

When I arrived [Stanford confided to Hopkins on the ninth], they thought they had it all their own way. Brigham was cold and close, but I have, I think, got pretty near to him. He and everybody here was dead set for the southern rout [sic; around the bottom end of Great Salt Lake]. How to meet this bothered me a good deal, but this afternoon, being pressed, I was able to find good reasons why they would be most benefited by the northern rout [sic]. There does not seem any of them to be aware of the location [the Central Pacific's surveyed line] from Humboldt Wells to the north of the Lake. I have not thought it advisable to enlighten them.[9]

Stanford's conversations with the U.P. men had unsettled him.

Col. Seymour told me [he wrote to Hopkins] they expected to be at the mouth of Weber [Canyon] by the first of January. They lay track night and day.

Have Charley double his energy, and do what is necessary to secure what labor is required to push the road to its utmost. Anything less than the utmost that can be done will very likely end in defeat, and, forewarned as we are, anything less than the utmost that can be done will merit it.

Stanford was shaken by his experience, and confessed to Hopkins that "it has been pretty difficult navigating here, and it requires care now to avoid getting into the breakers, which are devilish close, but I think I see the way out." [10]

Huntington, meanwhile, was expressing to Hopkins his doubts that Stanford and Grey were the best negotiators that could have been sent to Salt Lake City. "We need a bold, sharp man," [11] he grumbled. There's little doubt about whom he had in mind.

Yet Stanford found a way out. It was provided by the Mormon contracting firm of Benson, Farr & West. Ezra Taft Benson was a member of Brigham Young's original Council of Twelve and great-grandfather of a future Secretary of Agriculture. Lorin Farr was the Vermont-born mayor of Ogden. Chauncey W. West was a Mormon bishop. They engaged to build grade for the Central Pacific for 100 miles west from Monument Point. Hard-driving Bishop West, then a vigorous forty-three, was to be in active charge of the work.

At about the same time, Charlie Crocker decided to push his own Chinese graders as far out in front of him as possible. He dispatched 3,000 of them and a fleet of 400 carts to Palisades Canyon, on the Humboldt River, 300 miles in advance of his shuttling trains. There, among high, heavily eroded walls of brown rock, between which the track would wind intermittently for a total of 17 miles, these men and their horses began the most difficulty preparatory work that lay between Reno and the Salt Lake Valley. Their supply line was not only long; it was terribly costly. Strobridge once reported that distributing a single carload of tools and supplies from the end of the rails to the furthermost graders had cost $5,400.

On June 16th Judge Crocker sent a triumphant telegram to Huntington: "The track is connected across the mountains," it read. "We have one hundred and sixty-seven continuous miles laid." [12] He had originally added, "and can sell bonds accordingly," but had scratched out those words on the telegram blank. Of all people, Collis Huntington hardly needed to be reminded of this basic fiscal fact.

On June 18th the first passenger train from Sacramento arrived at Reno, bringing to the recent settlers of that rough-hewn community "tangible assurance that their confidence had not been misplaced." So an anonymous chronicler of the time put it.

> From that day on Reno counts its career as a business town.
> No sooner did trains begin to arrive from Sacramento with their loads of freight and passengers than Reno began to bustle with life and activity. Stages left daily for Carson and Virginia, crowded with passengers, and long trains of freight wagons were loaded with goods at the depot, from the scores of cars that arrived weekly, and defiled through the streets and out upon the roads that led to their destination.[13]

This meant rapidly rising revenues for the Central Pacific. By the time 1868 was over, Mark Hopkins and his accountants would find that the company had earned its biggest net profit for any year to date—more than $1,250,000.

Rail traffic became so heavy and complex, with its potpourri of scheduled passenger trains and freights and unscheduled construction trains, that an elaborate set of "Rules and Regulations for Employees" [14] was composed and printed. A surviving copy, larger than a page from a tabloid newspaper, provides entertaining and instructive reading.

Specially bold type carried a warning that stemmed directly from the unprecedented pressure of traffic movements:

> Carefulness is enjoined to prevent accidents when taking Wood and Water in obscure places. A man with a Red Flag by day, or a Red Light by night, must be stationed a sufficient distance in the rear to warn approaching trains. In such cases, TRAINS MUST ALWAYS BE EXPECTED.

Lest engineers be carried away by an undue sense of urgency between stops for Wood and Water, they were given notice that if they killed any farm animal en route, and it was found that they could have avoided hitting it, the value of the beast would be taken out of their pay. (One wonders what happened to the engineer of the locomotive Grizzly Bear, which hit a cow just east of Dutch Flat station and was derailed, sliding down into a deep gulley.)

Also, they were admonished to feel their way along in the tricky places. "Enginemen will enter all Tunnels with great caution," read the rules, "and no Train or Engine shall cross any bridge or trestle work at a rate of speed exceeding six miles an hour."

The fact that all the locomotives burned wood for fuel, and that crucial parts of the railroad were built of the same flammable material, led to another vital point to emphasize: "Dampers of ash pans *must in all cases be closed* while Engines are crossing bridges and passing wood yards."

There must be no casual abandonment of rolling stock, either. "Cars must *never* be allowed to *stand on the Main Track,* but must be placed on a siding, and the wheels must be securely blocked."

This was before the invention of air brakes, of course, and the process of bringing a train to a halt with the aid of hand brakes on each car and on the locomotive always involved unpredictable and uneven teamwork. The "Rules and Regulations for Employees" did its best to smooth the way for more finesse in this operation. "When the Engineman shuts off steam at Stations where the Train is to stop, the Brakemen must apply their brakes, and, using judgment, endeavor to stop at the Station without the necessity of the Engineer sounding his whistle," train crews were told. "Too much sounding of the whistle impairs its value as a signal of danger." On the other hand, "Brakemen must not *slip* the wheels, and it is the duty of the Conductor, and a very important one, to see to this matter."

Once the Central Pacific track was continuous from Sacramento to its easternmost rails, Charles Crocker was able to keep in much closer personal touch with his field forces. From mid-June on, he made the most of his opportunity. "Why," he once told an interviewer, "I used to go up and down that road in my car like a mad bull, stopping along wherever there was anything going amiss, and raising Old Nick with the boys that were not up to time." [15]

"The boys" were not the only sufferers. Mrs. Crocker felt the repercussions of her husband's increasing burden of worry and responsibility.

"When I came home to Sacramento," Crocker recalled, "my wife used to say, 'Why, Charlie, what is the matter? Why do you toss about so in bed?'

" 'I don't know,' said I, 'unless it is that I am getting old. I cannot sleep as I used to sleep.' "

But a restless occasional bedfellow wasn't Mrs. Crocker's only cause for complaint. Her husband had lost his genial disposition, too.

I became so that my wife used to be afraid of me. Said she, "Charlie, if you were going to build another railroad, I should just want to get away from you."

"Well," said I, "you know that I don't mean anything when I am abrupt with you."

"Well," said she, your manner is overbearing and gruff. That is the way you talk with me and with everybody."

I got so that I was really ashamed of myself. That sort of bearing was entirely foreign to me.[16]

Strobridge and his men needed no tongue-lashing from Crocker to put spirit into their efforts to lay the rails eastward that summer. They wasted no time congratulating themselves on reaching Reno, but went racing on down the Lower Canyon of the Truckee, through a narrowing meadow-land that lay between great, round, bare brown hills, until the river swung abruptly away from them and headed north for its outlet, Pyramid Lake. This point, the Big Bend of the Truckee, was about 35 miles east of Reno.

The construction superintendent's headquarters train, with additional crude dormitory cars for some of his Chinese, moved close on their heels. J. C. Lewis, editor of the days-old Reno *Crescent*, saw it roll through his town and was "struck all of a heap" by the strange sight. He wrote whimsically:

A locomotive came rushing down the track having in tow a string of boarding and lodging houses. One and four-story houses, which we called the Hotel de China. In the lower deck was cooking apartments; the second, third, and fourth decks were sleeping and eating rooms. Next, a three-decker, then a two-decker, and several houses of a superior quality for the officials of the company. These looked at first sight like a fleet of Merrimacs and Monitors going to get iron-clad. The windows of the four-decker looked like portholes; the heads of the John's sticking out of them looked in the distance like tompions of guns, with the tails for laniards. Altogether a novel sight and one we shall long remember. We are prepared for anything Charlie Crocker may do in the future.[17]

One thing not even Crocker himself was prepared to do at this point was hold a peace conference with an Indian chief, but he became obliged to.

Some Shoshones were in a mood to dispute the Chinese invasion of the Lower Truckee, and took a few pot shots at the track-builders. Crocker corraled the culprits and sent for their chief. Through an interpreter, he told this dignitary that he was a big chief himself, and could not stand for sniping. Crocker then produced two copies of a treaty of peace between his railroad and the Shoshone chief's tribe. The penalty for breaking the pact was death, he solemnly warned. On the other hand, lest the advantage seem one-sided, the Shoshones were assured of free passage in first-class cars (as soon as they began running through that territory) if they'd refrain from shooting at railroaders. Crocker signed one side of each copy of the agreement. The Shoshone chief made his mark on the other. Each document was then made to look suitably impressive by being stamped with a huge railroad seal.

"After this," commented Collis Huntington, who told the story of the pact, "the great army of laborers working on the railroad there had no more trouble with the Indians." [18]

The Piutes, a less disputatious tribe, considered to be lower on the social scale than Shoshones, were also given free rides on the railroad in return for their goodwill. But in their case the Central Pacific made a sharp distinction between its treatment of the chief, who was given a pass good on passenger cars, and his people, who were allowed to ride on freight trains only. Still, the policy worked well. "They have been very friendly ever since," Huntington said, "and in more than one case they have given the company notice of washouts on the road." [19]

By the time Strobridge began to lead his railroad-builders across northern Nevada, the Union Pacific's graders and tracklayers had had regular military escorts for three years. But when, in the summer of 1868, the War Department asked if the Central Pacific would like similar protection, and the question was referred to Strobridge, he said brusquely, "No guards. Damn the military!" [20] That ended the matter.

The Central Pacific's track crossed the Big Bend of the Truckee on July 9, 1868. There, 189 miles from Sacramento, the town of Wadsworth was founded, and it immediately became one of the most important points on the railroad, a base of supplies for the remaining 500 miles of construction. The route from here angled northeastward in a roughly straight line for 130 miles, mostly across the Great Desert, a vast waste of sand and sagebrush, spotted with glaring white alkali deposits. High mountain ranges, hazy with distance, marked the southern rim of the enormous, desolate plain. To the north, bleak, reddish hills brought the horizon somewhat closer, but there was no solace in that fact. Ahead of Strobridge and his main construction army of 5,000 men lay 100 miles of empty country almost devoid of flowing water. The area was so desiccated that, as a common saying of the day described it, "a jack rabbit had to carry a canteen and haversack" [21] to scamper across it.

At the Big Bend of the Truckee, westbound pioneers had found the first fresh water since leaving the slender Humboldt River, which simply disappeared into the sand 40 to 50 miles northeast of there. Crossing that "dark and fearful ground," as the editor of the Reno *Crescent* called it, had been one of the bitterest passages of the entire migration to California. Editor Lewis spoke feelingly of what it had been like to make one's way across the Great Desert "on the hurricane deck of a mustang, famished for water, eaten up with alkali dust, chilled by Washoe zephyrs, or petrified with blasts like simoons." He referred to it as "that country paved with the bones of animals that died from exhaustion in the great exodus to California." [22]

Now it was up to Charles Crocker and his men to build a railroad on which pioneers who survived that original crossing of the Humboldt Desert could have the wondrous satisfaction of going back over it in a few hours and in complete comfort.

Strobridge once remarked that it was curious, considering all the harrowing tales told of pioneer journeys across this desert, that his masses of graders had never uncovered a single bone or bit of discarded equipment. Neither, for that matter, he added ruefully, had his tunnelers ever blasted their way into a streak of gold or silver, or—of more usefulness to the Central Pacific—a vein of coal.

As far as Wadsworth, the C.P.'s construction force had had a plentiful and easily accessible supply of water, wood, and rock for all their purposes. From here on, wrote Engineer Lewis Clement, "there was not a tree that would make a board on over 500 miles of the route." Nor was there any worthwhile supply of building stone. "The country afforded nothing entering into the construction of the superstructure of a railroad," [23] Clement declared.

Costly attempts were made at well-digging, but thousands of dollars were spent with no results at all. Finally, "tunnels were bored into the mountains east of Wadsworth to develop small springs," Clement continued, "and when water was found, it was carefully protected and conveyed, in some cases, over eight miles in pipes to the line of the road." [24]

But these tapped springs provided such a skimpy supply that they were of small consequence. The Humboldt itself, once the railroad-builders

(Top) *Reno in its first summer (1868) was already an important rail center. The C.P. passenger station is in the distance, freight depot in foreground.*

(Bottom) *J. H. Strobridge's mobile headquarters during the construction of the Central Pacific from Truckee, California, to Promontory Summit, Utah.*

S.P.

STANFORD UNIVERSITY

(Top left) *C. P. tracklayers bend iron rails to form a curve beside the Humboldt River in Ten Mile Canyon, more than halfway across Nevada, in 1868.*

(Middle) *A typical summer camp of the Central Pacific's Chinese beside the track at Brown's Station, Nevada, in 1868.*

(Right) *C.P. passenger train moves along narrow roadbed shelf above Bear Valley, west of the summit of the Sierra.*

(Left) *C.P. rolling stock outside the new machine shops at Carlin, Nevada, end of line in 1868.*

HARPER'S WEEKLY

(Top) *Explosive rivalry between Irish and Chinese grading parallel routes on the east slope of the Promontory Range in the spring of 1869.*

(Bottom) *J. H. Strobridge (tall bearded man, lower foreground)* with some of *his men after their record day of tracklaying, April 28, 1869.*

SOC. OF CALIF. PIONEERS

reached it, was of no help—"meanest and muddiest, filthiest, of streams," [25] an early emigrant had called it. Most of the water needed for men, horses, and locomotives had to come from the Truckee, and was shipped across the desert in huge, semi-conical wooden vats on flatcars. The vats were equipped with big spouts, which worked like the spouts of railroad water towers. When the lip of the spout was yanked with a rope, water came pouring down its throat.

At the end of track, a great deal of the water had to be transferred to barrels and sent ahead by wagons to the distant graders.

Countless cords of firewood to feed the locomotives were sent forward on flatcars from Wadsworth, too, and stacked at intervals alongside the track as it advanced northeastward.

Wadsworth became the principal distribution point for these essential supplies and all the rest that must be forwarded ceaselessly to the end of track. Car shops were promptly set up, as well, to keep the busy rolling stock in constant repair.

So slick a working organization had Strobridge perfected by now, and so efficient was Crocker's supply system, that the tracklayers began making spectacular strides. The graders were moving even faster. One thing—the only thing—to be said in favor of the Humboldt Desert was that it was nearly flat. Beginning at Wadsworth, only slightly more than 4,000 feet above sea level, the route of the railroad inclined upward toward the east about as gently as the Nebraska plain uptilted toward the Rockies. As it wove its way between mountain ranges, some close at hand, others mistily far away, the line of track gained only 1,000 feet of altitude in the next 275 miles.

Far to the east of the graders, Butler Ives, with a party of twelve men, a mule team, several saddle horses, and four months' provisions, was making the final location for the railroad from Humboldt Wells to the Wasatch Mountains. "They keep me out in these infernal regions of salt and desolation because I am familiar with the country & don't fear the Indians," [26] he wrote to his brother. He was under most urgent orders from Montague.

The necessity for *pushing ahead* will compel us in many places to sacrifice good alignment & easy grades for the sake of getting light work [the chief engineer had written in mid-June]. Make temporary location by using sharp curves and heavy grades (keeping within the max.) wherever you can make any material savings on the work.

The line we want now is the one we can build the soonest, even if we rebuild immediately. Keep this in mind.[27]

To make sure that Ives never forgot it, Montague repeated his urging in every letter he sent him that summer.

Strobridge's men now were pounding over the sandy landscape so fast that on a single day in August, Monday the seventeenth, they laid 6 miles and 800 feet of track. The Reno *Crescent* proudly announced this striking fact, and then its editor immediately lapsed into a vivid complaint about the woes of life in a railroad town. He deplored "the strain of grim humor in locomotive engineers" that seemed to impel them to "exercise their steeds" the minute he had fallen into his first sound sleep each night. "Backward and forward" they went, he lamented,

up and down, blowing, hissing, rattling, screaming, snorting, puffing, panting, wheezing, straining, groaning, grating—a dead man could not sleep. Last night in particular the black disturber seemed dying of asthma.

We have written to Charley Crocker today. He has got to do one of three things: keep that particular machine off the track, get him a bottle of cough medicine, or move his old railroad.[28]

The Central Pacific was not the only disturber of peace in lusty Reno as the rising tempo of railroad-building lured more and more strangers into town.

"For the past two weeks, Reno has been enlivened with any number of fights," the *Crescent* had noted a few days earlier. "An attempt to record them has proved a total failure, so we have concluded to content ourselves with a summary of the killed and wounded at the end of the season." [29]

On August 22nd the rapidly advancing track was at a way station dubbed Browns, nearly 50 miles beyond Wadsworth and 235 miles east of Sacramento.

With Strobridge's force, now 6,000 to 7,000 strong, moving forward at a sprint, government-aid bonds were fairly streaming into Huntington's hands. The U.S. Treasury delivered packets of them to him thirteen times during 1868. The bonds had a total face value of $10,610,000. When Huntington had gone through the inevitable process of converting them into gold, however, they brought almost a third less to the Central Pacific's treasury.

In mid-August, Crocker received a warning letter from Huntington. The latter wrote that private information from a friend of the Central Pacific "in the camp of the enemy" [30] had enabled him to learn that the Union Pacific was sending a man out to Nevada and California that summer to find out how the C.P. was getting along.

"Now," Huntington continued, "you know how to handle him. I want you to take charge of him just as soon as he gets there. Just show him that we cannot build much road this summer."

Crocker immediately let Strobridge in on the plot.

If he stops at your camp, I want you to go to work and blast me and Huntington. Tell this man that we just don't seem to be up to the occasion at all, that we haven't any material, and that there isn't any on the way that you know of—all that sort of thing. Fix him up.

Not long afterward, "Stro" wired from the front that he had been told that the expected stranger had passed by, but he had not stopped long enough for a chat. He was on his way to Sacramento, though.

The Union Pacific's field scout soon presented himself at Crocker's office. "I took charge of him at once and invited him home to dinner," Crocker recalled later. The man began boasting about what the U.P. was going to accomplish that year, and how much material it had bought.

"The Doctor [Durant] just gave out advertisements," the garrulous stranger declared, "and he got all the iron there was to be manufactured."

"Oh, Lord!" groaned Crocker.

What was Huntington doing? Now, we could lay 250 miles of road if we had the material this year. But—I don't know—I sometimes think we won't get more than about 100 miles laid. . . . I telegraph Huntington every day to hurry up the cars and the iron and everything. We are short of cars, short of engines, short of iron and of everything.

Actually, Crocker explained to an interviewer long afterward,

we were expecting a ship in every minute, loaded down—three or four of them, following one after another—but I did not tell him that.

I took him down the next morning and showed him all the ties we had, and, said I, "There are ties enough to lay 10 miles of road. You see that little pile of iron? That is all the iron we have, and there are the spikes—not half enough to lay it."

He told me that he was sorry, but all the time he was chuckling.

The next day, Crocker and his guest boarded a train bound for the end of track, in order to let Strobridge play his part in the comedy of deception. When they found Stro, out in the middle of the Humboldt Desert, a wink from Crocker set him to ranting against Huntington.

"Crocker," said Strobridge, adding a few of his more picturesque oaths, "if you were there, we would have lots of material. But . . . I feel about like resigning."

"We have got to do the very best we can," said Crocker, sanctimoniously. "Don't let it be our fault. I think we will get to Winnemucca [132 miles from Wadsworth] this year. I believe that we can."

"How are we to get there," asked Strobridge scornfully, "when you have only got 10 miles of iron in the city?"

"Well," said Crocker, "I am not going to give up hopes yet. I think we can lay 150 miles this summer."

Having improvised dialogue that inwardly delighted them, since it was obviously impressing the Union Pacific's spy, Crocker and Strobridge eased the man on his way. But first—an inspired final touch—Crocker offered him a glass of heavily alkaline water, pretending that it was all the men had to drink. It was so bitter, the visitor spit out the first mouthful. "Cattle could not drink it at all," Crocker confided to posterity. "Horses would drink a little of it, but not much." [31]

The U.P. scout returned to his headquarters, and from there the word trickled back to Crocker that the game had worked. The Union Pacific officials had been told that the Central Pacific couldn't build more than 150 miles of track in 1868.

Instead, Strobridge and his men did more than twice as well as that. By the end of December, the rails had reached a point on the map just beyond the new settlement of Elko, "a great town of boards and tents, and the most hopeful and enthusiastic people in the world." [32] This spot, nearly at the upper end of the Humboldt River, was 470 miles from Sacramento and three-quarters of the way across northern Nevada.

The 3,000 graders whom Crocker had ordered forward to the canyons of the Humboldt River in mid-June had accomplished wonders. They had graded one 12-mile stretch between high bluffs in six weeks. Another section, 5 miles long, took them only three. Now they were streaking toward Wells, where the Humboldt rose. Wells was just a short distance from the Utah line.

Strobridge had remarkably few disciplinary problems that year with either his Chinese or his Irishmen. The latter had been cut off from liquor supplies by Stro's strong-arm squad when they were back in the Sierra. Now that they were far out in the arid wilderness of north-central Nevada, and thirstier than ever, liquor was kept from them by a more subtle but just as effective method. Whenever a vendor out of Reno showed up optimistically with a wagonload of whiskey at Wadsworth and sought to arrange with the railroad people to tap their supplies of water for himself and his team across the Humboldt Desert, they set such an exorbitant price on the commodity, which they controlled entirely, that he couldn't afford to make the trip.

"No 'local optionist' could wish for more," wrote Timothy Hopkins, after describing this arbitrary means of curtailing whiskey supplies, "and the camps at night when bedtime came were peaceful and quiet." [33]

Once there was a flare-up of opium-smoking among the Chinese track-layers. Strobridge, a very strong man, capable of formidable righteous fury, stamped this out alone. He had found, said a contemporary newspaper account, an improvised den where

some 40 Chinamen were elevating themselves to the seventh heaven of happiness. He drove them all out, confiscated their pipes and about $500 worth of opium. He had to make a desperate fight of it, though, for the keepers of the place, seeing, like the idol-makers encountered by St. Paul, that the hope of their gains was gone, pitched into him most furiously. But he handled and conquered them all single-handed. He treats the keepers of the gambling houses quite as roughly, and scatters tables, gamblers and money alike whenever he catches them.[34]

Charlie Crocker, meanwhile, was having trouble of a different sort, brewed, surprisingly enough, by that former cordial friend of the railroad, the Sacramento *Union*. Lauren Upson, Judah's particular admirer, had given up the editorship in 1864. James Anthony, one of the paper's owners, had taken his place. Anthony at first seemed to be as friendly to the Central Pacific as his predecessor, but in 1868 he abruptly turned hostile. From then on, the *Union* rarely had a good word for the C.P. or any of its principals.

Early in the fall of 1868, the *Union* began insisting that there was a 25-mile stretch of the Central Pacific's track, over in Nevada, that was so carelessly built as to be dangerous. The newspaper's voice was then listened to widely in the East, and especially in Washington. On October

15th Secretary of the Interior Browning appointed a special board of commissioners to come out and take a personal look at the C.P. There was the clear implication that the regular commissioners weren't doing an honest, or careful, job of inspecting each 20-mile section of track as it was completed.

Just by chance, the very next day, Browning received in his mail the map and profiles of the Central Pacific's proposed route from Monument Point to Echo Summit, submitted for his approval. The fact that he had just ordered investigators to look sharply at the part of the railroad that was already finished did not cloud his attitude toward its future plans. However, he noted in his diary that though he had the legal right to decide the matter himself, he thought it important enough to refer to the full Cabinet. This was done that day, but no decision was reached. Some members of the Cabinet suggested that since the Central Pacific and Union Pacific appeared to disagree on routes in Utah, Browning should send out a competent impartial engineer to locate a route for them. The Secretary of the Interior observed that such a course of action would delay the completion of the transcontinental railroad fully six months, and would not be warranted. So, he confided to his diary, if the Cabinet couldn't reach a decision at the next meeting, he'd settle the matter himself.

Four days later, when the Cabinet next convened, its members wasted little time in reaching a unanimous decision that the Central Pacific's proposed route should be accepted, so that work could be done on it throughout the winter. The Union Pacific didn't find out what had happened at that Cabinet meeting until two months later.

Meanwhile, Browning's special prowlers, appointed October 15th, arrived in Sacramento in mid-November, and rode all the way out to the end of track, accompanied by Charles Crocker and Chief Engineer Montague. They came back more slowly and critically. It was then that Crocker showed them how wrong the *Union* had been in its accusations.

When their train arrived at one end of the section of track that the *Union* had said was unsafe, Crocker announced this fact to his official guests. Then he said, "Here is a tumbler of water, which I'll set on the floor of the car. Now, gentlemen, take your watches." He told them how far it was to the next station. "Note the time when we leave this station and when we arrive at the other," he said, "so that you will know the rate of speed at which you have gone."

Crocker then told the conductor to pass the word to the engineer that he wanted to go over that piece of road at 50 miles an hour—20 miles faster than the regular passenger trains traveled over it.

"They made a little better time than that," Crocker recalled. "The tumbler was still standing, and but little water had been spilt. 'Now,' said I, 'gentlemen, there is your Sacramento *Union*,' and the commissioners all laughed, and said that was the strongest proof that could be given." [35]

On December 3rd the special commissioners sent a preliminary, highly favorable report to Secretary Browning by telegram. With particular reference to the *Union's* complaint, the message read, in part:

On the new portion of the road, through Humboldt Valley, cross ties, bridges, and rails are up to standard. Some minor defects, not of vital importance, exist in culverts, drains, width of embankments, and ballast, but these can be remedied at small cost when hurry of pushing forward the road is over. Heavy trains of rails, ties and fuel are running safely to the extreme end of the road, 445 miles from Sacramento. The road is being constructed in good faith, in a substantial manner, without stint of labor, materials or equipment, and is worthy of its character as a great national work. The telegraph line is first class.[36]

The Central Pacific's president, Leland Stanford, had been making his headquarters at Salt Lake City since November 1st. Stanford had been trying to learn what he could of the Union Pacific's progress and plans. More importantly, he had been arranging with his Mormon contractors to start grading east of Monument Point as soon as they completed their 100-mile section west of there. They expected to be finished with the latter by December 1st. Stanford then believed they should begin at Ogden and work backward toward Monument, thus establishing as soon as possible a firm claim to Ogden as a potential meeting place for the two railroads.

Huntington's letters at this time revealed him as obstinately in favor of placing the eastern end of the Central Pacific's roadbed at Echo Summit, to comply with the map Secretary Browning had already approved. Stanford disagreed, for he knew that Brigham Young already had graders at work there for the Union Pacific. He saw nothing to be gained by parallel grading in that rugged and costly terrain.

As the Governor went about his business and espionage, he watched the weather as anxiously as Noah, but with opposite emotions. He longed for heavy snows in the Wasatch Mountains, to bottle up the Union Pacific graders in Wyoming. "One good storm," he wrote wistfully to Hopkins on December 10th, "would settle the question of their coming through the Weber Canyon this winter." [37] Unfortunately, from Stanford's viewpoint, the weather remained dry in that vicinity right up to the year's end, though extreme cold began to trouble the U.P. graders.

Stanford peppered Hopkins with suggestions and alarms: (1) The C.P. should at once organize a scraper force to build grade over the rolling country between Humboldt Wells and the west end of the initial Mormon contract. (2) He had told Montague to send a team of surveyors to the mouth of Weber Canyon immediately, so that Stanford could put graders to work there as soon as possible. (3) "But now, as always, the great point is to push the track." (4) "The U. Pacific track is within eighty miles of mouth of Echo." (5) "I have telegraphed to Huntington to try and meet me at Omaha." (6) "If Charley would stay out to the front and on the line and see to pushing forward material, would not the thing go faster?" [38]

Thomas C. Durant was poking around the same locality that Stanford was patroling. The two men soon met. "We had general talk in the main," [39] wrote Stanford. Inevitably, though, they got onto the ticklish subject of competitive grading. Each railroad was now doggedly building grade across the wide gap between their converging tracks.

Earlier, Durant had boldly sent some of his toughest Irish graders all the way out to Humboldt Wells, 219 miles west of Ogden. When word of this last move reached Charles Crocker, he had flashed an alarm to Huntington. Huntington was unshaken.

"I received a telegram from Mr. Crocker saying that the Union Pacific was grading over to Humboldt Wells," Huntington recalled, years later. "But I answered, 'Don't let's bother ourselves about that, but lay the track right along. I am satisfied that you won't want to lay any rails after they have laid theirs.'" [40]

As Huntington surmised, the U.P. was not attempting to put down iron 300 miles ahead of its supply trains. But there seemed to be no reasonable limit to its ambition.

"Durant was going to the Pacific Ocean, I believe," Huntington once said. "He started for there, at any rate." [41]

In mid-October, spurred by these disorders, General Dodge did his best to persuade Durant to give up the irrational, wasteful effort involved in parallel grading. Let's settle on a reasonable meeting point with the C.P., he suggested. Durant at first indignantly refused, reminding Dodge that $32,000 a mile in subsidies was at stake, to say nothing of the land grants.

But for once Colonel Seymour, who was with them at Salt Lake City, sided with Dodge.

Finally, on October 12th, Durant sent a compromise offer to Stanford. He proposed that the two railroads establish an average cost per mile for their respective grading between Weber Canyon and Humboldt Wells, and each pay that price for as much as it could lay track on. Or, if Stanford preferred, he continued, they could arbitrarily agree to meet halfway between Weber and the Wells.

Stanford, fortified by his conviction that only the C.P. route was legitimate and that the U.P. was simply throwing away money and toil, gave an evasive answer. The situation was briefly allowed to drift. Before long, however, the Union Pacific gave up the futile attempt to grade back east from Humboldt Wells, and recalled its advance troops to join their compatriots near Ogden.

There, however, a new complication arose. Stanford, as he wrote Hopkins, had just "let the work from Ogden west to Monument to our old contractors Benson, Farr & West. Brigham Young has ¼ interest in the profits." [42] Practically alongside, another Mormon contractor, Bishop John Sharp, was grading for the Union Pacific. Brisk competitive bidding for the limited labor supply pushed up the cost of the job drastically for both roads. Itinerant laborers were wooed by both sides, and they, often inept and irresponsible, made the situation even worse.

It was this painful matter that Durant brought up in his conversation with Stanford when they met. The talk grew rather tense. "Durant said if we hired his men, he could play the same hinting game," [43] Stanford confided to Hopkins. Despite his bristling attitude, Durant got around to hinting once more that the two railroads ought to agree on a meeting place.

Stanford was still evasive. Bishop West's gangs were making fine progress with the C.P. roadbed between Ogden and Monument, working eight-hour shifts. Out in the desert country north of the lake, they graded at night by the light of big bonfires of sagebrush. Stanford felt under far less pressure to reach a compromise than Durant did.

With this second 100-mile section of Utah grading well under way, in mid-December, Stanford was much annoyed to learn that Huntington was still pushing his idea that the work should begin at Echo Summit, then 350 miles in advance of the Central Pacific's track.

In exasperation, Stanford wrote Hopkins, "To go to work at Echo

Summit seems to me such utter folly in every way that it can be viewed that either Huntington or I completely fail to comprehend the situation." [44]

Stanford was in Salt Lake City that day, December 13th, but on his way to Ogden. "If things are safe to leave," he told Hopkins, in conclusion, "I shall telegraph Huntington to meet me at Omaha, and start from Ogden, go up the Weber along the line of the U.P., and, if possible, along their entire line to the end of their track." [45]

Things were evidently safe to leave, for on December 19th Stanford was in Omaha, according to a dispatch telegraphed from there to the Sacramento *Union*. While waiting for Huntington to arrive from the East, he told local reporters that 10,000 Chinese and 1,500 white laborers were at work on the Central Pacific line between Ogden and Humboldt Wells. He didn't confide to them that the railroad was having a difficult time keeping any white workers on the job. The recent discovery of rich veins of silver in the White Pine district of Nevada, 75 to 100 miles southeast of Elko, was proving irresistible to many of them. At this time, the C.P. gave as many as 2,000 men free passage from Sacramento to Elko before it could get a hundred to stick with the railroad.

Huntington left New York on December 16th, and a last-minute wire from Hopkins—"We want three hundred thousand dollars more before you go West" [46]—almost missed him. He was soon off on a whirlwind journey, taking Mrs. Huntington with him.

"I made 1,400 miles by staging and the rest by rail," he said later. "Remained 10 days in California, and returned to my starting point in 31 days after leaving. I ran a line of special stages, which raced day and night. It cost something to make the trip, but I made it." [47]

Stanford had hoped to be home with his wife and baby [48] for Christmas, but his urgent journey to Omaha made that plan impossible to realize. He and Huntington conferred at length on their way back west, but they parted at Ogden. Stanford remained in Utah to cheer along his Mormon graders. Huntington rushed on to Sacramento for the first face-to-face conferences with his other chief partners since 1863.

As the year closed, the Central Pacific's track-builders had managed to make good Charlie Crocker's extravagant boast of January 1st. They had done more. They had added over 350 miles to the C.P.'s track, and they had had no serious interference from the weather, which remained benign to the year's end. Mark Hopkins sent a telegram on December 28th that closed with a kind of benediction: "No snow to impede progress." [49]

CHAPTER FOURTEEN

"WE'RE SAILING!"
SAID THE GENERAL

Early in January, 1868, the chief stockholders of the Credit Mobilier of America gathered in a private parlor at the Fifth Avenue Hotel, in New York, for a meeting that was to have notorious and pathetic consequences.

The corporation possessed only 650 shares of stock that had not yet been assigned to anyone. Three men now sought to distribute all or part of those uncommitted shares for political reasons. Thomas Durant, true to form, demanded the whole block. Oakes Ames said he must have enough shares to fulfil the promises he had made to various members of Congress during the previous month. Durant said, well, he'd made some promises, too. Besides, he felt that Ames could well afford to provide largesse to congressmen out of his own very ample holdings. The third applicant, Henry S. McComb of Wilmington, Delaware, declared that the company owed him 375 shares to complete a subscription he had applied for three years earlier. Nobody else remembered any such subscription, and McComb couldn't prove his claim. In fact, Sidney Dillon told him it was "so base and so fraudulent that, in presenting it, he had shown himself to be a scoundrel unworthy to associate with gentlemen, and he would not give such a bogus claim the slightest consideration." [1] The other shareholders present unanimously decided that he was not entitled to any extra stock. They voted to satisfy Durant's and Ames' claims by a compromise that roughly split the 650 shares between them, to be disposed of as they thought best. The decision was put in writing and signed by everyone in the room, including McComb. He later insisted he had no recollection of this.

By joining in the vote to reject McComb's claim, Oakes Ames made the second-biggest mistake of his life. The biggest had been his improper decision to offer, in December, 1867, to sell a few shares in the Credit Mobilier to receptive fellow-congressmen at par ($100), plus interest from the previous July. Up until the middle of 1867, stock in the Credit Mobilier had been hard to sell to anybody, even at prices way below par. But by December of that year, thanks to the signing of the Ames contract, it was generally felt to be worth more than $100 a share, and Ames knew it. (The stock was not listed on an exchange, so its market value at any time could not be determined except by infrequent individual sales.) The fact that he proceeded, despite this knowledge, to let various congressmen acquire the stock at par was interpreted as attempted bribery by the House committee that eventually looked into the transactions.

Most historians have agreed that Ames was sincere in protesting to that committee that he had seen nothing wrong in the course of action he began in December, 1867. He did not regard it as bribery.

"There is no law," he declared, when under investigators' fire, "and no reason, legal or moral, why a member of Congress should not own stock in a road, any more than why he should not own a sheep when the price of wool is to be affected by the tariff."

"Is that your conviction now?" asked one of the committee.

"Yes, sir," retorted Ames, "and always has been." [2]

The nation was aware, he said, that he was a major stockholder in the Credit Mobilier and the leading stockholder in the Union Pacific. Yet he had voted in Congress on legislation affecting the latter, and, as a member of the Pacific Railroad Committee of the House, had even helped frame the pertinent laws. No one had criticized him for that. Many people knew, too, that he had persuaded Senator J. W. Grimes, of Iowa, and Representatives John B. Alley and Samuel Hooper, of Massachusetts, all three of them wealthy men, to make large purchases of U.P. and C.M. stock at the time he bought his own. No one had taken conspicuous exception to that. As Ames pointed out, he and these other congressmen had been praised as patriotic for having made the investments when they were considered so risky. What was wrong, he asked, in effect, with interesting a few more congressmen in the ventures when they were no longer hazardous? Politicians of the day had a pretty relaxed attitude toward conflicts of interest.

The Union Pacific sought no more legislative favors, Ames declared. Congress had already done everything for the railroad that it needed. Furthermore, the congressmen to whom he offered to sell stock had all shown themselves to be friends of the U.P. anyway. What, he asked, was he supposed to have been bribing them to do? (He might better have asked himself why he should run the political risk of selling them Credit Mobilier stock at any price when their attitude toward the Union Pacific was already benevolent.)

The truth was that on December 9, 1867, when Representative C. C. Washburn suddenly introduced a bill to slash freight rates and passenger fares on the Union Pacific and Central Pacific, Ames had become unduly alarmed. (The bill, in fact, eventually died in the Senate's Pacific Railroad Committee.) He decided, ill-advisedly, that even friendly congressmen had better have their friendship reinforced. As Dr. Allan Nevins has put it, Ames sought "the negative favor of non-interference." He told his subsequent congressional inquisitors that he had found "there is no difficulty in getting men to look after their own property." [3] In the January, 1868, meeting at the Fifth Avenue Hotel, he was endeavoring to obtain the property for delivery to its new owners.

By voting against Henry McComb's petition at that meeting, though, Oakes Ames made a fatal enemy. McComb was a vengeful, unscrupulous man, already dirtied by contract scandals during the Civil War. He tried first by attempted blackmail and eventually by lawsuit to force Ames to give him the 375 Credit Mobilier shares that he claimed were his. Ames scorned the blackmail effort, but he could not escape the consequences of a whirlwind of unfavorable publicity eventually stirred up by the lawsuit. [4]

The sad and avoidable conclusion to the story of the Credit Mobilier still lay more than four years in the future when the executive committee of the Union Pacific drew up its building plans for the year 1868. Its ambitions, from General Dodge's point of view, were outlandish. The committee wanted him to have some of his engineers finish the final loca-

tion of the road to the Salt Lake Valley at once. They were then to continue it beyond there as far as Humboldt Wells, Nevada. Furthemore, as
soon as Reed's and General Casement's men were able to start work west
of Cheyenne, they were to plan to keep going, straight through the following winter, until they reached Humboldt Wells. The executive committee
not only wanted to shut the Central Pacific out of Salt Lake Valley but
collect the rich harvest of subsidies to be picked up by pushing 200 miles
west of there.

Dodge bleakly told the committee that its insistence on building
through the Wasatch Mountains in winter would run the costs up at
least $10 million more than necessary. Never mind, the committee de-
cided. Shrugging his shoulders, Dodge dispatched James R. Maxwell and
a survey crew toward Salt Lake in February. In sleighs, they crossed the
Wasatch Range on snow that covered the tops of the telegraph poles.

In describing to his superiors the territory that still stretched ahead of
the U.P.'s construction forces, then taking their ease at Cheyenne, Dodge
had called the Laramie Plains "a broad park, 200 miles long in latitude,
and 100 miles wide in longitude." [5] He explained that the Plains were
rimmed on the south and west by the main range of the Rockies, on the
north and east by the Sweetwater Mountains and the Black Hills, and
that the Medicine Bow Mountains and their northern extension, the
Rattlesnake Range, ran north and south through the middle of the huge
tableland. It was watered by tributaries of the North Platte, and its general elevation was 6,500 feet above sea level. The streams rose in the
Rockies or in the Medicine Bow Mountains, flowed northward, and
crossed the Union Pacific's route generally at right angles. This situation,
though it hampered the engineers' efforts to keep the line straight, had
one decided advantage. Ties could be cut in the ample forests on the
north slopes of the Rockies and in the Medicine Bow Mountains and
floated down to the U.P.'s grading.

Dodge had assured the railroad's directors that coal outcroppings were
frequent all across southern Wyoming, thus assuring a handy fuel supply,
and that sandstone and limestone were plentiful. "Material for building
the road is of easy access to the line," [6] he wrote.

On the western side of the Laramie Plains, the U.P.'s route crossed the
Continental Divide, but that would be no climb to worry about. In fact,
Dodge's Summit, at the watershed of the continent, was more than 1,000
feet lower than Sherman, at the summit of the Black Hills. As Jacob
Blickensderfer, Jr., had written in surprise about his travels through that

region with Dodge in 1867, the Continental Divide was a crest whose grade was barely perceptible. "The crest itself is a wide open plain," he wrote, "free from rocks or bold elevations, and the inclinations for miles of extent can be determined only by the aid of instruments." [7] It was almost like the Platte Valley on a higher level.

West of the Divide lay the Bitter Creek country, which Dodge described as "desolate, dreary, not susceptible of cultivation, and only portions of it fit for grazing." It had but one encouraging feature. "All of it is underlaid with immense beds of coal," said Dodge. But timber along that portion of the railroad's route, for a distance of 150 miles or more, was scarce, he wrote, "and the country has no inviting qualities." [8]

Green River, the southward-flowing main tributary of the Colorado River, marked the western boundary of this sun-withered region. After crossing Green River, the U.P. route followed the Black Fork for about 80 miles, and then began a gradual ascent into the Wasatch Mountains. From there, wrote Dodge, "until the valley of Salt Lake is reached, we are in a mountain country. Timber on this portion of the route abounds, coal is found, and there are indications of iron, silver, and oil." [9]

Between Ogden and Humboldt Wells, the problems involved could not be described until Engineer Maxwell and his party were able to report. At least, said Dodge, there were no serious obstacles to railroad construction to be encountered in Wyoming. There was just one small tunnel, 12 miles east of the second crossing of the North Platte. This was on a creek that Blickensderfer the summer before had named Mary's, in honor of his daughter. Perhaps owing to confusion on the part of the Irish graders, in 1868 it was mysteriously canonized. It became St. Mary's Creek that year, and has remained so ever since.

Contemplating the prospects for speed and profit during 1868, the trustees of the Ames contract were in such a sanguine mood that they declared a large dividend right away. It was issued on January 4th to all stockholders of the Credit Mobilier, and consisted of 80 per cent of their C.M. holdings in U.P. first-mortgage bonds and 100 per cent in U.P. stock. This was the onset of a streak of profligacy that would get the trustees into trouble before the year was over.

Out on the construction front, the effervescent viewpoint of the trustees was decidedly not reflected in Samuel B. Reed's thoughts.

"Nothing but the money I am earning from month to month keeps me in this dreary country," [10] he wrote from Cheyenne on January 14th, in the course of telling his wife his troubles. The 3,000 tie-cutters in the

Medicine Bow Mountains were floundering in 3 feet of snow. They wouldn't be able to float ties down the Laramie River to the railroad's line of grading until spring. Reed himself had just been marooned for two days at Fort Sanders by a blizzard that tapered off in temperatures sliding to 30 degrees below zero.

The U.P.'s construction superintendent had made his shivering way back to Cheyenne only to be greeted by an upsetting letter from General Dodge, in New York. Dodge wrote that certain members of the railroad's board of directors were dissatisfied with the construction record for 1867. "You, of course, have been blamed when you ought not to be," reported Dodge. The chief engineer offered reassurance, however. "Mr. Ames, Mr. Dillon, and I have now convinced a large majority of all of them on my statement of the case, an open, bold defense of you." Still, Dodge had some frank advice to give.

They want to build four hundred miles of road [in 1868] and you must do more head work and put the details on assistants. Keep as harmonious as possible with the Running Department [Reed often clashed with Webster Snyder, who headed Operations] . . . and steer clear of New York complications which we have no direct interest in.[11]

Reed enclosed Dodge's letter in the one he was writing to his wife, commenting:

I regret not resigning last year when I could have done so with a good reputation and not made half as many enemies as I now have. No one can tell by Mr. Durant's talk what he thinks of a man. His best friends may not know what he means when talking to them.

New York complications will crush any man that stands in the way, and it is impossible to steer clear of them all. I have the satisfaction of knowing that I have done my duty fearlessly and with fidelity to the whole interest of the company while in its service.[12]

In the midst of his brooding, Reed found one cause for cheer. Work on the masonry foundations for the big trestle that would cross Dale Creek, on the downgrade beyond Sherman Summit, was well along. Timbers for this highest of all Union Pacific bridges—126 feet above the slender creek and 700 feet long at grade line—had been bought and were to be shipped to the scene within two weeks. Though some pine logs had been felled for it in nearby mountains, most of the timbers were being cut to specification in Michigan's forests and would be shipped from Chicago. Already the second winter's temporary railroad bridge had been built across the Missouri's ice at Omaha, linking the Chicago & North Western with the U.P. Great volumes of materials were already moving over it and on out to Cheyenne.

By the first week in March, the weather was nearly as pleasant as May; the snow was gone and the frost was fast leaving the ground. During the winter, the Chicago & North Western had delivered 1,600 carloads of track iron to Council Bluffs. These cars had crossed the ice bridge, now about to be dismantled for the second time, and their cargoes had been stockpiled at Cheyenne.

Reed felt sufficiently encouraged in March to post a challenge to Charlie Crocker across the barren, snow-draped western mountains. "My men have stuck stakes in the Humboldt Mts.," wrote Reed. "We'll meet you there in 1871."

Crocker snorted when he read it. "He won't find his stakes when he arrives," he told Legh Freeman, who was off on a newsgathering jaunt for the *Frontier Index*. "I'll have trains running that far by the end of this year." [13]

The U.P.'s men were now blasting a path for the track through solid rock for a mile west of Dale Creek's ravine. The high bridge over the creek, which Engineer Hezekiah Bissell called "a big bridge for a small brook that one could easily step over," [14] was coming along fast. It had to be finished before General Casement's tracklayers could hit the westward trail again.

When it was half built, a violent wind nearly wrecked it. Bissell had been at work with his instruments west of the bridge that day. When the wind grew so strong that he could no longer use his surveying equipment, he started back to his camp in the Dale Creek ravine. He was appalled to discover that formidable gusts were throwing the bridge out of line. It was in imminent danger of being blown over.

The bridge men were scared out of their wits [Bissell related], and doing nothing to save the thing. I sent men to wherever contractors had derricks up, telling them to bring every rope and chain they could get hold of to the bridge as soon as possible. When the ropes first came, no one dared to go and put them on to guy the bridge. I finally induced two or three to go, and soon there were plenty of others. I probably saved the bridge. Had it been wrecked, there would have been a long delay in the tracklaying, at great cost. [15]

The bridge itself represented an outlay of $200,000. It consisted of double-framed trestles resting on granite masonry, with bents spaced 40 feet apart. In addition to replacing it, the Union Pacific would have been obliged to pay the Casements $3,000 a day, according to their latest contract, for every day their men were kept idle through no fault of their own.

"Bridge finished," Sam Reed was able to report from Cheyenne in a terse, triumphant note to his wife on April 23rd. Two weeks before, he had been complaining, "I have too much for any mortal man to do." Now, abruptly, the prospect was as bright as the spring morning on which he viewed it.

All excavations through the first range of mountains [Black Hills] done, track over bridge and through most of the rock cuts, great load off my mind. Work has been let nearly to Green River. I expect to go to Salt Lake in May to start work [from there East] as fast as possible. Carmichaels [a grading contractor] goes to heavy work on Green River, starts Monday next with three hundred men.[16]

Green River was then 300 miles beyond the end of track, but there were extensive rock cuts and fills to be made there, and at least one bridge to be built. Considering how General Casement's work troops would probably race through the Laramie Plains and across the Red Desert this summer, it was none too early to start preparing the way for them even as far in advance as Green River.

Carmichaels' men took several big teamloads of rails with them. They intended to lay track in the cuts and use dump cars to help carry off the debris of the blasts. This proved to be a sterile hope. When they got to Green River, they found no suitable timber near. Woodcutters went far upstream in search of ties. By the time they had them cut and ready to float down to Green River, the stream had dwindled until it was too low to provide transportation. Thus the rails, which had cost 9 cents a pound ($47 per rail) to cart 300 miles, were of no help at all to Carmichaels and his gang.

The Casements, meanwhile, were on the march.

I hope soon to get time to write you a good letter [Jack Casement scribbled to his adored wife from Cheyenne on April 21st], but I have never been hurried up more in my life. We are all ready at work. Have crossed the high Bridge today and want to commence laying three miles a day at once. Dillon and Durant are both here, feeling well. We will be at Fort Sanders next week.

We have taken more Grading and are Starting work 150 miles ahead of the track. Write to me often. I will drop you a line every day. Love to all and kisses to Johnny [his baby son]. God bless you.[17]

General Casement's remark about "work 150 miles ahead of the track" referred to the tunnel on St. Mary's Creek, 680 miles west of Omaha and close to the second crossing of the North Platte. Excavating on this tunnel, which was the first of four that the Union Pacific would encounter en route to Ogden, began on April 30th. Its final length was only 215 feet, but so fast did the Casements' main force move that it got there before the tunnel was ready for the track. The track-layers had to build a temporary line around it.

Keeping materials flowing toward the front threatened the life of the Dale Creek bridge before it was more than a few weeks old. One rainy day, a trainload of rails started down the 4-mile heavy grade from Sherman to the bridge with no brakemen on its flatcars. The locomotive was attached to the rear of the train. On the wet rails, its brakes alone were not adequate to hold back the cars. The train, out of control, slid at gathering speed toward the bridge, which, according to rules posted beside the track, was not supposed to be crossed faster than 4 miles per hour.

Hezekiah Bissell happened to be aboard. He had asked the conductor to drop him off at the east end of the trestle. Instead, Bissell later recalled, "the train went flying over the bridge, which swayed so that three or four of the guy ropes were broken." At the bottom of the grade, the cars rolled more than a mile on level track before they could be stopped. "For some seconds, my heart was in my throat," declared Bissell, "fearing train and all would land in the bottom of the ravine. While on the Union Pacific, I had many experiences that money would not hire me to repeat. This was one." [18]

Arthur Ferguson's engineering unit moved out from Omaha for the U.P.'s headlong advance of 1868 late in the afternoon of April 25th. Before the night was over, their train had been stopped for two hours because of telegraphed rumors of an Indian raid ahead. The rumors were true enough.

The first attack of the year had occurred only nine days earlier. Its victims had been five section men, killed at work on the track near Elm Creek, 80 miles east of North Platte. Later the same day, two off-duty conductors, fishing in Lodge Pole Creek within sight of Sidney station, had been cut off from retreat when marauding warriors suddenly filled the little settlement there. One of the conductors, Tom Cahoon, was shot and scalped, though not killed. The other, badly wounded, managed to stumble to the station, which had become a temporary fort. (Several years later, Jay Gould, while riding on the Union Pacific in western Nebraska, made some belittling remark about Indian yarns to his conductor. The latter merely lifted his cap and bowed a horribly scarred pate at Gould. He was Cahoon.)

President Johnson's Peace Commission, trying to wind up last season's unfinished business, was even then conferring with tribal chieftains on treaty terms at Fort Laramie. Recalcitrant parties of young warriors were still on the loose, however, ignoring the parleys of their elders. These unmanageable bucks made sporadic attacks on the Union Pacific through-out the summer. Less than a week after Ferguson rode over the line, U.P. passengers between Julesburg and Cheyenne were told to lie on the floors of the cars to avoid stopping stray arrows or bullets.

The Army did not relax its protection of the railroads, however, while treaties were being argued out between the Indians and the Peace Com-missioners. There were more than 5,000 troops scattered along the line of the Union Pacific between Omaha and Salt Lake Valley during 1868. Nearly a thousand were camped near Fort D. A. Russell, on the outskirts of Cheyenne, at the start of the construction season.

On May 6th Sam Reed set out for Fort Sanders and Salt Lake City. Durant was at Fort Sanders, outside Laramie, and he must confer with him. Reed's main goal, though, was to persuade Brigham Young to take grading and tunnel-building contracts for the Union Pacific in the Wasatch Mountains and begin them as soon as possible. He also wanted to arrange for Mormon graders to go to work for the U.P. as far west as Humboldt Wells, Nevada. At the same time, the railroad's directors did not want him to reveal to Brigham Young that the track was almost certainly not going to go through Salt Lake City. If Young found out, he might very well refuse to help the Union Pacific at all. Worse, he might shift his vital supply of labor, materials, food, and fodder to the Central Pacific.

Laramie, the sole town Reed would pass through until he got to Ogden, was only two weeks old, but already it had 2,000 residents. The Union Pacific's first train had reached there on May 4th. The rails were now streaking on up the Laramie Valley.

"Push is the word for this season," [19] Reed had written on May 5th. That same day, the *Frontier Index* reported, "The construction of the

U.P.R.R. goes on like a flash—three miles a day. The road will get to Green River early this fall." [20] Earlier in the week, General Casement had written jubilantly to his wife, "We are now *Sailing*. Mean to lay over three miles every day. Commenced yesterday. Laid 3 Miles and enough over to buy you a new Dress." [21]

With Sam Reed on his way to Salt Lake City and General Dodge still in Washington, Col. Silas Seymour, with Durant's connivance, now proceeded to make some drastic changes in the surveyed line. They were made in the broad Laramie Valley, through which General Casement's tracklayers were moving so rapidly.

From Sherman, at the summit of the Black Hills, 31 miles west of Cheyenne, the length of the Union Pacific's main line across Wyoming to the Utah border today is 383 miles. In the spring of 1868, thanks to Seymour's finagling, it became 20 miles longer than that.

After descending to the Laramie Plains from Sherman, the route ran northwestward as far as Rock Creek. There, it began swinging west around the Medicine Bow range. At Medicine Bow station, a few miles beyond, it commenced a long, wavery slant southwestward to the Utah line. Seymour's alterations affected only the portion of the line between Laramie and Rock Creek, making it snake-like instead of straight. The consulting engineer (and Durant) justified them by arguing that the shorter, straighter line that General Dodge had previously approved would have involved a good deal of expensive, time-consuming rock excavation. The fact that in skirting the rock work Seymour put enough curves in the route to make it 20 miles longer wasn't as foolish as it appeared. The longer line would be so much easier to build, he declared, that it would be finished sooner than the original one could have been. Besides, though Seymour didn't dare use this argument with Dodge, it enabled the Union Pacific to collect $640,000 more in U.S. subsidy bonds on that portion of the route than would otherwise have been possible.

When General Dodge found out what had been done during his enforced absence in Washington, he had no difficulty in divining at once that the lure of the enhanced subsidy had been at the root of the matter. He had a crashing showdown with Durant over it. But by then, Seymour's alterations had been incorporated into completed track. Dodge knew better than to try to persuade the U.P.'s executive committee to let him do this particular part of the job over again. They were obsessed by the urge to push the track forward with all possible speed. Dodge could do nothing but accept the 20 unnecessary miles with as good grace as he could muster. (When he was an old man, he finally got his revenge. Under E. H. Harriman's regime, in the first years of the twentieth century, the Union Pacific's track was relaid in that region just about as Dodge had intended it to be.)

T. C. Durant, that month, was quite carried away by the exhilarating prospect of high speed in construction across Wyoming. Jesse Williams, senior member of the U.P.'s roster of government directors and the best-qualified engineer among them, was less convinced.

"Mr. Durant talks (I think wildly) of reaching Salt Lake from the East during the season of 1868," [22] Williams wrote to the Secretary of the Interior on June 16th, from his home in Fort Wayne, Indiana. Williams was uneasy. He was convinced that the Union Pacific was being constructed too fast for its own good, and he was about to leave for Wyoming to find out for himself. He deplored the fact that the government directors, scattered from Massachusetts to Missouri, had had no recent chance to consult on the matter. There had been no U.P. board meeting since March.

In the course of this fretful letter to Secretary Browning, Williams said he had just warned Oliver Ames, Durant, and other members of the Union Pacific's executive committee that there ought to be a reserve fund to provide for correcting any deficiencies caused by hasty construction. They had said they agreed with him. Nevertheless, he told Browning, just to make sure there'd be money on hand, if needed, to bring the U.P. up to first-class standards at the end of the job, Williams thought the Pacific Railroad Act ought to be amended to allow the government to withhold part of its subsidies until the road was finished.

On the very next day, as if to underscore the validity of Director Williams' fears, the trustees of the Ames contract declared another whopping dividend for Credit Mobilier stockholders: 60 per cent of their C.M. holdings in cash, 40 per cent in U.P. stock. Two weeks later, on July 3rd, they voted still another: 75 per cent in U.P. first-mortgage bonds, 75 per cent in the railroad's stock. (The bonds were selling for around 80. The price of the stock per share ranged, during the construction period, from 9 to 40, but the stock paid no dividends in that period.)

This spasm of openhandedness had been inspired by the fact that President Oliver Ames, cautious Director John B. Alley, and the suspicious Jesse Williams were all safely out of the way. They were bound for Wyoming, where they were to join General Dodge. Dodge had applied for and been granted an indefinite leave of absence from the House of Representatives on June 17th. He had headed for the end of track as fast as he could get there.

In New York, with his chief opponents far removed from the scene and a working majority of cronies to do his bidding in the U.P.'s executive committee, Durant at once sought and obtained full authority to command construction work on the railroad. He then departed for Wyoming himself.

Dodge, fuming at the sinuous remodeling he had found applied to the main line from Laramie to Rock Creek, confronted Durant in Laramie's hot, powdery main street. Vehemently, the chief engineer told the railroad's vice-president that if he dared to order any more changes in the work, he'd find himself in dutch with the government. He'd also discover, swore Dodge, that the U.P.'s construction forces wouldn't obey him.

Durant stood slouching in the dust, his only answer an insolent look. Dodge turned and strode away. His angry words had been more than mere threats. Behind them lay the yeasty knowledge that he not only had the backing of Oliver Ames and Jesse Williams but General Grant's solid friendship and respect. Dodge had been with Grant frequently during the past six months in Washington, and felt closer to him than ever before. He knew he could count on Grant's support, and Grant was now the Republican candidate for President. Most people felt he was certain to be elected. Even Durant would not be likely to risk tangling with the next President of the United States. Dodge didn't doubt that Durant would heed his threats.

From Laramie, the U.P.'s chief engineer made his way along the line to Salt Lake City during July, admiring the pace of the Casement's track-layers, visiting sixteen camps of graders, and conferring with his engineers.

The relentless pressure on the builders to move ever faster had caused a flare-up of labor trouble at Green River, at the beginning of the month. Reed, on the spot at the time, settled it as brusquely as Charlie Crocker had dealt with his sole Chinese rebellion. The graders at Green River had demanded $4 a day. When they were rebuffed, they went on strike.

"At this place, there are five hundred that are being paid off," wrote Reed from Green River on July 6th. "The boarding houses will be closed tomorrow noon. I have troops to enforce orders and will starve them out unless they go to work. Wages are better here than at any other place in the country—three dollars per day." [23] The strike failed.

By the time Dodge reached Green River, the tempo of construction was as brisk as ever. His tour of inspection was heartening. Sam Reed's friendship and diplomatic graces had brought about a thoroughly satisfactory contract with Brigham Young to furnish graders and tunnel-builders for the railroad's line through the Wasatch Mountains to Ogden. Four thousand Mormons were at work there now. Blasting had just begun on the approaches to the U.P.'s lengthiest tunnel, 772 feet long, at the head of Echo Canyon.

Dodge found the Mormon workmen a diverting contrast to the roister-ing Irish farther east. They were teetotalers to the last man, tolerated no gambling, were quiet and law-abiding, devoutly said grace at meals, and concluded each day's labors with communal prayers and songs. They held religious services on Sunday and would do no work then.

Their favorite song was not pious, however. It was the jaunty tune to which they swung their picks and heaved their shovels. The first verse ran:

> At the head of great Echo
> The railway's begun.
> The Mormons are cutting
> And grading like fun.
> They say they'll stick to it
> Till it is complete,
> When friends and relations
> They're longing to meet.[24]

General Dodge had just arrived at Salt Lake City, on the distasteful errand of notifying Young, at last, that the U.P. was not headed his way, when he received a telegram from Sidney Dillon urging him to return to Fort Sanders at top speed. Generals Grant, Sherman, and Sheridan, the three chief heroes of the Civil War, would be there on July 26th and wanted to talk with him. Durant would be on hand, too, Dillon added. He warned Dodge, who hadn't heard the news before, that the U.P.'s executive vice-president now had enlarged authority.

It was an extraordinary conclave of military brass that cordially wel-comed their old comrade Dodge when he hurried into Fort Sanders on Sunday, July 26th, having rushed there by chartered stagecoach and by special train from the end of track, now across the North Platte at Rawlins. Grant was in the course of a campaign tour that consisted largely of his shaking hands with thousands of veterans. Sherman and Sheridan, both on duty on the plains, accompanied him part of the way while he was in their territory. Sherman, for one, had no doubt of the outcome.

"Of course Grant will be elected," he had recently written to his brother John. "I have just traveled with him for two weeks, and the curiosity to see him exhausted his and my patience." [25] They had come from triumphant stops at Denver and Cheyenne. They had ridden out to the end of the U.P.'s rails. Now, at Fort Sanders, they were joined by six more generals, including W. S. Harney, fresh from treaty-making with the Indians. Harney's massive figure, elongated by a top hat, made little Sheridan and Grant look like dwarfs.

Durant, flanked by his sly, bearded pawn, Colonel Seymour, and with Jesse Williams and Sidney Dillon in attendance, if not in agreement, unwisely chose this moment to try to get rid of Dodge and put Seymour in his place. In the presence of Grant and Sherman, Durant accused the Union Pacific's chief engineer of selecting costly routes, wasting money, ignoring sound (he meant Seymour's) advice, and dawdling over the final location into Salt Lake Valley.

Grant looked coldly at Durant, then asked Dodge what he had to say.

Dodge, speaking in a low, tense voice, said he had just one statement to make. If Durant or anybody else, on the railroad or in the government, changed his lines hereafter, he'd quit.

There was a brief, dramatic silence. Grant then began to speak. The government, he said, expected the road to be finished, and the Union Pacific to fulfil its obligations. Also, he added, with a grim glance at Durant, it expected General Dodge to stay on as its chief engineer until the job was done.[26]

Durant hastily backtracked. He wasn't through meddling, though. Within ten days afterward, government director Jesse L. Williams sent a telegram of protest to the Secretary of the Interior, deploring Durant's attempt to increase the grades over the Wasatch Mountains. Williams pointed out that the 90-foot grades located by Engineer Jacob Bickensderfer, Jr., and approved by Dodge were entirely feasible, could be achieved at reasonable cost, and would be ready in time to receive the rapidly advancing track. Durant was trying to change them to 110- and 116-foot grades in order to cheapen and speed up construction. Williams indignantly declared that to do so "would materially impair the efficiency of this continental road, injure both its stockholders and the commercial interest, and increase the hazard of travel over this snowy range, with only a paltry advantage to the contracting company." [27] Once more, Durant was forced to back down.

Just before the Fort Sanders conference began, President Ames and Director Alley had returned to the East. Alley was angered and alarmed to discover what Durant and his friends had done behind their backs. On July 25th, from Boston, he wrote in outrage to Oliver Ames, whose authority he felt was being flouted because of "the excessive amiability of his nature." [28]

Now, what do we find upon our return [wrote Alley]? The executive committee practically ignoring the board of directors, and no meeting of the board for four months; the chief engineer subordinate and insulted because he is fearless and honest and wishes to protect the rights of all; your authority very much impaired and crippled—in fact almost destroyed for the same reason. . . . I feel that you and I both have endeavored to do right and countenance no wrong; but just as sure as we acquiesce and help these people to carry out their designs, we shall be compromised and disgraced by their actions, as I fear we are already, to some extent. . . .

Now, Mr. Ames, I advise you, as a friend, and I earnestly implore you . . . to resist, by all the power which you possess, these encroachments upon your rights and ours. [29]

It was already too late. Alley, in his absence, had been dropped from the group of trustees of the Ames contract, in deference to Durant's wishes. John Duff, who would give Durant no trouble, had been put in Alley's place. Alley was also soon ousted from the directorate of the Union Pacific, as he foresaw. President Ames and Sidney Dillon henceforth were helplessly outvoted by Durant's henchmen in the governing circles of both the U.P. and the Credit Mobilier. Oliver Ames and his brother, Oakes, who was not an officer or director in either organization, could do little but hold on and endeavor to save the credit of the Union Pacific with their own, while Durant's reckless hand on the throttle nearly wrecked the railroad.

Sam Reed came close to quitting the U.P. during July, 1868. While he was in Salt Lake City the previous month, Durant had arbitrarily assigned supervision of construction between Laramie and Green River to James A. Evans, the engineer for whom the Black Hills pass was named. In fairness to Durant, it must be said that this was a reasonable move to lighten Reed's great load of work and responsibility, of which he had frequently complained to his wife. Durant undoubtedly felt that Reed would have enough to do if he concentrated on the line from Green River westward. Neither Reed nor Evans interpreted Durant's action as it was intended. Reed saw a plot to undermine his authority. Evans was embarrassed at being an apparent pawn in the plot. Both men sent in their resignations. Neither was accepted.

The matter was finally settled between Reed and Durant, face to face, at Laramie on July 30th. Durant had drawn up a paper renaming Reed as "superintendent and engineer of construction," but weakening his position with exceptions and restrictions. Reed perused the document, and crossed out all but the first sentence. "I accept this much," he said. Durant was angered. "What will you do if I refuse to agree?" he asked sharply. "I'll start for Salt Lake City tomorrow," [30] Reed retorted. His influence with Brigham Young and his ability as a railroad-builder were too valuable to lose. Durant gave in.

Later that day, Reed wrote cheerfully to his wife:

All is arranged satisfactorily. I will go west tonight. . . . I have no hopes that I may get time to visit home before winter. We shall soon have men at work two hundred miles west of Salt Lake, or to "Reed's Pass" of the Humboldt Mountains. The company is straining every nerve to build as much road as it is in the power of man to do before connecting with the Central Pacific.[31]

Trains started running to Benton, the next forward base, on July 20th. There, 700 miles west of Omaha, the Red Desert commenced. By the first of August, the track stretched 30 miles beyond. On that day General Casement summed up Benton for his wife. "This is an awful place," he wrote. "Alkali dust knee deep and certainly the meanest place I have ever been in. I am so thankful that my Darlings are where they are." [32]

On August 13th General Casement had just returned from inspecting the grading between Benton and Green River. "Rode 120 miles in 12 hours," he told his wife, "and hurt the Saddle some, as I felt it flinch when I sat on it." [33]

His tracklayers were moving toward Green River with gathering speed, despite interruptions that Durant permitted in the interests of publicity. "We are having a succession of excursion trains," Casement complained in his regular letter home on August 17th. "Today all the Professors of Yale College [an exaggeration] and a lot of Rail Road men with their Ladies have been here. It is a great nuisance to the work, yet we have laid over four miles of track today. . . . We haul all our water about Fifty Miles on the cars," the General continued. There was never enough of it, though, under the intense August sun in that "awfull [sic] country," as Casement called it. "We are loosing [sic] a great many Mules. Six nice fat ones died in less than an hour today." [34]

Though General Dodge was now in the oasis of Salt Lake City, he was almost as uncomfortable as Casement in the Red Desert. His discomfort was not physical, however. He had at last been obliged to tell Brigham Young that, much as the Union Pacific wanted to justify running its track through Salt Lake City, every engineering survey of 1867 and 1868 had made it obvious that the most practical route west was around the north end of Salt Lake.

Brigham Young, a 6-foot, 200-pound individual of commanding presence, was not an easy man to face with news he was bound to resent fiercely. "He has . . . secretive eyes, eagle nose, and mouth that shuts like a vice, indicating tremendous firmness," [35] wrote the New York *Tribune's* Bert Richardson.

He reacted as anticipated. Even though Dodge pointed out that the U.P. intended to build a branch from Ogden to Salt Lake City, Young would have none of it. He

appealed over my head to the board of directors [Dodge said later] who referred the question to the government directors, who fully sustained me. Then he gave his allegiance and aid to the Central Pacific, hoping to bring them around the south end of the lake and force us to connect with them there. He even went so far as to deliver in the tabernacle a great sermon denouncing me [on Sunday, August 16th], and stating a road could not be built or run without the aid of the Mormons.

When the Central Pacific engineers made their survey, they, too, were forced to adopt a line north of the lake. Then President Young returned to his first love, the Union Pacific, and turned all his forces and aid to that road.[36]

This last statement was far from exact, but by the time he made it, General Dodge's memory was undependable.

Casement's tracklayers advanced the U.P.'s rails more than 65 miles during August. It was their biggest achievement for any month since they began, two years earlier.

One traveler who found their work good was Senator Cornelius Cole. Reporting to his wife from Benton at 5 A.M. on August 19th, while homeward-bound for California, Cole wrote, "The Pacific RR is all the way *first rate*—smooth and safe. It is very different from the old way of traveling. We have had the best Pullman sleeping cars. Some of the stations are very fine and the scenery in the mountains rather grand." The track already stretched 60 miles beyond Benton, but none but construction trains were allowed over it. Senator Cole was now regretfully contemplating the big gap that still remained between the converging ends of the U.P. and C.P. "In an hour I take the stage—for a week," [37] he wrote.

Another traveler over the Union Pacific line that August had a reaction very different from Cole's. He was Jesse L. Williams, who wrote a long, critical report to the Secretary of the Interior, describing all the ways in which the U.P. was below the standards that the government expected of it.

Though Government Director Williams had found a good deal to admire, he deplored the emphasis on speed, and the resulting decline in the quality of the product. He declared that hardly any bridges or culverts on the entire road had stone masonry in them. Wooden bridges could be tolerated only as temporary structures, he warned. They were subject to fire and rot. At least 100 miles of the roadbed in the Platte Valley was a foot or two lower than it should be, Williams said, and too narrow to permit proper ballasting in many places. Also, he reported, as soon as tracklaying had reached an average pace of 2 miles a day, the company had stopped burnetizing the inferior cottonwood ties. Those that hadn't been treated wouldn't last more than four years, he insisted. Ties of mountain pine had been used west of the Black Hills, but, though better than cottonwood, they weren't as good as oak ones.

Williams, a fair-minded engineer, admitted that "taking the whole line in view, the trains pass over it more smoothly and with as high speed as on any new road over which I have traveled." But the scanty rainfall in the region was materially responsible, he added. As for the track, "on curved line time was not taken to bend the iron rails to suit the curves." [38]

The rolling stock, he said, though made by reputable manufacturers, was being worn out at such a rapid clip that by the time the road was finished, a lot of it would have to be replaced immediately.

All in all, Williams estimated that it would cost at least $3 million to bring the Union Pacific up to first-class condition from its present level.[39] He once again urged the prompt establishment of a reserve fund to meet that essential expense.

This report precipitated a stir in official Washington, and prompt action at U.P. headquarters in New York. On September 9th Williams was gratified to be able to tell Secretary of the Interior Browning that the railroad's board of directors had resolved on September 2nd to set aside $3 million worth of first-mortgage bonds for the purpose of correcting the deficiencies he had pointed out.[40]

Having made a move to appease the government, those U.P. directors who were also trustees of the Ames contract hastened to gratify the stockholders of the Credit Mobilier, as well, by distributing another large dividend. It amounted to 75 per cent in U.P. first-mortgage bonds and 100 per cent in the railroad's stock. The trustees voted for it on September 3rd.

By the middle of September, General Casement was boasting to his wife that not only had his men done "the largest month's work last month that has been done on the road" but he and Dan were expanding the scope of their activities. "We have taken sixty miles of grading west of Salt Lake," he wrote from the end of the track on September 19th, "and I am very busy fitting out parties to put on it." [41]

Late in September, hundreds of miles to the rear of the tracklayers, Indians wrecked their last Union Pacific train. The attack occurred between the stations of Alkali and Ogalalla, Nebraska, alongside the South Platte. Its pattern was similar to that of the Plum Creek raid of August, 1867. The warriors pried up rails and lashed them to a stack of ties with telegraph wire. A freight with one passenger car attached blundered into the barrier and was derailed.

The engineer was thrown from the cab when his locomotive left the track, and was barely hurt. The unlucky fireman was pinned against the firebox and slowly roasted to death. In his agony, he begged the engineer to shoot him. The latter, unable to bring himself to do this, became so distraught that he temporarily lost his mind.

The few passengers, including Father J. M. Ryan, a pioneer Catholic priest of Columbus, Nebraska, were besieged in their car, holding off the circling Indians with rifles snatched from overhead racks, where they were usually carried in U.P. passenger cars of the time. They were helpless to try to free the dying fireman. By the time the attackers tired of their battle with the beleaguered passengers and rode away, he had died. Another train was summoned by telegraph from Ogalalla station to come up and clear the track.

The railroad's Indian troubles flickered out after one more flare-up in early November. General Casement reported to his wife from Granger on November 6th, "The Indians are on the rampage east of us and are detaining trains." [42] Their only serious damage, though, was the burning of a small railroad bridge over Lodge Pole Creek, near Pine Bluffs, at the Nebraska-Wyoming line. "Bill Sherman had better send out a sheriff's posse to arrest them," [43] commented the *Frontier Index,* which had moved to Bear River City by then.

The Union Pacific's telegraph reached Green River on September 3rd, while the track was still 40 miles east. But the rails crossed the tandem bridges into town on October 6th, and General Casement's men celebrated their arrival by laying track for 5 miles beyond. Two weeks later, they had passed Bryan, then 856 miles west of Omaha.

General Casement's slickly functioning tracklayers outdid themselves in the easy reaches first encountered. On Monday, October 26th, they spiked down 7¾ miles of new rails. They swore they could have done even more if they hadn't run out of water. Three locomotives went dry at one time that day. A fourth jumped the track. For a time, the general couldn't move his train. He was so pleased with his men's fresh record, though, that he ignored the day's minor setbacks and generously paid everybody three days' wages.

Complications soon developed, however. "It is hard to get anything up the road except ties and iron," Jack Casement wrote his wife from Granger, 30 miles west of Green River, on October 31st.

Durant is here trying to hurry things up, but he only creates delays. We have held him level by keeping the track onto the Bridges and Our men idle more than half of the time. But as he claims to love to pay for those things, I propose to give him his fill of it. I expect to go up the line to start another gang of tie layers tomorrow. We have had one snow storm but it did not last long. I hope thirty days more of good weather will let us off for the winter.[44]

By now the Oakes Ames contract had run out. Ames refused to renew it, and the trustees had drawn up another to take its place. Durant and Sidney Dillon had persuaded James W. Davis, a tie contractor from Omaha, to lend his name to it, Hoxie-fashion, though he had no financial stake in the arrangement. Davis got no more than he already had—what he thought was going to be a lucrative contract for ties. It eventually transpired that he lost a good deal of money on it. Meanwhile, the construction of the railroad was managed precisely as before, by a board of trustees acting for the Credit Mobilier. It was completed to Promontory Summit under the Davis contract.

On November 6th, though still hampered by snags in the supply line from Omaha, General Casement had his men fully engaged in a powerful new forward thrust. "We are distributing and laying ties 40 miles ahead of the track," he wrote. "Are finishing grading and trying to accumulate winter supplies all at the same time." [45]

Samuel B. Reed, not long afterward, was congratulating himself at Bear River City that the grading was done at least that far. "Ten days of good weather and all will be clear to the heavy work in Weber Canyon," [46] he noted on November 17th.

By the end of the first week in December, Sam Reed was running into severe difficulties with the grading. "It goes very slowly," he wrote on December 6th, "on account of the hard frozen ground, which it is impossible to move without powder. We are working night and day without cessation." [47]

Reed's sorest burden was Durant, who had taken most of the graders off the line and sent them into the woods after ties and bridge timbers, of which there was a painful shortage. "The Doctor made a great mistake," declared Reed. "Had he left them [the graders] as they were, all the grading to Weber Canyon would have been done long ago, before there was frost in the ground to interfere with successful work." [48]

Ten days later, from his field office at the head of Echo Canyon, east of Weber, Reed was able to report that the grading was done to within 8 miles of where he sat, but he was still grumbling about Durant. "This work would all have been finished long ago if my arrangements had not been interfered with," [49] he told his wife on December 16th.

By now, General Dodge was back in Washington, for the third session of the Fortieth Congress. Sam Reed was the top field officer of the U.P.'s construction forces, and he felt woefully vulnerable with Durant rampaging around his vicinity.

Reed's last letter of 1868, written on December 28th, reported the track laid as far as the first stage station in Echo Canyon, and grading forces already being distributed farther west. However, those were the only cheerful notes in his message home.

"Doctor Durant arrived at the head of Echo on the twenty-fifth, will be here this evening," he told his wife. "You don't know how I want to be home. If anything goes wrong the H – – l is to pay, the same if all goes swimmingly. I do not care whether I remain another day or not." [50]

(Top left) *Aboard the U.P. directors' car in 1868. Rifles are handy above center mirror. At table, l. to r.: S. Seymour, S. Dillon, T. C. Durant, J. Duff.*

(Top right) *Generals Grant, Sheridan, and Sherman visited Dodge at Fort Sanders, Wyoming, in July, 1868. Durant (sixth from right) then tried and failed to oust Dodge (left end) as the U.P.'s chief engineer. Sheridan is third from left, Grant above dog, Sherman in center.*

(Bottom) *A Union Pacific train moves westward over the temporary bridge at Green River, Wyoming, late in 1868. Citadel Rock, famous landmark, is in the background.*

NATIONAL ARCHIVES

U.P.

(Top) *Bear River City, Wyoming, 965 miles west of Omaha, was one of the wildest temporary towns to prey on the U.P.'s construction workers.*

(Center) *A typical supply train for U.P. graders and bridge-builders moves through Echo Canyon, Utah, in 1868. Completed railroad grading is at right.*

(Bottom) *The Union Pacific's largest tunnel, 772 feet long, was at the head of Echo Canyon. A hazardous 8-mile track skirted it until finished.*

U.P.

(Top left) *An eastbound U.P. freight heads up Weber Canyon, Utah, after passing through Tunnel No. 3. There were but four tunnels on the whole railroad.*

(Top right) *A tremendous blizzard blockaded the Union Pacific's track in Wyoming for three weeks in February–March, 1869.*

(Bottom) *The last "hell on wheels" along the U.P. route was Corinne, Utah, already disintegrating when W. H. Jackson took this picture in July, 1869.*

(Top) *A U.P. excursion train heads westward across shored-up Devil's Gate Bridge, Weber Canyon, in May, 1869.*

(Bottom) *Union Pacific workmen ballasting track west of Green River in the summer of 1869, completing a job often slighted earlier to speed construction.*

CHAPTER FIFTEEN

1869

POLITICAL MANEUVERS
AND A RAID

The Union Pacific was nearly flat broke. At the same awkward moment, it was engaged in some of its most difficult and costly construction work. The weather high in the Wasatch Mountains was severe, and growing worse. Durant, according to Reed, who longed to see him depart for New York, was behaving like a wild man, indulging in prodigies of impracticality and extravagance. "He costs hundreds of thousands of dollars extra every month he remains here, and does not advance, but retards, the work," [1] Reed wrote to his wife early that month. The superintendent of construction was about at his wit's end, with Durant obsessively demanding speed and then so upsetting Reed's orderly organization that a slowdown resulted instead.

The Union Pacific's acute shortage of funds was partly the result of enormously increased expenditures. Dodge said that building the railroad at high altitudes in winter cost up to four times as much as it would have under favorable circumstances. Basically, however, the U.P.'s fiscal strait was the result of foolhardy decisions by the Durant-controlled majority among the Ames-contract trustees the previous year. Constructing the railroad across Wyoming had cost so much less than expected that the directors had joyously distributed all of their sudden surplus in dividends. (In December, topping off a profligate year, they had dispensed a bonus of 200 per cent in U.P. stock.) "In a short time," wrote Sidney Dillon, subsequently deploring this imprudence, "we were in greater distress than ever for money." [2] The distress was now at its worst. Contractors were failing to collect what was owed them. Their men weren't getting paid.

The problems that the Central Pacific and Union Pacific were encountering in the last months of their rush toward a meeting were both political and practical. They were occurring simultaneously but far apart, the political ones in Washington and New York, the practical ones in Wyoming and Utah.

In the political arena, Stanford and, particularly, Huntington were the most active Central Pacific participants. Stanford had been doing picket duty in Salt Lake Valley since the previous October, standing guard over his company's interests as best he could. Huntington was now 3,000 miles away from his usual beat. After sprinting across the continent with his wife in late December to see for himself what his colleagues had accomplished and what they had in mind for the finale of six years' all-out effort, he had arrived in Sacramento on the evening of January 2nd, home for the first time since 1863. Leaving Mrs. Huntington there for a long reunion with old friends and neighbors, he would soon be on his swift way back to New York. Stanford was eagerly awaiting his return passage through Salt Lake City, for another hurried exchange of late news and opinions.

There was ample cause for optimism and self-confidence among C.P. officials, but growing uncertainty over the status of the railroad's route in eastern Utah undermined their enthusiasm. The Central Pacific's position was that its own route was the only legitimate one west of Echo Summit. This was more than just an arbitrary point of view. A map and profiles of the route had been sent to Washington in the fall of 1868. They had been accepted and approved by President Johnson's Secretary of the Interior, Orville H. Browning, on October 20th. As far as the Central Pacific was concerned, that made its route official and beyond question.

The C.P.'s surveyed line entered Utah near the present settlement of Lucin, at the northwestern edge of Great Salt Lake Desert. Angling northeastward, it then climbed through a pass in the low Ombe Mountains and tilted down to an almost flat stretch of 25 miles along the north shore

of Great Salt Lake's Spring Bay. This was an unlovely and sterile area—
"a valley of alkali flats and salt beds of indescribable barrenness," proclaimed J. H. Beadle, who had looked it over for the Cincinnati *Commercial* in 1868, while trying to rid himself of asthma. "The spring rise of the
lake covers all the adjacent low lands, and retiring during the dry season,
leaves thousands of acres crusted with salt, and here and there a little
pond with deposits of the pure crystal a foot in depth." [3]

At Monument, the northernmost point of the lake, the Central Pacific
route swung gently southeastward. It soon began a climb of 685 feet in
16 miles to a bowl-shaped depression in the Promontory Range, which
thrusts its high, bony ridge far down into the lake, separating Spring Bay
from Bear River Bay. From Promontory Summit, in the midst of this
small, circular valley, the line slid down a gradual slope to skirt Bear
River Bay, cross the little Bear 10 miles north of its mouth, and then turn
firmly south and east to follow the western base of the Wasatch Mountains to Ogden. At Ogden, it curved eastward and ascended Weber and
Echo Canyons to the summit of the latter.

This was the route that had won Secretary Browning's approving
signature. On the basis of his favorable action, Leland Stanford had
placed Mormon graders along 200 miles of the line. Unfortunately, the
Union Pacific's gangs had built grade across much of the same territory,
and its track was already most of the way down Echo Canyon.

In point of fact, the Union Pacific's officers had first learned of Browning's acceptance of the Central Pacific's route on December 15th. On that
day, the secretary wrote to Oliver Ames, telling him what he had done
two months before, and asking him to see to it that the Union Pacific line
connected with that of the Central Pacific at Echo Summit. This caused
consternation and outrage at 20 Nassau Street.

Four days later, Oliver and Oakes Ames and General Dodge together
descended upon Browning in his Washington office. They vigorously protested his course of action. He told them they had the wrong idea of it.
His view, he said, was that the line he had approved was simply a general
route on which both roads were expected to lay track. The Central Pacific
certainly didn't feel that way about it, said Dodge. The Central Pacific
was wrong, snapped Browning.

In the course of their aroused discussion, Browning repeated his viewpoint of the situation "over and over again," [4] Dodge said later. Dodge
then asked him querulously if the U.P. had to conform to the grades and

alignment shown on the C.P. map. They were, he said, far inferior to the Union Pacific's own located line. No, answered Browning, that wasn't his intention at all. He wanted the best possible line. He didn't care who drew it, but he wanted both companies to adhere to it in a general way, so that they would meet, and not go shooting past each other. In the meantime, Browning told his callers, let the Union Pacific go ahead and lay track. *If* it met with the government inspectors' approval, he'd see to it that the railroad company got its subsidy bonds promptly.

The U.P. delegation had then departed, still ruffled and uncertain but not anticipating serious trouble. However, a disagreeable surprise was in store for them.

On January 5th President Ames wrote to Browning, asking that commissioners be sent out to report on construction work that had been done 60 miles in advance of the Union Pacific track. The railroad wanted to collect two-thirds of the subsidy bonds on that stretch, as the law allowed. Browning replied promptly and sharply that he wouldn't do a thing about Ames' request until the Union Pacific had filed a map with him indicating that its line would coincide with that of the Central Pacific from Echo Summit to Monument Point.

To quiet the furor that followed, Browning made a move that neither railroad would welcome. On January 14th he appointed three special commissioners to go to Utah and settle the troublesome question once and for all. He chose Maj. Gen. Gouverneur K. Warren, Lt. Col. R. G. Williamson, and Jacob Blickensderfer, Jr., all of them engineers. Warren's reputation was still somewhat shadowed by the fact that Sheridan had impetuously removed him from command after the Battle of Five Forks, in April, 1865. Colonel Williamson had already reported favorably on the Central Pacific's route only a month earlier, as a member of a previous special commission of Browning's. Blickensderfer was now an engineer in the Utah Division of the Union Pacific—a curious choice for arbiter, since he would naturally favor the line he had helped lay out.

Browning directed this commission to meet at Salt Lake City on January 25th. They were then to make a thorough examination of the ground between the approaching ends of the two railroads' tracks. If either company's surveyed line was "in all respects unobjectionable," [5] they were to adopt it as the one and only route. Otherwise, they were empowered to make an entirely new location. If the latter happened, all the grading already done by both railroads between Ogden and Monument Point might be a total loss.

The Central Pacific as yet knew nothing of these maneuvers. Huntington had lately been too far removed from his alert sources of information in Washington to learn of the trouble brewing, but he would soon find out.

"Huntington left Argenta for Salt Lake by stage today," [6] Hopkins wired Stanford on January 8th. On the same day, he telegraphed Fisk & Hatch, the C.P.'s leading bankers, and Brig. Gen. Richard Franchot, its chief lobbyist in Washington, that Huntington had started for New York. Franchot, a former New York congressman and longtime friend of Huntington's, was now being paid $20,000 a year—twice as much salary as any Central Pacific official drew—to be the railroad's confidential agent in the national capital.

Huntington met briefly with Stanford in Salt Lake City on his return journey, and then went bucketing up through the Wasatch Mountains in his private stagecoach to board the first U.P. train he could catch. In Echo Canyon he saw an arresting sight: some of Casement's tracklayers warming themselves at hot bonfires of railroad ties. Those ties, Huntington found out by asking, had cost the Union Pacific $1.75 apiece. It made him shudder to witness such waste, even when it was hurting his rival.

Back in Salt Lake City, Stanford recorded his pleasure over Huntington's visit. "It has been a great satisfaction to me that he has been out and learned the true state of matters," [7] Stanford wrote Hopkins on January 15th.

By January 18th Huntington was back in New York. For the period, his speed had been extraordinary. It was a foretaste of the lively pace of travel that would be possible for every cross-country traveler soon, when that particular journey could be made entirely by rail.

Huntington found an alarming document waiting at his office. Franchot had sent him the text of Browning's instructions to his latest trio of special commissioners, now already en route to Utah. Huntington mailed the ominous tidings to Stanford at once. He then composed a bitter letter of protest to the President of the United States. It was a long, indignant recital of grievances. Toward the end, he made his crucial point: "We respectfully submit and insist that the Union Pacific R.R. Company are not entitled to, and should not receive, any subsidies, either of bonds or lands, on any work done, or road constructed by them, west of Echo Summit." [8]

Huntington mailed the letter on January 19th. That same day, Charles Crocker sent an anxious telegram to Stanford. "Col. Williamson, one of the new Commissioners, started today for Salt Lake City," it read, "ordered there by telegraph to receive instructions from Secretary of Interior on RR matters. Be sure to see him early as possible." [9]

Neither Crocker nor Stanford knew then what the disquieting instructions were, but Stanford conferred with Williamson as soon as he could, and learned what was afoot. Here was one commissioner whom the Central Pacific felt it could count on. Only the other day, he had signed his name to a report that stated that the C.P.'s route was "remarkable among railroad examples." [10] He had joined with the other members of Browning's last previous special commission in marveling that it never deviated more than 55 miles from a straight line between Sacramento and Monument, Utah, and did that but once in a total distance of 662 miles. Considering the terrain it crossed—"including high and rough mountains, and a broad desert plain intersected with numerous ranges of hills whose crooked canyons afforded the only means of passage"—that was amazing. The verdict of Williamson and his fellow-commissioners had been that "the best general location for a great National Railroad between those two points is probably the one that has been adopted." [11]

It seemed most unlikely that Colonel Williamson would change his opinion. But Stanford was gloomy and suspicious about the other members of the new commission. "From the instructions and straws, I fear the thing is set up against us," he wrote morosely to Hopkins on January 29th. "The far off distance of our track and slow progress makes against us with great force. It is trying to ones nerves to think of." But there was nothing Stanford could do but cooperate. "On Monday, Feb. 1st, we start to examine the lines from end of U.P. track in Weber Canyon through to our track. It is not expected that we will make more than twenty miles a day." [12]

Huntington, meanwhile, was doing his best to foil the Union Pacific in Washington. He had in mind a move that, if successful, would cut the ground out from under the U.P. He would apply to Hugh McCulloch, Secretary of the Treasury, for two-thirds of the subsidy bonds due on the Central Pacific's advance construction work as far east as Ogden. After all, the Secretary of the Interior had approved the route. Huntington believed his railroad was legally entitled to the bonds. If McCulloch would issue them, that would settle the route controversy. Obviously, the Union Pacific couldn't collect bonds on a second line through the same territory.

Huntington didn't know that a reversed version of his scheme had occurred earlier to Oliver Ames, whose very first move had been brusquely rejected by the Secretary of the Interior on January 6th. But the Central Pacific had two important assets that the Union Pacific didn't have at this moment: an officially accepted route and a clean reputation. The Credit Mobilier was a growing scandal in Washington and elsewhere, and its bad name was tarnishing the Union Pacific.

That same month, in an article in the influential *North American Review*, young Charles Francis Adams, Jr., a grandson and great-grandson of U.S. Presidents, and now a new member of the Massachusetts Board of Railroad Commissioners, had made a resounding attack on the Credit Mobilier.

It is but another name for the Pacific Railroad ring [he wrote]. The members of it are in Congress; they are trustees for the bondholders; they are directors; they are stockholders; they are contractors; in Washington they vote the subsidies, in New York they receive them, upon the plains they expend them, and in the "Credit Mobilier" they divide them.[13]

Adams, who eventually, by an odd quirk of chance, became president of the Union Pacific and helped it climb to respectability, continued:

Ever-shifting characters, they are ever ubiquitous; they receive money into one hand as a corporation and pay it into the other as a contractor. Humanly speaking, the whole thing seems to be a species of thimble-rig, with difference from the ordinary arrangement, that whereas commonly "the little joker" is never found under the thimble which may be turned up, in this case he is sure to be found, turn up which thimble you may. Under one name or another, a ring of a few persons is struck at whatever point the Union Pacific is approached.[14]

With that sort of press, it wasn't going to be easy for Ames to prevail against Huntington.

Still, Secretary McCulloch proved to be uncommonly elusive. Huntington called at his office several days in a row, but the Secretary was always out or too busy to see him.

On January 25th, Stanford wrote worriedly to Hopkins:

I fear he [Huntington] is having a hard time in trying to save what a want of foresight has jeopardised if not lost. I tell you, Hopkins, the thought makes me feel like a dog; I have no pleasure in the thought of Railroad. It is mortification.[15]

Collis Huntington was not one to tolerate frustration for long, however.

I commenced to bring different influences to bear on the Secretary [he recalled subsequently]. I got a report from the Attorney-General that I was entitled to the bonds under the law. I obtained another of the same tenor from the Solicitor of the Treasury.[16]

While these schemes were unfolding, Stanford and Secretary Browning's latest board of inquiry headed for Sacramento. That had not been the intention of the special commissioners, nor what they had been instructed to do, but somehow Stanford had persuaded them to examine the Central Pacific from its starting point. He might well have reasoned that when they saw what difficulties the C.P. had already overcome and how skillfully the great problems had been solved, their judgment of its proposed route across Utah could become much more sympathetic. There was another reason for the change in itinerary. General Warren was suffering from snow-blindness. The white canyons of the Wasatch Mountains, where he and his colleagues were to have begun their inspection of the ground between the two railroads, were no place for him now. A short rest in California, on the other hand, would doubtless soothe his sore eyes.

Stanford and his not particularly welcome guests arrived in Sacramento on February 6th. The doting Governor was able to see his son for the first time in three months.

Two days later, he telegraphed the disagreeable tidings to Huntington that Jacob Blickensderfer, Jr., was a Union Pacific engineer, who had assisted in locating the U.P. line from Ogden to Humboldt Wells. "Justice demands that L. M. Clement, our first assistant and locating engineer, be added to the Commission," Stanford's wire concluded.[17]

Huntington promptly rounded up three California congressmen to support his appeal, and applied to Secretary Browning to appoint Clement. Browning took the application along to a Cabinet meeting on February 12th. The timing was most auspicious. That very day, Browning had in hand the freshly arrived report of his earlier special commission, which was highly favorable to the Central Pacific. He read it to the Cabinet, all members of which were present. Afterward, there was no objection to approving Clement's appointment to the investigating commission. Browning noted in his diary that he made the appointment by telegram when he got back to his office.

Where he sent it, he did not say, but it must have gone astray. Ten days later, after reporting to Huntington that the commissioners were still in Sacramento, Hopkins wired, "Has Clement been appointed? If so, has he been advised of it, and on what portions is he authorized to act?" [18]

There must have been a prompt and illuminating answer from Huntington, for the next day Hopkins telegraphed that Stanford, Montague, and the special commissioners were on their way at last.

Whether or not Huntington's canvassing of top-lofty Washington legal opinions in his favor spurred Browning or McCulloch into action—he later boasted that it had—the Central Pacific's request for subsidy bonds was brought up for discussion in a Cabinet meeting on February 26th. The matter wasn't settled that day, though Browning recorded in his diary that both he and McCulloch favored issuing the bonds. The decision was made on the following Monday, March 1st. On that day, the Cabinet members voted their unanimous approval of the C.P.'s appeal, and Secretary McCulloch was formally directed to release the bonds.

"But McCulloch still refused to let me have them," Collis Huntington declared at a later time. His theory was that the Secretary "had had a talk with Ames and had agreed not to deliver them." [19] The only plausible basis for this suspicion was that General Dodge's close friend Ulysses S. Grant would become President on Thursday, March 4th, and if the delivery of the bonds could be delayed until after his Administration took office, a way might be found to reroute them into the Union Pacific's treasury.

Huntington was taking no chances. He went to McCulloch's office and stayed there until he was able to confront the Secretary. He told him he'd sit in his anteroom for two weeks, if he had to, but he wasn't going to leave without the bonds—or a good reason why he couldn't have them.

McCulloch called fretfully to one of his assistants. "Mr. Jordan," he said, "Mr. Huntington is worrying me to death. He says that he wants those bonds. What do you think of it?"

"I have given you a written opinion, Mr. Secretary," replied Jordan, "that he is entitled to the bonds under the law."

"Well," said McCulloch, with a sigh, suddenly weary of fending off this tireless petitioner any longer, "he shall have them."

In reporting the conversation, many years afterward, Huntington said, "I went out, and by eight o'clock I found the bonds in my room. They amounted to over $2,400,000." [20] His memory was just a trifle askew. The true figure was $2,399,000.

Eleven days later, Stanford told Hopkins he believed that the Union Pacific hadn't yet found out what had happened. Writing from Salt Lake City on March 14th, he said:

I am strongly of the opinion that if it were known that we had the bonds for unfinished work that the U.P. would call off their graders. . . . Just now, as we have those bonds, it seems to me we had better keep quiet, if they do not crowd too hard, and get our track forward as fast as possible. [21]

Hopkins had just sent him an impatient telegram: "Will Commissioners' report be for CPRR interest?" [22] In this letter, Stanford replied, "I don't think any report will be ready to mail for a week or more. Then there will be disagreement and two reports probably." He continued:

Our work is going well, and is so far advanced that there need be no delay in track laying from end of present track to Ogden in consequence of grading. The U.P. have changed their line so as to cross us five times, with unequal grades, between Bear River and the Promontory. They have done this purposely, as there was no necessity for so doing.

I think they have calculated on a report of the Special Commission favorable to this line, and but for the addition of Clem[ent] to the Commission, would have got it. That the thing was set up with Warren and everything understood as to what the U.P. needed, I have no doubt. His behavior has indicated that he had a part to fill. B——— [Blickensderfer] was safe to adopt his own line; besides, his friendship for Dodge was another strong reliance. . . .

If the U.P. could have got report favorable to their line, I conclude their intention to have been to deny that we had the right of way and claim it for themselves, and that we must not get on it. Hence their crossing us and at unequal grades. They have laid track about three miles west of Ogden. I do not intend to finish up our line, but keep men scattered along it until our track is close upon them. I don't think there will be any attempt to jump our line while it is unfinished and we are working it. . . .

They [the Union Pacific] commenced to break ground last Monday on the heavy work at Promontory. We shall serve notices for them not to interfere with our line, and rest there for the present. [23]

At this time, according to some penciled reminiscences of Timothy Hopkins', Stanford and Montague were doing their scouting in a 4-horse wagon, driven by a boy. They had no tent with them, and usually slept on the ground, rolled up in blankets. They were much amused, therefore, upon visiting General Dodge in one of the U.P.'s construction camps, to find that he and his men still had a sizable escort of soldiers in this tranquil land.

That evening Dodge returned the call, for Stanford and Montague had halted their wagon within sight of the Union Pacific's many campfires. The general suggested that the Central Pacific's envoys move into his enclave for the night. They politely declined. After the general had left, Montague drily remarked, "I'm sorry we didn't arrange some signals with Dodge. I think he needs protection." [24]

Before Secretary Browning's special commissioners could make up their minds about the respective merits of the Central Pacific and Union Pacific routes in Utah, the whole matter was taken out of their hands and tossed into the halls of Congress. This came about accidentally, and because of the scheming of that obstreperous and unsavory Wall Street plunger, James Fisk, Jr.

Early in 1869, Fisk bought a small amount of Union Pacific stock and proceeded to sue the company. He claimed that, as a stockholder, he was being deprived of his rights because the Credit Mobilier was absorbing all the profits and assets of the Union Pacific. In fact, he maintained, the Union Pacific was actually bankrupt. Through the cooperation of two powerful and notoriously corrupt friends in New York, "Boss" Tweed and State Supreme Court Justice Barnard, Fisk managed to have the U.P. declared bankrupt and a receiver appointed. Not surprisingly, the receiver was William M. Tweed, Jr., son of the "Boss."

Young Tweed sent in sheriff's deputies to break up a Union Pacific stockholders' meeting on March 10th, before those assembled had had a chance to elect directors for the coming year. The company then appealed to Congress to permit it to move its headquarters to another state, out of reach of Fisk, Tweed, and Barnard.

Representative John A. Bingham of Ohio promptly introduced a joint resolution in the House "to protect the interests of the United States in the Union Pacific, and for other purposes." [25] By April 9th the House and Senate had given the Union Pacific the right to establish its head office wherever it liked, and it had chosen Boston. In the meantime, however, the members of Congress warmed to the occasion and gave the affairs of the Union Pacific and Central Pacific an unpleasantly thorough airing.

While the rancorous debate was proceeding, an absurd and humiliating scene occurred in the Union Pacific's office in New York.

For several days and nights, deputy sheriffs had been besieging 20 Nassau Street, declaring that they had been ordered to see to it that no records or securities were removed from the premises. On April 1st the Union Pacific sued Fisk for trespass, asking $1 million damages. At 11 A.M. on April 2nd, William Tweed, Jr., entered the U.P. office, accompanied by a squad of eight deputies armed with sledgehammers and chisels. Tweed announced that his men were going to break open the company's safe.

The safe was huge, and snugly bricked up except for its doors. While Tweed sat on an office stool, tranquilly smoking a cigar, his men began flailing away at the doors. This accomplished little besides agitating the clerks and company officers, and attracting a crowd of spectators from outside.

Just before noon, while Tweed had stepped out for a moment, Charles Tracy, one of the Union Pacific's lawyers, strode into the office and shouted, "I order all you burglars to cease this work and leave the building within five minutes, or I shall proceed against you both civilly and criminally." [26]

The bystanders scattered like frightened pigeons, but the men at the sledgehammers refused to scare. By mid-afternoon, they had made a small hole in one door. The builder of the safe, who dropped by, said it would take at least four days of constant work to broach it that way. He seriously doubted that it could be done even then. Tweed, who had now returned, said he would break the safe open if it took ten years.

Durant, back in the city briefly from his frenetic expeditions to various parts of the construction front, remarked sarcastically to Tweed that his men were damaging the safe so badly, even the company officers wouldn't be able to open it. He added that he hoped Tweed would feel rewarded for his trouble when he succeeded in getting at the contents. Tweed replied amiably that he ought to be, unless somebody had already removed them. With these "Erie thugs" [27] on the premises night and day, nobody had a chance, Durant retorted.

When the safe finally yielded to its attackers, there was a frenzied scramble between clerks and deputies for possession of the contents. A few securities disappeared in the melee, but somehow most of the Union Pacific's most valuable papers were rescued and stealthily transferred to New Jersey. From there they traveled unmolested to Boston.

A different sort of free-for-all fight over the Union Pacific now took place in Congress. There, beginning on April 5th, Senator William M. Stewart, the celebrated lawyer from Virginia City, Nevada, and staunch friend of the Central Pacific, derived considerable relish from telling his colleagues what a dreadful mess the Union Pacific was. He was seconded by Senator James W. Nye, also of Nevada. The chief defender of the Union Pacific was Senator John M. Thayer of Nebraska, who got an occasional assist from Senator John Sherman of Ohio. Michigan's Senator Jacob M. Howard, powerful chairman of the Pacific Railroad Committee, tried to be impartial, but his distrust of the Union Pacific showed through.

The battling Senators quickly disposed of the U.P.'s plea to move its headquarters to another state. As far as they were concerned, it could move anywhere it liked.

But these charges of Fisk's were another matter. Fisk, as Senator Stewart said, might well be "a great rascal," and Justice Barnard might preside over "a very rascally court," but if the Credit Mobilier were making off with all the profits and assets of the Union Pacific, "Congress had better find out about it." [28]

Then, foreshadowing the sensational scandal that wracked the Republican party in 1872–73, Stewart declared:

I have heard it stated that leading members of Congress, members of the Committee on the Pacific Railroad in the House, were not only in the Union Pacific but in this identical Credit Mobilier, and were the recipients of enormous dividends, and I have not heard it denied.[29]

The threat of further development of this theme passed. The debate swung to the controversy between the U.P. and C.P. over the last miles of their respective routes.

Senator Thayer read an affidavit from General Dodge, who declared that the Central Pacific's map filed in the Interior Department the previous October was "false and fraudulent." He said he had met the C.P. engineers while they were running it, "and they never pretended that the line that had then been filed was anything but a trial line." Furthermore, he said, the map

was intentionally so made that it is perfectly useless in an engineering point of view or for the purpose of retracing it upon the ground. It has no topography, no stations, no courses, no angles, no scale—nothing by which any line could be identified by it on the ground.[30]

Senator Howard said that the Central Pacific people claimed their surveyors' stakes had been pulled up by persons unknown, and that the line was "perfectly useful." [31]

Why argue, asked Senator Nye, when "the Government has already issued bonds to the Central Pacific to Ogden"? [32] Yes, retorted Senator Thayer. How come? Nobody supplied an answer.

By now, Senator Stewart was off the route and into more damaging particulars. The fact that Representative Oakes Ames had just come into the Senate Chamber and was sitting near him did not subdue Stewart a particle.

The Union Pacific [he said] have run their road as rapidly as they could without making their location in advance and having it approved. In order to make distance, they have skipped a very important tunnel, and laid a very precipitous track around it. . . . They have got the Government commissioners to call that a road, and they have got their Government bonds on that road. They have not dug out the tunnel. They have no continuous line to Ogden, or within many miles of Ogden. That is the course they have taken to get distance, so that they could claim that they might go on toward Ogden. They did attempt to jump over four or five hundred miles, and spent some $200,000 at Humboldt Wells, in my state, last July, August, and September, but they saw they could not cover up that distance, and abandoned it. They played these games, and they put their adversaries on guard.[33]

He then read into the record a corrosive recent letter to the Chicago *Tribune,* signed by fifty disgruntled Union Pacific passengers, many of whom Stewart said he knew personally.

"The officers in the employ of the company and the workmen on the road openly state that for near three months the men have not been paid," the letter said, in part, "and that there is general dissatisfaction and demoralization throughout that end [western] of the road." As for the roadbed, embankments were "in many places so narrow that the ties overlap the earthwork, which, when subjected to the dissolving injury of spring weather, will mostly disappear." Mark their words, said the letter-writers, when the roadbed thawed, the Union Pacific would become "simply an elongated human slaughter house." [34]

By now, the attentive Senate had nearly lost sight of what it had gathered to decide. At the start of an evening session on April 9th, however, Senator Howard abruptly announced that the Central Pacific and Union Pacific had agreed to a point of meeting, and he proposed to incorporate it in the joint resolution the senators were debating.

Then came the phraseology that fixed the place where the rails would join, and also where the respective railroads would end—not the same spot at all.

> Resolved [read Senator Howard], that the common terminal of the Union Pacific and Central Pacific Railroads shall be at or near Ogden; and the Union Pacific Railroad Company shall build, and the Central Pacific Railroad Company shall pay for and own, the railroad from the terminus aforesaid to Promontory Summit, at which point the rails shall meet and connect and form one continuous line.[35]

The Sacramento *Union's* Washington correspondent afterward reported that certain signs of a compromise had been clearly visible that morning. "C.P. Huntington was discovered to be on most cosy terms with Oakes Ames of the Credit Mobilier of the Union Pacific." [36]

The terms had not been so cozy at first. Huntington had made the initial move, an offer to buy the U.P. track between Promontory Summit and Ogden, but he coupled it with a threat. If the Union Pacific refused to accept his proposition, he said, the Central Pacific would build a track of its own into Ogden. The U.P. could take its choice.

"I offered them $4 million," he later asserted. That was what the Union Pacific estimated it had cost to build that particular stretch of track. "They did not want to sell," Huntington continued, "but at length accepted the proposition. It was this payment that saved them from breaking down utterly." [37]

As it turned out, Huntington's deal with the Union Pacific cost considerably less than $4 million. Before payment was made, the government stepped in and trimmed the price, declaring that it had been set too high. The final settlement, made in November, 1869, comprised $2,840,000, in nearly equal amounts of C.P. first-mortgage bonds and U.S. government 6's. This paid for 47½ miles of track. The Central Pacific, for reasons not disclosed, chose to lease the last 5 miles of track leading into Ogden from the west—for 999 years.

The glad news from Washington put an immediate end to Charlie Crocker's insomnia, which had harried him for months. He said later, "When Huntington telegraphed me that he had fixed matters with the Union Pacific, and that we were to meet on the summit of Promontory, I was out at the front, and went to bed that night and slept like a child." [38]

The dreams of other officials of both railroads were presumably less blissful that night, for the Senate had not bestowed its blessing without serious reservations. The joint resolution that was passed and sent to the President for signing on April 9th approved the Union Pacific's move to Boston and the details of rail-joining and terminus, but it added three most disturbing clauses:

1. It authorized the President to appoint a board of five to examine both railroads and determine how much money was still needed to make them "first class."

2. It authorized the President to withhold subsidy bonds in amounts sufficient to cover the cost of raising the railroads to that status. If there weren't enough subsidy bonds still due to pay the bill, he was empowered to collect the sum in the railroads' first-mortgage bonds, or make other requisition on them for it.

3. It authorized the U.S. Attorney General to investigate both companies to see if fraud had been committed, illegal dividends distributed, or if agents or employees had violated penal laws.[39]

In New York, Justice Barnard aimed one more blow at Durant's retreating coattails. He issued an injunction forbidding the Corn Exchange Bank to pay out any more money to him. But Durant was already on his way back West, to be present when the rails met.

On April 22nd, in the safe and steady city of Boston, the stockholders of the Union Pacific met for the annual meeting that had been so shockingly postponed. Their mood was jaunty, for on the day before, "Boston parties," said a dispatch in the papers, had bought all the company's first-mortgage land grants and bonds, "thus providing funds sufficient to complete and equip the road perfectly, pay the floating debts, and build the Denver branch." [40] The reference to the Denver branch was cleared up after the meeting. The official report announced that the stockholders had decided to purchase that persistent threat to their future traffic, the Kansas Pacific (formerly the Union Pacific Railway, Eastern Division), the road from Kansas City to Denver. The "Denver branch" would link the K.P. to the Union Pacific's main line at Cheyenne.

Then Jesse L. Williams, the dean of the government directors of the U.P., declared, after denigrating Fisk and Justice Barnard, that the company didn't object to a legal examination of its affairs "by a *competent* tribunal." [41]

The meeting ended on a cheery note from Utah. A telegram from General Dodge was read aloud. "The Central Pacific is 18 miles from Promontory Summit," he wired, "and the Union Pacific only 12." [42]

The next day, the C.P.'s "Clem" Clement, Montague's first assistant, read a copy of the same telegram in Washington, where he was fuming over the absurd predicament of the special commission to which he had been appointed. He was glad to hear the news, he wrote to his friend Butler Ives, but his thoughts were mostly angry.

We the commissioners are simply wasting our time, in endeavoring to ascertain the best location from North, or Ives, Pass to Ogden, a fact already firmly established by the bond of iron which is to hold our glorious country in one eternal union. . . .

I don't know how this commission will end nor how it will make its report. Suffice it to say that I am heartily sick of such d——d nonsense and sincerely hope that this illegal, unjust, and humbugging posse will soon end.[43]

CHAPTER SIXTEEN

1869

THE C.P. SETS A
TRACKLAYING RECORD

Thirty-five ships bound for San Francisco were bringing essential construction materials, including eighteen locomotives, to the Central Pacific as the year 1869 opened. The sawmills around Truckee were buzzing away at C.P. orders for a million more ties. Charlie Crocker and Strobridge felt well prepared for their final dash in the race with the Union Pacific. Yet track-building, for a variety of reasons, was limping.

Stanford, irked at his own railroad's laggard pace and hoping the heavens would fall on Casement and his men, was still moaning about the "remarkably good" weather in eastern Utah on January 15th. He observed wistfully in a letter to Hopkins that day that "Ives says two years ago last September, when he was at Echo Summit, snow fell four feet. Such a fall of snow this year would have saved us, notwithstanding the slow progress of our track." [1]

The Central Pacific's tracklaying was no more sluggish than the grading in Utah.

Our work from Ogden to Monument goes very slowly [Stanford continued]. Our contractors have many excuses. But the real trouble is they are trying to do the work too close. But I have started Brigham after them, and they give indications of doing better. I will get all done here that I can, but we must rely upon Strobridge's forces to finish up the work and to have the grade ready for the track.[2]

Strobridge's forces, already somewhat hobbled by a mild smallpox epidemic, were now struggling with a deep freeze. The winter of 1868–69 had begun mildly enough in northern Nevada, but in mid-January there was a bitter change. Temperatures dropped to unprecedented lows. Between Humboldt Wells and Cedar Pass, where Stro's graders were at work, thermometers registered 18 degrees below zero on January 18th. The frigid weather lasted an entire week. By the end of it, the soil was frozen solid to a depth of nearly 2 feet.

The C.P. graders were not deterred by the fact that they couldn't dig up the icy ground with pick or shovel. Instead, they blew it up, using vast quantities of powder to split the earth into chunks with which they could build at least a temporary base for track. It was a poor substitute, and a very expensive one, but it worked as long as the cold weather lasted.

Later, when the soft breezes of spring blew across that land, and the sunlight grew ardent, the Central Pacific paid a stiff additional price for the hasty expedient of building grade out of "chunks of ice," as Crocker described it.

"This all melted," he recalled, "and down went the track. It was almost impossible to get a train over it without getting off the track." [3] The 100-mile stretch between Elko and Montello, Nevada, close to the Utah line, became particularly wobbly.

When Henry George, the future economist, then a thirty-year-old San Francisco reporter, rode over it that spring, he wrote grumpily that it had been "thrown together in the biggest kind of a hurry," [4] and his train often could move no faster than an ox team.

Obstructions in the flow of track-building materials occurred that Crocker was helpless to prevent. The vagaries of ocean travel around the Horn led to unexpected shortages of supplies.

"We have in Cal. 183 miles iron and only 89 miles spikes," he telegraphed Huntington on January 20th, "and 81 miles iron and 75 miles spikes to arrive in sixty days. It is very unsafe to half-spike track at this season of the year." [5] On the same day, Hopkins asked Huntington by wire, "Will you send spikes by steamer to make up deficiency?" [6] That meant a stiff boost in their cost.

Eight days later, a less predictable but serious shortage was discovered.

"Unless you send us chimneys for kerosene burners, we cannot use our headlights," Hopkins telegraphed Huntington. "Chimneys can't be had here." [7]

The most frequent obstacles to progress were railroad accidents.

On January 21st, a new C.P. locomotive named Blue Jay, which had arrived in Reno three days earlier, looking "prettier than a spotted mule, or a New York schoolma'am," ran into a stalled lumber train on its way back over the mountains with a few carloads of passengers. "Bruised, broken, and crippled, it was then taken limping to Sacramento for repairs," the Reno *Crescent* reported. Some of the cars on both trains were smashed, "but fortunately nobody was killed or even wounded." [8]

One heavily loaded construction train uncoupled in the middle as it started down the long, curving grade from the Nevada line to Reno. The break wasn't discovered until the front half of the train had pulled a considerable distance ahead of the abandoned rear. Then it was too late to forestall disaster. The aft cars rapidly gained momentum as they rolled unchecked in pursuit of the forward ones. The engineer dared not go fast enough to match their speed before they hit the last car of his section. When they did overtake it, the violent collision splintered eleven cars. Two brakemen were crushed.

During the same week, and almost in the same spot, 10 miles west of Reno, an overloaded eastbound freight with too few brakemen ran a mile past the Verdi station before it could be brought to a stop. The engineer then climbed out to give his locomotive some badly needed lubrication. While he was at it, a following construction train rounded a curve not far behind and plowed into the halted freight. Again, nearly a dozen cars were wrecked.

Accidents had become so frequent that it was now a matter of routine to split up smashed cars for locomotive firewood. Fuel always seemed to be in short supply, even though 30,000 cords of pine and fir logs were stacked up along the track as it stretched ever farther away from the Sierra forests. Engineers sometimes even had to pull up sagebrush to keep their charges chuffing across the Nevada desert.

Nature interfered with the construction schedule, too, by other means than frost and hindering winds at sea.

A great storm has overtaken us during the past week [the Reno *Crescent* reported on February 13th], and from appearance it has not yet spent its force. The Rail Road is blocked, and we have not had any California papers for three days. The storm on the mountain is described as something awful, but the company hope to be able to be running again in a day or two.⁹

The C.P. locomotives Mountaineer ("a very titan of iron and fire") and Toyabie, "making a gay old double-ender," had managed to slip through the Summit blizzard on the twelfth. They "came down with iron enough to lay two miles of track—sixteen cars loaded with ties, four cars loaded with bridge timber, a caboose and passenger cars." With a slap at the prophets of doom—notably the Sacramento *Union*, which had repeatedly stated that part of the roadbed in Nevada was unsafe—the *Crescent* continued, "They were going to the front over that terrible road which was to float away like water after a two days storm." ¹⁰

The present Sierra storm was the worst of the winter. A big snowslide knocked out a trestle near Cisco and caused a blockade above there. Several passenger trains were snowbound. Even nine locomotives couldn't push one of the largest plows through the drifts. Freight clerks at Sacramento had an unexpected holiday after every last freight car the railroad had available west of the Sierra had been loaded and dispatched to the western foot of the mountains, where they waited on sidings for the snow blockade to be broken and the empties to come rolling back from Nevada.

But the snowsheds, of which the final 14 miles would be built this year, had staunchly held against the onslaught, and in no more than four days the road was open again.

The Union Pacific had begun the year facing a construction task that General Dodge considered remarkable for paradoxical reasons. The 120-mile portion of road yet to be built appeared to offer enormous difficulties —dropping, as it did, down through the deep gorges of the Wasatch Mountains for 60 miles, descending from nearly 7,000 feet to 4,300—yet Nature had made it unexpectedly easy for the engineers to overcome most of the obstacles. The formation of the countryside was generally obliging. "By a skillful location," wrote Dodge, "the work per mile in cubic yards was rendered very light." ¹¹

Still, it was undeniably awkward that whereas the Union Pacific had only four tunnels in its entire length, as against the Central Pacific's fifteen, three of them should lie in the way just now. The longest, 772 feet, was up at the head of Echo Canyon. A temporary track of 8 miles had been built around it, zigzagging perilously down into the gorge. The remaining two tunnels, considerably shorter, were only three-quarters of a mile apart, in Weber Canyon. The track had quite a distance yet to go before it would reach them. Excavation of all three tunnels had been begun the previous fall and was well along.

The great difficulties that arose to confront the U.P. in 1869 were in large part financial. At the very start, the construction profits of the previous year had already been dissipated. The railroad had had to borrow so much money to keep going that its interest charges alone amounted to $500,000 a month. Soon, the Central Pacific would snatch away nearly $2,400,000 of anticipated subsidies. With them would go the right to market an equal amount of first-mortgage bonds. The U.P. was so far behind on payments to contractors that, in turn, the contractors' men weren't getting paid. They were becoming sullen and inefficient.

It was so vital to the railroad that each completed 20-mile stretch of track be approved by the government inspectors that when an unscrupulous commissioner, Cornelius Wendell, refused his approval unless he was given $25,000, the rattled superintendent of operations, Webster Snyder, hastily paid the bribe, without consulting anyone. His excuse was that he knew the railroad *had* to have the commissioner's O.K. He got off with a reproof from headquarters. Before the track was laid to Promontory Summit, the Ameses and their staunchest associates would assume personal debts of $5 million in order to save the Union Pacific's credit.

Many of the U.P.'s troubles that year, however, were due to the weather. The Wasatch Mountains were decidedly not the place to build a railroad in winter, as General Dodge had warned.

At the end of the first week in January, the snowy grade in Echo Canyon, beneath high cliffs eroded so strangely that they looked like a display of primitive sculptures, was covered by a swarm of Casement's men around the clock. Through the nights, reported a traveler, they worked "by the light of numberless lanterns." [12]

Already, though, many miles behind them, the attrition of blizzards in Wyoming was beginning to thin their vital supply line from the East. On January 10th snow fell so heavily in western Wyoming, and the wind tore at it so viciously, that a freight train bound for Echo took fourteen hours to crawl the 40 miles from Bryan to Evanston, at the Utah line.

By the middle of the month, when the bridgebuilders had finished most of the thirty-one trestles that crisscrossed Echo Creek in the course of 26 miles, the savage cold wave that had nearly paralyzed Strobridge's Chinese plunged down upon the Wasatch.

Only a couple of days earlier, Sam Reed had written his wife, "The Doctor himself, I think, is getting frightened at the bills." [13] Now they would mount spectacularly.

For a week, the thermometer never climbed as high as zero. On the seventeenth, it sank to 20 below. Up at the "wicked city" [14] of Wasatch, winter headquarters of the construction forces, just beyond the head of Echo Canyon, men were frantically trying to board up the rough-hewn settlement of 1,500 against the cruel cold. All around them, snow lay more than 2 feet deep.

"The sound of hammer and saw was heard day and night," [15] wrote J. D. Beadle, who shivered through a miserable breakfast in a cafe whose weatherboarding was being applied while the customers ate. Meanwhile, there were half-inch gaps in the outer walls of the room, and the temperature inside was 5 degrees below zero. Spilled coffee congealed on the tabletops; gravy and butter froze on the plates.

Casement's graders had to work all day long in their overcoats, and this slowed them down appreciably. The sun shone with a frosty brilliance, and the air was still, but so intensely cold that the ground froze deep and had to be blasted to shape it into a roadbed.

The U.P.'s men resorted to building grade out of "chunks of ice," as Crocker's had. Only, they had worse luck with the result. An entire train and the track beneath it slid off one slippery embankment into a gulley.

More routine accidents were frequent. One morning, a train of sixteen flatcars, loaded with rails and ties, had just started down the long grade from Castle Rock station when the last four cars parted from the rest. This happened in a section that was fairly flat, and the main part of the train had pulled ahead half a mile before a Casement foreman up front noticed the break. By then, the derelict cars were really beginning to roll. There were two German workmen aboard them, who might have applied the brakes, but they were sound asleep.

The foreman yelled to the engineer to go as fast as he could. The engineer took one startled look around and grabbed for the throttle. The train surged forward, its whistle now shrieking the signal for "Switches open," and Echo Canyon truly lived up to its name. The banshee cries were heard for miles, and caused a panicky scramble downtrack to clear the way.

The foreman, meanwhile, had run back to the rear car of his section of the train and ordered some graders huddled there to start tossing ties into the path of the pursuing cars. They did so in frantic haste. A couple of minutes later, the berserk cars struck a tumbling cluster of ties and made a contorted leap into a deep ditch. The two men aboard them had slept through all the noise, but their snoozes were now terminated in shocking fashion. They were hurled into a snowbank, however, and escaped with mere bruises.

Despite harrowing incidents of this sort, the track reached the hamlet of Echo City, only 8 miles from the mouth of Echo Canyon, on January 15th. The first locomotive got there at eleven o'clock in the morning, "and Echo City held high carnival and general jubilee on the occasion." [16]

The next day, Sam Reed was angrily spilling his troubles to Mrs. Reed:

Doctor Durant is still here, and of all men to mix accounts and business, he is the chief. My matters are in good shape, and if they could be let alone, more work would be done for less money and in less time under the present system.[17]

Much to Reed's relief, Durant departed for Omaha and New York on January 23rd. The burdens of the superintendent of construction would grow no less, but at least he would be in full control of them now.

The track by this time had reached a tall, ancient pine that stood close to the line of grade in Weber Canyon, a lordly gorge from whose heights the Mormons had contemplated rolling huge boulders down upon Gen. Albert Sidney Johnston and his expedition that came out to investigate them in 1857. The pine marked precisely the 1,000th mile from Omaha.

On January 30th light shone through the big tunnel at the top of Echo. The headings had met. The bottoms would not be completely blasted out until April 3rd. Excavating that tunnel consumed 1,064 kegs of powder. No nitroglycerin was used.

Nitroglycerin was briskly clearing out the two tunnels in Weber Canyon, however. It had been substituted for powder in the first one the day Durant left, but with his consent, in order to speed up the work. Promptly, a fifth of the tunnel men walked off the job and refused to return. They were afraid of the new explosive. It didn't matter. Nitroglycerin helped the rest do their work so much faster that the quitters weren't missed. Even so, the track got there before the tunnel was finished. A short temporary track, incorporating a 22-degree curve, was built around it. By the time the rails reached the last tunnel, it was ready for them. Nitroglycerin had ripped out the bottoms of it at a record pace of 8 feet a day.

By February 10th Engineer Mark Seymour, a cousin of the colonel's, was predicting that the U.P. track would be in Ogden in a month. It got there two days sooner than that. Beyond Ogden, there were 1,000 graders at work on the line to Promontory Point.

Out on the rocky eastern slope of the Promontory Range, a large gang of Strobridge's Chinese were patiently grading in the opposite direction. The two lines of embankment at times were within 100 feet of each other. Then tempers flared among the U.P.'s Irish. Obviously, one side or the other was just wasting its labor, and these Irishmen were in no mood to be made fools of.

At first, they tried to shake the bland persistence of the Chinese by jeering and by tossing frozen clods at them. When those tactics had no restraining effect, they staged sudden raids with pick handles. The Chinese fought back with unexpected vigor and accuracy. Then the Irish tried stealth. They set off heavy powder charges without warning their nearby rivals, and timed them to explode when the closest part of the C.P. grade was swarming with Chinese. As a result, several Chinese were critically hurt. The Central Pacific made official protests to the Union Pacific, which, according to General Dodge, gave sharp orders to its grading contractors to stop the guerrilla warfare. The contractors' men ignored the command. They soon received a much more effective warning.

A day or two later, at a point where the respective grades nearly crossed, and the Central Pacific's was the higher of the two, a sudden, unheralded explosion on the C.P. line deposited a huge cascade of dirt and rocks on the heads of the U.P. graders. Several of them were buried alive. This ended the war. The Irishmen abruptly abandoned their bullying when they found they had met their match.

In mid-February, the Union Pacific suffered its heaviest physical setback of the year, the worst storm it had known since its beginning. The disturbance may have been part of the same great blizzard that struck the Sierra and blockaded the Central Pacific at about this time. In Wyoming, at any rate, it created far more trouble. Ninety miles of the U.P. line, between Rawlins and Laramie, were snowbound for three weeks. Two hundred eastbound passengers were marooned at Rawlins. Six hundred others gradually clotted at Laramie, waiting for transportation west. The eastbound travelers stalled in the snow included a number of prominent Californians who had hopefully set out for Washington to see Grant inaugurated. The general had become President even before they got as far as St. Louis.

On February 20th the Salt Lake *Telegraph* reported that "the most terrific storm for years" [18] was then in progress, and that no mail had come through from Omaha for ten days. Supplies for the Union Pacific were cut off altogether.

On the twenty-seventh, Sam Reed wrote his wife that it might be four weeks before the snow blockade was raised. He was already running short of ties, but, thank heavens, had enough other supplies to last awhile longer. Otherwise, "we would be starved out." [19]

Dan Casement and a road-clearing crew with a big plow had set out for Laramie from Echo nearly ten days earlier. When they got to Percy, they found the cuts filled with 25 feet of snow. In the following three days, through a constant whirl of flakes and wind, they moved forward only 5 miles. Then Casement and some companions decided to walk the rest of the way to Laramie—77 miles. Dan almost died of exhaustion—"came near going up," [20] said his brother Jack—before he got there.

In the meantime, the eastbound passengers marooned in the Rawlins station had exhausted the local supply of antelope meat and were down to soup, coffee, and bad biscuits. A few were able to buy slices of bread with molasses on them, for $1.50 apiece.

The train crews, overwhelmed by their massive predicament, sought solace in whiskey, and became drunk and insolent. The passengers were soon in a desperate mood to break out of this sordid prison, so they volunteered to help dig their way through the drifts to Laramie, where the track was clear. By telegraph, they won reluctant permission from the superintendent of the Laramie Division, provided that they set out at their own risk and came armed with enough food, at least one hundred shovels, and a locomotive and plow to break a path.

The expedition began in high spirits, but had progressed only about 1,000 feet when a telegram from H. M. Hoxie, assistant general superintendent, arrived to countermand its permission to go farther. The frustrated passengers stalked back in dismay and anger to the station, which now had four dead men laid out in it. The boiler of Engine No. 112, overtaxed by the strain of its struggle with the snow, had exploded, killing the engineer, fireman, and conductor. The fourth man had been crushed when a car overturned.

Finally, the would-be spectators at Grant's inaugural were mad enough to break out, with or without leave. They stumbled and waded along the line of track for four days, stopping at night in stations, and finally reached Laramie, some of them with frostbitten feet. The temperature had never risen above freezing during their journey, and once it plunged to 33 below zero.

When a handful of the escapees straggled into St. Louis on March 5th, and told their tales of woe to the *Dispatch*, one said, "Most of us are much the worse for wear, and we think it will be a long time before we take another ride over the mountains on the Union Pacific Railroad." [21]

But the U.P. builders, undeterred by catastrophe at their rear, were now moving down upon Ogden at a lively rate. On the morning of March 8th, the tracklayers came marching into that little town of log and adobe houses, whose wide streets, people said, became the muddiest in Utah when it rained or thawed. Still, Ogden was fast growing up. There was no longer a local bounty on wolves, and for two years now, farmers had been forbidden to let their livestock roam at will among the populace. Ogden had 1,500 citizens, and most of them turned out to welcome the first locomotive, which puffed into their midst at 11:20 A.M.

The rest of the day was given over to wild celebration, or as unbridled festivity as the abstemious Mormons would permit themselves. Casement's men undoubtedly made up for any shortage of zest.

Captain Pugh's band serenaded the grimy tracklayers and Captain Wadsworth's artillery fired salutes in their honor. By five o'clock in the afternoon, a full-blown civic ceremony had been improvised, with long official speeches, and welcoming banners stretched between the arching trees.

From here on, the going would be easy, except for some sizable trestles and heavy rock work out at Promontory.

It was about time. Reed was exhausted. Three weeks before, he had confided to his wife, "I wish the last rail was laid; too much business is unfitting me for future usefulness. I know it is wearing me out." Only the other day, he had declared to her that when the long, gruelling job was done, "I shall want to leave the day after for home, and hope to have one year's rest at least." [22]

On the day the track entered Ogden, General Casement was in a wistful mood, too. "I am perfectly homesick," he wrote to Mrs. Casement, "and think I would like to work in the garden or drive on the flatts or build a house." [23]

But this mood passed as the track leaped forward toward Promontory Summit. "The weather is delightful," he noted exuberantly on March 12th. "Frogs singing and birds yelping." [24]

Life was taking on a far sunnier aspect in the Central Pacific camp also. After several weeks of halting, shivering progress in January and February, Strobridge had now stepped his track-builders up to an awesome pace. The Chinese had given him a spot of trouble once, when he had forbidden them to take time off for the usual prolonged celebration of their belated New Year's, but their grumbling had stopped.

On March 12th Hopkins was able once more to telegraph to Huntington the stimulating message "Roving Delia Fish Dance," [25] which, decoded, meant "Laying track at the rate of 4 miles a day."

The endless procession of construction trains from Sacramento to the end of track and back again drained the Central Pacific's shops of rolling stock as fast as it could be assembled. The editor of the Reno *Crescent* fondly noted each new locomotive as it hooted through his disorderly town, and called the roll of their names to his readers: Fire Fly, Grey Eagle, Verdi, Roller, White Eagle, Tiger ("a monster freight machine"),[26] Hurricane, Jupiter, Mercury, Herald, Heron. There seemed to be no limit to the outpouring of freshly minted engines, all of them "beauties."

Each night, Strobridge telegraphed back to the nearest station where materials were stockpiled, ordering as many cars of ties and rails and track hardware as he expected to use the following day, and specifying the order in which he wanted the supplies to arrive at the front. Crocker, meanwhile, roved the completed line night and day, vigilantly prodding the materials forward.

This system worked splendidly most of the time, but under the fierce pressure of full steam ahead, mistakes were sometimes made.

Crocker told of one major sin of omission that he converted into an effective object lesson. On this occasion, he was with Strobridge at dawn when a trainload of supplies that Stro had ordered the previous night came chugging up to the end of track with nothing on it but ties. The essential rails were missing.

"Of course, Strobridge was angry," Crocker recalled. "He could not lay any track."

Crocker at once rode a locomotive back to the closest supply depot and sought out the materials forwarder, an unfortunate named McWade.

McWade tried to blunt the superintendent's wrath with an immediate apology. As soon as he saw him coming, he called out, "Mr. Crocker, I know about it. Mr. Strobridge has telegraphed me, and I know it was all wrong and I am sorry."

Crocker was not appeased.

"Mac," he exclaimed, "a mistake is a crime now. You know what we have been trying to do. You know how I have been going up and down this road trying to get the material to you. And here it is—and you have made a mistake and thrown us out of two miles of track today. Now, just take your bundle and go. I cannot overlook it."

"McWade just burst out crying," Crocker reported. " 'Well,' said he, '. . . it is pretty hard on me. I have been a good, faithful man.' "

"I answered, 'I know you have, but there has got to be discipline on this road, and I cannot overlook anything of that kind. You must go. Send your assistant to me.' And I put the assistant in charge."

Charlie Crocker was basically a kindhearted man, however. He soon relented.

"I let him lay off a month," he said of McWade, "and put him back again. But it put everybody on the alert, and kept them right up to their work. And it did good, because everybody was afraid, and when I came along they were all hard at work, I can tell you." [27]

After April 9th, when Congress affirmed where the Union Pacific and Central Pacific rails were to meet, the C.P. halted all construction between Ogden and Blue Creek and withdrew its entire force west of Promontory Summit. Crocker now began thinking seriously of trying to set a track-laying record that the U.P. couldn't beat. This special rivalry to determine which road could move forward farthest in a single day had begun one day in 1868, when Jack Casement's men advanced the U.P. track 4½ miles.

"They bragged of it," declared Charles Crocker, in telling the story years afterward, "and it was heralded all over the country as being the biggest day's tracklaying that ever was known.

"I told Strobridge that we must beat it," he continued, "and we got together the material and laid six miles and a few feet.

"They came back at us afterwards, and made eight miles and a fraction." To accomplish this, the Union Pacific's track-builders had had to begin that day's work at three o'clock in the morning, laboring by lantern light until dawn, and had kept at the urgent task until midnight.

Crocker was determined that his Chinese could beat that.

" 'Now,' said I to Strobridge," he subsequently recalled, " 'we must take off our coats. But we must not beat them till we get so close together that there is not enough room for them to turn around and outdo us.' " 28

Before long, the Central Pacific's track had nosed to within 14 miles of Promontory Summit. The Union Pacific had but 12 miles to go, but its tracklayers had been obliged to slow down to about half a mile a day, for they were right on the heels of the graders. Some of the U.P.'s heaviest work in Utah was up the approach to Promontory.

The time seemed ripe for the Central Pacific's maximum effort.

The story has persisted down the years that Durant had bet Crocker $10,000 that his men couldn't top the Union Pacific's best day of track-building. Crocker was said to have taken the bet. However, in telling his version of the race to one of Historian H. H. Bancroft's interviewers, many years later, he made no mention of a wager.

I was not educated as a railroad man [Crocker told his questioner], and Strobridge was. And he said to me, "Mr. Crocker, we cannot get men enough onto the track to lay 10 miles."

Said I, "We are going to lay 10 miles of track. You must make up your mind to that."

"How are we going to do it? The men will all be in each other's way."

Said I, "We must organize. You don't suppose we are going to put two or three thousand men on that track and let them do just as they please? I have been thinking over this for two weeks, and I have got it all planned out." 29

Strobridge's own terse, and much more probably true, account of how the contest came about was laughably different. "I said to Mr. Crocker, 'We can beat them, but it will cost something,'" he recalled. "'Go ahead and do it,' said Crocker." 30

Eager as Charlie Crocker was to take credit for the historic achievement that followed, he deserved but part of it. Strobridge had trained the Central Pacific's track-builders. In months of steady progress across Nevada, they had developed remarkable proficiency. During those same months, Crocker had built a superlatively efficient supply organization. Faultless teamwork between the two resulted in building more railroad track on a single day, April 28, 1869, than was ever built before. (The achievement has been exceeded only once since, and then by but a few hundred feet. It happened August 15, 1870, on the Kansas Pacific, near Strasburg, Colorado.)

There was an embarrassing false start on April 27th, when a locomotive went off the track and stalled the first try for a record. Unfortunately, a few Union Pacific engineers were on hand to watch, at Crocker's invitation, and some Army officers en route to a West Coast fort had stopped to see the fun. Worse still, there were several newspaper correspondents in the casual audience.

Crocker made light of the mishap, while his guests needled him. "His face clouded for a moment when he heard the engine had got off the track," wrote the *Alta California's* reporter, ". . . but in a few minutes his merry laugh was ringing out as if nothing to annoy him had recently occurred." [31] He was soon happily engaged in another contest—competing with his guests in shooting at a cigar box, set up in the sand 100 yards away. Some of the visitors had decided to stick around for one more day.

Meanwhile, the offending locomotive was righted, and elaborate preparations made to stage the Central Pacific's record-breaking exhibition of tracklaying on April 28th.

Long ago, Crocker's supply staff had learned how to load sixteen flatcars with every last item needed to lay 2 miles of track. Five such trains had now moved up to the front, and stood on the main line or handiest sidings, waiting to be summoned. Strobridge had already sent a squadron of two-horse teams ahead, distributing ties along 10 miles of completed grading. In fact, most of the ties had been dropped approximately in final position along the path the rails would follow.

Very early the next morning, a wagonload of Union Pacific officials—Durant, Dodge, Reed, Dillon, Duff, and Seymour—arrived on the scene, in the hope of seeing Crocker's bluff called.[32]

At seven o'clock, the Central Pacific's well-drilled construction forces began their greatest day's march. At this moment, the first of five supply trains was already panting at the railhead. When the whistle of its locomotive screamed for the contest to begin, a swarm of Chinese leapt onto the cars and began hurling down kegs of bolts and spikes, bundles of fish plates, and iron rails. "In eight minutes, the sixteen cars were cleared, with a noise like the bombardment of an army," [33] wrote the San Francisco *Bulletin's* correspondent.

That train was then pulled back to a siding to make way for the next. As it chuffed away, 6-man gangs lifted small openwork flatcars onto the track and began loading each of them with sixteen rails, plus kegs of the necessary hardware to bolt the rails together and fasten them to the ties. These little flatcars, called "iron cars," had rows of rollers along their outer edges, to make it easier to slide the rails forward and off when they were needed. Two horses, in single file, with riders on their backs, were then hitched to each car by a long rope.

While this was being done, three men with shovels, who formed the army's advance guard and were called pioneers, moved out along the grade, aligning the ties. They did this by butting them to a rope stretched out parallel to a row of stakes that the railroad's surveyors had driven to mark the center line of the track.

At rails' end stood eight burly Irishmen, armed with heavy track tongs. Their names were Michael Shay, Patrick Joyce, Michael Kennedy, Thomas Dailey, George Elliott, Michael Sullivan, Edward Killeen, and Fred McNamara. They waited now beside a portable track gauge, a wooden-framed measuring device for making sure that the rails they laid were always 4 feet, 8½ inches apart. Two additional men handled the gauge, moving it just ahead of the tracklayers all day long.

As soon as the first iron car had been hauled forward, with a Chinese gang aboard, its horses were released and led aside. The Chinese quickly stripped the car of its kegs of spikes, bolts, and fish plates, and broke them open. They poured the spikes over the stack of rails, so that they would dribble onto the ground as the rails were removed. The bolts and fish plates were loaded into hand buckets to be carried where they were needed.

The Irish tracklaying team split in half, two men taking up positions at each end of the rail car on both sides. As each forward pair grabbed one end of a rail and quickstepped ahead with it, the rear pair guided the other end along the car's rollers and eased it to the ground with their tongs. Each rail, 30 feet long and weighing an average of 560 pounds, was in place within 30 seconds.

Behind the rail handlers followed a gang that started the spikes—eight to a rail—and attached fish plates to the rail joints by thrusting bolts through them. After them came a crew that finished the spiking and tightened the bolts. In their rear moved the track levelers, who hoisted tie ends and shoveled dirt under them in order to keep the rails on an even keel. They were guided by the gestures of a surveyor—a "reverend-looking old gentleman," [34] noted the *Bulletin's* reporter—who kept sighting along the finished track. At the back of the line tramped the biggest contingent of all—400 tampers, with shovels and tamping bars to give the track a firm seating.

As each iron car was unloaded, it was lifted and turned around. The horses were rehitched to it and hauled it back to the supply dump at a run. It was lifted off the track whenever it got in the way of a full car headed for the front, and in time to prevent the latter from having to slow down.

The scene was an animated one [wrote the man from the *Bulletin*]. From the first "pioneer" to the last tamper, about two miles, there was a line of men advancing a mile an hour; iron cars with their load of rails and humans dashed up and down the newly-laid track; foremen on horseback were galloping back and forth. Keeping pace with the track layers was the telegraph construction party. Alongside the moving force, teams were hauling food and water wagons. Chinamen with pails dangling from poles balanced over their shoulders were moving among the men with water and tea.[35]

When the whistle blew for the midday meal, Crocker's "pets," as the Chinese were often called, and their Irish advance guard had built 6 miles of railroad. Strobridge insisted on fresh horses for the iron cars every 2½ miles. He also had a second team of tracklayers in reserve, but the proud gang that had laid 6 miles of rails before lunch insisted on keeping at it throughout the rest of the day.

Stanford and Montague joined Crocker's guests at lunch. As he munched boiled beef, the top-ranking Army officer present told his host, "Mr. Crocker, I never saw such organization as that. It was just like an army marching over the ground and leaving the track built behind them." [36]

The better part of an hour was lost after lunch at the tedious job of bending rails, for the remainder of the 10-mile stretch was a steady climb and full of curves. This was done in a crude way: by placing each rail between blocks and hammering a bend into it.

When the curved rails were ready, the construction army resumed its march. By seven o'clock in the evening, the Central Pacific Railroad was 10 miles and 56 feet longer than it had been 12 hours earlier.

Each man in Strobridge's astonishing team of tracklayers had lifted 125 tons of iron in the course of the day. The consumption of materials was even more impressive: 25,800 ties, 3,520 rails, 28,160 spikes, 14,080 bolts.

As soon as the epic day's work was done, Jim Campbell, who later became a division superintendent for the C.P., ran a locomotive over the new track at 40 m.p.h., to prove that the record-breaking feat was a sound job as well. Then the last emptied supply train, pushed by two engines, was backed briskly down the long grade to the construction camp beside the lake, with 1,200 men riding on its flatcars.

Strobridge got lasting satisfaction from General Casement's comment to him about the achievement of April 28th. "He owned up beaten," [37] said Strobridge. Not so the general's peppery little brother, Dan. He was so sure that his men could exceed the Central Pacific's mark, given room enough to do so, that he begged Durant for permission to tear up several miles of track in order to prove it. Durant said no.

After witnessing Stro's triumph, the watchers from the Union Pacific camp departed for Ogden in a subdued mood. At Promontory, on the way, Durant left orders to haul rails and ties up to the Summit by wagon and start immediately to lay track back eastward from there. Never mind waiting for the trestles east of Promontory to be finished before Union Pacific rails could reach the agreed point of junction with the Central Pacific.

Wagons began hauling U.P. iron up the slope the next morning. It was just as well. On April 30th the C.P. finished a continuous line of track from Sacramento to Promontory Summit, a distance of 690 miles. Only a rail's length now separated it from where the U.P. would end.

Strobridge, uneasy about possible contamination of his men by the blatant sinners who were already setting up saloons in tents in the neighborhood, at once sent the bulk of his construction forces many miles back down the line. They had lots of ballasting still to do there, anyway.

On May 2nd, General Dodge wrote home in a bleak frame of mind.

I never saw so much needless waste in building railroads. Our own construction department has been inefficient. There is no excuse for not being fifty miles west of Promontory Summit. Everything connected with the construction department is being closed up, and closing the accounts is like the close of the Rebellion.[38]

However, the U.P. had only 5 miles of track to put down before it met the Central Pacific. "There will not be much of a time here," wrote the general, "no demonstration. But in the East and farther West I expect they will celebrate. You'd better put your flags on the outer wall." [39]

CHAPTER SEVENTEEN

STUMBLING STEPS
TO A MEETING

In his old age, General Dodge tried to recall exactly what happened at Promontory Summit on May 10, 1869, and who was there. He wrote that Leland Stanford arrived that morning "accompanied by Messrs. Huntington, Hopkins, Crocker, and trainloads of California's distinguished citizens." [1] His memory was sadly faulty. Huntington was in New York. Crocker and Hopkins were in Sacramento. Stanford brought with him not trainloads of Western notables but a single carload, consisting of nine men besides himself.

One of the nine was his close friend Dr. J. D. B. Stillman, who had migrated to California from New York on the same ship with Mark Hopkins, in 1849, and was now city coroner of San Francisco. Dr. Stillman wrote the only substantial contemporary account of the Last Spike ceremony by any member of the group of official guests. Dr. John Todd, the eminent Congregational minister who delivered the dedicatory prayer that day, also described the occasion, but his comments, though illuminating, were brief. When General Dodge and Sidney Dillon eventually produced their respective recollections of the ceremony, they were both aged and inclined to be forgetful. Stillman's and Todd's descriptions were written very soon after the event, and from privileged vantage points not shared by the professional reporters present.

Twenty newspapers were represented at Promontory Summit, but their correspondents, some of whom were covering the ceremony for more than one editor, had to elbow their way through crushes of workmen and soldiers at crucial moments. Most of them couldn't half see what went on or hear what was said. Luckily for their dispatches, they had obtained copies of the few, short speeches in advance. It seems likely that they wrote some of their descriptive passages ahead of time, too. Most of them told how gaily decorated the featured locomotives were, but the photographs taken of the engines that day fail to show a shred of bunting or a single American flag on either of them. Perhaps a festive scheme had been abandoned at the last moment, or the rough crowd had seized the decorations as souvenirs, or, quite possibly, the strong wind had already blown them off into the sagebrush.

Stanford's party left Sacramento for Promontory by special train shortly after 6 A.M. on Wednesday, May 5th, following not far behind the regular morning passenger train for Reno and points east. It was then expected that the Central Pacific and the Union Pacific would meet on May 8th. The Governor's guests included Associate Justice Silas W. Sanderson, of the California Supreme Court; the newly appointed Governor of Arizona Territory, A. P. K. Safford; the three current government inspectors of the Central Pacific, William G. Sherman, J. W. Haines, and F. A. Tritle, who was soon to become Governor of Nevada; and Edgar Mills, a son of Darius Ogden Mills, the leading banker on the West Coast. There were "a few others," wrote Dr. Stillman, "who, like myself, were not particularly distinguished but born to good luck." [2] One of them was Dr. W. H. Harkness, editor of the Sacramento *Press*.

The special train on which they rode had only two cars, but they were unique. One was the Central Pacific's plushiest piece of equipment, Superintendent Crocker's private car. It had a kitchen, a dining room, a lounge, and places for ten people to sleep. The other car, completed in mid-February, was called a tender, but it was really a food storehouse on wheels, intended to provision the first through train east when the railroad was finished. It had many compartments. One, lined with zinc, was for meat. Another, with a wire door, was intended to hold live poultry. There were many bins for groceries and vegetables, large tanks for fresh water, a commodious icebox, and, at one end of the car, several berths to accommodate members of the crew. When the Stanford special pulled out of Sacramento that morning, this car contained several cases of champagne and a large assortment of California fruit in addition to the necessary staples.

Aboard Crocker's car were also three symbolic railroad spikes, about 6 inches long. Two, presented by individuals, were made of gold. The third, a gift from Arizona Territory, was a mixture of gold, silver, and iron. The state of Nevada had promised to add a pure silver spike to the collection. It was to be delivered to the train at Reno.

One of the golden spikes had been contributed to the occasion by David Hewes, a product of Andover and, briefly, of Yale, who was rapidly becoming rich in San Francisco by leveling sand dunes and creating new building lots for the city. Hewes, previously a resident of Sacramento, had been friendly with all the principal men of the Central Pacific for many years. Not having had money to spare to help them start their railroad, he had now been moved to make a $414 gesture in celebration of their having completed the job. The Hewes spike, which weighed 18 ounces, had appropriate inscriptions on all four sides. Across its top was engraved, in a combination of script and block capitals, "The LAST SPIKE." There was a rough nugget of gold attached to its other end. Later, that was broken off, and Hewes had finger rings fashioned from it for President Grant, Secretary of State William H. Seward, Oakes Ames, Stanford, and Dr. Todd. In sentimentalized reference to the joining of the two railroads, Todd's ring was inscribed, as presumably they all were, "The Mountain Wedding, May 10, 1869." [3]

The other gold spike on Crocker's car as it rolled out of Sacramento on the lovely morning of May 5th had been given to Stanford by Frank Marriott, owner of the San Francisco *News Letter*. It was somewhat shorter, lighter, and less valuable than the Hewes spike.

Along with his small burden of precious spikes, Stanford was carrying to Utah a handsome railroad tie of polished laurel wood. This was to be the symbolic last tie in the first transcontinental railroad, and it bore an inscribed silver plate to that effect. Though Hewes, many years afterward, claimed he donated it, contemporary newspaper accounts announced that it was the gift of West Evans, a former Sacramentan, who had supplied the Central Pacific with its first regular tie and 250,000 more. Evans was aboard the special this morning.

Stanford was also supposed to have with him a silver-plated sledge, given to him by the Pacific Express Co., of San Francisco, but it missed his train and had to be specially forwarded to Promontory Summit the following day.

Writing of some of these matters when he was an old man, David Hewes declared that he had felt that "the rich men of the Comstock" [4] ought to have supplied last rails of solid silver, but he had been unable to enlist support for this whimsy. He had better luck with another imaginative scheme. It was he, so he claimed, who suggested to Stanford the arrangement to inform the nation by telegraph of the actual sledge blows that drove the last spike. The same arrangement was to fire a 15-inch Parrott rifled cannon at San Francisco's Fort Point, guarding the south shore of the Golden Gate. That shot would begin a salute of one hundred guns.

As Leland Stanford's special train set off for Utah, Dr. Stillman luxuriated in the setting and the mood of the day.

Stretching myself out on a sumptuous lounge [he wrote, not long afterward], I looked out on the brimming, turbid river and breathed the morning air laden with the perfume of a city full of roses. The pulse of life beat high, the town was on tip-toe of expectation and gushing with the enthusiasm of triumph. The crowds cheered as we passed, and President Stanford on the platform bowed his thanks.[5]

Sacramento was expecting a delicious deluge of free-spending tourists. The Union Pacific had just announced that 15,000 people had already booked passage over its road. And why not? As the Sacramento *Union* pointed out,

To cross the continent will be to our own countrymen in the East a novelty more exciting than Saratoga, more useful than basking in sloth by the seaside, more stimulating than the old retreats of fisherman or hunter, and more becoming the dignity of an American than to play the snob in foreign cities.[6]

Early in the first afternoon of its journey, Stanford's special was nearly wrecked.

Up on the steep, forested slopes south of Donner Lake, a gang of Chinese woodcutters was at work. As they felled and stripped trees, they slid them down a slippery trough of mud and snow to be hauled away by teams at the foot of the incline. The railroad track passed directly beneath them, but most of the logs bounded across it on their swift way down.

When the woodsmen saw the first eastbound passenger train of the day go past, they assumed there was none other to worry about. Nobody had warned them about the special, tagging along behind.

Just before the second train appeared, the woodcutters launched downward a 50-foot log, more than 3 feet thick at its base. Instead of leaping the track, it buried its tip between the rails and leaned against the high south bank of the cut.

The track was full of blind curves in this section. The engineer of the Stanford special had only a moment's warning of the danger in his path. Fortunately, the train was not moving fast, but Dr. Harkness was riding out on the pilot, as the government inspectors usually did when they were on official business. Harkness took an appalled look and jumped, while the engineer tooted for brakes. It was too late, of course. The locomotive whammed into the tree trunk with enough force to break the log in the middle and toss the halves aside. The heavier part fell into the narrow ditch to the right of the track, ripping off the starboard steps of both cars as it fell. The pilot was demolished.

Harkness escaped with but slight injuries. Had he not jumped, he almost certainly would have been killed.

There was a considerable delay, while the badly shaken passengers collected their fallen friend and regained their composure, and the train crew assessed the damage to the locomotive's battered nose. It was found that the engine could still move, though at reduced speed.

It limped down into Reno, where Stanford telegraphed ahead to hold the advance train at Wadsworth until his cars could be hitched to it. The delay had been useful in one respect. It gave Nevada's silver spike, late in getting started on its buggy ride down the mountains from Virginia City, just time to catch the Stanford special.

At Wadsworth, about sunset, "our crippled locomotive was sent to the hospital," reported Dr. Stillman, "and our cars were made fast to the regular train." [7] That train happened to be drawn by Jupiter, the C.P.'s Engine No. 60, built in Schenectady. It was now headed for a permanent place in railroad history.

The first night of the trip to Utah was wretched for Dr. Stillman. "It was too much like being tossed in a blanket," he wrote. He was up at dawn. "The air was cold, and snowy mountains were in sight—one is never out of sight of them." [8] (It is regrettable today, especially in early spring, that the Southern Pacific's through trains always pass that noble scenery during the night.)

At Elko, toward the second day's end, most of the passengers in the cars up front debarked. They were bound for the scene of the latest silver discoveries, White Pine, 100 miles south. Empty cars were sloughed off into the Elko yard, and Stanford and his party proceeded into another night's journey.

On Friday morning, May 7th, they were at the Central Pacific's construction camp, on the shore of Great Salt Lake at Monument Point, and creeping past Strobridge's curious boarding train. The day was wet and dreary. After a week of weather so warm that it had swollen the streams of the Wasatch with melting snow, a cold rain was now falling.

At Promontory Summit, there was no sign of Union Pacific officialdom. "Two or three tents were pitched in the vicinity," Stillman reported, "for the rendezvous of those ruffians who hang about on the march of industry and flourish on the vices of men." [9] In other words, the first bars were open. But there were no customers. The only potential clients were the telegraph operators of the respective railroads. They had sent up tents and tables and keys within a few yards of each other. They were damp and unhappy, but the U.P.'s man obligingly put Stanford in touch with Ogden.

Then came distressing news indeed. "Heavy rains," [10] Stanford was told, had obstructed Union Pacific traffic to such an extent that Durant and his colleagues and guests could not possibly reach Promontory Summit before Monday. It was true that downpours in the Wasatch Mountains and western Wyoming had caused washouts and disrupted travel, but the chief—and as yet undisclosed—reason why Durant and his friends were missing was that they were prisoners. They were being held for ransom by several hundred irate tie-cutters, who hadn't received any pay since January and thought there was no better time than the present to collect it.

Durant, Duff, and Dillon had traveled back as far as Piedmont, 40 miles east of Wasatch, to greet the train that was bringing their guests from Eastern cities. The U.P. directors, in their elegant special car, had pulled into Piedmont on Thursday, May 6th, but the westbound train had not yet arrived. Instead, the station was overflowing with an angry crowd of laborers.[11] These men demanded their back wages. Durant gave them only flustered promises in return. Then he told the conductor to move his train out of Piedmont. The locomotive started up, but the mob had already uncoupled the directors' car. When the conductor ran back, demanding to know who was responsible, two stern-looking men aimed pistols at him and told him to skedaddle. He did.

A forthright delegation then stormed in upon Durant and said they'd take him up into the mountains and feed him salt horse and sagebrush if he didn't telegraph for their money right away. Durant stoically wrote out a dispatch calling upon Oliver Ames for the amount due, though he had no idea where the money might be found.

Members of the mob rushed the dispatch to the telegraph operator in the Piedmont station, warning him that they'd hang or shoot him if he sent for troops instead of money. Threats were not necessary. He was in full sympathy with them.

The message was flashed to Boston. Ames' first reaction was to wire Dodge at Salt Lake City, telling him to organize a rescue party. Dodge at least tried. He telegraphed Fort Bridger, Wyoming, the Army post nearest the scene of the trouble, to send a company of troops to deal with the kidnappers. But the telegraph operator at Piedmont intercepted the message. It never reached Fort Bridger, but it was carried promptly to the leaders of the mob. They at once responded to Dodge, warning him that they would stir up a general strike all the way from Ogden to Omaha if their demands weren't met within twenty-four hours.

Meanwhile, the train of excursionists had rolled in from the East and was immobilized. No one from it was allowed to visit the marooned directors' car, nor was the train permitted to proceed westward. Scouts were sent out to warn of approaching soldiers or armed railroad employees attempting to intervene.

Even without knowing that troops were not on their way from Fort Bridger, General Dodge capitulated. The next morning, May 7th, he wired Ames, "You must furnish funds on Dillon's call." [12] Ames did so, using his own and his brother's money for the purpose, and Durant and his friends were soon freed to start for Promontory Summit.

Trouble of a different sort was just ahead. At Devil's Gate Station, 13 miles short of Ogden, the heavy rains and run-off from melting snow had so weakened the railroad bridge that no train could cross it until it had been fortified. In a persistent downpour, the desolate party waited many hours while 200 men strained to shore up the bridge.

At Promontory, at one o'clock that afternoon, Leland Stanford had had the disagreeable duty of telegraphing the parade chairmen in Sacramento and San Francisco that the celebration was unavoidably off until Monday,

May 10th. The chairmen were not long in replying that festivities would begin on the eighth, as planned. It would be impossible to alter the elaborate preparations or halt the momentum of impending jubilee at this late hour, they said. Never mind, the chairmen cheerfully added, the two cities would simply keep on celebrating until the happy event really did take place.

That was all very well for the fortunate citizens of Sacramento and San Francisco. At Promontory Summit, however, the Stanford party looked around them dejectedly. Dr. Stillman summed up their mood. "To spend three days in this desolate spot, surrounded by sage-brush," he wrote, "with only such neighbors as would make it dangerous to venture away from the car, lest we have our throats cut on the suspicion that we might have a spare quarter in our pockets, was not charming." [13] They did not relapse into sulking, though. Half the group rustled up a wagon and rode down the east slope of the Promontory range to the Union Pacific's nearest construction camp, a few miles away. There, hospitable General Jack Casement provided a train to take them into Ogden for a short visit.

The next morning, the general rode a caboose, drawn by locomotive No. 117, out to the end of track and offered it to Stanford and his guests for a day's excursion on the U.P. This group included Stillman, and he said the offer was gratefully accepted. They rode as far as Weber Creek station, in the Wasatch Mountains. There, only a few miles from Durant's stalled and disconsolate party, they thrilled at the sight of "some of the finest mountain scenery in the world." [14] "They are the very ideal of inaccessible snow-covered mountains," wrote Dr. Stillman, "set off by the green fields and blushing tints of the peach orchards just coming into flower." [15]

At five o'clock that morning, May 8th, the first trainload of celebrants, a large delegation from Nevada, had pulled into Sacramento. Led by the Virginia City and Gold Hill firemen, they tramped away from the C.P. station to the sharp-voiced brasses of their bands, a no-nonsense challenge to the sleeping town. The slumberous leaves soon stirred to the belching voice of Mr. Siddons' Union Boy, the brass cannon that had saluted the first shovelful of earth hoisted for the Central Pacific and was now prematurely signaling the end of the job. Sacramento's jubilation was well begun. A mammoth parade would start later.

San Francisco, too, had awakened to the clumping of guns, and had looked out to see every ship in the sun-flooded harbor flaunting all its flags.

It had been originally announced that the Central Pacific and Union Pacific would be linked at noon. So, promptly at 11 A.M.—allowing for the time differential between Utah and California—Sacramento and San Francisco pretended that the last spike had been driven. In Sacramento, twenty-three locomotives, led by the C.P.'s first, the Governor Stanford, especially burnished for the occasion, let loose with a shriek of whistles that drowned out every other sound in the city for 15 minutes.

San Francisco's din, a medley of fire bells and steam whistles—on foundries, machine shops, steamers, and the U.S. Mint—lasted a full hour. Then the city settled down to watch one of its biggest and longest processions.

Far east of this tumult, General Dodge, at the end of the U.P. track, was sending a distressed and urgent telegram to Oliver Ames:

Trouble at Piedmont will cause trouble on running department unless Snyder gets immediate help. If you wait until trains are stopped it will be too late to release them until we are forced to pay, in fact, everything due on the line. Half million at once will relieve necessities and enable me to keep moving. Actions at Piedmont known everywhere and all know Company was obliged to pay before officers were released. Answer care Snyder.[16]

No telegraphed response from Ames has been preserved, but a letter he wrote to Dodge a few days later reveals how stirred he had been by the chaos and anarchy in Utah:

We have raised a large amount of money on land grants and other bonds and sent it out, but there seems to be no relief, and we feel that the vortex out there will swallow all that can be raised out of our securities, and then perhaps the mobs on line of road will stop the trains and the next thing we shall hear is that the trains have been stopped and passengers robbed to pay starving men. It would have been better to have called out the military and stopped this first mob, and then we should have had no more trouble. [Ames evidently didn't know that Dodge had tried.]

I am informed that Davis and associate men were the parties stopping the train. Could it be one of Durant's plans to have the men get their pay out of the road and we suffer for his benefit? Durant is so strange a man that I am prepared to believe any sort of rascality that may be charged against him.[17]

At three o'clock in the afternoon of May 8th, while Stanford and his party were riding back toward Promontory Summit after their drizzly visit to Weber Canyon, Charlie Crocker, at Sacramento, was telling California's assembled legislators, "My heart is full—boiling over." [18] The Senate and the Assembly had just given him and the Judge and Uncle Mark a splendid luncheon, and were expecting a few suitable remarks.

Judge Crocker had already responded, with a particularly fitting sentiment:

In the midst of our rejoicing at this event, I wish to call to your minds that the early completion of this railroad we have built has been in great measure due to that poor, despised class of laborers called the Chinese—to the fidelity and industry they have shown.

Charlie followed, in his usual folksy style.

When he asked for help, who met us and responded to our calls? The men of Sacramento. [Loud cheers.] They loaned us their money, and they gave us their confidence, which was better than money [cheers], and when others traduced us—when others said we intended to perpetrate a great swindle—that we did not intend to build a railroad—that all we intended to build up was a poor, little, miserable wagon road, the people of Sacramento would not believe them, but believed we were in earnest—that the railroad would be built—and went heart and hand with us in assisting in the prosecution of this great work. [Loud cheers.]

The response was even louder, a few minutes later, when he promised that freight rates would soon be lower.

Then the legislators gave three cheers for each of the Central Pacific's principals, in turn, winding up with Huntington.

As the last shout died, Charlie Crocker called out:

In connection with the name of C. P. Huntington, allow me to say a word. He is not here today. I tell you there is no man in the United States that has done so much to build this railroad as C. P. Huntington. He has raised money; he has exhibited an energy, ability, a knowledge of men and measures superior to anything his friends could have supposed, highly as they estimated his abilities, and today he stands among New York capitalists A No. 1. [Loud cheers.] [19]

The luncheon broke up without a single mention of Theodore Judah, the man whose motivating vision had now been fulfilled, and without a call for comments from Mark Hopkins, who doubtless was greatly relieved.

By now, nearly 700 miles east of there, Stanford and his friends had returned to Promontory Summit and were wondering what to do tomorrow. And in Weber Canyon, the foreman of the emergency repair crew was assuring Durant that before long his train would at last be able to cross the threatened bridge at Devil's Gate.

It was dark, however, before the stranded cars could be moved over the thundering stream, 50 feet below. Even then, the train crew did not dare risk sending the heavy locomotive across. Instead, each car was uncoupled and given a gentle shove, to roll across the bridge by itself. Another locomotive had been sent up from Ogden to pull the train westward, once it was reassembled on that side of the bridge.

There is no record of where Durant and his friends spent Sunday, May 9th, but they probably took stages down to Salt Lake City from Ogden, that being the obvious tourist attraction. There was no point in their hurrying out to Promontory. Casement's men were still hard at work there, laying the last few hundred feet of the U.P. track and putting in sidings and switches.

Stanford had his cars pulled back 30 miles to Monument Point, on that cloudy Sunday, and treated his guests to several hours by the shore of Great Salt Lake. At least, the day produced a meal worth remembering. Stanford's cook, a resourceful type, took a gun out into the nearby marshes and shot enough snipe for dinner.

The *Alta California's* correspondent, from San Francisco, spent Sunday poking around at Promontory Summit, looking for copy, and he was glad he had, for two sights interested him very much. One was the arrival of O. Vedder, who was just completing his official assignment of measuring with a chain the entire length of the Union Pacific main line from Omaha to this point, a distance of 1,086 miles. The other scene had more historical and social significance. The reporter watched Wells, Fargo's Overland Stage No. 2, Eastern Division, come lumbering up into the summit valley with its last load of mail for the West Coast.

The four old nags were worn and jaded [he wrote], and the coach showed evidence of long service. The mail matter was delivered to the Central Pacific Co., and, with that dusty, dilapidated coach and team, the old order of things passed away forever.[20]

On Sunday night, the sky cleared. Monday, May 10th, dawned bright and chilly. There was a skim of ice on the puddles. A brisk wind tore at a small American flag that at 7 A.M. had been hoisted to the top of the telegraph pole nearest the spot where the rails would meet.

The line of track ran roughly northeast-southwest, and along it fourteen tent saloons, on opposite sides of the rails, by now had sprung up to sell Red Cloud, Red Jacket, Blue Run, and other varieties of rot-gut to the expected throng. Where the track disappeared into the southwest, the land swelled toward a pass that seemed a gateway to probable enchantment. There were still patches of snow on the cedar-sprinkled high slopes of the Promontory Mountains, which walled in the plateau on the east. Across the northeast horizon stood the white-topped rampart of the Wasatch Range, a view to lift the heart. The mountains that sheltered the little valley on the west were bare.

Stanford's special had moved up to within sight of the point of juncture during the previous evening. As his guests now peered out upon the early-morning scene, they saw U.P. workmen hurrying to complete the last few yards of their track, leading up to the gap that two rails would soon fill ceremoniously. The two final lengths of iron already lay beside it in the dirt. All ties were in place on the grading except the last. There was a space left for the 8-foot length of polished laurel wood.

"About ten o'clock," Dr. Stillman wrote, "the whistle announced the long-expected officers from the other side. We went over at once to meet them." [21]

The U.P.'s official train, drawn by locomotive No. 119, a spanking new coal-burning engine with a straight, slender smokestack, consisted of but two cars. One was a sleeper. The other, according to Dr. Stillman, was "a superb piece of cabinet work they called a 'Pullman car.'" In the latter,

we met Vice President Durant, of whom we had heard so much, with a black velvet coat and gay necktie . . . gorgeously gotten up. General Dodge was there, and he looked like business. The veterans, Dillon and Duff, were there to give away the bride. General Dodge, on the part of the Union Pacific, and Edgar Mills, on the part of the Central Pacific, were appointed to arrange the preliminaries.[22]

Though Stillman failed to mention them, General Patrick E. Connor, Silas Seymour, the Casement brothers, and Samuel B. Reed were also in the official U.P. party. So were Bishop John Sharp, of the Church of Jesus Christ of Latter Day Saints, who had been one of the grading contractors for the Union Pacific, and Lorin Farr, mayor of Ogden. These Mormons represented President Brigham Young, who was away on business in southern Utah.

The chief officials of the Central Pacific and Union Pacific had been far too busy with construction and other pressing problems to plan in advance an order of ceremony for the act of joining their tracks. When Dodge and Mills began to improvise a plan, only an hour and a half before the event, they promptly clashed over a crucial detail. Mills declared that since Leland Stanford was the highest official present and had tossed the first shovelful of earth in the construction of the transcontinental railroad, and since the Central Pacific had been incorporated earlier than the Union Pacific, Stanford was the logical man to drive the last spike. Dodge disagreed. Durant should do it, he said. The Union Pacific was much the longer railroad, with the Grant Administration and a far greater proportion of the nation's population vitally interested in it.

"At one time the Union Pacific positively refused connection," wrote the reporter for the San Francisco *News Letter,* "and told the Central people they might do as they liked, and there should be no joint celebration." [23]

While Dodge and Mills haggled over the order of ceremony, the audience was assembling. Construction trains brought a swarm of U.P. workmen up to the Summit from their camp below. A few curious settlers straggled in on horseback and in wagons. Almost at the last minute, three companies of the 21st U.S. Infantry and a few men from the 32nd Regiment, who had been camped near Devil's Gate two nights before and were en route to the Presidio, at San Francisco, arrived on a U.P. train. They had a band with them, and some of the officers had brought their wives along on the overland journey.

The band, the array of blue uniforms, and the presence of ladies, however sparse, brightened the occasion considerably. Until then, it had threatened to have no more flair than an ordinary piece of tracklaying.

Three photographers were present: Colonel Charles R. Savage, of Salt Lake City; A. J. Russell, the U.P.'s official photographer; and A. A. Hart, of Sacramento, who served the Central Pacific in a like role. They were busy setting up their bulky, slow, wet-plate cameras on the east side of the gap in the track, where the sun would be largely behind them. Dodge and Mills had agreed that the ceremony of driving the last spike should take place on that side of the track, and that the crowd would be moved back so as not to obstruct the photographers' field of vision.

Within a few minutes of the start of the program, Stanford and Durant themselves settled the controversy over who would drive the last spike. Since they had two gold spikes for the purpose, they would each drive one, and they would do it simultaneously, at opposite ends of the laurel tie. "Drive" was hardly the word for the action. Holes had already been bored in the tie, so that the precious spikes would slip in easily (and be extracted without damage afterward). All that Durant and Stanford were required to do was tap them. The only advantage Stanford had over his rival was that the telegraph wires that would let the waiting nation know that the great task was finished would be connected to his spike and his silver-plated sledge. When he tapped his spike, a circuit would be closed, and the signal would be flashed across the United States and as far as Halifax, Nova Scotia. Durant, who was developing a bad headache from the glare of the sun and the rapidly rising temperature, was willing to concede that much.

A slicked-up team of the Union Pacific's best Irish tracklayers had already swung the west rail across the gap in the track and spiked it down, except on the missing tie. Now a gang of Chinese, in clean blue jackets, moved out to put the final, east rail in place. As they did so, someone shouted at Colonel Savage, "Now's the time, Charlie! Take a shot." [24] These Chinese had never seen a camera before, and knew only one meaning for the word "shot." In instant alarm, they dropped the rail and scurried into the crowd, which howled with glee and quickly pulled them back to their task. They finished it nervously.

At about noon, when a jampacked thanksgiving service in honor of the occasion had already begun in Trinity Church, at the west end of Wall Street, in New York City, prepared telegrams were sent to President Grant and to the Associated Press of New York, announcing the meeting of the rails. General Jack Casement then climbed up on the pilot of No. 119 and yelled to the crowd to move back and make room for the spike-driving.

Western Union had arranged that news from Promontory would have priority over all other telegraph traffic at this hour. The chatter of instruments was stilled across the land, and the circuits so arranged that when the awaited signal came—three dots and the word "Done"—it would set fire bells ringing in every major city in the United States and launch a national rejoicing. There were only a few hundred people gathered at Promontory Summit, but, thanks to the telegraph, "in reality, the millions of our country were present," [25] as Dr. Todd later wrote.

After the crowd had responded to Casement's call, Strobridge and Reed solemnly carried the laurel tie to the track and slid it under the rails. Tritle, of Nevada, and Safford, of Arizona, then made brief, graceful pres-

U.P.

(Top) *This is the largest group of U.P. construction workers ever photographed. The time, April, 1869; the place, Blue Creek Station, Utah; the occasion, payday.*

(Right) *Some of the heaviest rock excavation between Omaha and Promontory cleared this path for the U.P. track down the western slope of Sherman Summit, Wyoming.*

NATIONAL ARCHIVES

(Left) *The Union Pacific's locomotive No. 119, about to play a more historic role, chugs across a trestle just east of Promontory Summit early in May, 1869.*

(Top) *Leland Stanford's special train, drawn by Jupiter (No. 60), idles for a picture at Monument Point, Utah, May 9, 1869, while awaiting "last spike" ceremony.*

(Bottom) *Early in the morning of May 10, 1869, Stanford's special waits near the gap between C.P. and U.P. (left) tracks, soon to be formally filled.*

(Top) *After the "last spike" ceremony, Stanford (left) and Durant prominently hoisted sledgehammers with which they had gently tapped two gold spikes into prepared holes.*

(Bottom) *Luxury soon supplanted crudity in Union Pacific, as shown in print, and Central Pacific rolling stock when the first transcontinental railroad was at last complete.*

entations of their respective silver spikes, Tritle handing his to Durant, Safford giving his to Stanford. They were placed in the holes bored for them.

By this time, telegraph operators in the East were getting restless. Several of them broke in to ask what was going on. Omaha shushed them with To everybody: keep quiet. When the last spike is driven at Promontory Point, we will say "Done." Don't break the circuit, but watch for the signals of the blows of the hammer.

At 12:27, the Promontory operator tapped, "Almost ready. Hats off. Prayer is being offered." [26]

Dr. John Todd, sixty-nine, of Pittsfield, Massachusetts, a Congregational pastor whose renown had spread far beyond his parish, stepped forward. The author of more than two dozen moralistic books, some of them best-sellers that had been translated into several languages, and a friend and fellow-townsman of Durant's in earlier years, Dr. Todd yet felt awed and strange in his present role.

"What a place in which to pray!" he exclaimed in a book he hastened to write afterward. "Was prayer ever offered there before?" Then, thinking of the vast reach of continent between Halifax and San Francisco, he added, "Was ever prayer heard by mortal ears 4,000 miles away before?" [27] (Dr. Todd was misled by his imagination. The listening continent had been told he was praying, but only those within earshot knew what he said.)

Though greatly moved, Todd managed to limit his invocation to two minutes. When he finished, the Western Union's operator told the waiting telegraphers everywhere, "We have got done praying. The spike is about to be presented." [28]

This was not the moment to be chatty, but Chicago eagerly cut in with "We understand. All are ready in the East." [29]

Dr. Harkness handed one gold spike to Durant, the other to Stanford, and addressed some flowery, but commendably brief, remarks to the latter.

General Dodge made a two-sentence response for Durant, who perhaps felt too miserable by this time to speak his piece, and Stanford acknowledged all the spikes in a short talk that contained just one interesting sentence. "The day is not far distant," he said, "when three tracks will be found necessary to accommodate the commerce and travel which will seek a transit across this continent." [30]

As Stanford concluded, the telegraph operator, sitting at a table in the open within a few feet of him, told his national audience, "All ready now. The spike will soon be driven. The signal will be three dots for the commencement of the blows." [31]

According to the New York *Tribune's* correspondent, who, since he represented the nation's leading paper at the time, was probably one of the most reliable reporters there, Stanford stood beside the east rail, Durant at the west one, and, "on the signal of 'OK' from the telegraph officer," [32] simultaneously tapped their respective spikes.

Dr. Todd's eyes were upon Stanford, who had "a telegraph wire coiled around his silver hammer." [33]

"That gentle tap," Todd wrote, "fired the big gun which the officer was watching at the Fort [in San Francisco], and instantly set all the bells in the land a-ringing, and announced that the greatest work ever attempted in railroads was a success." [34]

Hezekiah Bissell, who was watching from the top of No. 119, said the only photograph taken of that historic moment's action was lost, because the plate got broken.[35]

"In three minutes," continued Dr. Todd, "the telegrams came back from all the cities—'The bells are ringing, and the people rejoicing.' The whole thing seemed a wild dream." [36]

At Promontory Summit, the little crowd made the biggest noise it could muster, assisted by the whistles of at least four locomotives. Stanford and Durant shook hands, the latter remarking, "There is henceforth but one Pacific Railroad of the United States." [37]

The principal guests then jokingly vied with one another in tapping the gold and silver spikes into their loose holes. Mrs. J. H. Strobridge, one of the few ladies present, was allowed to deliver the last soft blow to one of them, as befitted her position as "Heroine of the Central," which her companions had just dubbed her.[38] Everybody then posed for a few pictures.

Jupiter and No. 119, with men clinging to them like swarming bees, next moved forward until their pilots touched. Champagne was poured upon the engines, the rails, and down the throats of all the thirsty bystanders who could grab a bottle. Then each locomotive, in turn, backed up to let the other puff across the spot where the rails met.

With this ritual complete, Stanford had the gold and silver spikes gently pried out of the laurel tie, and the tie itself removed to his car. The Central Pacific's Chinese produced a redwood tie to take the place of the laurel one. To the crowd's raucous amusement, Stanford and Durant then took a few wild swings at the iron spikes that would pin the rails to it. They both missed every time. The Chinese had to finish the job. When they were through, they tramped off to Strobridge's boarding car, where they were his honored guests at lunch and were cheered as they entered.

Durant, his head splitting, walked wearily to his sleeper to lie down. Fifteen days later, his career as a power in the Union Pacific came to an end. At President Grant's specific, testy suggestion, he was abruptly dropped from the board of directors. He then sold all his stock in the railroad, leaving to the Ameses the enormous burden of restoring the U.P.'s credit.

The Chinese had scarcely turned away from completing the track before the tie they had just laid "was attacked by hundreds of jack-knives, and soon reduced to a mere stick," wrote the San Francisco *News Letter*'s reporter. And when he last looked at the spot, he said, "soldiers were hammering away at the flanges of the rails, and had carried off all the pieces they could break, so that a new rail will soon be necessary." [39] Only a few days later, J. H. Beadle was told that six ties and two pairs of rails had already been consumed by souvenir hunters.

After what Colonel Leonard H. Eicholtz, one of the Union Pacific engineers, dismissed in his diary as "a great deal of speechyfying and wine drinking," [40] the principals at the May 10th ceremony adjourned to the U.P. directors' car to read some of the congratulatory telegrams that were streaming in. Then Stanford invited his fellow-notables to his own car for an elaborate lunch. It was followed by rather bibulous speeches. Stanford startled everyone by declaring that he wished the Central Pacific had never had any government aid, that it would have been better off without it. He was doubtless thinking worriedly about the forthcoming investigation by special commission that Grant's Secretary of the Interior, Jacob D. Cox, had just ordered. But Dan Casement couldn't let the remark go unchallenged. He popped up and asked why Stanford didn't give his subsidy bonds back, if they were such a burden to him. Stanford flushed, and abruptly concluded his talk. The party split up.

By four-thirty, Durant's train had headed East. A half-hour later, the Stanford special left for California, hauling two extra cars—brand-new first-class passenger cars, made in Springfield, Massachusetts, and delivered to Promontory by the Union Pacific that afternoon. In Stanford's car were the gold spike donated by David Hewes and the silver spike that was Nevada's gift. Both eventually landed in the Stanford University

Museum, where they are now, together with the silver-plated sledge. The laurel tie for years reposed in the headquarters building of the Southern Pacific in San Francisco, but was destroyed, along with all of the Central Pacific's records and the building itself, in the fire that followed the earthquake of 1906. Stanford gave the second gold spike to General Dodge. Arizona's gold, silver, and iron spike was cut in half. Part of it was given to Sidney Dillon. The other half disappeared without record.

Throughout the United States, on May 10, 1869, there was an explosion of jubilation that hadn't been matched since Lee's surrender. More cannon were fired than ever took part in the Battle of Gettysburg. No city's celebration was greater than Chicago's, where, it was said, nearly every vehicle in the place joined an impromptu parade that stretched more than seven miles, and was paced along Michigan Avenue by a string of fifty tugboats in the lake.

The only melancholy observance of the day that has been recorded was Anna Ferona Judah's. Deliberately alone in her home in Greenfield, Massachusetts—"I refused myself to everyone that day," she said. "I could not talk of the common events of daily living"—she sat thinking of what it would have meant to Theodore to see his dream come true. The day was doubly lugubrious to Mrs. Judah because it was also, by sad coincidence, the anniversary of her wedding. "It seemed as though the spirit of my brave husband descended upon me," she wrote, "and together we were there unseen, unheard of men." [41]

That night, while fireworks blazed in the sky, Schuyler Colfax, Vice-President of the United States, told an audience of Chicago's most prominent and fashionable citizens what the completion of the first transcontinental railroad meant to the nation. He foresaw a future "beyond the portrayal of language, beyond any words my heart could devise or that my tongue can express to you upon this joyful night, the opening of the new history of the American republic." [42]

And on the following morning, General Sherman, who at first had expected this "work of giants" would hardly be finished in time for his grandchildren to ride on, paid earnest tribute to the giants who had made it possible.

"All honor," he said, concluding a telegram to Dodge, ". . . to the thousands of brave fellows who have wrought out this glorious problem, spite of changes, storms, and even doubts of the incredulous, and all the obstacles you have now happily surmounted." [43]

APPENDIX

Author's Note: The Collis P. Huntington and Charles Crocker Manuscripts repeatedly referred to in the Appendix are transcripts of firsthand interviews with those gentlemen in the early 1880s. The interviewers, who recorded the conversations verbatim in shorthand, were members of Hubert Howe Bancroft's staff of history researchers.

The Mrs. Theodore D. Judah Manuscript cited below is a reminiscent essay about her dead husband, in the form of a personal letter to an old friend in California.

The Gen. G. M. Dodge Manuscript cited is the original typescript of Dodge's unpublished autobiography. This memoir was never finished. Dodge had brought the account of his career only up to 1871 at the time of his death.

NOTES

CHAPTER I

1. Bertha Berner, *Mrs. Leland Stanford; An Intimate Account.*
2. Charles Crocker Manuscript, Bancroft Library.
3. *Ibid.*
4. Sacramento *Union,* Jan. 9, 1863.
5. *Ibid.,* Apr. 14, 1869.
6. *Ibid.,* Jan. 9, 1863.
7. *Ibid.*
8. B. B. Redding, *A Sketch of the Life of Mark Hopkins, of California.*
9. New York *Tribune,* May 8, 1869.
10. Thomas G. Cary, "Pacific Rail Road" (essay), Manuscript Division, Library of Congress.
11. *Ibid.*
12. Thomas Hart Benton, *Letter from Col. Benton to the People of Missouri.*
13. Testimony of D. W. Strong in Report of the Commission and of the Minority Commissioner of the United States Pacific Railway Commission, vol. V, p. 2840.
14. *Ibid.*
15. Collis B. Huntington Manuscript, Bancroft Library.
16. *Ibid.*
17. *Ibid.*
18. Crocker MS.
19. Mrs. Theodore D. Judah Manuscript, Bancroft Library.
20. *First Annual of the Territorial Pioneers of California.*
21. Maj. Gen. Grenville M. Dodge, *Personal Recollections.*
22. *Congressional Globe,* May 7, 1862.
23. *Ibid.*
24. "Report of the Chief Engineer of the Central Pacific Railroad Company of California, on his Operations in the Atlantic States," 1862.

CHAPTER II

1. Testimony of Leland Stanford, in Report of the U.S. Pacific Railway Commission, vol. V, p. 2621.
2. *Ibid.*
3. Crocker MS.
4. Huntington MS.
5. Sacramento *Union,* July 1, 1863.
6. Huntington-Hopkins Letters, Dept. of Special Collections, Stanford University.
7. Huntington MS.
8. Henry Clews, *Twenty-eight Years in Wall Street.*
9. Huntington MS.
10. Alfred A. Cohen's testimony in Report of U.S. Pacific Railway Commission, vol. V, p. 2400.
11. Letter from Josiah D. Whitney in testimony of Edward H. Miller, Jr., Report of Pacific Railway Commission, vol. V, p. 3569.

12. Sacramento *Union*, Feb. 22, 1864.

13. *Ibid.*, Apr. 29, 1863.

14. *Ibid.*

15. Huntington MS.

16. *Ibid.*

17. Mrs. Theodore D. Judah MS.

18. Testimony of D. W. Strong in Report of U.S. Pacific Railway Commission, vol. V, p. 2965.

19. Report of U.S. Pacific Railway Commission, vol. VIII, p. 4527.

20. Testimony of D. W. Strong in Report of U.S. Pacific Railway Commission, vol. V, p. 2966.

21. Huntington MS.

22. *Ibid.*

23. *Ibid.*

24. E. H. Miller, Jr., *Ledger, 1862-71*, Hopkins Transportation Library, Stanford University Libraries.

25. Articles of Association, Dutch Flat and Donner Lake Wagon Road Co., Hopkins Transportation Library.

26. Document of Conveyance, Hopkins Transportation Library.

27. Mrs. Theodore D. Judah MS.

28. *First Annual of the Territorial Pioneers of California.*

29. Mrs. Theodore D. Judah MS.

30. Testimony of D. W. Strong in Report of U.S. Pacific Railway Commission, vol. V, p. 2967.

31. Mrs. Theodore D. Judah MS.

32. Sacramento *Union*, Oct. 27, 1863.

33. Huntington MS.

34. Sacramento *Union*, Nov. 11, 1863.

35. Annual Report of the Secretary of the Interior for 1863.

CHAPTER III

1. Boston *Olive Branch,* Mar. 29, 1851.

2. William E. Hayes, *Iron Road to Empire.*

3. Maj. Gen. Grenville M. Dodge, *How We Built The Union Pacific Railway,* p. 116.

4. G. M. Dodge, Autobiography (manuscript), Council Bluffs Public Library.

5. *Ibid.*

6. John P. Usher's testimony, Report of Pacific Railway Commission, vol. III, p. 1675.

7. Dodge MS.

8. *Ibid.*

9. Henry W. Farnam, *Memoir of Henry Farnam.*

10. Dodge MS.

11. *Ibid.*

12. *Ibid.*

13. *Ibid.*

14. "Report of the Organization and Proceedings of the Union Pacific Railroad Co.," 1864.

15. William O. Stoddard, *Lincoln's Third Secretary.*
16. Testimony of John P. Usher, Report of U.S. Pacific Railway Commission, vol. III, p. 1676.
17. Dodge MS.
18. *Ibid.*
19. J. Sterling Morton, *Illustrated History of Nebraska.*
20. Council Bluffs *Bugle,* Dec. 10, 1863.
21. *Ibid.*
22. Dodge Letter Books, Council Bluffs Public Library.
23. "Report of the Organization and Proceedings of the Union Pacific Railroad Co.," 1864.

CHAPTER IV

1. A. A. Sargent to Cornelius Cole, Jan. 3, 1864; Cornelius Cole Papers, Department of Special Collections, U.C.L.A.
2. *Congressional Globe,* Feb. 24, 1864.
3. *Ibid.,* May 18, 1864.
4. A. A. Sargent to C. Cole, May 11, 1864, Cole Papers.
5. Huntington MS.
6. *Congressional Globe,* May 23, 1864.
7. *Ibid.,* June 19, 1866.
8. *Ibid.,* May 23, 1864.
9. Cornelius Cole, "The Central Pacific Railroad Co.," (handwritten essay) Cole Papers.
10. Cornelius Cole to H. G. Otis, draft of letter, April 14, 1890, Cole Papers.
11. Cornelius Cole, Handwritten essay on his achievements in Congress, Cole Papers.
12. E. B. Crocker to Cornelius Cole, March 2, 1864, in *ibid.*
13. Cornelius Cole to Mrs. Cole, June 22, 1864, in *ibid.*
14. John P. Davis, *The Union Pacific Railway: A Study in Railway Politics.*
15. *Congressional Globe,* June 21, 1864.
16. *Ibid.*
17. Davis, *op. cit.*
18. *Congressional Globe,* June 21, 1864.
19. *Ibid.*
20. *Ibid.*
21. *Ibid.*
22. *Ibid.,* July 1, 1864.
23. *Ibid.*

CHAPTER V

1. Sacramento *Union,* Feb. 18, 1864.
2. *Ibid.*
3. Report of U.S. Pacific Railway Commission, vol. VIII, p. 4528.

4. *Ibid.*, p. 4530.
5. *Ibid.*, p. 4529.
6. Sacramento *Union,* Mar. 21, 1864.
7. Crocker MS.
8. Report of U.S. Pacific Railway Commission, vol. V, p. 3114.
9. Crocker MS.
10. *Ibid.*
11. Sacramento *Union,* Mar. 26, 1864.
12. E. B. Crocker to C. Cole, Apr. 27, 1864, in Cole Papers.
13. Timothy Hopkins Papers, Hopkins Transportation Library.
14. *Ibid.*
15. C. Cole to Mrs. Cole, July 12, 1864, in Cole Papers.
16. C. Cole to Mrs. Cole, July 13, 1864, in *ibid.*
17. Francis B. Carpenter, *The Inner Life of Abraham Lincoln.*
18. Crocker MS.
19. *Ibid.*
20. Huntington MS.
21. "Statement Made to Nevada Constitutional Convention, July 4, 1864, by Hon. Leland Stanford," California Division, California State Library.
22. Crocker MS.
23. *Ibid.*
24. *Ibid.*
25. Sacramento *Union,* Oct. 10, 1864.
26. E. B. Crocker to C. Cole, Dec. 26, 1864, in Cole Papers.

CHAPTER VI

1. S. B. Reed to Mrs. Reed, April 5, 1864, in Samuel B. Reed Letters, U.P. Historical Museum, Omaha.
2. *Ibid.*, Apr. 5, 1864.
3. *Ibid.*, May 7, 1864.
4. *Ibid.*, May 21, 1864.
5. *Ibid.*, May 26, 1864.
6. *Ibid.*, June 12, 1864.
7. *Ibid.*
8. *Ibid.*
9. *Ibid.*
10. *Ibid.*, June 18, 1864.
11. John D. Cruise, "Early Days on the Union Pacific," *Collections of the Kansas State Historical Society,* 1909–10, vol. XI.
12. *Ibid.*
13. Testimony of Oliver Ames, House of Representatives Report No. 78, 42nd Congress, 3rd Session, p. 256.
14. Dodge MS.
15. House of Representatives Report No. 78, Part 2, 42nd Congress, 3rd Session, p. 2.
16. *Ibid.*, p. 3.
17. *Ibid.*, p. 4.

18. House of Representatives Report No. 78, 42nd Congress, 3rd Session, p. 670.
19. *Ibid.*, p. 669.
20. *Ibid.*, p. 670.
21. *Ibid.*
22. *Ibid.*
23. *Ibid.*, p. 652.
24. *Ibid.*

CHAPTER VII

1. Sacramento *Union,* Jan. 7, 1865.
2. Testimony of Frederick F. Low, Senate Report No. 689, 44th Congress, 2nd Session.
3. Crocker MS.
4. *Ibid.*
5. Testimony of Charles Crocker in Senate Report No. 689, *op. cit.*
6. Timothy Hopkins Papers, Hopkins Transportation Library.
7. Testimony of Charles Crocker in Senate Report No. 689, *op. cit.*
8. *Ibid.*
9. E. B. Crocker to C. Cole, Apr. 12, 1865, in Cole Papers.
10. Sen. John Conness and Rep. A. A. Sargent were the only political friends of the Central Pacific ever to have locomotives named for them. Oddly, Cornelius Cole, a singularly accommodating congressman, was never accorded this apt distinction. The C.P.'s nomenclature for locomotives at first drew largely on mythological and Biblical sources: Hercules, Ajax, Samson, Goliath, Achilles, Jupiter. Then came a phase in which names of birds and beasts were favored. Finally, a more poetic mood seized the engine-namers, and they christened locomotives Storm, Growler, Whirlwind, Terrible, Hurricane, Tempest, and the like.
11. Sacramento *Union,* Mar. 17, 1865.
12. *Ibid.*
13. Huntington MS.
14. E. B. Crocker to C. Cole, Apr. 12, 1865, Cole Papers.
15. *Ibid.*
16. Timothy Hopkins Papers.
17. Quoted in Sacramento *Union,* June 16, 1865.
18. Testimony of Thomas H. King, Senate Report No. 689, *op. cit.*
19. Rev. O. Gibson, *The Chinese in America.*
20. *Ibid.*
21. Rev. A. W. Loomis, "How Our Chinamen Are Employed," *Overland Monthly,* March, 1869.
22. Sacramento *Union,* Aug. 3, 1865.
23. Albert D. Richardson, *Beyond the Mississippi.*
24. *Ibid.*
25. *Ibid.*
26. C. P. R. R., "Statement Made to the President of the United States, and Secretary of the Interior, on the Progress of the Work, Oct. 10th, 1865," California Division, California State Library.
27. Report of U.S. Pacific Railway Commission, vol. V, p. 3608.

CHAPTER VIII

1. Winthrop Ames, *The Ames Family of Easton, Massachusetts.*
2. *Ibid.*
3. *Ibid.*
4. S. B. Reed to Mrs. Reed, Apr. 20, 1865, Reed Letters.
5. *Ibid.*
6. G. M. Dodge to N. P. Dodge, May 3, 1865, Dodge Letter Books.
7. D. H. Ainsworth, *Recollections of a Civil Engineer.*
8. Samuel Bowles, *Across the Continent.*
9. *Ibid.*
10. *Ibid.*
11. S. B. Reed to Mrs. Reed, June 4, 1865, Reed Letters.
12. Senate Executive Document No. 69, 49th Congress, 1st Session, p. 5.
13. Omaha *Weekly Republican,* July 12, 1865.
14. Gen. W. T. Sherman, *Memoirs,* 2nd ed.
15. G. M. Dodge, Autobiography (manuscript).
16. *Ibid.*
17. *Ibid.*
18. *Ibid.*
19. *Ibid.*

CHAPTER IX

1. C. Huntington to M. Hopkins, Jan 3, 1866, in Huntington-Hopkins Correspondence, Dept. of Special Collections, Stanford University.
2. Quoted in Sacramento *Union,* Nov. 25, 1865.
3. Crocker MS.
4. Testimony of J. H. Strobridge in Senate Report No. 689, 44th Congress, 2nd Session.
5. Timothy Hopkins Papers, Hopkins Transportation Library.
6. Testimony of Lewis M. Clement in Report of U.S. Pacific Railway Commission, vol. V, p. 3206.
7. Testimony of Edward H. Miller, Jr., in *ibid.,* p. 3052.
8. San Francisco *Alta California,* Apr. 16, 1866.
9. Sacramento *Union,* Apr. 17, 1866.
10. *Ibid.,* Apr. 20, 1866.
11. *Ibid.,* Apr. 21, 1866.
12. B. W. Brooks to C. Cole, Apr. 17, 1866, in Cole Papers.
13. Samuel Bowles, *Across the Continent.*
14. Cited in testimony of Edward H. Miller, Jr., Report of U.S. Pacific Railway Commission, vol. V, p. 3050.
15. New York *Herald* report, cited in Sacramento *Union,* Oct. 18, 1866.
16. Testimony of Edward H. Miller, Jr., in *op. cit.*
17. Huntington MS.
18. *Congressional Globe,* June 19, 1866.
19. Huntington MS.
20. *Congressional Globe,* June 19, 1866.
21. Huntington MS. Huntington remembered the date incorrectly, though.

22. Sacramento *Union,* July 6, 1866.
23. Huntington MS.
24. *Ibid.*
25. C. Cole to Mrs. Cole, June 18, 1866, in Cole Papers.
26. *Ibid.,* Aug. 6, 1866.
27. Crocker MS.
28. "Report of the Acting Chief Engineer to the Board of Directors of the Central Pacific Railway Co. of California, Jan. 5, 1867."
29. Testimony of Leland Stanford, Report of U.S. Pacific Railway Commission, vol. V, p. 2626.
30. Quoted in Sacramento *Union,* Aug. 20, 1866.
31. *Ibid.,* Oct. 23, 1866.
32. *Ibid.,* Nov. 16, 1866.
33. *Ibid.,* Nov. 12, 1866.
34. *Ibid.,* Nov. 27, 1866.
35. Wilder Manuscript, Department of Public Relations, Southern Pacific Co.
36. Crocker MS.
37. *Ibid.*
38. Sacramento *Union,* Dec. 10, 1866.

CHAPTER X

1. *History of the State of Nebraska,* 1882.
2. Painesville (Ohio) *Telegraph,* July 5, 1939.
3. *Union Pacific Magazine,* February, 1931, p. 4.
4. *Ibid.,* p. 36.
5. U.P. Historical Museum, Omaha.
6. *Ibid.*
7. G. M. Dodge to N. P. Dodge, Jan. 26, 1866, Dodge Letter Books.
8. Dodge MS.
9. *Union Pacific Magazine,* February, 1931, p. 4.
10. W. H. Jackson, *Diary,* July, 1866, Manuscript Division, N.Y. Public Library.
11. *Union Pacific Magazine,* February, 1931, p. 4.
12. Arthur N. Ferguson, *Journals,* June 25, 1866, U.P. Historical Museum.
13. Dodge MS.
14. *Ibid.*
15. *Union Pacific Magazine,* February, 1924, p. 10.
16. Hezekiah Bissell MS., Wyoming State Archives and Historical Department, Cheyenne.
17. U.P.R.R., "Report of the Chief Engineer, with Accompanying Reports of Division Engineers, for 1866."
18. *Union Pacific Magazine,* February, 1931, p. 24.
19. *Ibid.*
20. S. B. Reed to Mrs. Reed, Aug. 16, 1866, Reed Letters.
21. Quoted in letter of Gen. W. T. Sherman to Gen. J. A. Rawlins, Aug. 17, 1866, House of Representatives Executive Document No. 23, 39th Congress, 2nd Session.
22. *Ibid.*
23. Otis E. Young, *The West of Philip St. George Cooke, 1809–1895.*
24. *Diary of Gideon Welles,* vol. II.

25. Letter of Gen. W. T. Sherman to Gen. J. A. Rawlins, Aug. 17, 1866, *op. cit.*

26. *Ibid.*

27. Letter of Gen. W. T. Sherman to Gen. J. A. Rawlins, Aug. 21, 1866, in House of Representatives Executive Document No. 23, *op. cit.*

28. Brig. Gen. James F. Rusling, *Across America, or, The Great West and the Pacific Coast.*

29. Letter of Gen. W. T. Sherman to Gen. J. A. Rawlins, Aug. 31, 1866, in House of Representatives Executive Document No. 23, *op. cit.*

30. Rachel Sherman Thorndike, editor, *The Sherman Letters, 1837–91.*

31. Albert D. Richardson, *Garnered Sheaves.*

32. Albert D. Richardson, *Beyond the Mississippi.*

33. *Ibid.*

34. *Ibid.*

35. *Ibid.*

36. S. B. Reed to Mrs. Reed, Sept. 23, 1866, in Reed Letters.

37. *Ibid.*

38. Silas Seymour, *Incidents of a Trip through the Great Platte Valley.*

39. Dodge MS.

40. *Ibid.*

41. *Ibid.*

42. *Ibid.*

43. Seymour, *op. cit.*

44. John Adams Dix, *The Memoirs of John Adams Dix,* compiled by Morgan Dix.

45. U.P.R.R., "Report of the Chief Engineer, with Accompanying Reports of Division Engineers, for 1866."

46. A. N. Ferguson, *Journals,* Nov. 13, 1866.

47. *Ibid.,* Nov. 14, 1866.

CHAPTER XI

1. John R. Gilliss, "Tunnels of the Pacific Railroad," *Transactions, American Society of Civil Engineers,* vol. I.

2. *Ibid.*

3. *Southern Pacific Bulletin,* November, 1923, p. 25.

4. Cited in testimony of Leland Stanford in Report of U.S. Pacific Railway Commission, vol. V, p. 2581.

5. C. Huntington to M. Hopkins, Mar. 12, 1867; Huntington-Hopkins Correspondence.

6. A. A. Partridge MS., Dept. of Public Relations, Southern Pacific Co.

7. Gilliss, *op. cit.*

8. Erle Heath MS., Dept. of Public Relations, Southern Pacific Co.

9. Brig. Gen. James F. Rusling, *Across America.*

10. *Ibid.*

11. Quoted in Sacramento *Union,* Apr. 10, 1867.

12. Sacramento *Union,* July 3, 1867.

13. Testimony of Charles Crocker, Senate Report No. 689, 44th Congress, 2nd Session.

14. Crocker MS.

15. A. D. Richardson, *Beyond the Mississippi.*

16. *Railroad Communication with the Pacific, with an Account of the Central Pacific Railroad, etc.,* Fisk and Hatch, 1867.

17. B. Ives to W. Ives, June 8, 1867, Montague-Ives Correspondence, Hopkins Transportation Library, Stanford University.

18. *Ibid.,* Nov. 17, 1867.

19. S. S. Montague to B. Ives, Sept. 13, 1867, Montague-Ives Correspondence.

20. Testimony of Leland Stanford, Report of U.S. Pacific Railway Commission, vol. V, p. 2624.

21. *Ibid.,* p. 2637.

22. *Ibid.*

23. Sacramento *Union,* Aug. 30, 1867.

24. *Ibid.,* Nov. 30, 1867.

25. *Ibid.,* Dec. 9, 1867.

26. *Ibid.*

27. *Ibid.*

28. John R. Brown Diary, California Division, California State Library.

29. Quoted in Sacramento *Union,* Dec. 9, 1867.

CHAPTER XII

1. C. G. Coutant, *The History of Wyoming.*

2. Maj. Gen. G. M. Dodge, *Personal Recollections.*

3. *Ibid.*

4. *Ibid.*

5. *Ibid.*

6. *Ibid.*

7. *Ibid.*

8. *Ibid.*

9. Brig. Gen. J. H. Simpson, quoted in Silas Seymour, *The Great Union Pacific Railroad; Excursion to the Hundredth Meridian.*

10. Henry M. Stanley, *My Early Travels and Adventures in America and Asia.*

11. S. B. Reed to Mrs. Reed, Mar. 25, 1867, in Reed Letters.

12. *Ibid.,* Mar. 27, 1867.

13. Gen. J. S. Casement to Mrs. Casement, Apr. 13, 1867, in Casement Letters, Dr. J. V. Easterling, N. Oklahoma Junior College, Tonkawa, Okla.

14. S. B. Reed to Mrs. Reed, Apr. 25, 1867, Reed Letters.

15. *Ibid.,* Apr. 27, 1867.

16. *Ibid.,* May 4, 1867.

17. James W. Savage and John T. Bell, *History of the City of Omaha, Nebraska.*

18. Testimony of John B. Alley, House of Representatives Report No. 78, 42nd Congress, 3rd Session, p. 87.

19. Testimony of John M. S. Williams, House of Representatives Report No. 78, p. 163.

20. A. D. Richardson, *Garnered Sheaves.*

21. Dodge MS.

22. S. B. Reed to Mrs. Reed, May 6, 1867, in Reed Letters.

23. Dodge MS.

24. *Ibid.*

25. *Ibid.*

26. *Ibid.*

27. Oliver Knight, *Following the Indian Wars.*

28. Dodge MS.

29. *Ibid.*

30. *Ibid.*

31. Quoted in "Union Pacific Railroad Company, Chartered by the United States; Progress of their Road West from Omaha, Nebraska, Across the Continent," June 18, 1868.

32. S. B. Reed to Mrs. Reed, July 30, 1867, in Reed Letters.

33. Stanley, *op. cit.*

34. Dodge MS.

35. *Ibid.*

36. *Ibid.*

37. *Ibid.*

38. *Ibid.*

39. *Ibid.*

40. Testimony of Thomas C. Durant, House of Representatives Report No. 78, 42nd Congress, 3rd Session, p. 120.

41. John Adams Dix, *The Memoirs of John Adams Dix,* compiled by Morgan Dix.

42. S. B. Reed to Mrs. Reed, Oct. 21, 1867, in Reed Letters.

43. S. B. Reed to Mrs. Reed, Oct. 2, 1867, in Reed Letters.

44. Rachel Sherman Thorndike, editor, *The Sherman Letters, 1837–91.*

45. A. N. Ferguson, *Journals,* Oct. 1, 1867, U.P. Historical Museum.

CHAPTER XIII

1. Crocker MS.

2. Quoted in testimony of Leland Stanford, Report of U.S. Pacific Railway Commission, vol. V, p. 2580.

3. Robert L. Fulton, *Epic of the Overland,* p. 38.

4. Quoted in Sacramento *Union,* Feb. 3, 1868.

5. Most of the messages flowing over the single thread of communications between Charlie Crocker's field forces and Sacramento would have baffled any wiretapper, as they were intended to do. Now that the race between the Central Pacific and Union Pacific was in its most hectic phase, each road was trying to hide from the other just how well or badly things were going. Officials of both companies had developed codes to cloak their most intimate telegraphic conversations.

The Union Pacific's attempt at secrecy was to a large degree foiled by one of its own engineers, F. C. Hodges, chief of a survey party. Hodges corresponded with Butler Ives, of the C.P.'s engineering staff, telling him all he knew about the U.P.'s plans and progress. Ives promptly passed along the information to Sacramento.

The Central Pacific had two codes, one of which consisted of capital letters only. There is no key to it in existence. The other code consisted of symbolic words, obviously devised by a person with both imagination and satirical wit. "Yelp," for example, was the code name for Brigham Young; "Riddle," for William C. Ralston, mogul of the Bank of California, whose financial help was so desired and yet so seldom certain. The key to this entertaining code is available at Stanford University, in Mark Hopkins' handwriting, in two books of copies of Central Pacific telegrams (Dept. of Special Collections) that have survived the strenuous attrition of the years.

Hopkins, always cautious, was the only one among the C.P.'s top brass who habitually sent his messages in code. About the only time he flung caution to the winds was when he dispatched the forthright but solitary word "No" to Huntington one day in 1868. He evidently felt that was sufficiently cryptic even in plain English.

6. Annie Estelle Prouty, "The Development of Reno," *Nevada Historical Society Papers*, vol. IV, 1923–24.

7. Thompson & West, *History of the State of Nevada*.

8. S. B. Reed to Mrs. Reed, June 7, 1868, in Reed Letters.

9. L. Stanford to M. Hopkins, June 9, 1868, in Huntington-Hopkins Correspondence.

10. *Ibid.*

11. C. Huntington to M. Hopkins, June 11, 1868, in Huntington-Hopkins Correspondence.

12. Telegram from E. B. Crocker to C. Huntington, June 16, 1868, Stanford Collection, Stanford Univ.

13. Thompson & West, *History of the State of Nevada*.

14. Bancroft Library, University of California, Berkeley.

15. Crocker MS.

16. *Ibid.*

17. Reno *Crescent*, July 14, 1868.

18. Huntington MS.

19. *Ibid.*

20. Robert L. Fulton, *The Epic of the Overland*, p. 39.

21. Reno *Crescent*, Nov. 28, 1868.

22. *Ibid.*

23. Quoted in Stanford testimony, Report of U.S. Pacific Railway Commission, vol. V, p. 2578.

24. *Ibid.*

25. Dale L. Morgan, *The Humboldt: Highroad of the West*.

26. B. Ives to W. Ives, July 19, 1868, in Montague-Ives Correspondence.

27. S. S. Montague to B. Ives, June 16, 1868, in *ibid.*

28. Reno *Crescent*, Aug. 22, 1868.

29. *Ibid.*, Aug. 15, 1868.

30. Crocker MS.; evidently a reference to U.P. engineer F. C. Hodges. See Note 5.

31. Crocker MS.

32. Reno *Crescent*, Dec. 28, 1868.

33. Timothy Hopkins Papers, Hopkins Transportation Library.

34. Unidentified clipping in Hayes Scrapbooks, No. 89, Bancroft Library.

35. Crocker MS.

36. Copy of telegram in Hopkins Transportation Library, Stanford University.

37. L. Stanford to M. Hopkins, Dec. 10, 1868, Huntington-Hopkins Correspondence.

38. *Ibid.*, various letters, November–December, 1868.

39. L. Stanford to M. Hopkins, Nov. 9, 1868; Huntington-Hopkins Correspondence.

40. Huntington MS.

41. Huntington's testimony, Report of U.S. Pacific Railway Commission, vol. I, p. 11.

42. L. Stanford to M. Hopkins, Nov. 21, 1868, Huntington-Hopkins Correspondence.

43. *Ibid.*, Dec. 6, 1868.

44. *Ibid.*, Dec. 13, 1868.

45. *Ibid.*

46. Telegram from M. Hopkins to C. Huntington, Dec. 16, 1868, Stanford Collection.

47. Huntington MS.

48. Leland Stanford, Jr., the Stanfords' ill-fated only child, was born May 14, 1868. The Governor was so grateful to his wife for producing a son that, two weeks later, he gave her approximately a million dollars. The gift took the form of 9,000 shares of Contract & Finance Co. stock. In the light of Stanford's eventual protest to the U.S. Pacific Railway Commission that the stock was practically worthless at the time, his note accompanying the gift is most revealing. (It's among Stanford correspondence, Dept. of Special Collections, Stanford University.)

"These Shares of Stock," he wrote on May 30th, "are very valuable, worth in all probability much more than par [$100 a share]. . . . They are for you and will secure you a competence in case of accident to your Devoted Husband." The following day, May 31st, he toted up what he had left in his safe. It was a comforting residue. The value of the remaining securities, he estimated, was $1,198,052.54.

It is particularly interesting that in a memo he wrote to himself that day (Stanford correspondence, Stanford University), he based his judgment of the much-more-than-par value of the Contract & Finance Co. stock on the fact that "the Co. now hold of the full paid stock of the Central Pacific R.R. ($10,000,000) ten millions." Yet, he later told the Pacific Railway Commissioners that C.P. stock had then been worth barely 10 cents a share.

49. Telegram from M. Hopkins to C. Huntington, Dec. 28, 1868, Stanford Collection.

CHAPTER XIV

1. Testimony of John B. Alley, House of Representatives Report No. 77, 42nd Congress, 3rd Session, p. 91.

2. Testimony of Oakes Ames, House of Representatives Report No. 77, 42nd Congress, 3rd Session, p. 46.

3. *Ibid.*, p. 22.

4. In the summer of 1872, McComb introduced in a Pennsylvania court some personal letters that Ames had written to him during the first months in 1868. Those letters discussed placing the disputed Credit Mobilier shares in Congress "where they will do the most good for us." Ames did not name any recipients in writing. McComb, however, had jotted down a list of prominent congressmen whom he claimed Ames had mentioned as his leading sales prospects.

The letters and McComb's list of names found their way into the New York *Sun* on Sept. 4, 1872. They were published under the sensational heading "The King of Frauds: How the Credit Mobilier Bought Its Way into Congress." Grant's second campaign was then at its peak. The *Sun's* disclosures created a political ruckus of colossal proportions. Every man on McComb's list who was running for re-election promptly denied the story in its entirety. Oakes Ames at once was deserted by most of his fellow-Republicans and became the target of greatly exaggerated slander.

As soon as the next Congress convened, Speaker of the House James G. Blaine, who was one of the most reputable men on McComb's damning list, at once demanded an investigation. The Poland Committee of the House, named for its chairman, looked into the scandal involving Ames and certain other members of the House and Senate. The Wilson Committee of the Senate, also bearing its chairman's name, at the same time investigated the interrelationship of the Credit Mobilier and the Union Pacific, seeking to find out whether or not the government had been defrauded.

Speaker Blaine's name was cleared promptly and legitimately. Other men on the McComb list faired less well. Oakes Ames confounded most of them by telling the whole truth, as well as he could remember it, which was entirely in keeping with his character and past reputation. Several of the other witnesses were thereby obliged —to their humiliation—to correct their own evasive stories under cross-examination. One who, to his lasting misfortune, did not revise his testimony was Vice-President Schuyler Colfax. It became apparent to everyone in the course of the investigation that Colfax was lying. As a result, his political career was ruined. The testimony of Representative James A. Garfield, of Ohio, was also at variance with Ames', in part, and the Poland Committee did Garfield's reputation no good by accepting Ames' version of the story. Senator James W. Patterson, of New Hampshire, emerged from the investigation with his prestige badly rumpled.

Representative James Brooks, of New York, was found to have been guilty of discreditable conduct both as a member of Congress and as one of the U.P.'s government directors. He was bracketed with Ames when the Poland Committee announced its verdict.

Ames was found "guilty of selling to members of Congress shares of stock in the Credit Mobilier of America for prices much below the true value of such stock, with intent thereby to influence the votes and decisions of such members in matters to be brought before Congress for action." (Report No. 77, House of Representatives, 42nd Congress, 3rd Session) The fact that no member had held his few shares very long or obtained more than small financial benefit at best was brushed aside. The point that no one could prove that the involved members' brief connection with the Credit Mobilier had influenced a single vote was not considered important. The fact that the whole sorry episode had come to its natural end long before the investigation began, and had taken place during an earlier Congress, was blinked at in the Republicans' urgent need to have a scapegoat.

The Poland Committee first recommended expelling both Brooks and Ames from the House. Almost immediately, though, it softened that to a recommendation of censure, which the House endorsed.

Oakes Ames looked pale and stunned when the censure vote was announced. Colleagues tried to comfort him. A swarm of members clustered around his seat, assuring him of their unshaken confidence and devotion, begging him to understand how political expediency had forced them to vote for his shame. By then, though, the grave financial burdens and worries that he and his brother had borne for the Union Pacific, beginning in the winter of 1868–69, had exacted a critical physical toll. Public humiliation, which he (and many an eminent politician) so stoutly felt he did not deserve, aggravated the strain. Ames went sadly home to Massachusetts, and died of a stroke a few weeks afterward. By a melancholy coincidence, Representative Brooks had died even sooner. On the other hand, the tarnish that the Republican party had acquired in the scandal survived for nearly a generation.

The Wilson Committee, meanwhile, had decided that the government had been defrauded in the building of the Union Pacific (Report No. 78, House of Representatives, 42nd Congress, 3rd Session). Oakes Ames had denied this, declaring that the Credit Mobilier made less than $10 million on the U.P.'s outlay of $70 million.

The financial records of the Union Pacific and Credit Mobilier had been sloppily kept. Auditors hired by the Wilson Committee reported that the bookkeeping systems used were disgraceful. In consequence, it was impossible even then to find out precisely how much the Union Pacific had cost to build and how much profit had been made on the job. Down the years, a number of literary probers have taken varying approaches to the task of trying to capture those elusive figures. Their findings have differed widely, and most seem to have been flavored by bias or made suspect by guesswork.

In the latest, and by far the most penetrating and closely reasoned, study of the financial aspects of building the Union Pacific, Robert W. Fogel, an economist at the University of Rochester, has produced what appear to be the most reliable answers. He has estimated that it cost slightly more than $57 million to build the railroad from Omaha to Promontory Summit, and that the stockholders of the Credit Mobilier made not less than $13,000,000 or more than $16,500,000 on what their trustees charged the Union Pacific for its construction. Professor Fogel goes beyond these findings to conclude, in an impressive analysis of the nature and extent of the risk the promoters ran, that $11,100,000 would have been a "reasonable" profit. He points out, further, that that figure is conservative. (Robert W. Fogel, *The Union Pacific Railroad: A Case in Premature Enterprise,* Johns Hopkins Press.) It appears probable, therefore, that the Credit Mobilier, in the freebooting times in which it existed, would never have caused a sensation at all if it had not become accidentally embroiled in political warfare.

5. U.P.R.R., "Report of G. M. Dodge, Chief Engineer, with Accompanying Reports of Chiefs of Parties for 1868–69."

6. *Ibid.*

7. *Ibid.*

8. *Ibid.*

9. *Ibid.*

10. S. B. Reed to Mrs. Reed, Jan. 14, 1868, Reed Letters.

11. Quoted in letter from S. B. Reed to Mrs. Reed, Jan. 11, 1868, Reed Letters.

12. S. B. Reed to Mrs. Reed, Jan. 11, 1868, Reed Letters.

13. *Frontier Index,* Mar. 18, 1868.

14. Hezekiah Bissell MS., Wyoming State Archives and Historical Dept., Cheyenne.

15. *Ibid.*

16. S. B. Reed to Mrs. Reed, Apr. 23, 1868, in Reed Letters.

17. Gen. J. S. Casement to Mrs. Casement, Apr. 21, 1868, in Casement Letters.

18. Bissell MS.

19. S. B. Reed to Mrs. Reed, May 5, 1868.

20. *Frontier Index,* May 5, 1868.

21. Gen. J. S. Casement to Mrs. Casement, May 2, 1868, in Casement Letters.

22. Williams letter, June 16, 1868, contained in Senate Executive Document No. 69, 49th Congress, 1st Session, p. 37.

23. S. B. Reed to Mrs. Reed, July 6, 1868, in Reed Letters.

24. *Union Pacific Magazine,* December, 1923, p. 12.

25. Rachel Sherman Thorndike, editor, *The Sherman Letters, 1837–1891.*

26. Dodge MS.

27. Williams telegram reproduced in Senate Executive Document No. 69, p. 46.

28. Testimony of John B. Alley, House of Representatives Report No. 77, 42nd Congress, 3rd Session, p. 89.

29. *Ibid.*, pp. 89–90.

30. Editorial note by S. B. Reed's son-in-law, appended to Reed Letters, U.P. Historical Museum.

31. S. B. Reed to Mrs. Reed, July 30, 1868, in Reed Letters.

32. Gen. J. S. Casement to Mrs. Casement, Aug. 1, 1868, University of Wyoming, Laramie.

33. Gen. J. S. Casement to Mrs. Casement, Aug. 13, 1868, in Casement Letters.

34. *Ibid.*, Aug. 17, 1868.

35. A. D. Richardson, *Beyond the Mississippi.*

36. Maj. Gen. G. M. Dodge, *How We Built the Union Pacific*, pp. 27–28.

37. Cornelius Cole to Mrs. Cole, Aug. 19, 1868, in Cole Papers.

38. Williams report to Secretary of Interior, Aug. 15, 1868, contained in Senate Executive Document No. 69, *op. cit.*, p. 42.

39. *Ibid.*, p. 45.

40. *Ibid.*, p. 48.

41. Gen. J. S. Casement to Mrs. Casement, Sept. 19, 1868, in Casement Letters.

42. *Ibid.*, Nov. 6, 1868.

43. *Frontier Index*, Nov. 6, 1868.

44. Gen. J. S. Casement to Mrs. Casement, Oct. 31, 1868, in Casement Letters.

45. *Ibid.*, Nov. 6, 1868.

46. S. B. Reed to Mrs. Reed, Nov. 17, 1868.

47. *Ibid.*, Dec. 6, 1868.

48. *Ibid.*

49. *Ibid.*, Dec. 16, 1868.

50. *Ibid.*, Dec. 28, 1868.

CHAPTER XV

1. S. B. Reed to Mrs. Reed, Jan. 12, 1869, in Reed Letters.

2. Sidney Dillon, "Historic Moments: Driving the Last Spike of the Union Pacific," *Scribner's Magazine*, August, 1892.

3. J. H. Beadle, *The Undeveloped West.*

4. *Congressional Globe*, Apr. 5, 1869.

5. *Ibid.*

6. Telegram from M. Hopkins to L. Stanford, Jan. 8, 1869, Stanford Collection.

7. L. Stanford to M. Hopkins, Jan. 15, 1869, in Huntington-Hopkins Correspondence.

8. C. Huntington to President Andrew Johnson, Jan. 19, 1869, in Andrew Johnson Papers, Manuscript Division, Library of Congress.

9. Telegram from C. Crocker to L. Stanford, Jan. 19, 1869, Stanford Collection.

10. Report by U.S. Commissioners, San Francisco, Jan. 25, 1869, copy in Hopkins Transportation Library.

11. *Ibid.*

12. L. Stanford to M. Hopkins, Jan. 29, 1869, in Huntington-Hopkins Correspondence.

13. Charles Francis Adams, Jr., "The Pacific Railroad Ring," *North American Review*, January, 1869.
14. *Ibid.*
15. L. Stanford to M. Hopkins, Jan. 25, 1869, in Huntington-Hopkins Correspondence.
16. Huntington MS.
17. Telegram from L. Stanford to C. Huntington, Feb. 8, 1869, Stanford Collection.
18. Telegram from M. Hopkins to C. Huntington, Feb. 22, 1869, Stanford Collection.
19. Huntington MS.
20. *Ibid.*
21. L. Stanford to M. Hopkins, Mar. 14, 1869, Huntington-Hopkins Correspondence.
22. Telegram from M. Hopkins to L. Stanford, Mar. 8, 1869, Stanford Collection.
23. L. Stanford to M. Hopkins, Mar. 14, 1869, in Huntington-Hopkins Correspondence.
24. Timothy Hopkins Papers, Hopkins Transportation Library.
25. *Congressional Globe,* Mar. 10, 1869.
26. N.Y. *Post,* Apr. 2, 1869.
27. *Ibid.*
28. *Congressional Globe,* Apr. 5, 1869.
29. *Ibid.*
30. *Ibid.*
31. *Ibid.*
32. *Ibid.*
33. *Ibid.*
34. *Ibid.*
35. *Ibid.,* Apr. 9, 1869.
36. Sacramento *Union,* Apr. 10, 1869.
37. Huntington MS.
38. Crocker MS.
39. *Congressional Globe,* Apr. 9, 1869.
40. Sacramento *Union,* Apr. 21, 1869.
41. Sacramento *Union,* Apr. 22, 1869.
42. *Ibid.*
43. L. M. Clement to B. Ives, Apr. 23, 1869, in Montague-Ives Correspondence.

CHAPTER XVI

1. L. Stanford to M. Hopkins, Jan. 15, 1869, Huntington-Hopkins Correspondence.
2. *Ibid.*
3. Crocker MS.
4. Sacramento *Union,* Apr. 15, 1869.
5. Telegram from C. Crocker to C. Huntington, Jan. 20, 1869, Stanford Collection.
6. *Ibid.*
7. Telegram from Crocker to Huntington, Jan. 28, 1869, Stanford Collection.
8. Reno *Crescent,* Jan. 23, 1869.
9. *Ibid.,* Feb. 13, 1869.
10. *Ibid.*

11. U.P.R.R., "Report of G. M. Dodge, Chief Engineer, with Accompanying Reports of Chiefs of Parties for 1868–69."

12. Sacramento *Union*, Jan. 8, 1869.

13. S. B. Reed to Mrs. Reed, Jan. 12, 1869, in Reed Letters.

14. J. H. Beadle, *The Undeveloped West*.

15. *Ibid.*

16. Sacramento *Union*, Jan. 19, 1869.

17. S. B. Reed to Mrs. Reed, Jan. 16, 1869, in Reed Letters.

18. Salt Lake *Telegraph* dispatch to Sacramento *Union*, Feb. 20, 1869.

19. S. B. Reed to Mrs. Reed, Feb. 27, 1869, in Reed Letters.

20. Gen. J. S. Casement to Mrs. Casement, Mar. 12, 1869, in Casement Letters.

21. Quoted in Sacramento *Union*, Mar. 6, 1869.

22. S. B. Reed to Mrs. Reed, Feb. 10, 1869, in Reed Letters.

23. Gen. J. S. Casement to Mrs. Casement, Mar. 8, 1869, in Casement Letters.

24. *Ibid.*, Mar. 12, 1869.

25. Telegram from M. Hopkins to C. Huntington, Mar. 12, 1869, with translation in Hopkins' handwriting on the copy, Stanford Collection.

26. Reno *Crescent*, Mar. 20, 1869.

27. Crocker MS.

28. *Ibid.*

29. *Ibid.*

30. Robert L. Fulton, *Epic of the Overland*.

31. San Francisco *Alta California*, Apr. 29, 1869.

32. Col. L. H. Eicholtz, *Diary*, quoted in Elmer O. Davis, *The First Five Years of the Railroad Era in Colorado*.

33. San Francisco *Bulletin*, Apr. 29, 1869.

34. *Ibid.*

35. *Ibid.*

36. Crocker MS.

37. Fulton, *op. cit.*

38. Dodge Letter Books, Council Bluffs Public Library.

39. *Ibid.*

CHAPTER XVII

1. Maj. Gen. G. M. Dodge, *How We Built the Union Pacific Railway*.

2. Dr. J. D. B. Stillman, "The Last Tie," *Overland Monthly*, July, 1869.

3. John Todd, D. D., *The Sunset Land; or, The Great Pacific Slope*.

4. David Hewes, "An Autobiography," essay included in *Lieutenant Joshua Hewes, a New England Pioneer*.

5. Stillman, *op. cit.*

6. Sacramento *Union*, May 4, 1869.

7. Stillman, *op. cit.*

8. *Ibid.*

9. *Ibid.*

10. *Ibid.*

11. San Francisco *Alta California*, May 10, 1869.

12. Telegram from G. M. Dodge to O. Ames, May 7, 1869, in Dodge Letter Books.

13. Stillman, *op. cit.*

14. *Ibid.*
15. *Ibid.*
16. Telegram from G. M. Dodge to O. Ames, May 8, 1869, Dodge Letter Books.
17. Letter from O. Ames to G. M. Dodge, May 12, 1869, Dodge Letter Books.
18. Sacramento *Union,* May 10, 1869.
19. *Ibid.*
20. San Francisco *Alta California,* May 10, 1869.
21. Stillman, *op. cit.*
22. *Ibid.*
23. San Francisco *News Letter Supplement,* May 15, 1869.
24. Dale L. Morgan, *The Humboldt: Highroad of the West.*
25. Todd, *op. cit.*
26. New York *Tribune,* May 11, 1869.
27. Todd, *op. cit.*
28. New York *Tribune,* May 11, 1869.
29. *Ibid.*
30. Reno *Crescent,* May 11, 1869.
31. New York *Tribune,* May 11, 1869.
32. *Ibid.*
33. Todd, *op. cit.*
34. *Ibid.*
35. Bissell MS.
36. Todd, *op. cit.*
37. New York *Tribune,* May 11, 1869.
38. Todd, *op. cit.*
39. San Francisco *News Letter Supplement,* May 15, 1869.
40. Diary of Col. L. H. Eicholtz, quoted in Elmer O. Davis, *The First Five Years of the Railroad Era in Colorado.*
41. Mrs. Theodore D. Judah MS.
42. New York *Tribune,* May 11, 1869.
43. Quoted in Maj. Gen. G. M. Dodge, *How We Built the Union Pacific Railway.*

BIBLIOGRAPHY

Adams, Charles Francis, Jr., "The Pacific Railroad Ring," *North American Review*, January, 1869.

Ainsworth, D. H., *Recollections of a Civil Engineer*. Newton, Iowa: Privately printed, 1893.

Alter, J. Cecil, *James Bridger*. Salt Lake City: Shepard Book Co., 1925.

Ames, Oakes: A Memoir. Cambridge, Mass.: Riverside Press, 1883.

Ames, Winthrop, *The Ames Family of Easton, Massachusetts*. Privately printed, 1938.

Appleton's Cyclopaedia of American Biography. 6 vols. New York: D. Appleton & Company, 1888.

Athearn, Robert G., *William Tecumseh Sherman and the Settlement of the West*. Norman, Okla.: University of Oklahoma Press, 1956.

Avery, B. P., "The Building of the Iron Road," *Overland Monthly*, May, 1869.

Bailey, W. F., *The Story of the First Trans-continental Railroad*. Pittsburgh: Pittsburgh Printing Company, 1906.

Bancroft, Hubert Howe, *Chronicles of the Builders of the Commonwealth*, vols. VI, VII. San Francisco: The History Company, 1890.

——— *History of California*, vol. VII, 1860–90. San Francisco: The History Company, 1890.

——— *History of Nevada, Colorado, and Wyoming*. San Francisco: The History Company, 1890.

Barnes, Demas, *From the Atlantic to the Pacific, Overland*. New York: D. Van Nostrand Company, 1886.

Beadle, J. H., *The Undeveloped West, or, Five Years in the Territories*. Philadelphia: National Publishing Company, 1873.

Bell, William A., *New Tracks in North America*. London: Chapman and Hall, 1869.

Benton, Thomas Hart, *Letter from Col. Benton to the People of Missouri*. Washington: Privately printed, 1853.

Berner, Bertha, *Mrs. Leland Stanford; An Intimate Account*. Stanford University, Calif.: Stanford University Press, 1935.

Biographical Directory of the American Congress, 1774–1949. Washington: U.S. Government Printing Office, 1950.

Biographical History of Eminent and Self-Made Men of the State of Indiana, A, vol. II. Cincinnati: Western Biographical Publishing Company, 1880.

Bowers, Claude G., *The Tragic Era*. Cambridge, Mass.: Houghton Mifflin Company, 1929.

Bowles, Samuel, *Across the Continent*. New York: Hurd & Houghton, 1866.

——— *Our New West*. Hartford: Hartford Publishing Co., 1869.

——— *The Pacific Railroad—Open; How to Go; What to See*. Boston: Fields, Osgood & Company, 1869.

Brace, Charles Loring, *The New West, or, California in 1867–1868*. New York: G. P. Putnam & Sons, 1869.

Brodie, Fawn M., *Thaddeus Stevens: Scourge of the South*. New York: W. W. Norton & Company, 1959.

Browning, Orville H., *The Diary of Orville Hickman Browning*, vol. II, 1865–81. Springfield, Ill.: Collections of the Illinois State Historical Library, vol. XXII, 1933.

Bruce, Robert, *The Fighting Norths and Pawnee Scouts*. Lincoln, Neb.: The Nebraska State Historical Society, 1932.

Bulletin, The. San Francisco: Southern Pacific Company.

Burch, John C., "Theodore D. Judah," *First Annual of the Territorial Pioneers of California*, 1877.

Burton, Sir Richard Francis, *The City of the Saints*. London: Longman, Green, Longman, and Roberts, 1861.

Carpenter, Francis B., *The Inner Life of Abraham Lincoln; Six Months at the White House*. New York: Hurd & Houghton, 1868.

Central Pacific Railroad, The, or, '49 and '69, by "Old Block." San Francisco: White & Bauer, 1868.

Chambers, William N., *Old Bullion Benton: Senator from the New West*. Boston: Little, Brown & Company, 1956.

Clampitt, John W., *Echoes from the Rocky Mountains*. Chicago: Bedford, Clarke & Company, 1889.

Clews, Henry, *Twenty-Eight Years in Wall Street*. New York: Irving Publishing Co., 1888.

Cook, Rev. Joseph W., *Diary and Letters*. Laramie, Wyo.: Laramie Republican Company, 1919.

Coolidge, Mary Roberts, *Chinese Immigration*. New York: Henry Holt & Company, 1909.

Coutant, C. G., *The History of Wyoming*. Laramie, Wyo.: Chaplin, Spafford & Mathison, 1899.

Coy, Owen C., *The Humboldt Bay Region, 1850–1875*. Los Angeles: California State Historical Association, 1929.

Cruise, John D., "Early Days on the Union Pacific," *Collections of the Kansas State Historical Society*, vol. XI, 1909–10.

Dana, Charles A., *Recollections of the Civil War*. New York: D. Appleton & Company, 1898.

Davis, Elmer O., *The First Five Years of the Railroad Era in Colorado*. Privately printed, 1948.

Davis, George T. M., *Autobiography of the Late Col. George T. M. Davis*. New York: "Published by His Legal Representatives," 1891.

Davis, John P., *The Union Pacific Railway; A Study in Railway Politics, History, and Economics*. Chicago: S. C. Griggs & Company, 1894.

Devens, R. M., *Great Events of Our Past Century*. Springfield, Mass.: C. A. Nichols and Company, 1879.

Dictionary of American Biography, 20 vols. New York: Charles Scribner's Sons, 1928.

Dillon, Sidney, "Historic Moments: Driving the Last Spike of the Union Pacific," *Scribner's Magazine*, August, 1892.

Dix, Morgan, compiler, *The Memoirs of John Adams Dix*. New York: Harper & Brothers, 1883.

Dodge, Maj. Gen. Grenville M., *Biographical Sketch of James Bridger*. New York: Unz & Company, 1905.

—— *How We Built the Union Pacific Railway, and Other Railway Papers and Addresses*. Washington: U.S. Government Printing Office, 1910.

—— *Personal Recollections*. Council Bluffs, Iowa: The Monarch Printing Company, 1914.

Dodge, Col. Richard I., *Our Wild Indians*. Hartford: A. D. Worthington & Company, 1882.

Evans, John H. and Minnie E. Anderson, *Ezra T. Benson, Pioneer-Statesman-Saint*. Salt Lake City: Deseret News Press, 1947.

Farnam, Henry W., *Memoir of Henry Farnam*. New Haven: Privately printed, 1889.

Farquhar, Francis P., "Exploration of the Sierra Nevada," *California Historical Society Quarterly*, vol. IV, March, 1925.

Farrell, Dennis, "Adventures on the Plains, 1865–67," *Collections of the Nebraska State Historical Society*, vol. XVII, 1913.

Fisk, Harvey E., "Fisk & Hatch, Bankers and Dealers in Government Securities, 1862–1885," *Journal of Economic and Business History*, vol. II, August, 1930.

Fogel, Robert W., *The Union Pacific Railroad: A Case in Premature Enterprise*, Baltimore: The Johns Hopkins Press, 1960.

Galloway, John D., *The First Transcontinental Railroad*. New York: Simmons-Boardman Publishing Corporation, 1950.

Ghent, W. J., *The Road to Oregon*. New York: Longmans, Green & Company, 1929.

Gibson, Rev. O., *The Chinese in America*. Cincinnati: Hitchcock & Walden, 1877.

Gilliss, John R., "Tunnels of the Pacific Railroad," *Transactions, American Society of Civil Engineers*, vol. I, 1872.

Goodwin, C. C., *As I Remember Them*. Salt Lake City: Salt Lake Commercial Club, 1913.

Grinnell, George B., *The Fighting Cheyennes*. Norman, Okla.: University of Oklahoma Press, 1956 (c) 1913.

―――― *Two Great Scouts and Their Pawnee Battalion*. Cleveland: The Arthur H. Clark Company, 1928.

Gudde, Erwin D., *California Place Names*. Berkeley and Los Angeles: University of California Press, 1949.

Hayes, William E., *Iron Road to Empire*. New York: Simmons-Boardman Publishing Corporation, 1953.

Hewes, David, "An Autobiography," in *Lieutenant Joshua Hewes, a New England Pioneer, a genealogical history*. Privately printed, 1913.

Hill, Thomas, *The Last Spike, a Painting by Thomas Hill*. San Francisco: E. Bosqui & Company, 1881.

"Historical Sketch of Weber County," *Utah Historical Records Survey*, 1940.

"History of Ogden, A," *Utah Historical Records Survey*, 1940.

History of the State of Nebraska. Chicago: The Western Historical Company, 1882.

History of the State of Nevada. Oakland, Calif.: Thompson & West, 1881.

Hittell, Theodore H., *History of California*, vol. IV. San Francisco: N. J. Stone & Company, 1897.

Hoar, George F., *Autobiography of Seventy Years*. New York: Charles Scribner's Sons, 1905.

Holbrook, Stewart H., *The Story of American Railroads*. New York: Crown Publishers, 1947.

Holland, Rupert S., *Historic Railroads*. Philadelphia: Macrae-Smith Company, 1927.

Hoyt, A. W., "Over the Plains to Colorado," *Harper's New Monthly Magazine*, June, 1867.

Humason, W. L., *From the Atlantic Surf to the Golden Gate*. Hartford: Press of Wm. C. Hutchings, 1869.

Hungerford, Edward, *Men and Iron: The History of the New York Central*. New York: Thomas Y. Crowell Company, 1938.

Hunter, Milton R., *Beneath Ben Lomond's Peak; a History of Weber County, 1824–1900*. Salt Lake City: Deseret News Press, 1944.

Hyde, George E., *Pawnee Indians*. Denver: The University of Denver Press, 1951.

Jackson, William Henry, in collaboration with Howard R. Driggs, *The Pioneer Photographer*. Yonkers-on-Hudson, N.Y.: World Book Co., 1929.

Jackson, William Henry, *Time Exposure*. New York: G. P. Putnam's Sons, 1940.

James, Marquis, *They Had Their Hour*. Indianapolis: The Bobbs-Merrill Company, 1934.

Knight, Oliver, *Following the Indian Wars; The Story of the Newspaper Correspondents Among the Indian Campaigners*. Norman, Okla.: University of Oklahoma Press, 1960.

Larson, Henrietta M., *Jay Cooke, Private Banker*. Cambridge, Mass.: Harvard University Press, 1936.

Lewis, Lloyd, *Sherman, Fighting Prophet*. New York: Harcourt, Brace & Company, 1932.

Lewis, Oscar, *The Big Four*. New York: Alfred A. Knopf, 1938.

Loomis, Rev. A. W., "How Our Chinamen Are Employed," *Overland Monthly*, March, 1869.

Low, Frederick F., *Reflections of a California Governor*, edited, with preface and notes, by Robert H. Becker. Sacramento: Sacramento Book Collectors Club, 1959.

McClure, Alexander K., *Three Thousand Miles through the Rocky Mountains*. Philadelphia: J. B. Lippincott & Company, 1869.

McLeod, Alexander, *Pigtails and Gold Dust*. Caldwell, Idaho: The Caxton Printers, Ltd., 1947.

Majors, Alexander, *Seventy Years on the Frontier*. Chicago: Rand, McNally & Company, 1893.

Morgan, Dale L., *The Humboldt: Highroad of the West*. New York: Farrar & Rinehart, Inc., 1943.

Morse, Frank P., *Cavalcade of the Rails*. New York: E. P. Dutton & Company, 1940.

Morton, J. Sterling, *Illustrated History of Nebraska*. 3 vols. Lincoln, Neb.: Jacob North & Company, 1906.

"Nebraska History and Record of Pioneer Days," *Collections of the Nebraska State Historical Society*, vol. VII, April–June, 1924.

Nichols, Joseph, *Condensed History of the Construction of the Union Pacific Railway*. Omaha: Klopp, Bartlett & Company, 1892.

Nordhoff, Charles, *California: for Health, Pleasure, and Residence*. New York: Harper & Brothers, 1873.

North, Edward P., "Blasting with Nitro-Glycerine," *Transactions, American Society of Civil Engineers*, vol. I, 1872.

Oberholtzer, Ellis P., *A History of the United States Since the Civil War*. vols. I–II. New York: The Macmillan Company, 1917.

Olson, James C., *History of Nebraska*. Lincoln, Neb.: University of Nebraska Press, 1955.

Ostrander, Alson B., *An Army Boy of the Sixties*. Yonkers-on-Hudson, N.Y.: World Book Co., 1924.

"Pacific Railway, The," *Engineering*, vol. IV, Nov. 8, 1867.

Park, William Lee, *Pioneer Pathways to the Pacific*. Clare, Mich.: Privately printed, 1938.

Paxson, Frederic L., *The Last American Frontier*. New York: The Macmillan Company, 1928.

Peattie, Donald Culross, "Tracks West," *The Saturday Evening Post*, Nov. 5, 1949.

Pence, Mary Lou and Lola M. Homsher, *The Ghost Towns of Wyoming*. New York: Hastings House, 1956.

Perkins, J. R., *Trails, Rails and War*. Indianapolis: The Bobbs-Merrill Company, 1929.

Phelps, Alonzo, *Contemporary Biography of California's Representative Men*. San Francisco: A. L. Bancroft & Company, 1881.

Poppleton, Andrew J., *Reminiscences*. Omaha: Privately printed, 1915.

Priest, Loring B., *Uncle Sam's Stepchildren*. New Brunswick, N.J.: Rutgers University Press, 1942.

Prouty, Annie Estelle, "The Development of Reno," *Nevada Historical Society Papers*, vol. IV, 1923–24.

Quiett, Glenn Chesney, *They Built the West*. New York: D. Appleton-Century Company, 1934.

Rae, W. F., *Westward by Rail: The New Route to the East*. New York: D. Appleton-Century Company, 1871.

Redding, B. B., *A Sketch of the Life of Mark Hopkins, of California*. San Francisco: A. L. Bancroft & Company, 1881.

Rhodes, James F., *History of the United States from the Compromise of 1850 to the Final Restoration of Home Rule at the South in 1877*, vol. VII. New York: The Macmillan Company, 1906.

Richardson, Albert D., *Beyond the Mississippi*. Hartford: American Publishing Company, 1867.

—— *Garnered Sheaves from the Writings of Albert D. Richardson*, collected and arranged by his wife. Hartford: Columbian Book Company, 1880.

Riegel, Robert E., *America Moves West*. New York: Henry Holt & Company, 1930.

Rusling, Brig. Gen. James F., *Across America, or, The Great West and the Pacific Coast*. New York: Sheldon & Company, 1874.

Russell, A. J., *The Great West Illustrated in a series of Photographic Views Across the Continent; taken along the line of the Union Pacific Railroad, west from Omaha, Nebraska*, vol. I. New York: Union Pacific Railroad Company, 1869.

Sabin, Edwin L., *Building the Pacific Railway*. Philadelphia: J. P. Lippincott Company, 1919.

Sandburg, Carl, *Abraham Lincoln: The War Years*, vol. II. New York: Harcourt, Brace & Company, 1936.

Sandmeyer, Elmer Clarence, *The Anti-Chinese Movement in California*. Urbana, Ill.: University of Illinois Press, 1939.

Savage, James W. and John T. Bell, *History of the City of Omaha, Nebraska*. New York: Munsell & Company, 1894.

Scientific American, 1866–69.

Seymour, Silas, *Incidents of a Trip Through the Great Platte Valley, to the Rocky Mountains and Laramie Plains in the Fall of 1866, with a synoptical statement of the various Pacific Railroads, and an account of the Great Union Pacific Railroad Excursion to the One Hundredth Meridian of Longitude*. New York: D. Van Nostrand Company, 1867.

Sherman, John, *Recollections of Forty Years in the House, Senate, and Cabinet.* Chicago: The Werner Company, 1895.

Sherman, Gen. William T., *Memoirs.* 2nd ed. New York: D. Appleton & Company, 1887.

Shuck, Oscar T., *Representative Men of the Pacific.* San Francisco: Bacon & Company, 1870.

Sillcox, L. K., *Safety in Early American Railway Operation, 1853–1871.* Princeton, N.J.: Princeton University Press, 1936.

Smith, W. H. B., *Small Arms of the World.* Harrisburg, Pa.: The Military Service Publishing Company, 1957.

Stanley, Henry M., *Autobiography of Sir Henry Morton Stanley, G. C. B.* Boston: Houghton Mifflin Company, 1909.

—— *My Early Travels and Adventures in America and Asia,* vol. I. New York: Charles Scribner's Sons, 1895.

Starr, John W., Jr., *Lincoln and the Railroads.* New York: Dodd, Mead & Company, 1930.

Stillman, Dr. J. D. B., "The Last Tie," *Overland Monthly,* July, 1869.

Stoddard, William O., *Lincoln's Third Secretary: The Memoirs of William O. Stoddard.* New York: Exposition Press, 1955.

Stone, Irving, *Men to Match My Mountains.* Garden City, N.Y.: Doubleday & Company, Inc., 1956.

Stokes, Anson Phelps, *Stokes Records.* New York: Privately printed, 1910.

Taft, Robert, *Photography and the American Scene.* New York: The Macmillan Company, 1938.

Thorndike, Rachel Sherman, editor: *The Sherman Letters; Correspondence between General and Senator Sherman from 1837 to 1891.* London: Sampson Low, Marston & Co., 1894.

Todd, John, D. D., *The Sunset Land; or, The Great Pacific Slope.* Boston: Lee & Shepard, 1870.

Transactions, American Society of Civil Engineers, vol. XXXVI, December, 1896: Brief biographies of Sidney Dillon and Thomas C. Durant.

Trottman, Nelson, *History of the Union Pacific.* New York: The Ronald Press Company, 1923.

Union Pacific Magazine. Omaha: Union Pacific Railroad Company.

Warman, Cy, *The Story of the Railroad.* New York: D. Appleton & Company, 1898.

Welles, Gideon, *Diary of Gideon Welles.* 3 vols. Boston: Houghton Mifflin Company, 1911.

Wells, Rev. Charles W., *A Frontier Life.* Cincinnati: Jennings & Pye, 1902.

Wenzel, Caroline, "Finding Facts about the Stanfords in the California State Library," *California Historical Society Quarterly,* vol. XIX, September, 1940.

Wheat, Carl I., "A Sketch of the Life of Theodore D. Judah," *California Historical Society Quarterly,* vol. IV, September, 1925.

White, Henry Kirke, *History of the Union Pacific Railway.* Chicago: University of Chicago Press, 1895.

Wilson, Neill C. and Frank J. Taylor, *Southern Pacific.* New York: McGraw-Hill Book Company, 1952.

Young, Otis E., *The West of Philip St. George Cooke, 1809–1895.* Glendale, Calif.: The Arthur H. Clark Company, 1955.

GOVERNMENT DOCUMENTS

Affairs of the Union Pacific Railroad Company, Report No. 78, House of Representatives, 42nd Congress, Third Session, 1873.

Annual Reports of the Secretary of the Interior, 1863–69.

Annual Reports of the Secretary of War, 1863–69.

Credit Mobilier Investigation, Report No. 77, House of Representatives, 42nd Congress, Third Session, 1873.

Protection Across the Continent, House Executive Document No. 23, 39th Congress, Second Session, 1867.

Report of the Commission and of the Minority Commissioner of the United States Pacific Railway Commission. 5 vols. 1887.

Reports of the Government Directors of the Union Pacific Railroad Company, 1864–1884, Senate Executive Document No. 69, 49th Congress, First Session, 1886.

Report of the Joint Special Committee to Investigate Chinese Immigration, Senate Report No. 689, 44th Congress, Second Session, 1877.

Report of U.S. Special Commissioners to Hon. Orville H. Browning, Secretary of the Interior, on the Central Pacific and Western Pacific Railroads, San Francisco.

Report on Transcontinental Railways, 1883, by Col. O. M. Poe, U.S. Engineers. House Executive Document No. 1, Part 2, 48th Congress, First Session, 1884.

RAILROAD DOCUMENTS

Central Pacific Railroad: *Letter to Hon. C. A. Sumner and H. Epstein, Chairmen of R.R. Committees, Nevada State Legislature, from Leland Stanford, Pres., Central Pacific R.R., Feb. 14, 1865.*

———— *Railroad Communication with the Pacific, with an Account of the Central Pacific Railroad of California: The Character of the Work, Its Progress, Resources, Earnings and Future Prospect, and the Advantages of Its First Mortgage Bonds.* Fisk & Hatch, 1867.

———— *Report of the Chief Engineer of the Central Pacific Railroad Company of California, on his Operations in the Atlantic States, 1862.*

———— *Report of the Chief Engineer to the Board of Directors and President, Central Pacific Railroad Co., July 1, 1863.*

———— *Report of the Chief Engineer upon Recent Surveys, Progress of Construction, and Estimated Revenue of the Central Pacific Railroad of California, December, 1864.*

———— *Report of the Chief Engineer upon Recent Surveys and Progress of Construction of the Central Pacific Railroad of California, December, 1865.*

———— *Report of the Acting Chief Engineer to the Board of Directors of the Central Pacific Railroad Co. of California, Jan. 5, 1867.*

———— *Rules and Regulations for Employees* (c. 1868).

———— *Statement Made to the President of the United States, and Secretary of the Interior, on the Progress of the Work, Oct. 10, 1865.*

———— *Statement Made to Senate Committee of the Nevada Legislature, Jan. 14, 1865.*

Pacific Railroad Convention: *Memorial to the President of the United States, Heads of Departments, Senate and House of Representatives, 1859.*

Pacific Railroad Convention: *Report of Theodore D. Judah, accredited agent Pacific Railroad Convention, Upon His Operations in the Atlantic States, August, 1860.*
Union Pacific Railroad: *Report of the Chief Engineer, with Accompanying Reports of Division Engineers, for 1866.*
———— *Report of G. M. Dodge, Chief Engineer, with accompanying Reports of Chiefs of Parties for 1868–69.*
———— *Report of the Organization and Proceedings of the Union Pacific Railroad Co.,* 1864.
———— *Union Pacific Railroad Company, Chartered by the United States; Progress of their Road West from Omaha, Nebraska, Across the Continent,* June 18, 1868.

MANUSCRIPTS AND LETTERS

Bissell, Hezekiah, *Recollections,* Wyoming State Archives and Historical Department, Cheyenne.
Browne, John Ross, *Diary,* California Section, California State Library, Sacramento.
Cary, Thomas G., "Pacific Rail Road," Manuscript Division, Library of Congress, Washington.
Casement, Brig. Gen. John S., *Letters,* Dr. V. R. Easterling, President, Northern Oklahoma Junior College, Tonkawa, Okla.
Central Pacific Railroad, *Telegram Copies, 1868–69,* Stanford Collection, The Stanford University Libraries, Stanford.
Cole, Cornelius, *Papers,* Department of Special Collections, University of California Library, Los Angeles.
Conness, Sen. John, *Letter,* to James McClatchy, Dec. 18, 1863, California Section, California State Library, Sacramento.
Crocker, Charles, *Reminiscences,* Bancroft Library, University of California, Berkeley.
Dodge, Maj. Gen. Grenville M., *Autobiography, 1831–71,* Free Public Library, Council Bluffs, Iowa.
———— *Transcribed Letter Books,* Free Public Library, Council Bluffs, Iowa.
Ferguson, Arthur N., *Journals,* Union Pacific Historical Museum, Omaha.
Hopkins-Huntington Letters, Hopkins Transportation Library, The Stanford University Libraries, Stanford.
Hopkins, Timothy, *Random Notes on Central Pacific History,* Hopkins Transportation Library, The Stanford University Libraries, Stanford.
Huntington, Collis P., *Reminiscences,* Bancroft Library, University of California, Berkeley.
Jackson, William Henry, *Diary,* Manuscript Division, N.Y. Public Library.
Judah, Anna Ferona, *Reminiscences,* Bancroft Library, University of California, Berkeley.
Miller, E. H., Jr., *Ledger, 1862–71,* Hopkins Transportation Library, The Stanford University Libraries, Stanford.
Montague, Samuel S., *Letters,* Hopkins Transportation Library, The Stanford University Libraries, Stanford.
Partridge, A. A., *Reminiscences,* The Southern Pacific Company, San Francisco.
Reed, Samuel B., *Transcribed Letters,* Union Pacific Historical Museum, Omaha.
Stanford, Leland, *Letters,* Stanford Collection, The Stanford University Libraries, Stanford.

Towne, A. N., *Letter*, to H. H. Bancroft, April 16, 1889, Bancroft Library, University of California, Berkeley.

NEWSPAPERS

Cheyenne *Daily Leader*.
Chicago *Tribune*.
Congressional Globe.
Council Bluffs *Bugle*.
—— *Nonpareil*.
Frontier Index, The
Frank Leslie's Illustrated Newspaper.
New York *Post*.
—— *Tribune*.
Painesville (Ohio) *Telegraph*.
Reno *Crescent*.
Sacramento *Union*.
Salt Lake *Tribune*.
San Francisco *Alta California*.
—— *Chronicle*.
—— *Newsletter*.

INDEX

ABOUT THE AUTHOR

Mr. Griswold was born in Middletown, Connecticut, in 1909. After graduating from the University of North Carolina he worked as a reporter on the Hartford (Connecticut) *Courant*. He served three years in the Air Force, and after that was hired as a copy editor for the *New Yorker*. He stayed with the *New Yorker* for five years, at the end of which time he joined the staff of *Popular Science* and became the magazine's first Midwestern editor. Since January, 1955, he has been its West Coast editor.

Exploring the West in the course of scouting for stories for *Popular Science* gave the author his first look at the country through which the builders of the Central Pacific and Union Pacific fought their way. In 1957 the idea of writing an account of this "work of giants" developed into an obsession. It took five years to research (Mr. Griswold has traveled all over the country in search of material) and write—between his articles for *Popular Science*. *A Work of Giants* is Mr. Griswold's first book.

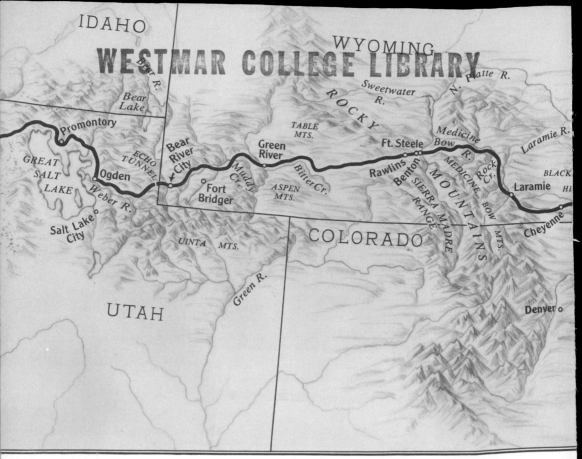

Bear R.

Bear Lake

Promontory

ROCKY

Sweetwater R.

N. Platte R.

GREAT SALT LAKE

ECHO TUNNEL

Bear River City

TABLE MTS.

Green River

Ft. Steele

Medicine Bow R.

Laramie R.

Ogden

Muddy Cr.

BitterCr.

Rawlins

MEDICINE

Rock Cr.

BLACK

Weber R.

Fort Bridger

ASPEN MTS.

Benton

SIERRA MADRE RANGE

MOUNTAINS

Laramie

Hi

Salt Lake City

UINTA MTS.

COLORADO

Cheyenne

BOW MTS.

UTAH

Green R.

Denver o